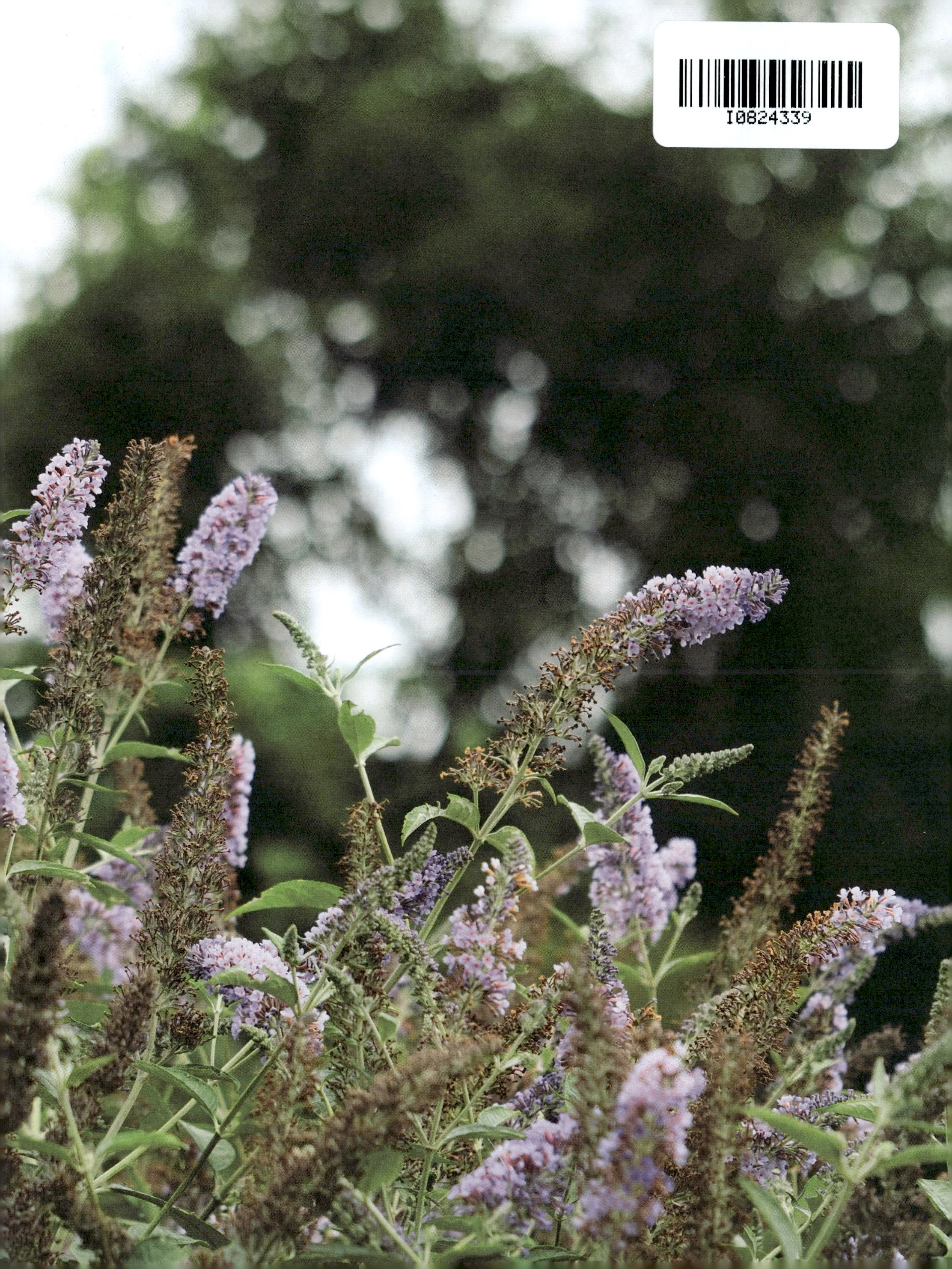
I0824339

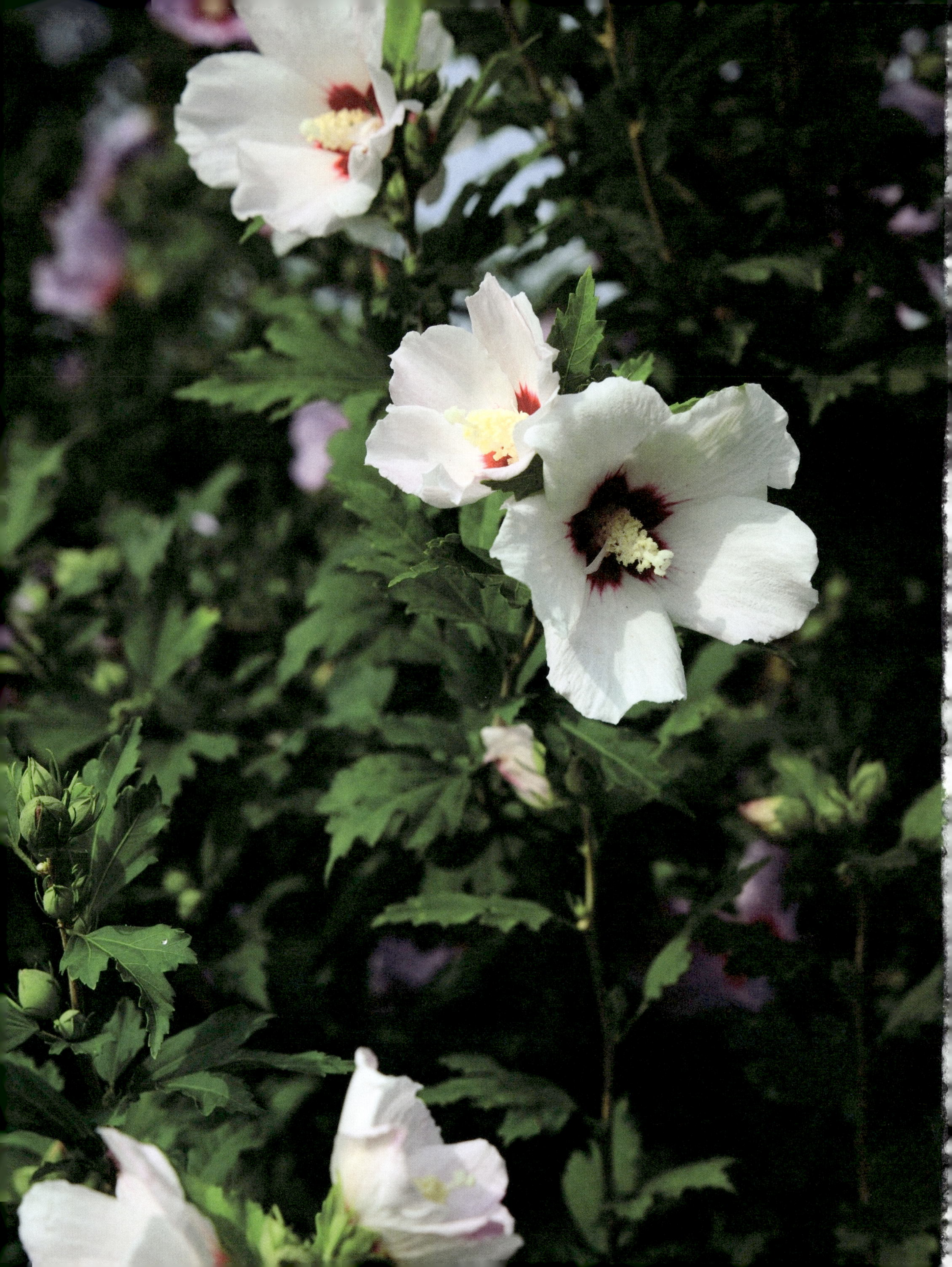

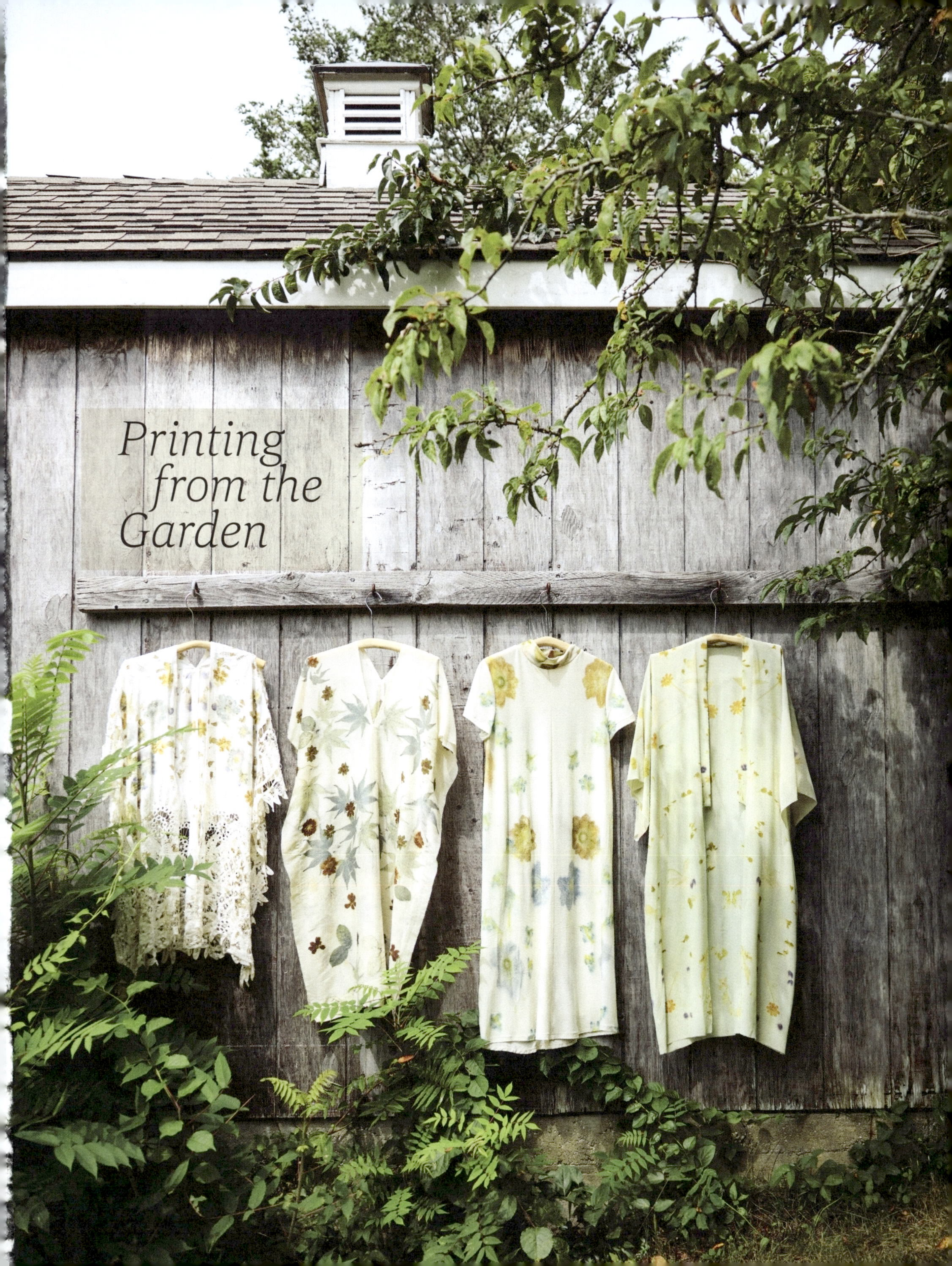
Printing from the Garden

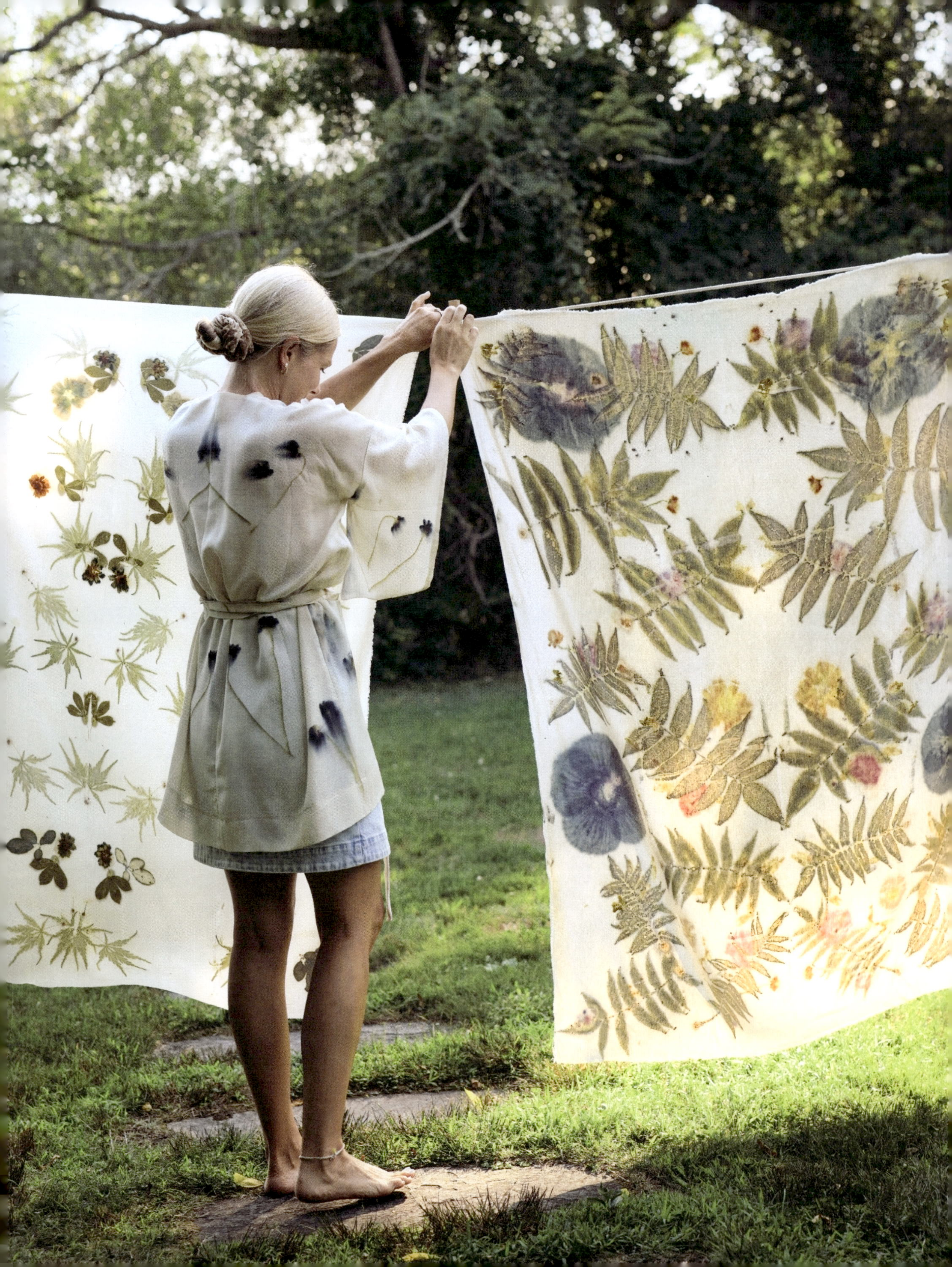

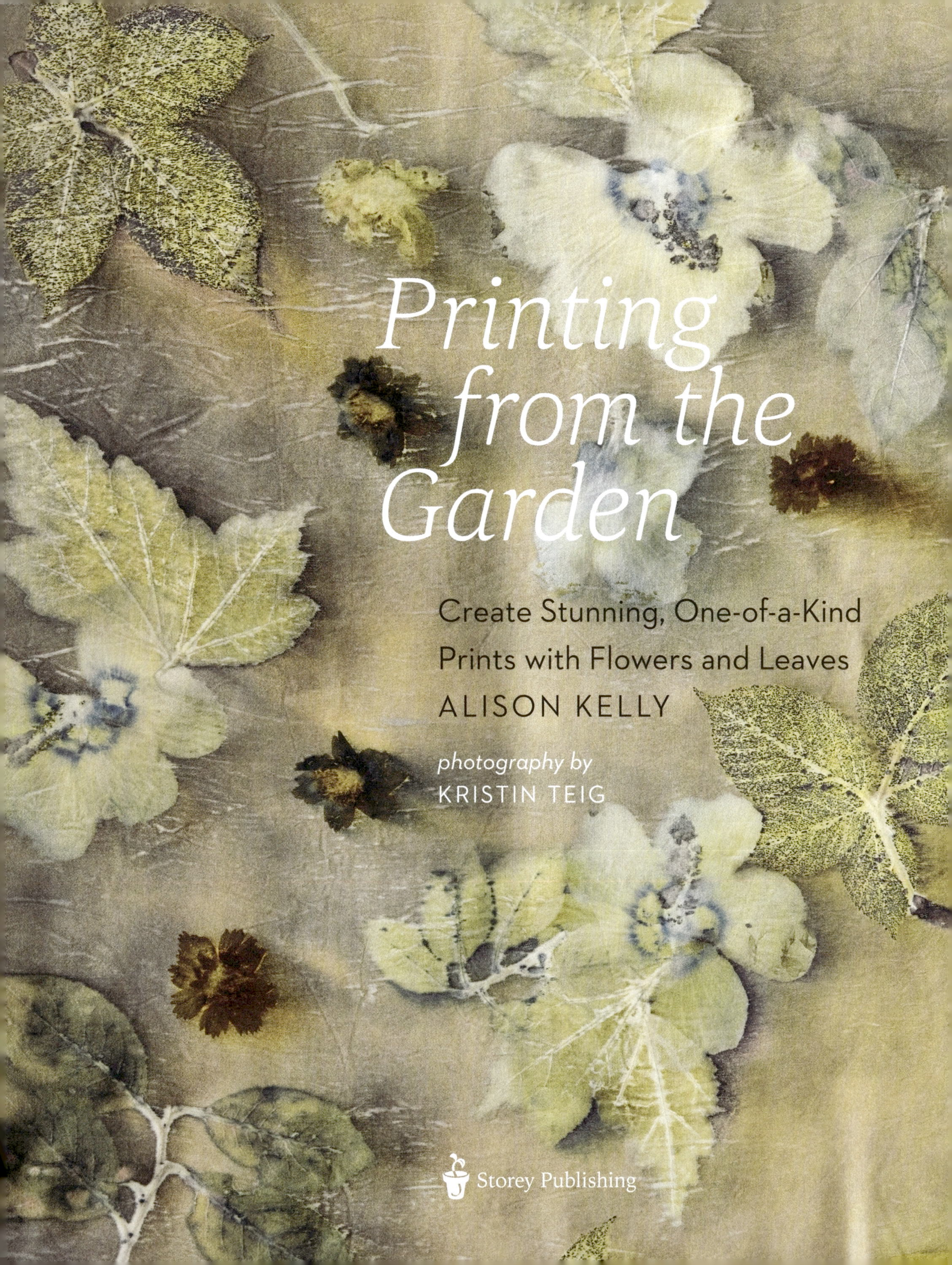

Printing from the Garden

Create Stunning, One-of-a-Kind Prints with Flowers and Leaves

ALISON KELLY

photography by
KRISTIN TEIG

Storey Publishing

The mission of Storey Publishing is to serve our customers by publishing practical information that encourages personal independence in harmony with the environment.

EDITED BY Lisa Hiley and Diana Rupp
ART DIRECTION AND BOOK DESIGN BY Carolyn Eckert
TEXT PRODUCTION BY Jennifer Jepson Smith

COVER AND INTERIOR PHOTOGRAPHY BY © Kristin Teig
ADDITIONAL PHOTOGRAPHY BY © Abinieks/Shutterstock.com, 42 t.; Courtesy of Alison Kelly, 52 t., 99; Cory Maylett/CC BY-SA 3.0/Wikimedia Commons, 51 t.r.; Denis Conrado/CC BY-SA 3.0/Wikimedia Commons, 58 t.; Emily Dickinson, Herbarium, circa 1839–1846, 1 vol. (66 pgs.), pg. 62. MS Am 1118.11, Houghton Library, Harvard University, 35; © Fatim NoE/Shutterstock.com, 87 t.; George Chernilevsky/Public domain/Wikimedia Commons, 60 t.; © John A. Anderson/Shutterstock.com, 66 t.; © Kabar/Shutterstock.com, 91 t.; © Marinodenisenko/Shutterstock.com, 74 t.; Mmrsafy/CC BY-SA 4.0/Wikimedia Commons, 84 b.r.; © olko1975/Shutterstock.com, 36 t.r.; R. A. Nonenmacher/CC BY-SA 4.0/Wikimedia Commons, 44 t.r.; © Robert Buchel/Shutterstock.com, 81 t.; © Subbotina Anna/Shutterstock.com, 63 t.; Thelmadatter/CC BY-SA 4.0/Wikimedia Commons, 8 t.; Vinayaraj/CC BY-SA 4.0/Wikimedia Commons, 104 t.; © weha/Shutterstock.com, 57 t.; © weruu/Shutterstock.com, 40 b.r.
PHOTO STYLING BY Ann P. Lewis

Be sure to read all the instructions thoroughly before undertaking any of the projects in this book and follow all of the safety guidelines summarized on page 21.

Storey Publishing
210 MASS MoCA Way
North Adams, MA 01247
storey.com

Storey Publishing is an imprint of Workman Publishing, a division of Hachette Book Group, Inc., 1290 Avenue of the Americas, New York, NY 10104. The Storey Publishing name and logo are registered trademarks of Hachette Book Group, Inc.

ISBNs: 978-1-63586-876-0 (hardcover); 978-1-63586-877-7 (ebook)

Printed in China through Asia Pacific Offset on paper from responsible sources
10 9 8 7 6 5 4 3 2 1

APO

Library of Congress Cataloging-in-Publication Data on file

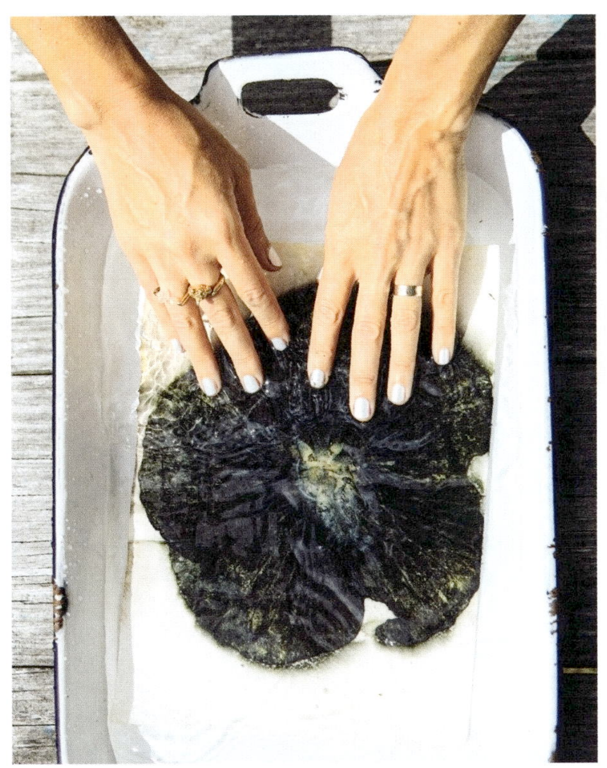

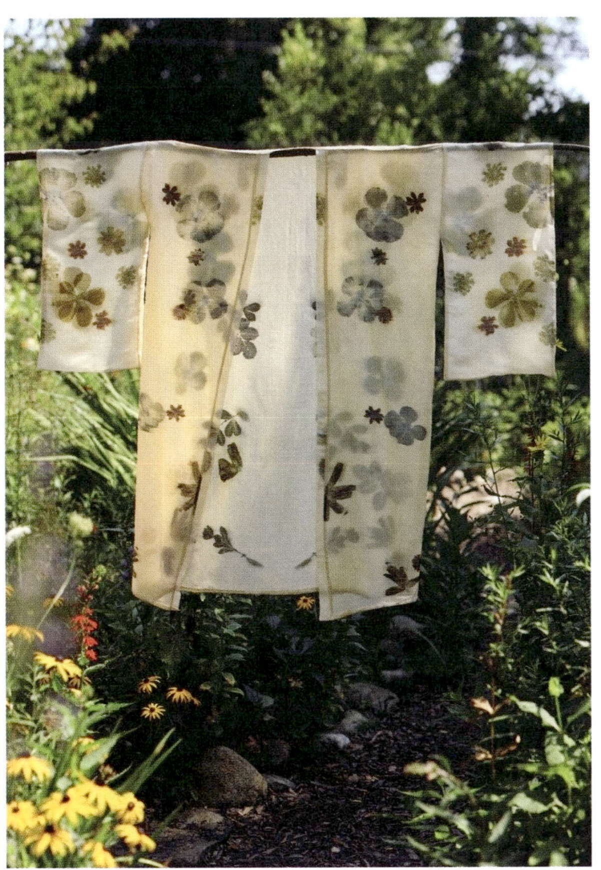

Contents

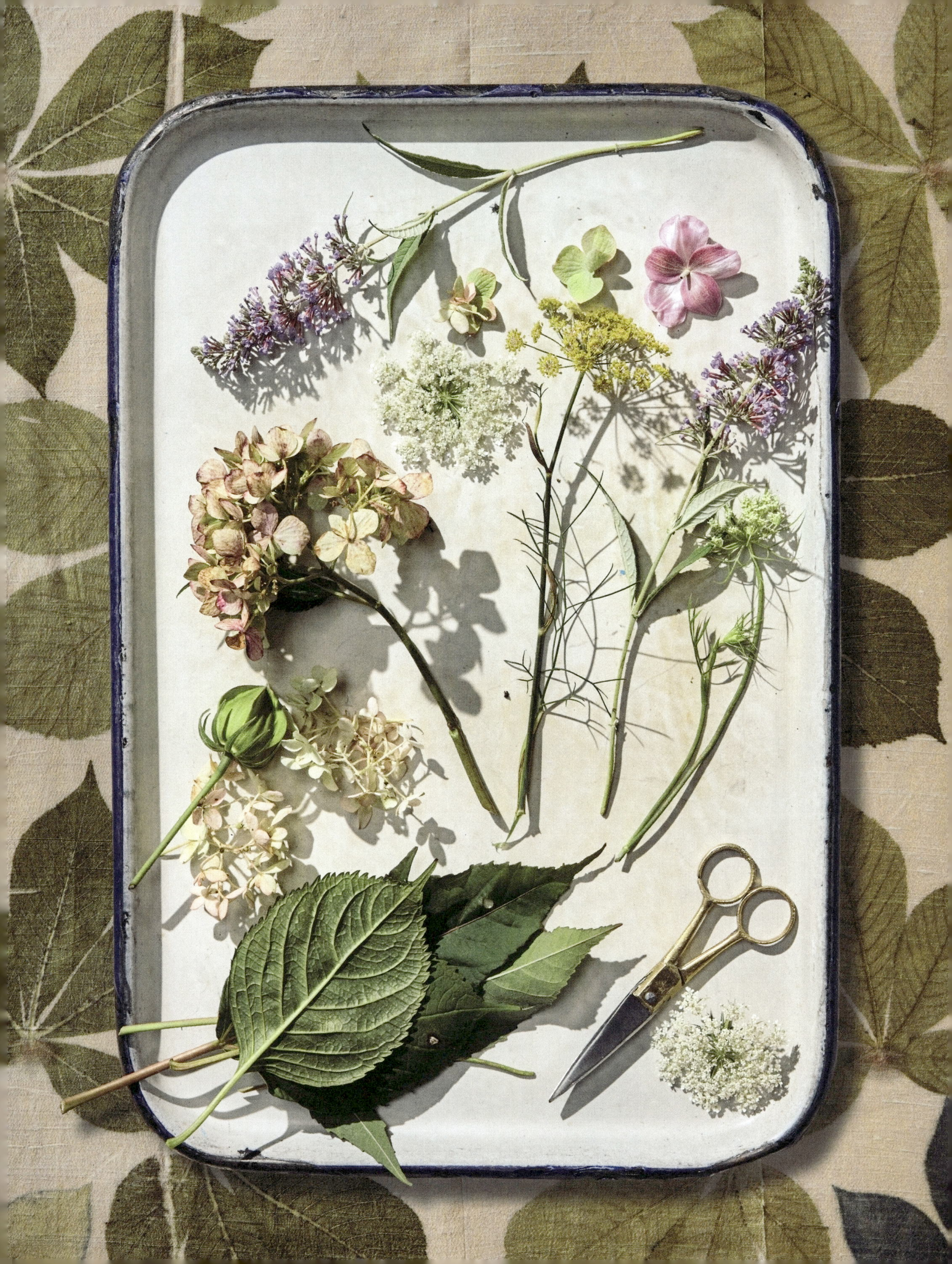

Preface: A Botanical Life

My connection to nature took root in childhood. Growing up in the lush green mountains of Vermont and along the sandy beaches of Cape Cod, I have always been enchanted by the tiniest wonders of the natural world. Evergreen forests, soft winding paths blanketed with pine needles and the heady scent of pitch, snowy white mountains, sugar-sand beaches, and deep blue Atlantic waters.

Nature was my playground, bursting with vegetation and color, inspiring awe. My mother tended to a vegetable and flower garden, showing me what an interdependent relationship with nature can look like. In addition to being a painter, she was always sewing: holiday dresses, patchwork quilts, matching quilted jackets for me and my sister and our dolls. My deep connection to textiles was ignited early, as was a preference for customized clothing. My first experiments were in high school, when I altered vintage pieces sourced from thrift shops and vintage boutiques because the fashion trends that reached our local department stores didn't suit me at all. Picking apart the seams to enhance the fit was an excellent method in understanding how clothing is pieced together, a puzzle far more complex and compelling than you may think.

This perspective led me to pursue an art degree specializing in fashion, silversmithing, and textiles, with nature as the driving force behind my creations.

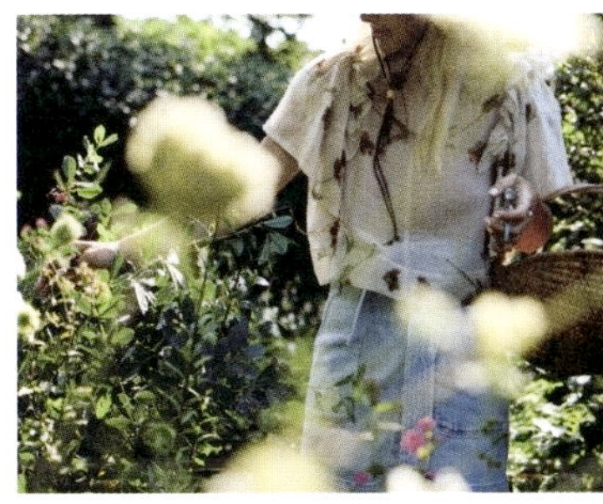

Until we can comprehend the beguiling beauty of a single flower, we are woefully unable to grasp the meaning and potential of life itself.

—VIRGINIA WOOLF

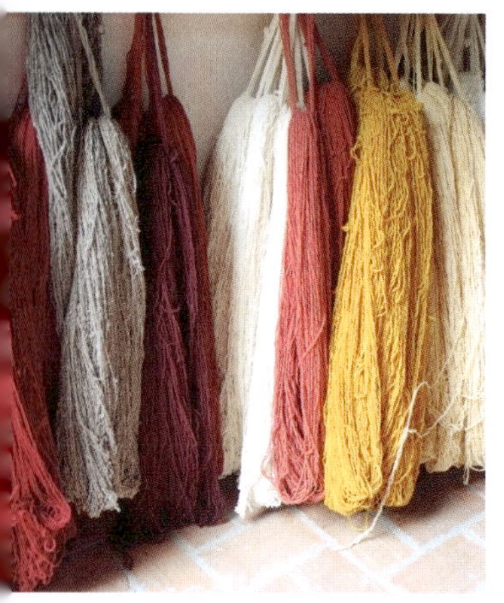

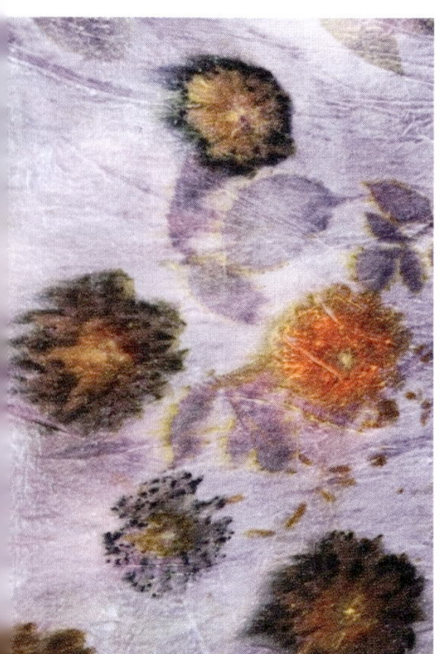

I first encountered the fascinating history of botanical dyeing on a trip to Oaxaca in 1999. In this vibrant region, 16 Indigenous groups, each with their distinct culture and dialect, share a storied history of arts, natural dyes, and weaving. The Zapotec-style textiles captivated me as I wandered the zócalo, where local artisans proudly exhibited their craftsmanship. Each intricate rug and shawl, adorned with distinctive diamond and geometric patterns, told a story of cultural heritage. The weavers employed backstrap looms—one of humanity's oldest weaving methods dating back to the Aztecs—infusing each piece with a sense of tradition and artistry. While many contemporary Oaxacan weavers had turned to synthetic dyes for their affordability and ease of use, the gorgeous hues and rich narratives of the natural dyes of the region were impossible to overlook. That experience left a lasting impression on my 18-year-old mind, but it wasn't until years later that I began integrating botanical dyes into my own creative processes, reigniting the passion I felt in Oaxaca.

When I moved to New York City in 2006, I was cast in the third season of Bravo TV's *Project Runway*. Although this experience opened doors in the fashion industry, I quickly realized I didn't fit into the cutthroat, unsustainable, fast-paced world around me. In response, I chose to forge my own path, designing independently with a focus on creating editions of clothing made from vintage and run-off fabrics. A sense of incompleteness lingered, however—I wanted my creations to tell a story. I yearned to craft my own prints and color palettes, deepening my connection to each garment. This desire aligned with my growing awareness of the detrimental impact of fast fashion on the environment and the workers whose labor fuels it, prompting me to seek a more sustainable and meaningful approach to my craft.

I began experimenting with alternative methods for dyeing textiles by looking to the past, where ancient natural dye practices relied solely on botanicals to create color. I started with shibori, a celebrated Japanese technique that allows for intricate patterns on fabric through folding, clamping, or stitching, creating resist patterns that leave those areas untouched when submerged in dye, like tie-dyeing.

While pregnant with my daughter, I discovered a world of beauty that would change my perspective on textiles forever. In the pages of *Eco Colour: Botanical Dyes for Beautiful Textiles* by India Flint, I encountered stunning pieces imprinted with eucalyptus leaves. The natural elegance of these fabrics captivated me and inspired a passion for the art of printing with plants. Although the book lacked precise recipes, the emotionally stunning visuals increased my eagerness to further explore the art of imbuing fabric with botanicals. The term *eco-printing* was introduced in the book to describe this intricate process. The prefix *eco-* (not harming the environment) seemed far too broad to describe the artful act of laying, compressing, and steaming plants into fiber.

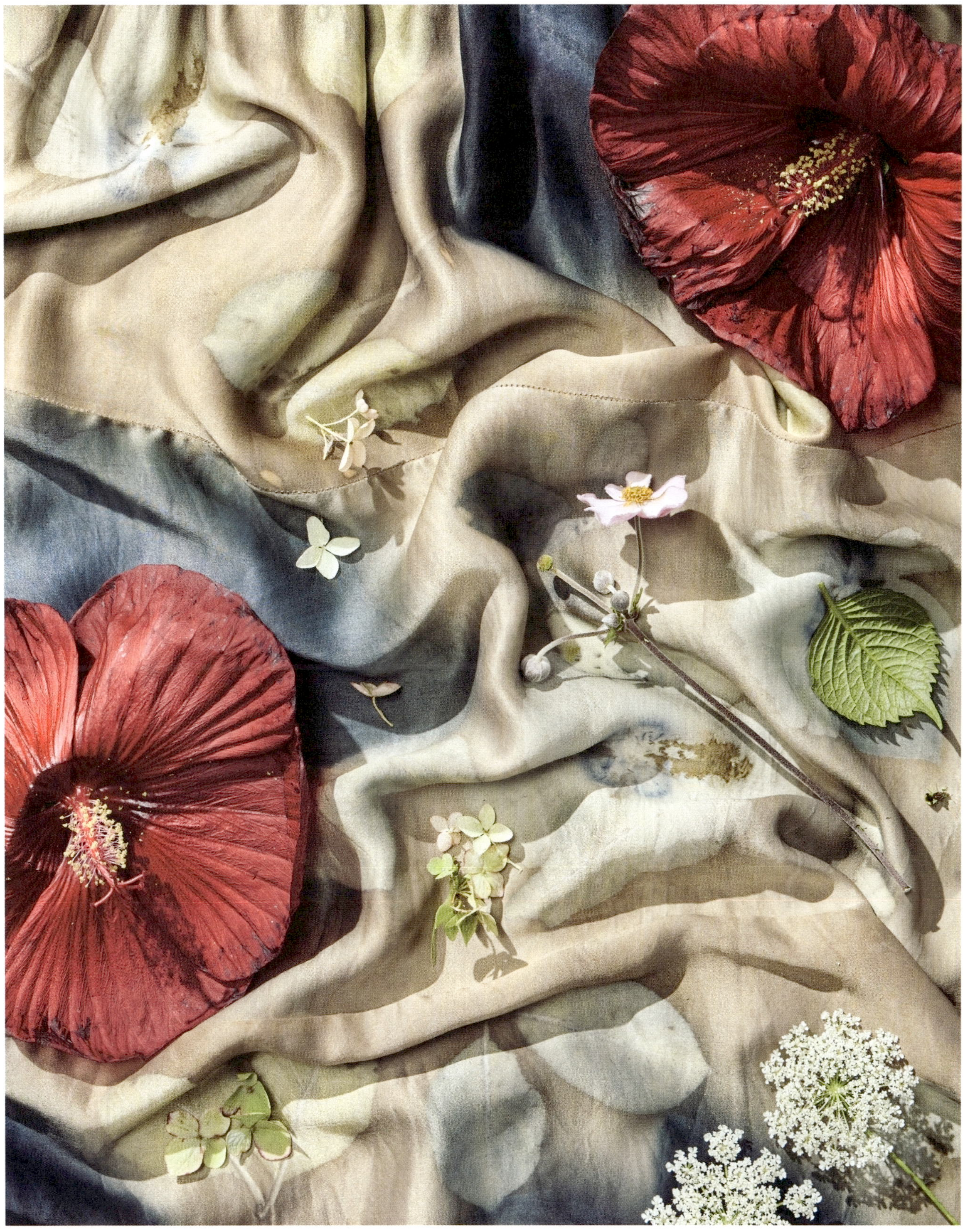

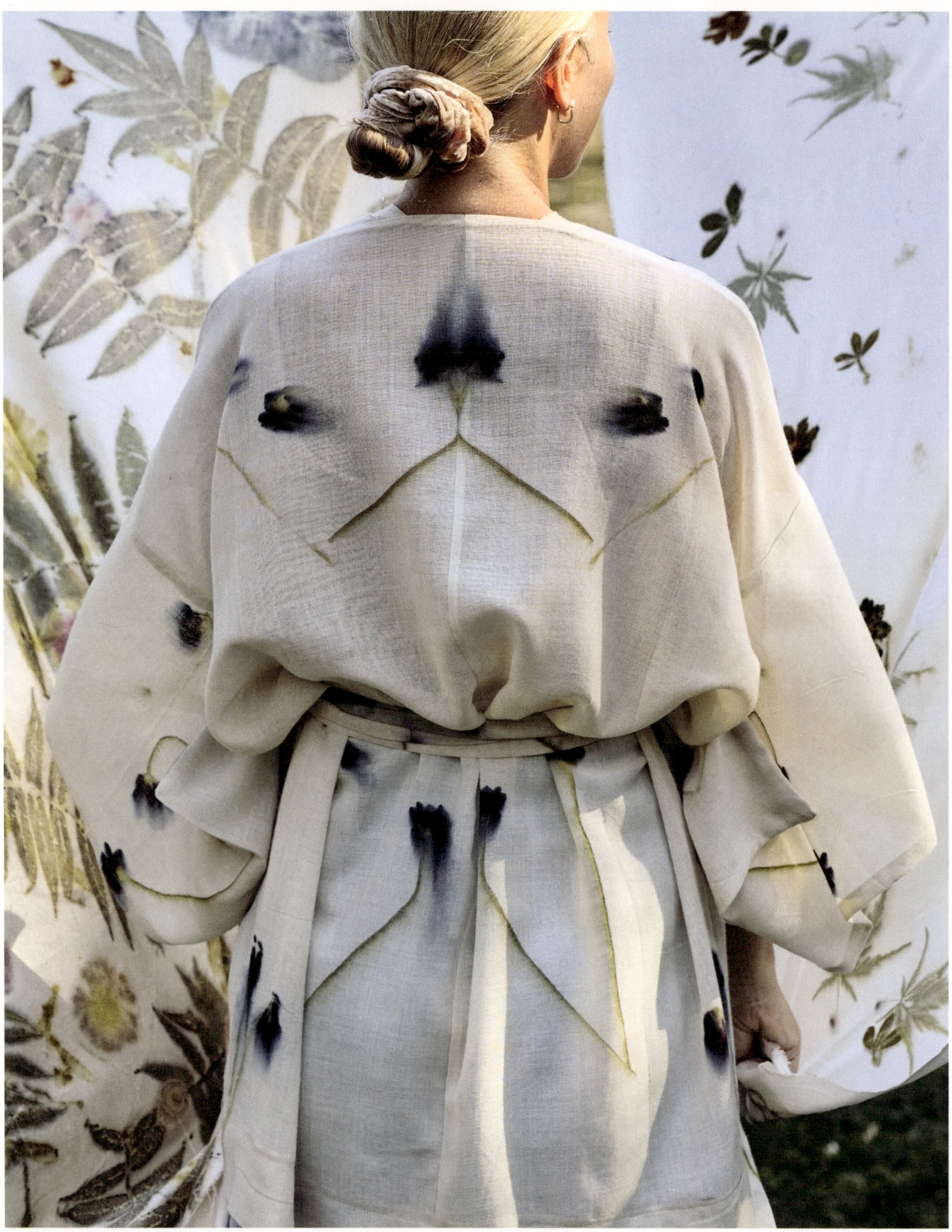

In response, I began calling this process botanical contact printing, a more accurate description. At the time, Israeli artist Irit Dulman maintained a blog dedicated to botanical printing, where she openly shared the results of her workshops and experiments. Her insights provided invaluable guidance to many, helping them push forward in a medium that had little published information available. I set out to use plants that could be found locally in my biomes, or local habitats, of Brooklyn and Cape Cod. My first experiment was a silk slip printed with foraged tulips, violets, and dried roses, and the results were unlike anything I'd seen before. The highly anticipated moment of unwrapping the bundle led me to insights into how we interact with plants and the emotions they cultivate in us.

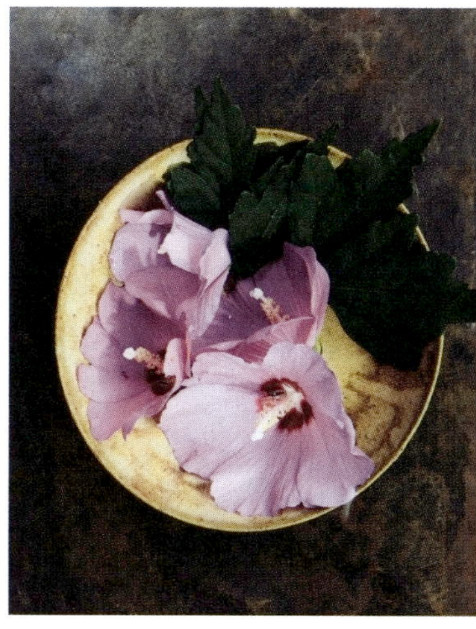

That experiment changed everything.

I had finally found a comfortable niche working in an art form that existed at the intersection of fashion, textiles, art, and nature. Quietly, I began to build a body of work under the label Flora Obscura, a journey that allowed me to deepen my understanding and refine my craft. What started as a simple exploration of the symbiotic relationship between natural fibers and plants evolved into a profound expression of creativity.

Flora Obscura, derived from the scientific term for plants—*flora*—and the word *obscura*, meaning "shadow" or "dark," encapsulates my mission: to capture the essence or shadow of a plant on textile or paper. Through this work, I aim to celebrate nature's beauty while fostering a deeper connection to sustainable practices in both art and fashion, creating pieces that resonate with the stories of the natural world. Flora Obscura has provided me with a deep sense of purpose as an artist and has brought many blessings, from exhibitions to collaborations, bespoke commissions to hosting group workshops.

Today fiber artists have access to an expansive array of resources for sourcing botanical dyes, mordants—the metallic salts we use to fix color to fiber—and undyed natural fibers. Embracing plant-based dyes not only enhances your artistic palette but also deepens your connection to nature. As you work with organic materials, you become more attuned to the delicate shifts of the natural world, revealing a stunning biodiversity of color. Replacing synthetic dyes with natural alternatives will open up a world of inspiration and creativity. It fosters a profound appreciation for the plants around us and emphasizes the importance of protecting and preserving them.

This book serves as a catalyst to ignite your passion for plants, inviting you to not only appreciate the beauty of textiles but to engage with the natural world in a mindful and respectful way.

> When you take a flower in your hand and really look at it, it's your world for the moment. I want to give that world to someone else. Most people in the city rush around so, they have no time to look at a flower. I want them to see it whether they want to or not.
>
> —GEORGIA O'KEEFFE

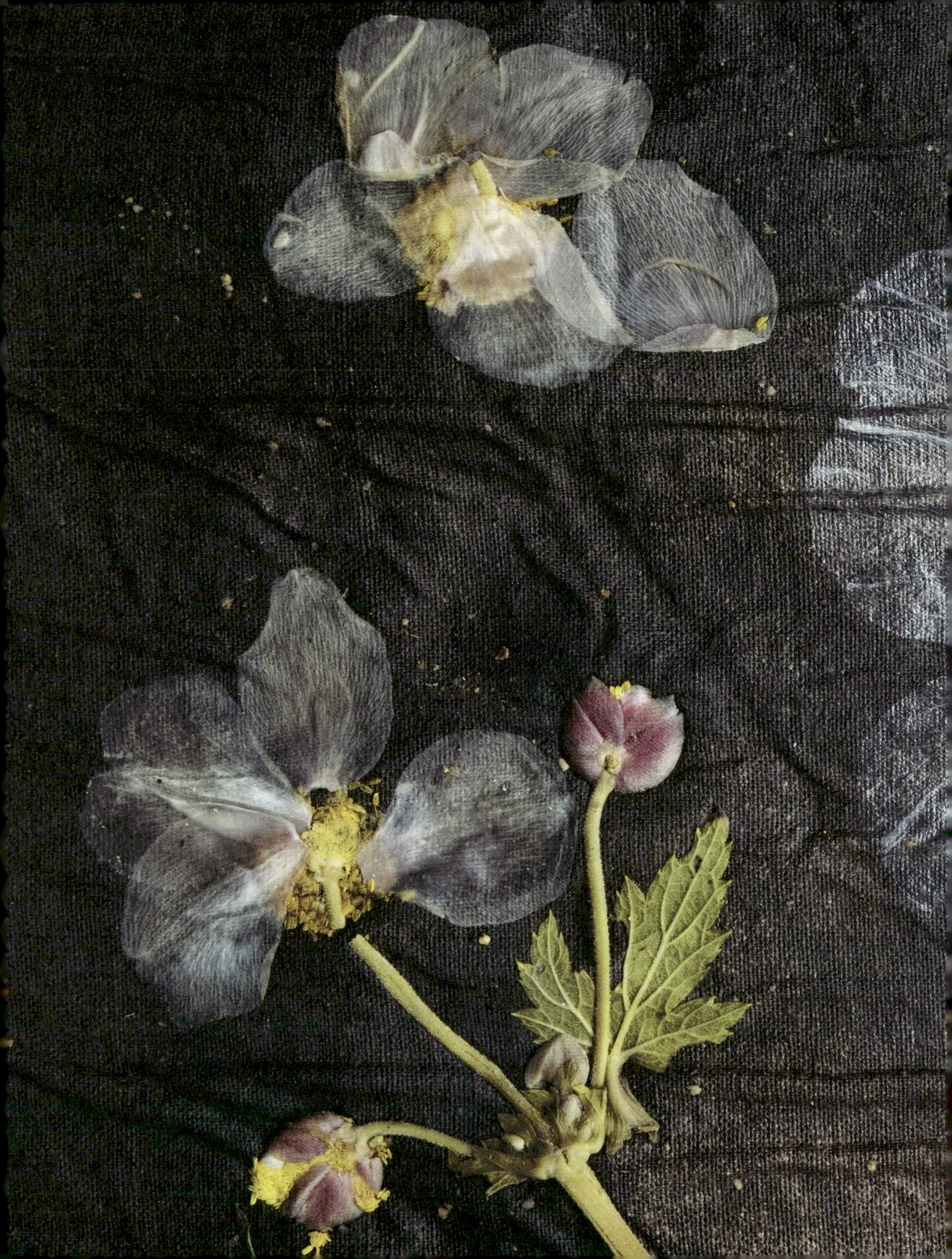

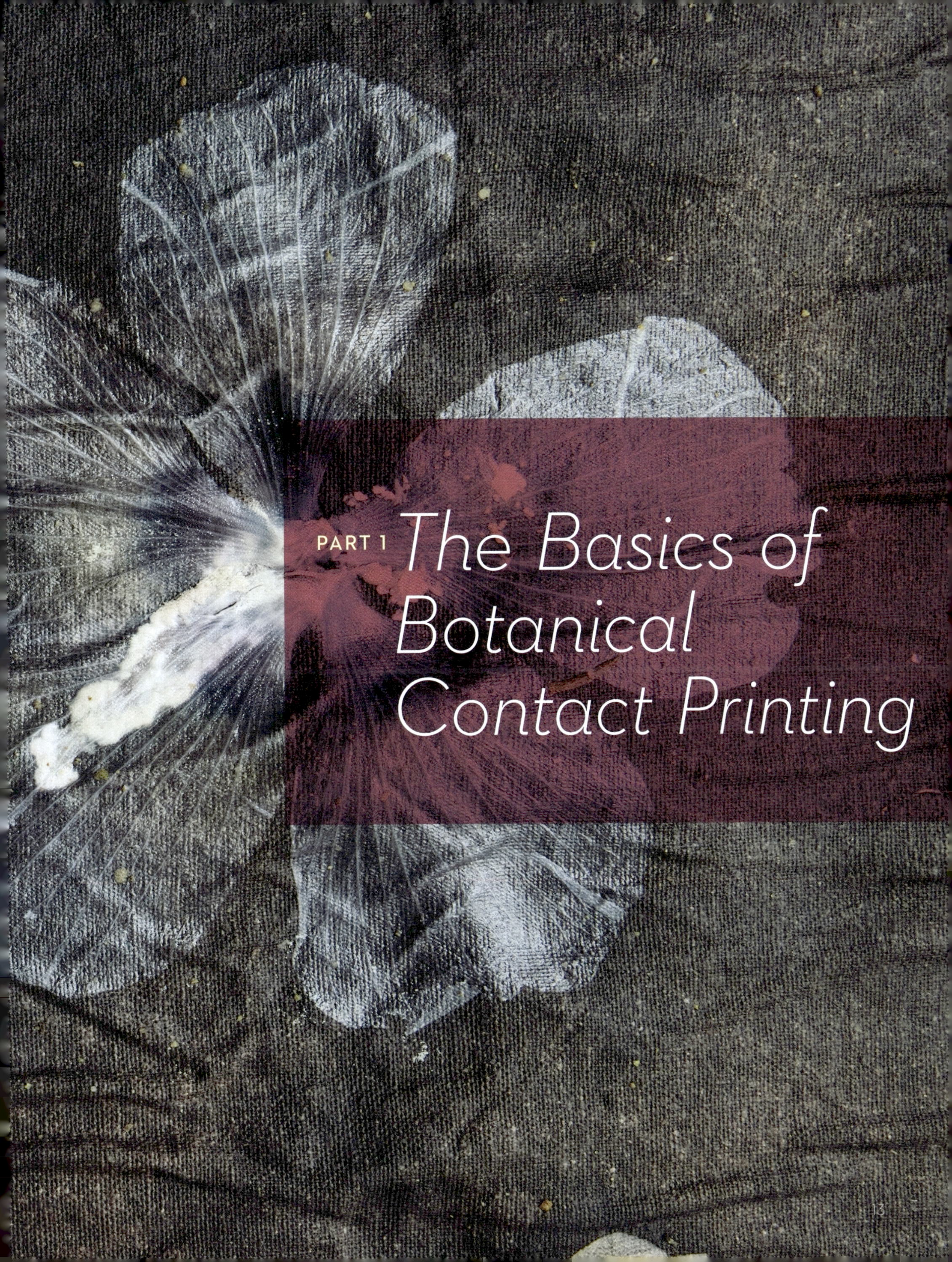

PART 1 The Basics of Botanical Contact Printing

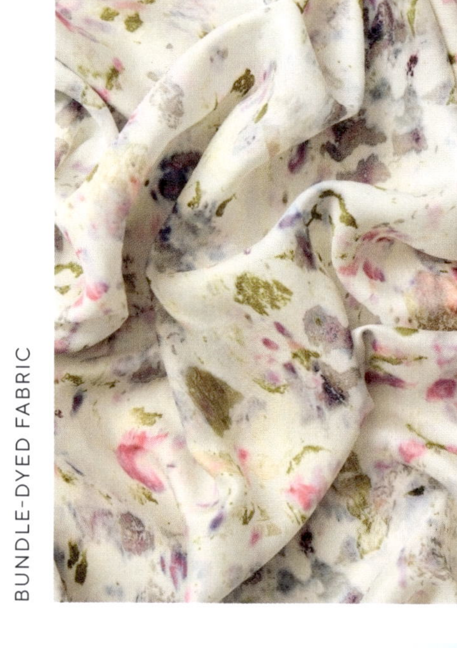

BUNDLE-DYED FABRIC

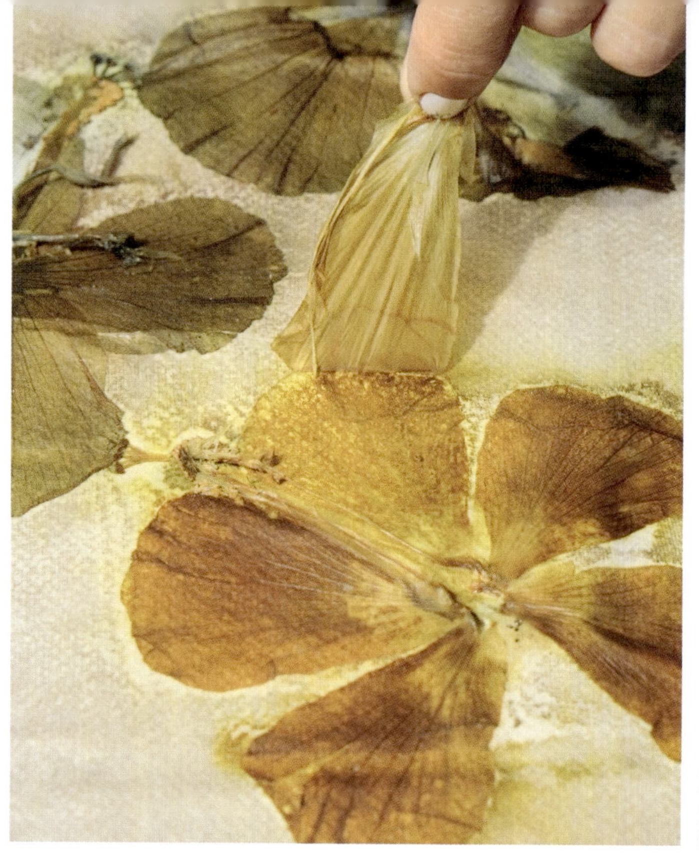

THE REVEAL

HIBISCUS: PRINTED & FRESH

Botanical contact printing is a delicate dance between chemistry, botany, and art. A seemingly magical process of transformation takes place when these elements interact. Using four key components—moisture, compression, heat, and botanicals—you can transmute the pigment, the spirit, and the essence of plants into fiber.

Adapted from ancient natural-dyeing traditions, this art form invites you to discover the vibrant potential of plant pigments. Through a series of crucial yet straightforward steps, you'll learn how to harness nature's colors effectively. While the outcome can be unpredictable, the methods presented in this book serve as a reliable foundation for achieving more consistent results. Embrace the journey, and let these techniques encourage you to explore your own creative path in the world of botanical printing.

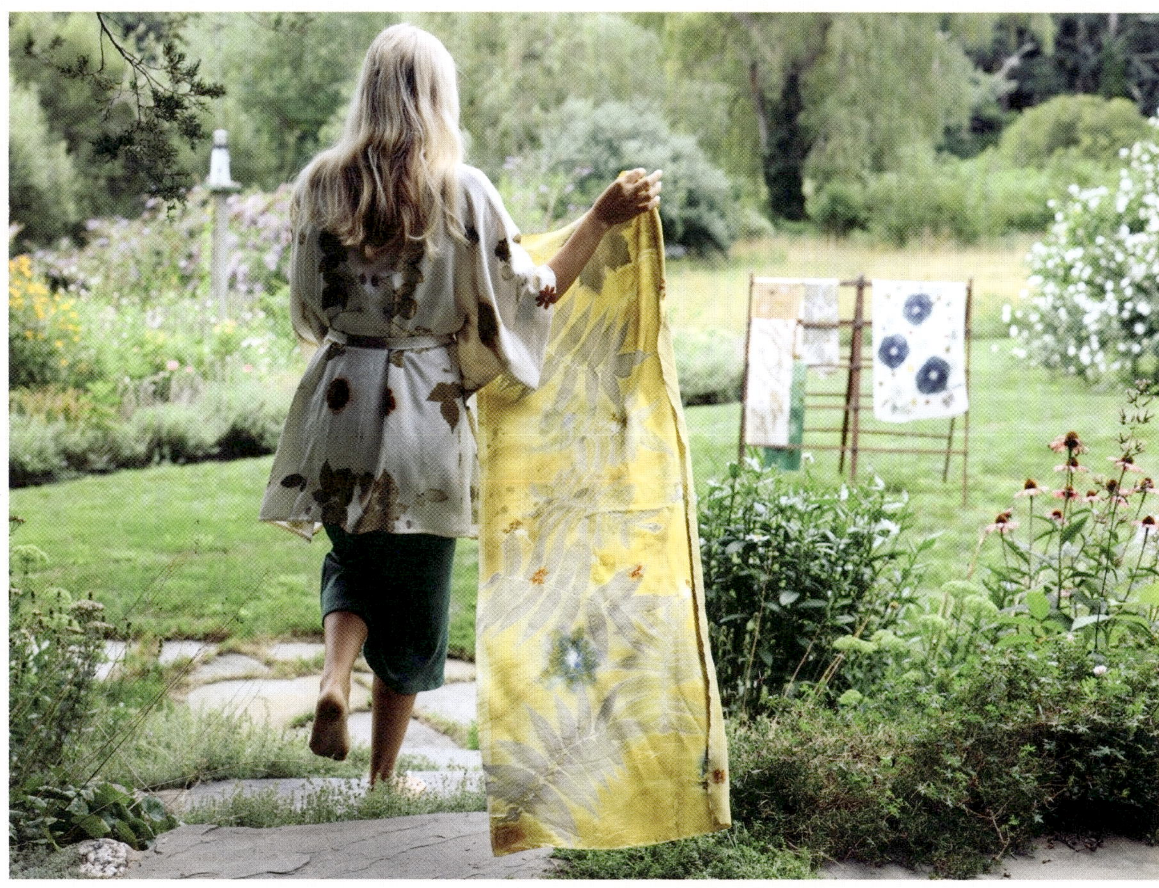

A Brief History of Dyeing with Plants

Evidence of botanical dyeing has been found across many ancient cultural artifacts from around the world. Anthropologists believe that many dye materials were discovered by accident: Perhaps a berry caused a dark plummy stain on skin or clothing, and admiration for the surprising coloration led to further experimentation and application of dyes. It appears that botanical and other natural dyes—pigments derived from plants, barks, roots, berries, fungi, mosses, insects, minerals—were being used to dye textiles as long as five thousand years ago. Ancient madder root was discovered in a belt found at the grave of the Egyptian pharaoh Tutankhamen, dating back to circa 3000 BCE. Some evidence suggests that the practice goes back even further to the New Stone Age or around 10200 BCE. The earliest evidence—artifacts containing a reddish brown dye, possibly derived from iron oxide pigments found in clay—was unearthed in the region of Çatalhöyük in southern Anatolia.

Historically speaking, botanical dyes are divided into two categories: substantive (or direct) dyes, which require no mordant, or "fixer," to permanently imbue color into fiber, and adjective dyes, which require a mordant to fix color to the fiber. Most botanical dyes are adjective dyes, but there are notable exceptions: Indigo (*Indigofera tinctoria*) is still used to achieve colors ranging from light Botticelli blue to deep navy, as well as alluring greens when overdyed with yellow or orange-hued botanicals. Other historical substantive dyes include cochineal, a tiny cactus-dwelling insect that is small but mighty, rich in carminic acid and plucked from the prickly pear cactus to be used today as a food and cosmetic dye. Safflower (*Carthamus tinctorius*), black walnut (*Juglans nigra*), and some lesser-known fungi also fall into this category.

Indigo was used to dye the denim of the original Levi's blue jeans, as it has excellent fastness properties.

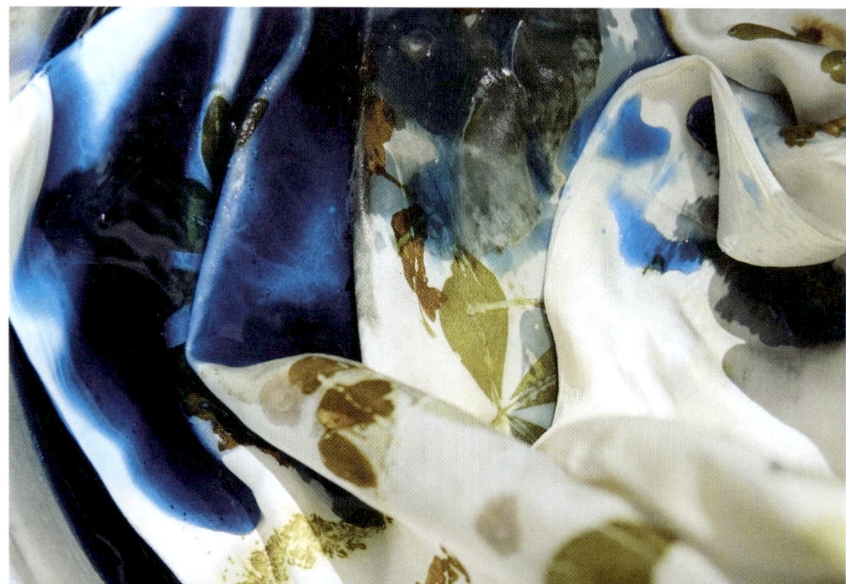

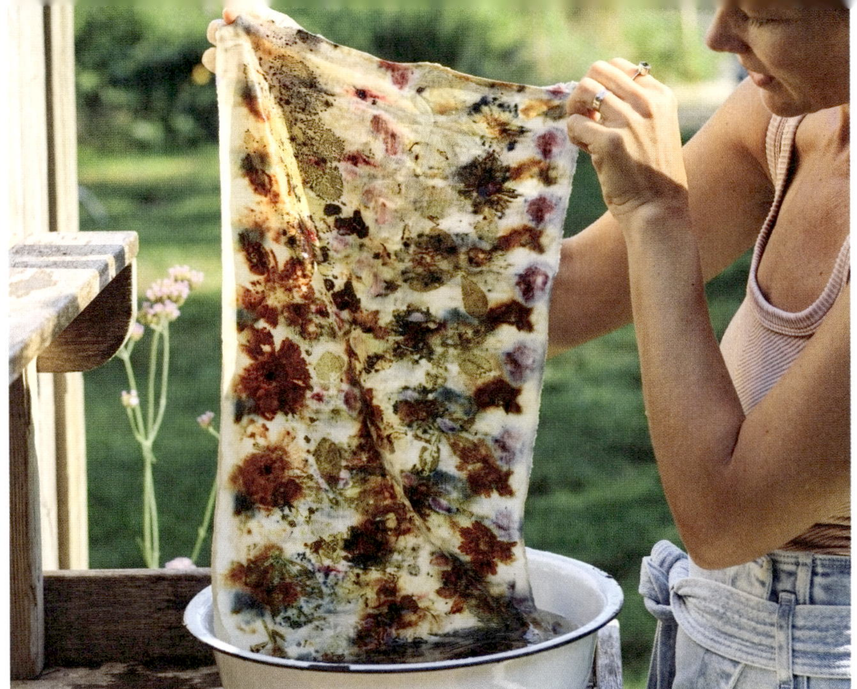

An Overview of the Process

With just a few mordant recipes and techniques, the world of plant printing offers endless possibilities and outcomes. The intriguing variety of the craft has captivated countless enthusiasts over the years. By simply altering the vegetation or the hue of a dye bath, you can unlock a spectrum of unexpected and beautifully varied results. Each experiment invites new creativity, as the inherent qualities of the plants interact with the materials, revealing stunning imprints and colors that reflect the natural world.

At first you may feel overwhelmed as you read through the recipes and techniques, but it's essential to fully grasp the process before jumping in, as each step is important, and materials need to be gathered ahead of time. The mordanting process, which prepares fabric and paper fibers to accept pigment, requires a couple of days to fully implement. The good news is that you can prepare a quantity of material at once and store it for future projects.

Before cutting into expensive fabrics or printing on fine papers, I suggest experimenting on fabric scraps and inexpensive or recycled paper. This approach not only builds your confidence but also provides valuable insights into how various plants and mordants react. By freeing yourself from the pressure of costly materials, you can fully explore your artistic vision and develop your skills, paving the way for beautiful, successful projects in the future.

The Printing Process

1 Wet Out the Fiber (page 113)

Soaking fabric in water before scouring, mordanting, or printing is referred to as "wetting out" the fiber. The fabric must be completely saturated with water before moving on to the next step, allowing for full uptake of mordant ingredients and plant pigments.

2 Scour the Fabric (page 114)

It's critical to wash your fabric before printing in order to remove residue, such as oils or sizing, that can interfere with achieving clear prints. This step does not apply to paper.

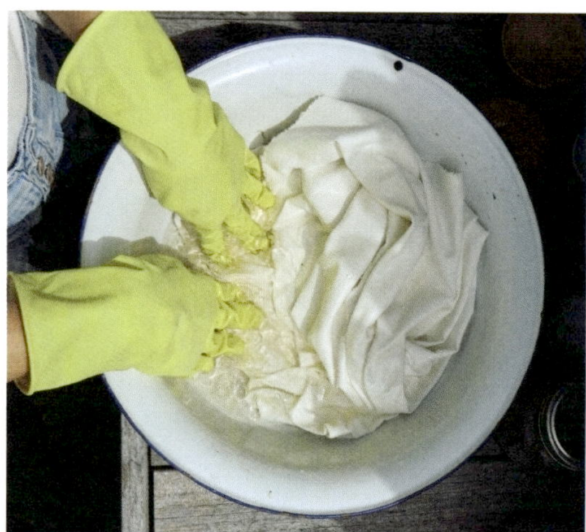

3 Mordant the Fabric (page 118) or Paper (page 170)

Soaking fabric or paper in a solution of metallic salts gives it the capacity to accept pigmentation. The substrate is soaked in a mordant solution, and in some cases, allowed to dry completely. Different mordant recipes produce different results. Some processes require a second bath in phosphorus-rich oatmeal to fully fix the mordant to the fibers.

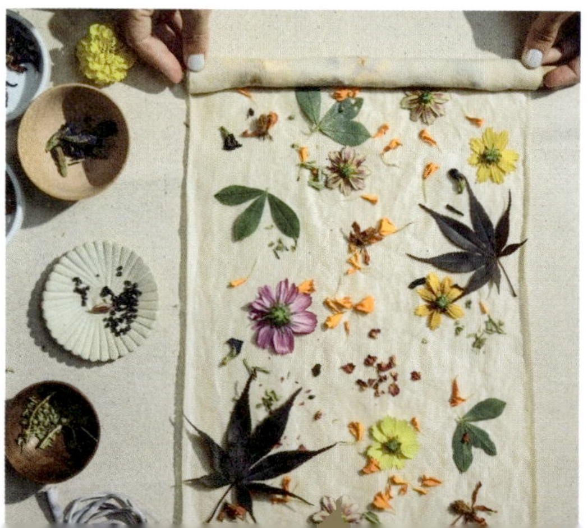

4 Lay Out the Design (page 132)

Before starting a new project, choose which technique you want to use and think of the colors and shapes you wish to achieve. Techniques include creating an allover print by bundle dyeing, creating a mirror-image print, or using a carrier blanket to impart a background color to the target (the piece of fabric or paper). Often before creating a print, I have an outcome in mind, such as turning the textile into a garment or pillowcase. I think about where on the body the imprints may fall or what I want to be centered on a square pillowcase. You can also print on clothing, though this usually takes more planning.

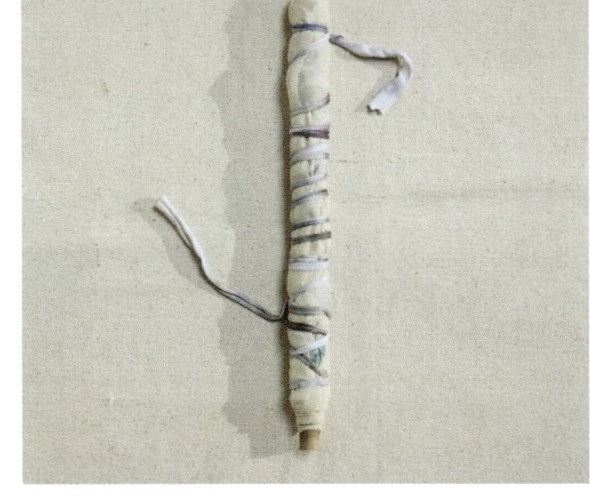

5 Bundle the Project (page 136)

The target, if fabric, is rolled around a thick wooden dowel. If paper, the target is wrapped around a larger cylindrical form, such as a clean coffee can or a steel pipe. Care must be taken to avoid wrinkles and bubbles while rolling. The bundle is tightly bound with bandage or stretchy T-shirt yarn.

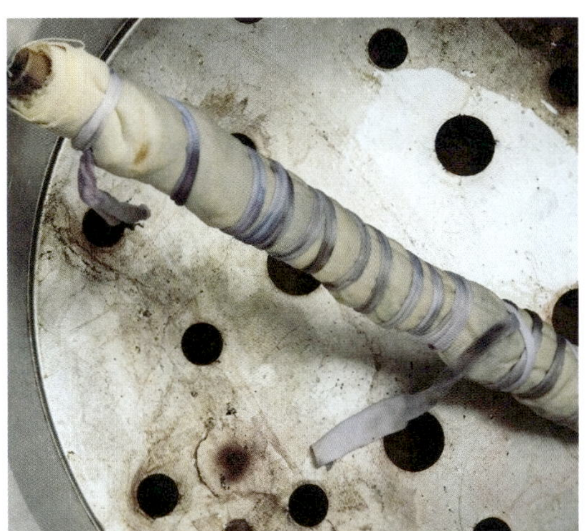

6 Steam to Fix the Color (page 138)

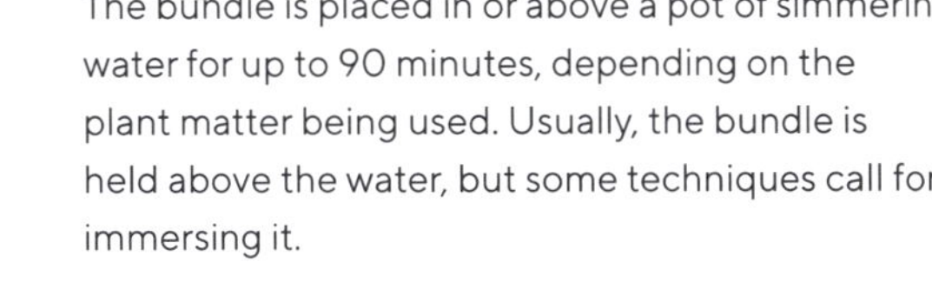

The bundle is placed in or above a pot of simmering water for up to 90 minutes, depending on the plant matter being used. Usually, the bundle is held above the water, but some techniques call for immersing it.

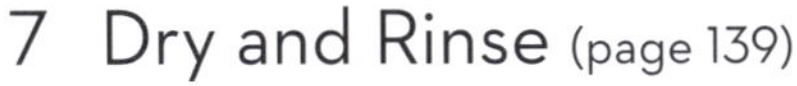

7 Dry and Rinse (page 139)

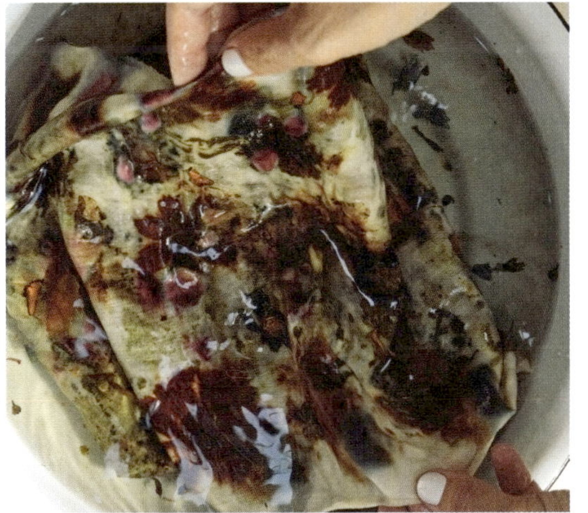

The bundle is removed from the steam bath and allowed to cool before being unrolled (this is the "reveal"—the best part!) and hung to dry. Once the fabric has dried, it is rinsed using cold water and a dash of pH-neutral soap to remove any remaining botanical particles.

8 Caring for Printed Pieces

To refresh printed fabrics, iron with steam on the wrong or backside of fabric to smooth out any wrinkles. Paper can be ironed from the back with a piece of muslin between the iron and paper.

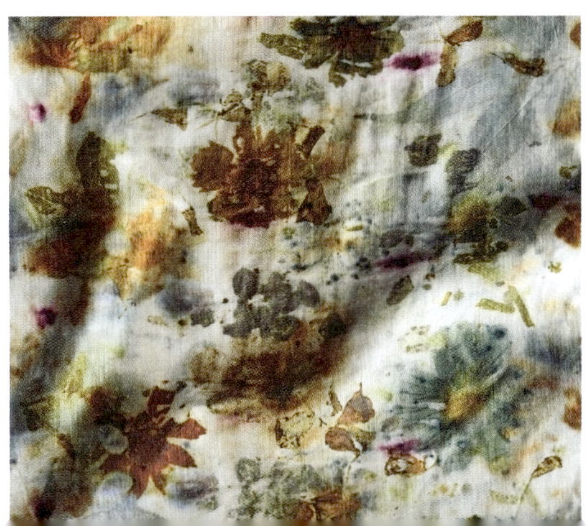

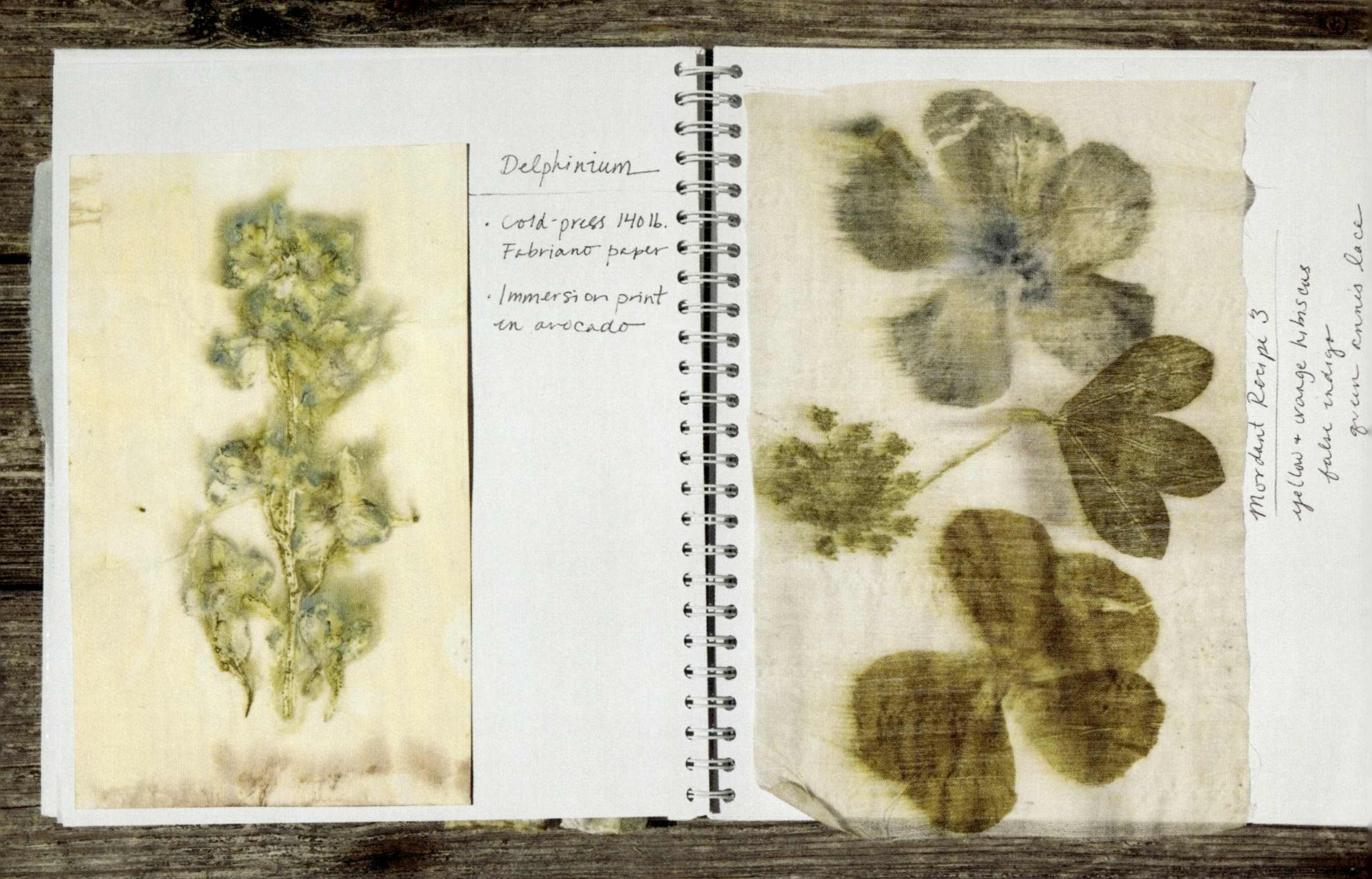

KEEP GOOD PROCESS NOTES

While it's important to trust in the process, allowing the unpredictability of the dyeing journey to inspire you, a logbook can become an indispensable companion for keeping track of successes and failures. Keeping notes will help you refine your techniques and understand the nuances of different plants and fibers. Here are some things to jot down about each project.

- Type of target (e.g., silk charmeuse, hot-pressed watercolor paper)
- Weight of target
- Type of mordant
- Technique used for printing
- Carrier blanket and dye if applicable
- Vegetation used
- Steaming or immersion bundling
- Type of immersion liquid if applicable
- Steaming time

Use a method that works for you and will make filling out the details of your projects a joyful ritual. You might also plot out a plan *before* you begin by recording weights and type of fiber and noting the intended process steps, plant matter, dye blankets, and more.

I keep photographic records and written notes in my phone. This also comes in handy when I'm working with compositions that won't fit into a swatch book. A photo is the perfect replacement.

Safety Precautions

When practicing any of the methods and techniques in this book, please practice caution. Follow all manufacturer's instructions for operating any equipment and be careful when handling potentially harmful ingredients, such as metallic salts and powdered dyes. Read safety data that accompanies any of your selected ingredients.

Know your materials. Be sure to clearly identify your plants before handling them or using them in the printing process; some are toxic and may cause irritation, blistering, or rashes.

Protect your lungs. Wear gloves and a mask (N95 or similar) when handling and weighing metallic salts and powders to avoid breathing in particles.

Protect work surfaces. Especially if working in your kitchen, be aware that powder residue can accumulate on surfaces. Cover workspaces well and clean up thoroughly. Better yet, work outside or at a dedicated location away from food prep areas.

Beware of heat. Steaming is integral to the botanical printing process. Protect your hands, arms, face, and feet around vessels of boiling water. Wear long pants and closed-toe shoes. Let pots of water cool before moving or emptying them.

Pay attention. An insistent timer that you cannot ignore is an invaluable tool to avoid letting pots simmer too long, which can lead to burning, melting, or worse.

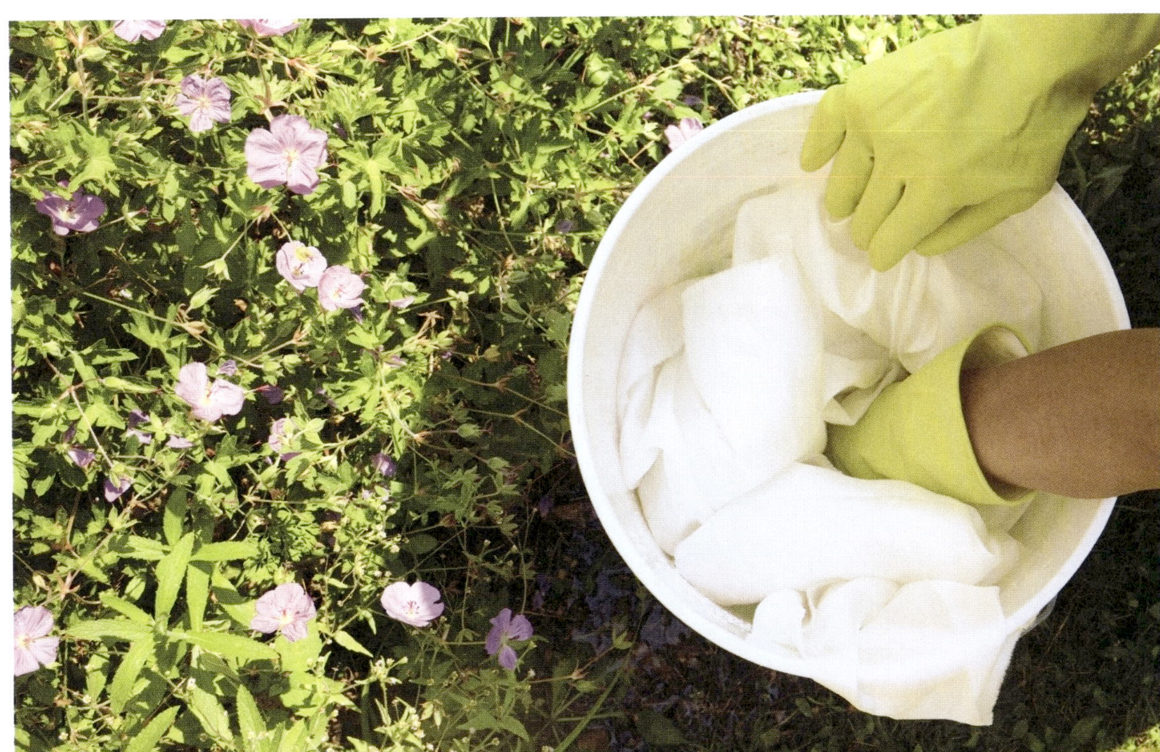

Glossary

Glossaries are usually located at the back of a book, but it's important to be familiar with the technical terminology before you begin printing.

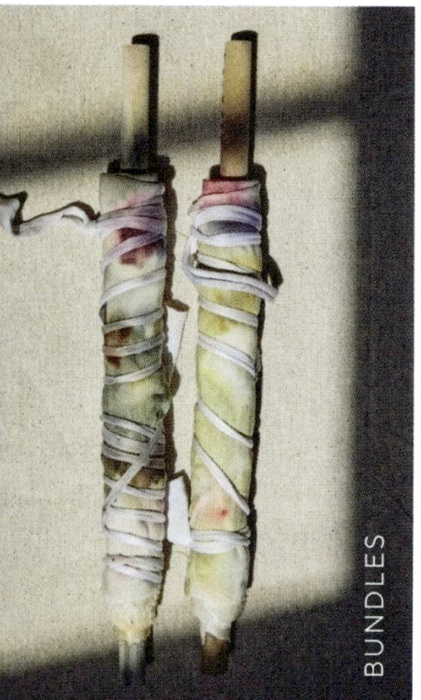

BUNDLES

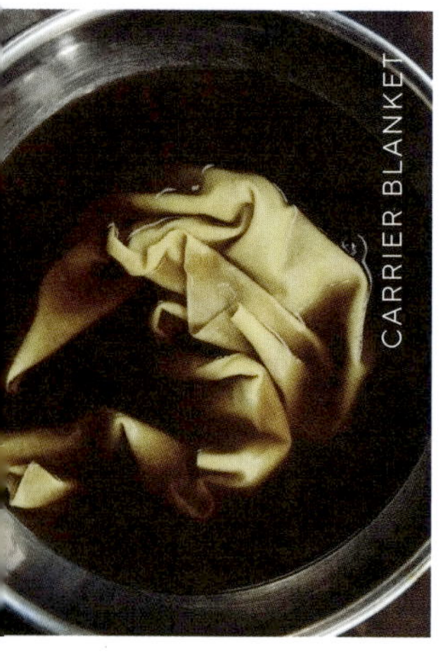

CARRIER BLANKET

MORDANT INGREDIENTS

Aluminum acetate (AA). A metallic salt used to mordant cellulose fibers such as cotton, linen, hemp, bamboo, viscose, and paper. AA is a more refined and therefore more expensive version of potassium aluminum sulfate, or PAS.

Aluminum triformate (ATF). A powerful metallic salt used to mordant both protein and cellulose fibers to achieve vivid and saturated coloring.

Calx (calcium hydroxide, hydrated lime, or slaked lime). A mordant ingredient for cellulose and protein fibers. It serves as an alkali in many dye recipes, raising the pH level of the mordant, and also acts as a preservative.

Iron (ferrous sulfate). A mordant ingredient for cellulose and protein fibers. It acts as a color modifier and makes the color more washfast. Must be used with care on protein fibers, as it can make them brittle.

Potassium aluminum sulfate (PAS). A metallic salt used to mordant both protein and cellulose fibers, it is a chemical compound made up of potassium, aluminum, and sulfate ions.

Soda ash/sodium carbonate (Na_2CO_3). An alkaline modifier ingredient for cellulose and protein fibers that increases the effectiveness of a mordant. Soda ash can enhance the coloration of plant pigments. It is also used in combination with soap to scour cellulose fibers.

PRINTING TERMINOLOGY

Barrier. A layer of a nonporous material placed on top of the target before bundling. A barrier, which is optional, helps create clear and crisp prints by eliminating multiple repeats and bleed-throughs of color onto the adjacent fiber. Many people use painter's plastic, large sheets of reusable plastic that come in panels that can be perfectly cut to size. Parchment paper is another option.

Bundle. (v) To roll the target tightly around a dowel and secure it for steaming. (n) The rolled and secured target.

Carrier blanket. Also known as a tannin blanket. A piece of cloth that transfers a background color onto the target when rolled and steamed.

Cellulose fiber. A structural fiber made by plants (vegetable fibers), including cotton, linen, rayon, bamboo, hemp, and viscose, among others.

Cushioning blanket. A piece of cloth that is placed over the target before bundling. A blanket can be cut from pure white cloth and is used to provide cushioning when rolling the bundle, which can contribute to enhanced plant prints. A blanket soaked in dye is called a carrier blanket.

Dowel. Round cylindrical stick of wood, pipe, tin can, or metal around which the target is wrapped.

Extract. A concentrated form of a botanical substance, in this case plant- and animal-based dyes.

Fastness. The resistance of a dyed fiber to lose color by fading or running.

Mordant. A metallic salt that binds to fiber and makes it possible for pigment to be absorbed, increasing both color- and washfastness.

pH-neutral soap. A plant-based soap with a pH of 7 to 10 used for scouring fabric. The level indicates that the soap is neutral, meaning there is an even balance of hydroxide and hydrogen. Castile soap is a good choice—made with 100 percent olive oil, it has a pH level of around 8.

Prepared for dye (PFD). A term applied specifically to silk protein fibers, indicating that the textile has been washed and does not need to be scoured, though it will need to be mordanted.

Protein fiber. Animal-based fibers, such as silk, wool, mohair, cashmere, and angora, that are made primarily of protein.

Ready-to-dye. A term applied to fabrics in general. Indicates that the textile has been washed and does not need to be scoured (but it will need to be mordanted).

Scour. Washing fabric, particularly ones made of cellulose or vintage fiber, in a bath of pH-neutral soap and soda ash to remove any buildup, grease, or sizing and to better aid the target in accepting mordants and plant pigment.

Simmer. To stay just below the boiling point where bubbles are present but the water is not at a full boil. Aim for 180 to 200°F (82–93°C).

Tannins. Powerful compounds found in bark, leaves, and fruits that enhance the dyeing process by forming chemical complexes with dye molecules and mordants in the fiber. Acting as a bridge between the dye and the material, tannins significantly improve the adhesion of dyes, ensuring more vibrant and long-lasting colors.

Target. The surface, or substrate, typically fabric or paper, onto which vegetation is being printed.

Weight of fiber (WOF). A convenient way to state how much dye is needed for a given color. The measure is a percentage of the dry weight of fiber; it remains constant regardless of whether you are dyeing a few ounces or a few grams.

Wetting out fiber. To saturate fabric with water before dyeing or printing so the pigment can adhere to the fabric more easily. Dry fabric may not absorb color evenly, resulting in streaks.

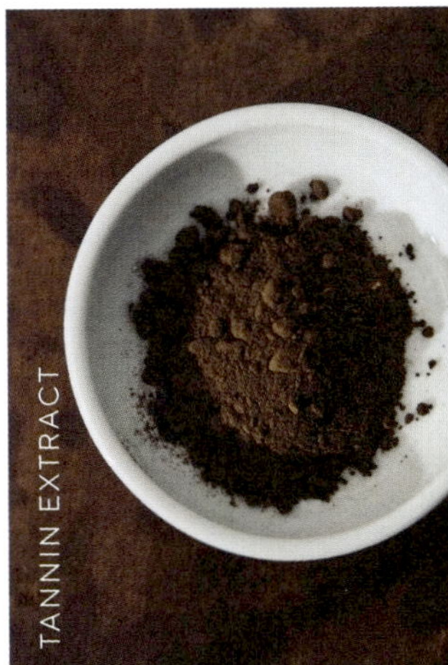
TANNIN EXTRACT

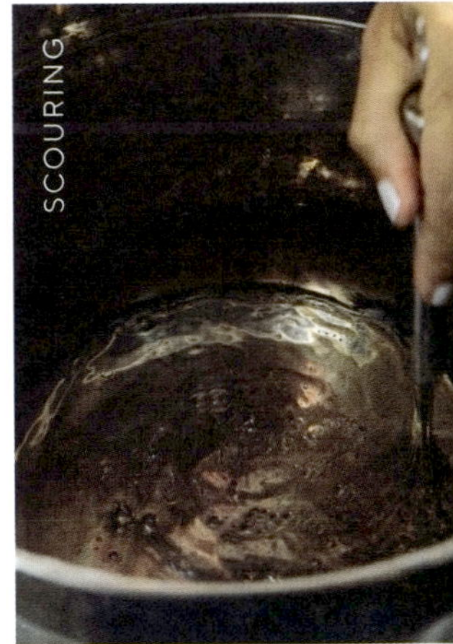
SCOURING

Preparing Your Workspace

Creating a botanical printing studio at home involves a few key elements that will enhance your overall process. If you don't have a studio, you can work in your kitchen, using dedicated dye-only equipment and protecting all surfaces from contamination, or you may opt for a garage, a shed, a dedicated community workspace, or an outdoor area.

Your workspace must be well ventilated and easily accessible. Ensure you have a sturdy table for your projects. A functional setup not only aids in organization but also promotes a seamless and enjoyable creative experience.

In the summer I set up a worktable in a garage; this allows me to close the doors when decorating fabric and open them for airflow during the steaming process, which creates heat and moisture. I use portable electric burners to steam the bundles on a separate table near a window for ventilation.

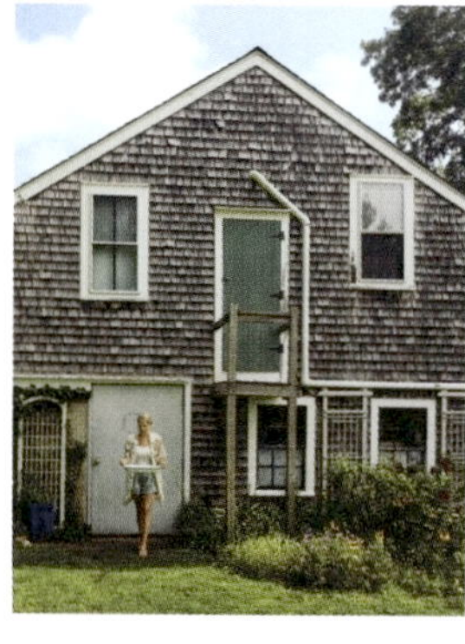

I love to work outdoors in warmer months. Mordanting and hanging fabrics in the sun speeds the drying process.

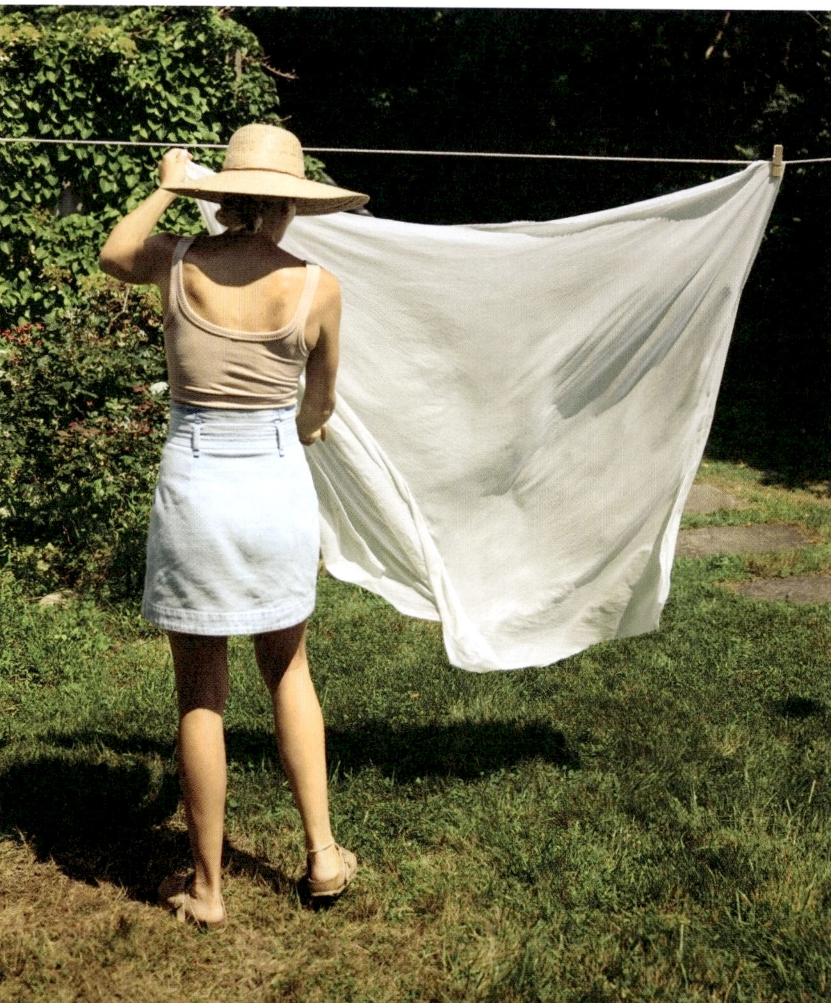

When possible, I prefer to work outdoors when mordanting fabric and paper, setting up a clothesline or a drying rack to allow the targets to quickly dry in the sunlight and wind. (While it can be quite liberating to work outside, be sure to measure powdered mordant ingredients in a wind-free area.) If you're working indoors, a drying rack with a drop cloth beneath it will work just fine. Here is what you need to set up your workspace for printing.

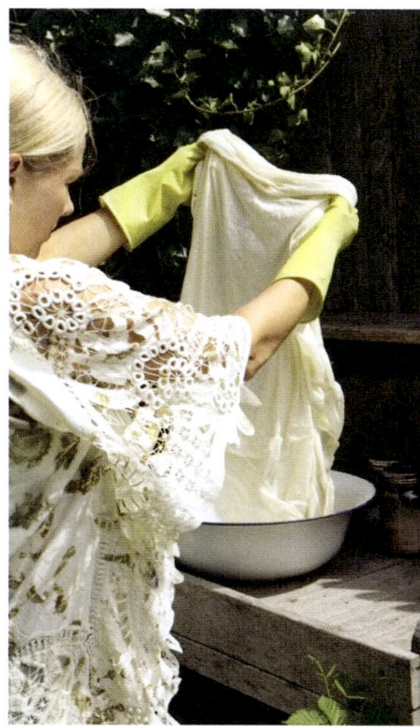

Work surface. You need a counter or worktable large enough to accommodate your projects. If you start small, you don't need much space at all. Protect the surface with reusable painter's plastic, a drop cloth, or a waterproof mattress pad, which is my preference. The cushiony surface absorbs drips from carrier blankets and excess water, but it also provides a buoyant surface for flattening and rolling bundles. It's easy to wash when it gets marked up with dye.

Heat source. You will need a heat source for steaming bundles and making carrier blanket dyes; use a gas stove, electric burner, induction burner, camping stove, or propane stove.

Dedicated dyeing and steaming vessels. Stainless steel, aluminum, and unchipped enamel pots with tight-fitting lids are ideal for processing dyes and steaming bundles. I prefer a Mexican vaporera pot, also called a tamalera. These pots include a steaming tray with a catch so that your bundles can rest just above the water level. They are wide and quite tall, which makes them ideal for accommodating numerous bundles at once. A large double boiler or covered roasting pan with a rack can work well, too. Label all vessels and utensils used for dyeing and store them away from containers used for food preparation.

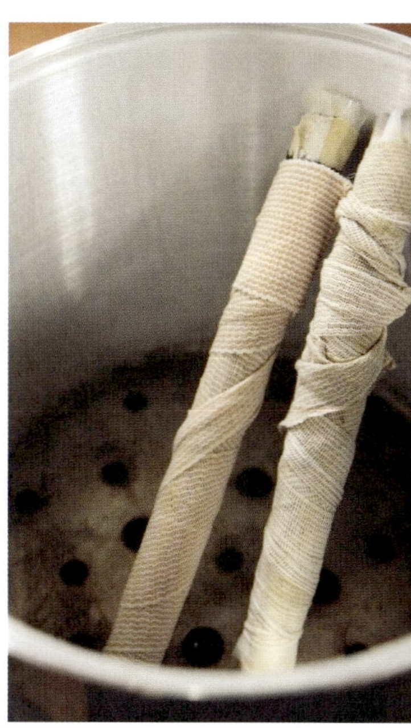

A tamalera pot is deep and comes with a catch tray to hold dowels during steaming.

Plastic buckets. These are great for mordanting large batches. Buckets with lids can be sealed to store mordant for some time. Look for 5- to 12-gallon buckets. The larger ones allow for ease of movement when mordanting your fibers. Some metals may interact with the mordant salts, so I don't use those for mordanting.

Dowels for bundling fabric. Wooden dowels from 1 to 2 inches in diameter are a good choice, but I also use clean paintbrush rollers that are 2 to 3 inches in diameter and at least 12 inches long. A dowel needs to be slightly longer than the target is wide. The dowels must also fit into the steaming vessel with the lid on. They can rest directly on top of the steamer, or at an angle. I rest the base of the dowel on the steamer tray and lean the bundle upright at an angle.

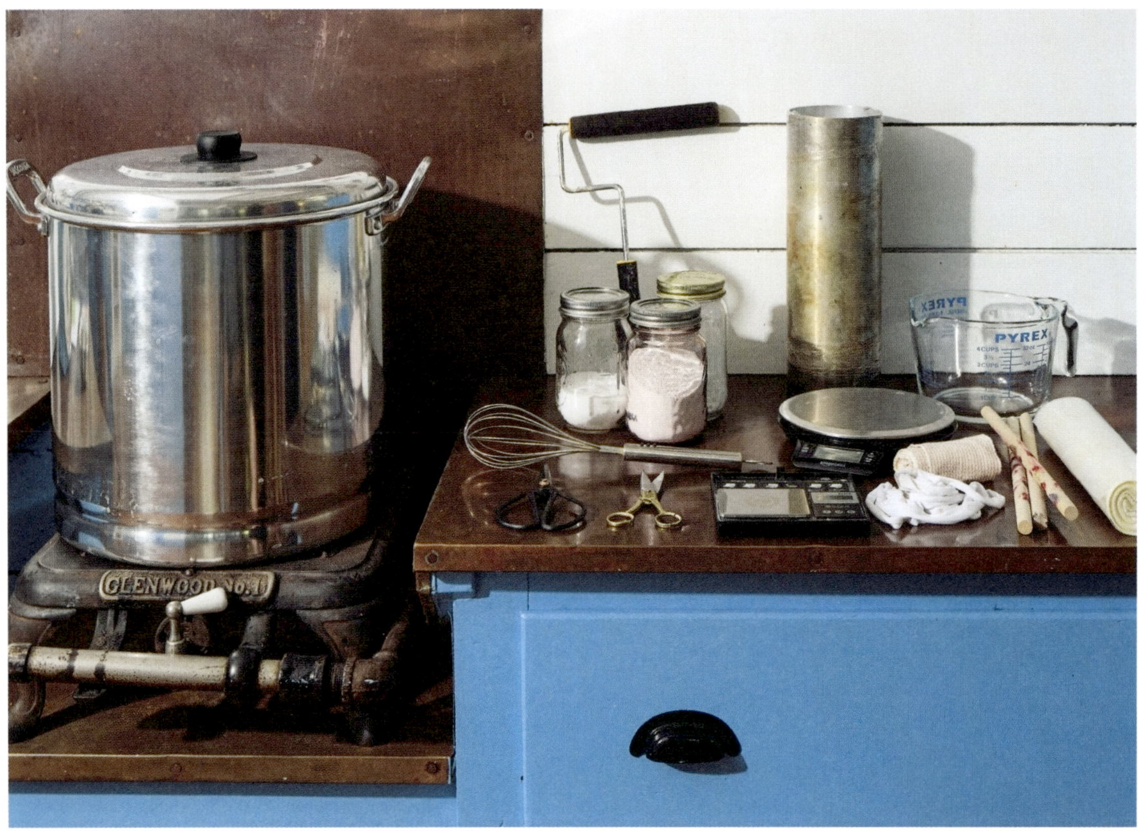

Be sure to keep all equipment used for botanical printing separate from similar items used for preparing food, to avoid cross contamination.

Dowels for bundling paper. A larger dowel makes it easier to roll the paper while providing more surface contact with the dye bath if using the immersion method. My preferred instrument is a metal pipe that measures 7 inches in diameter and is 12 inches long. Empty tomato sauce or coffee cans with the labels peeled off can be used as well. Using old copper or rust-covered pipes may create striking interactions between the rust, mordant, and vegetation. Just be cautious and wear gloves when handling any rusty objects.

Designated drying area. This could be an outdoor area or a well-ventilated indoor space with room to hang or lay out your projects to dry. Lay wet fabric on clean surfaces to avoid any transfer of markings.

Other Necessary Materials

Thrift shops, consignment stores, and estate and yard sales are great places to source many of these items.

- Small glass, enamel, plastic, or stainless steel bowls for diluting mordants and dyes
- Whisk for preparing mordants
- Mask (N95 or similar) for measuring mordant powders
- Scissors for cutting flowers and leaves
- Precision scale that measures in grams
- Measuring cups and spoons
- Heat-resistant tongs
- Nonstick compression bandage or store-bought T-shirt yarn (stretchy, flat yarn made from recycled textiles) to wrap bundles
- Heat-resistant, waterproof gloves that come at least halfway up your arms
- Reusable painter's plastic for bundling
- Clothesline and clothespins, or drying rack
- Timer for steaming bundles (one loud enough that you cannot ignore it!)
- Paintbrush roller for compressing and smoothing out plant material in a design
- Liquid Scour, Synthrapol, and Orvus Paste Soap are products particularly suited for use with dyed fabric. The first two are used for scouring and to increase the bond of natural dyes to cellulose fibers, deepening the color. Orvus Paste Soap is a gentle, pH-neutral detergent that dissolves easily to create an effective solution for washing delicate fabrics. It restores luster and conditions wools and silks.

TIME MANAGEMENT

Some of the processes outlined in this book are indeed time-consuming and require significant setup and planning. As your familiarity with these practices grows, however, the workflow will become more efficient. If time is a constraint, consider spreading tasks over several days, starting with the scouring process. For projects involving more than just small samples of fabric or paper, working in batches is advisable; scour, mordant, and fix your materials in groups so that these steps don't need to be repeated often. While these processes can be both beautiful and tedious, the rewards of your patience and effort will ultimately enhance your textile crafting experience.

The recipes I have provided can be used to scour and mordant many grams of fiber or paper at one time. Choose your materials and weigh them *dry*. Make a note of the weight. Scour and mordant as much as you can in each batch, according to the dry weight of the materials. You can always allow items to dry completely and store for later use. Simply wet them out when it is time to print.

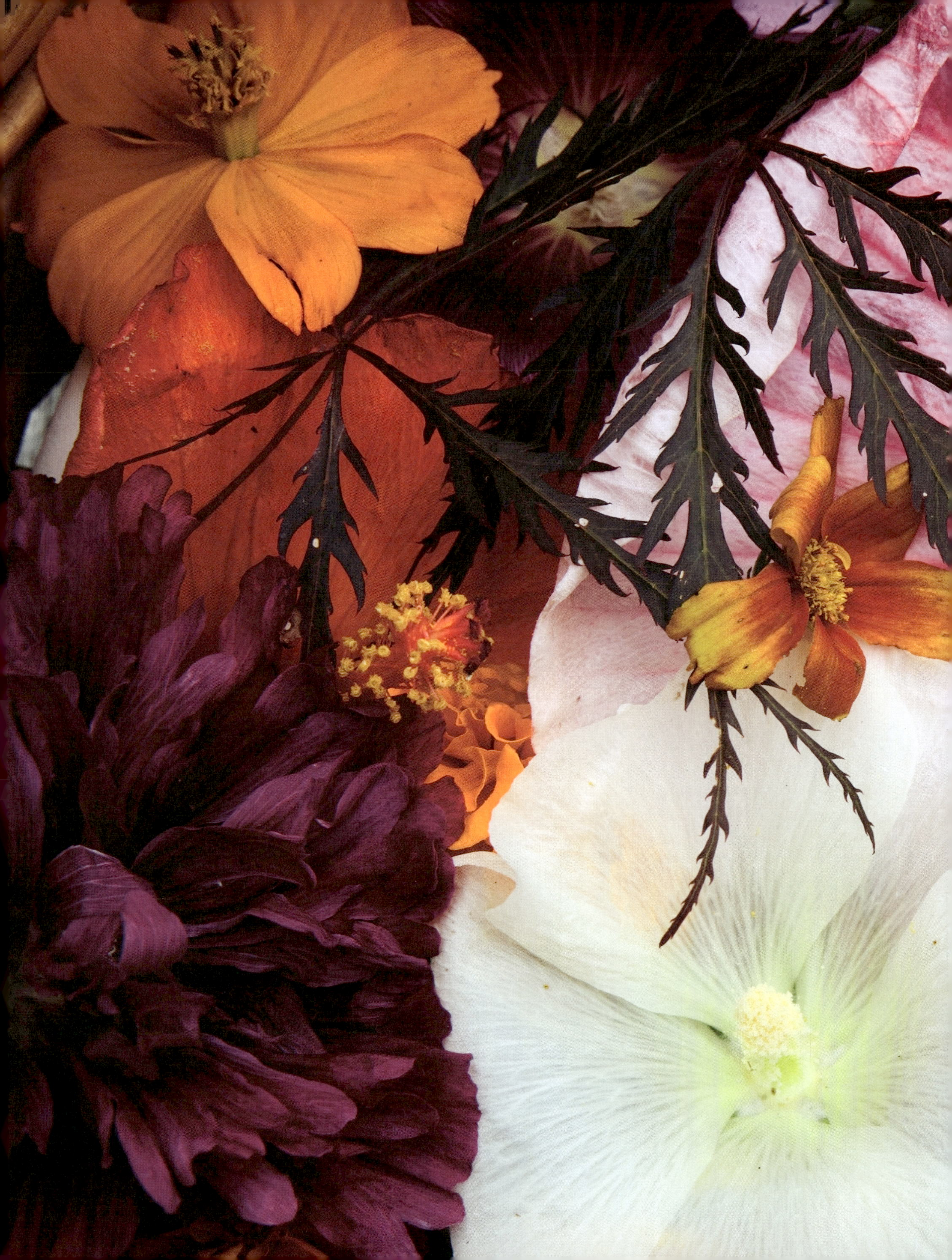

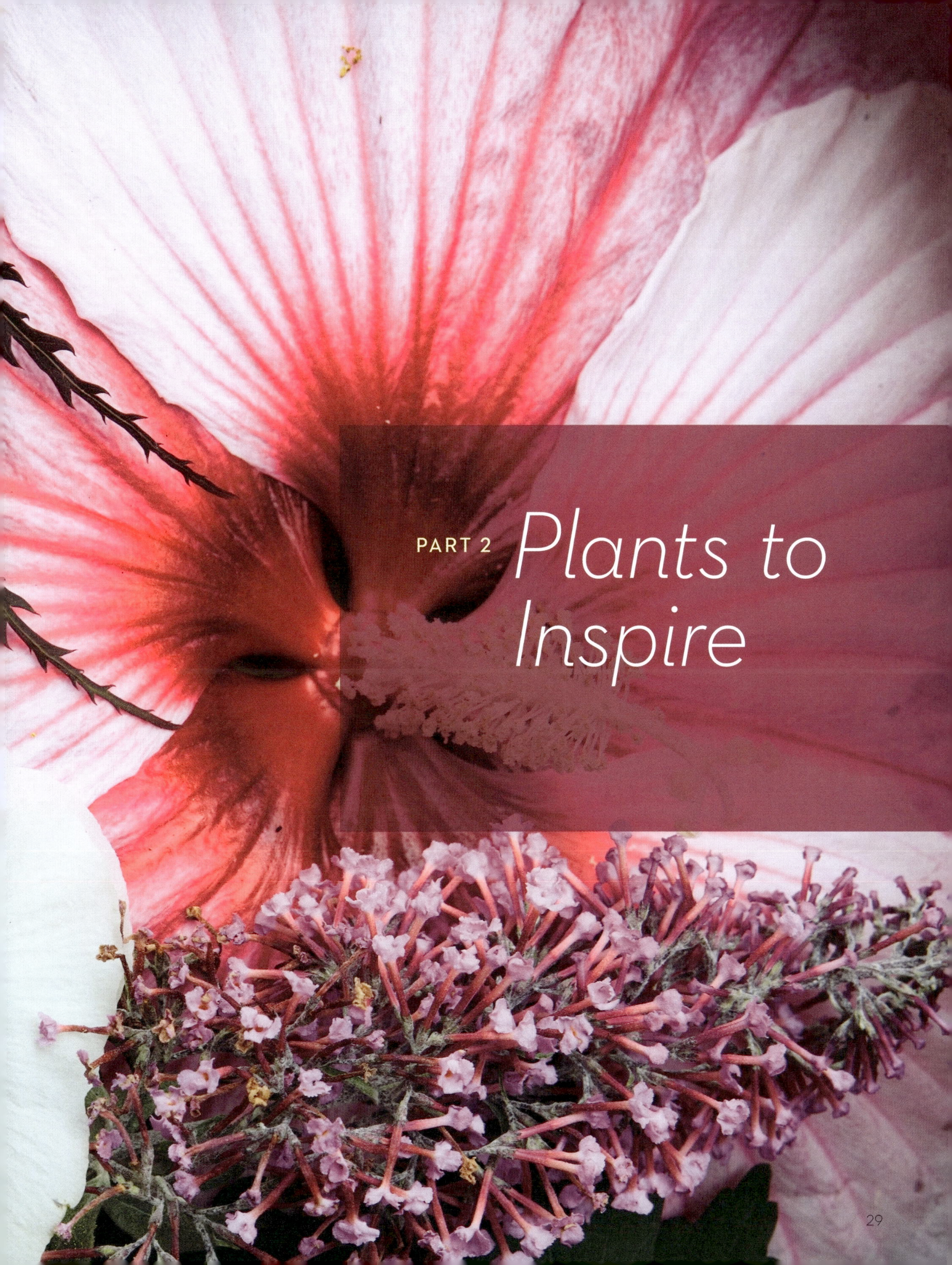

PART 2

Plants to Inspire

Once you put your botanical printing methods into practice and you're comfortable with them, you will likely notice a shift in your relationship with the natural world. What you used to perceive as a vague mosaic of color in the plants nearby, for example, can transform into a visual of individual leaves and flowers; it can be like putting on much-needed glasses for the first time. This renewed sight reveals fresh potential in the world around, igniting inspiration.

Wherever you live, I encourage you to discover, and learn about, what grows around you. Here I offer suggestions based on personal experimentation, using what I've been able to source locally and inspired by the results I've seen from printers around the world.

While I can't possibly name every plant one should try, I hope there is enough vegetation proposed within these pages to get one started. In my garden on Cape Cod and on my stoop in Brooklyn, I aspire to plant a pollinator's paradise among botanical print heroes. I grow coreopsis, cosmos, marigolds, dahlias, hibiscus, bidens, hollyhock, sunflowers, impatiens, begonias, indigo (both false and Japanese), bee balm, and roses. A walk around the yard or in nature yields the discovery of perennials planted long ago, such as fruit trees, dogwood, rose of Sharon, Japanese maple, oak, staghorn sumac, rugosa rose, goldenrod, butterfly bush, and much more.

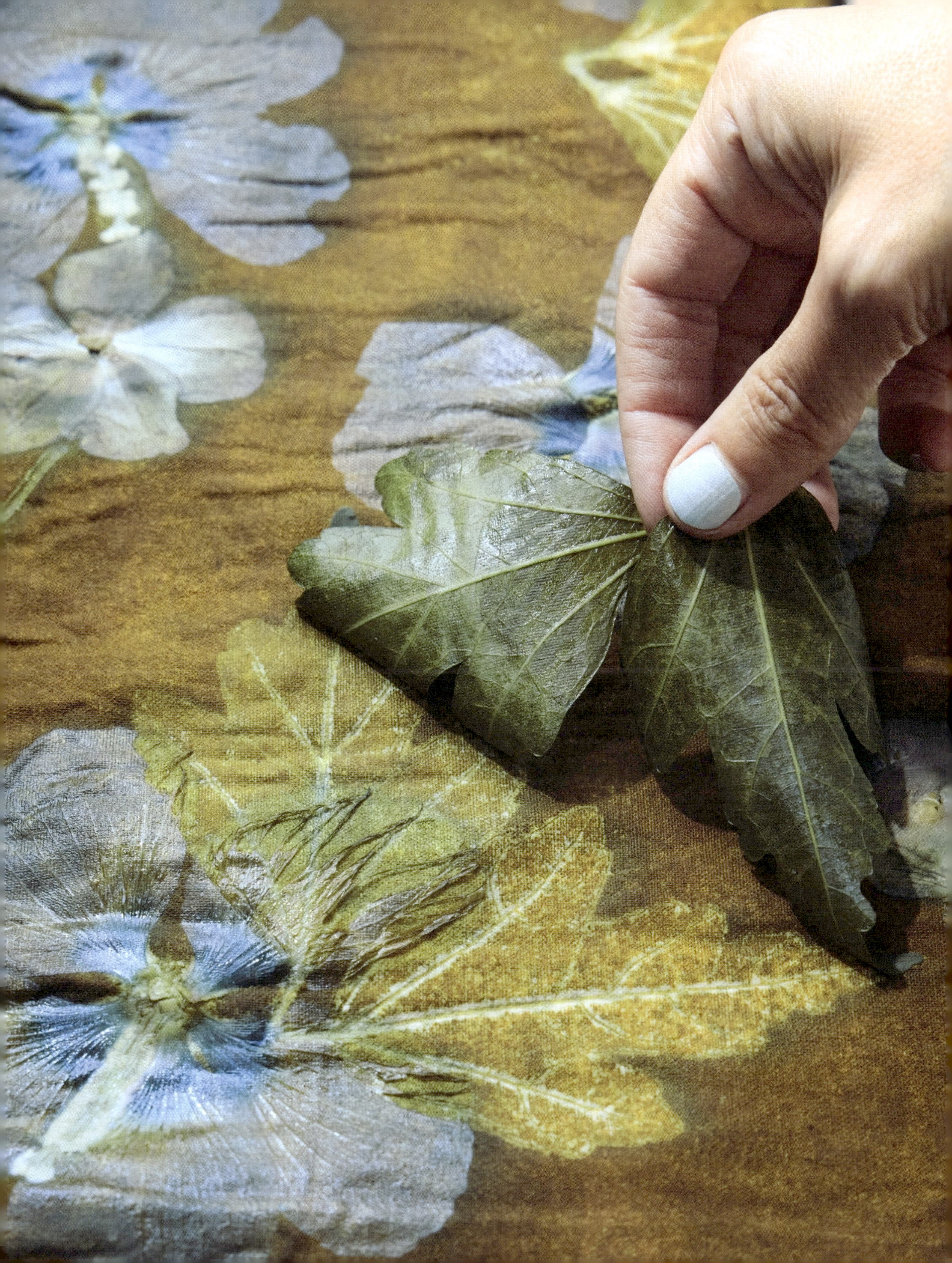

A Guide to Harvesting Botanicals

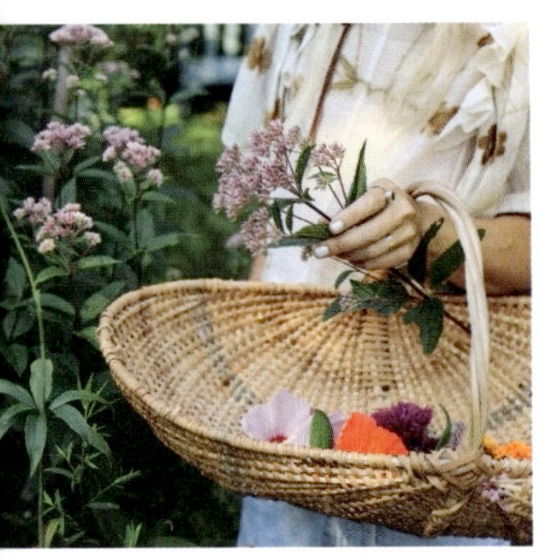

I encourage you to go out into nature and discover what grows around you.

Autumn is an excellent time to gather windfallen leaves to store and rehydrate for later use. I also visit the flower district and florists during the colder months, not only to be immersed in a riot of color, steeped in sweet scents and humidity, but to source fresh flowers and leaves. No matter where you are, be mindful of what you're gathering. Be sure to identify what you're looking at to confirm whether the plant is toxic or endangered, in which case it's best to leave it be.

If you find a wild species of plant, don't take too much of it. The rule among conscious botanical dye artisans is to not take more than 10 percent of a living plant. Remember that birds, bees, insects, and mammals rely on plants for food. Use scissors to carefully cut trimmings instead of tearing, snapping, or ripping. Start small and experiment with a few flowers or leaves to test the print quality before harvesting too many.

Collecting Materials

Collecting vegetation can be a peaceful and thoughtful part of the practice. Planting and keeping your own garden can create a greater connection to nature, but materials can be sourced by foraging and through donations from friends, as well as from florists, natural dye vendors, and markets.

Throughout the growing cycle, the chemical makeup of plants changes dramatically. For example, the tannin-rich leaves of wild staghorn sumac produce a delicate, fresh green imprint in spring, while those collected in late September yield a much darker hue due to increased tannin accumulation. Conversely, flowers generally provide a more consistent color throughout their life cycle; some become more vibrant and have increased saturated tones when dried. Understanding these nuances opens up a world of possibilities, allowing for the creation of unique textiles with each seasonal harvest.

Factors such as location, time of year, soil composition, water quality, and weather patterns all play crucial roles in the printing process. Keeping detailed records of the dates and locations where various plant materials are collected can lead to deeper insights into their printing potential.

Some flowers, including asters, bidens, marigolds, coreopsis, cosmos, hollyhocks, hibiscus, dahlias, impatiens, sunflowers, Jerusalem artichokes, anemones, and rose of Sharon, are excellent candidates for printing when fresh. Other flowers may impart far more concentrated color when dried. Roses appear to be packed with tantalizing color, but fresh rose petals do not produce quality prints and are best used dried. Dried rose buds, the pink and red varieties used to make rose tea, can be broken into bits to create pops of color. Pea flowers, hibiscus, marigold, pincushion, sulfur cosmos, and coreopsis work dried as well.

Seasonal flowers can be picked, dried, and stored for a long time if kept away from light and moisture. Flowers can be dried and pressed flat with the aim of retaining their original shape, or simply left to dry more organically and used for adding further color in a print, such as in bundle dyeing. Try to pick flowers when they first bloom so they are more likely to retain their original shape.

Aside from providing colorful options for winter projects, preserved dried flowers are less bulky, can be easier to place within a composition, and often bleed less during steaming. Fresh flowers and stems are bulkier and contain more moisture; they may shift when rolling the bundle, sometimes leading to undesirable markings. One downside of using pressed flowers is that they can be incredibly delicate and require the utmost care when handling. Be sure to stay away from any drafts when placing them on a target.

Storing Flowers and Leaves

Pick flowers when they are dry, not immediately after watering or rainfall. To press them, place the flowers between paper towels or sheets of parchment paper within the pages of heavy books. The same technique can be applied to leaves, especially the more delicate types that won't hold up well to freezing, such as the feathery leaves of cosmos. These will store for a long time if kept away from moisture. You can invest in or make your own flower press, which can be super helpful for bulkier blooms; the press aids in flattening and preserving their natural shape. Keep dried and pressed flowers out of direct sunlight and away from moisture.

Leaves can also be pressed and dried, though the sturdier types (such as those from eucalyptus, oak, maple, smoke bush, plum, or ginkgo) can simply be hung upside down to dry. However, to keep leaves as fresh and intact as possible, I highly recommend freezing them. I layer leaves flat in a large freezer bag, filling it about halfway, and add about ¼ cup of water to retain moisture. When it's time to print, the frozen leaves can be easily thawed by running the bag under hot water, and they may print as if they were just picked. For the leaves, it can be helpful to dip them in cool water prior to printing to regain some moisture, as a very dry leaf can crumble or fail to impart much color.

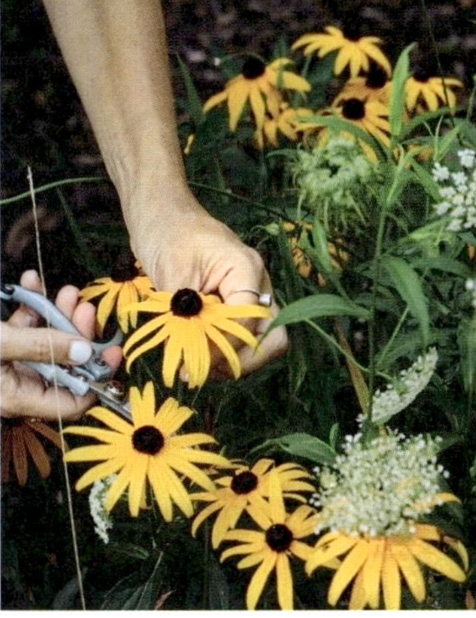

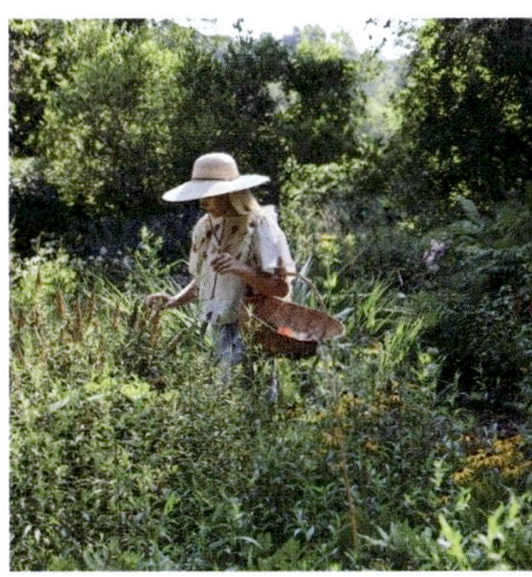

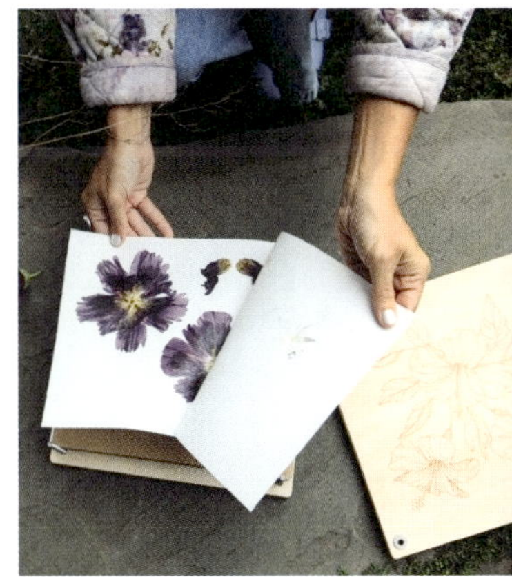

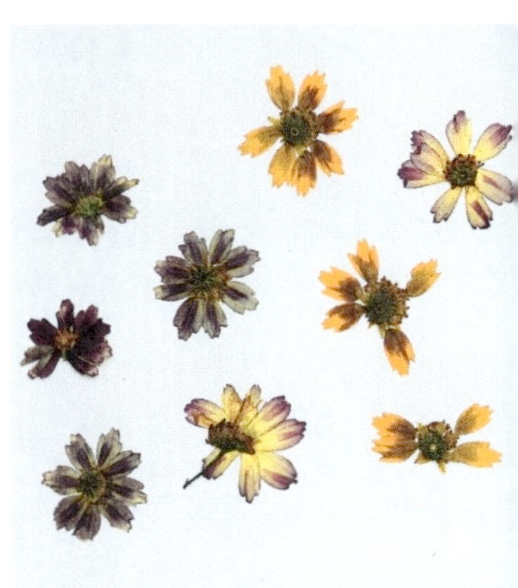

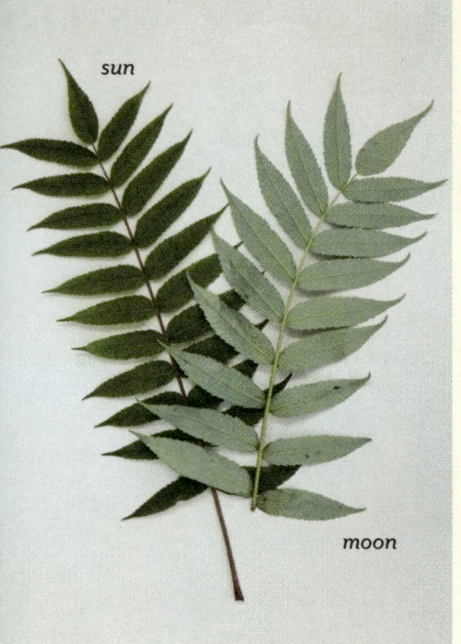

THE TWO SIDES OF LEAVES

Most leaves have a distinct "sun" side that faces toward the sun and a "moon" side that faces the earth. Each side imparts color differently in the printing process. In most cases, the moon side, which sometimes exhibits visible veins, will impart a darker, more dramatic imprint, sometimes even black, if iron was used in the mordanting process and the leaf is rich in tannin. Rose leaves, for instance, will print from olive green to grayish black on the moon side in combination with iron, but impart a more verdant green when using the sun side.

Using both sides of the leaves can create a more colorful and harmonious composition, but be sure to test them to ensure each side will print. If creating a mirror-image design, decorate one side of the target with both sides of the leaves, to ensure balance of color and strength of the imprint. Both sides of eucalyptus leaves create a similar imprint.

In this mirror-image print, the moon side of the leaves is on the left.

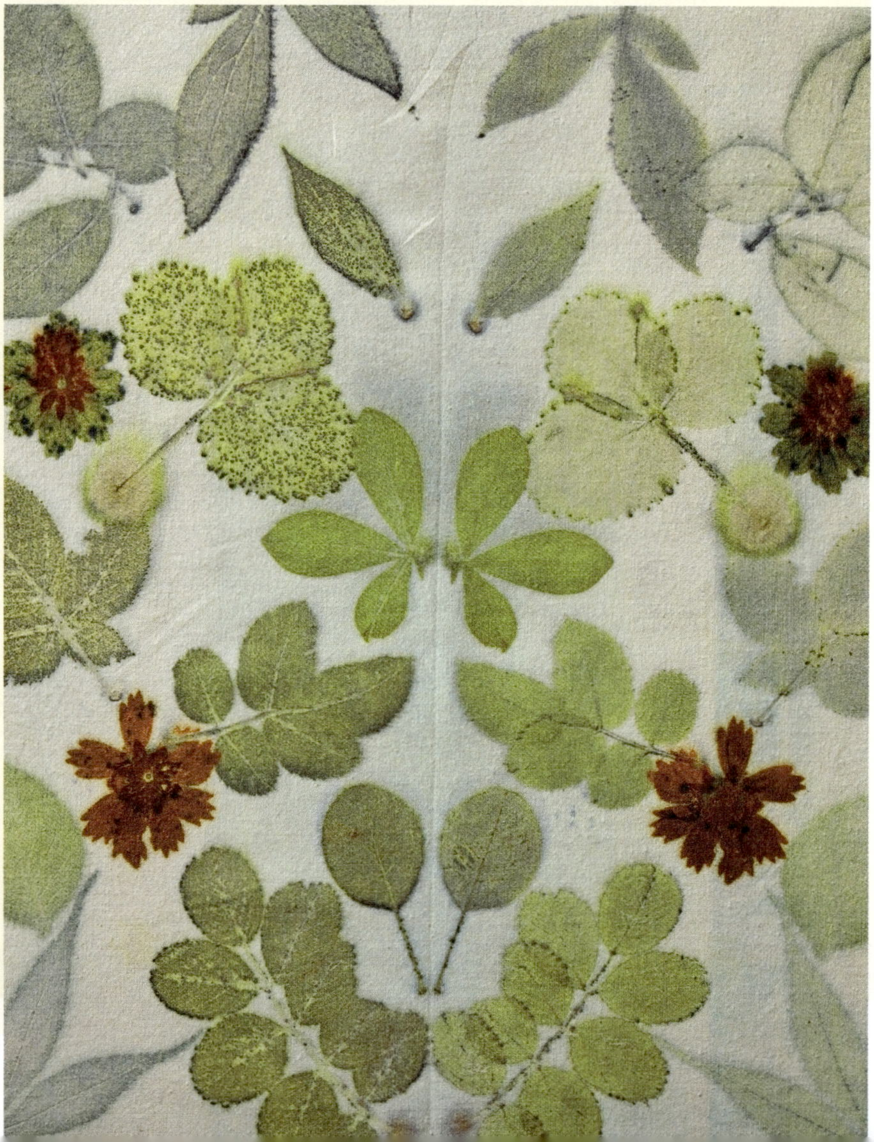

A Compendium of Plants

The following compendium draws inspiration from the intricate herbarium of Emily Dickinson, who meticulously documented 424 wildflowers from New England in her famed, green-bound album, as shown in these examples. The poet and dedicated gardener lived closely with her flowers, and her words have resonated with many. This section aims to illuminate the profound relationship we share with nature, showcasing how these botanical specimens can enhance our own creativity. By exploring the vibrant hues and unique characteristics of these plants, I invite you to discover the beauty of natural inspiration and its power to fuel your artistic endeavors.

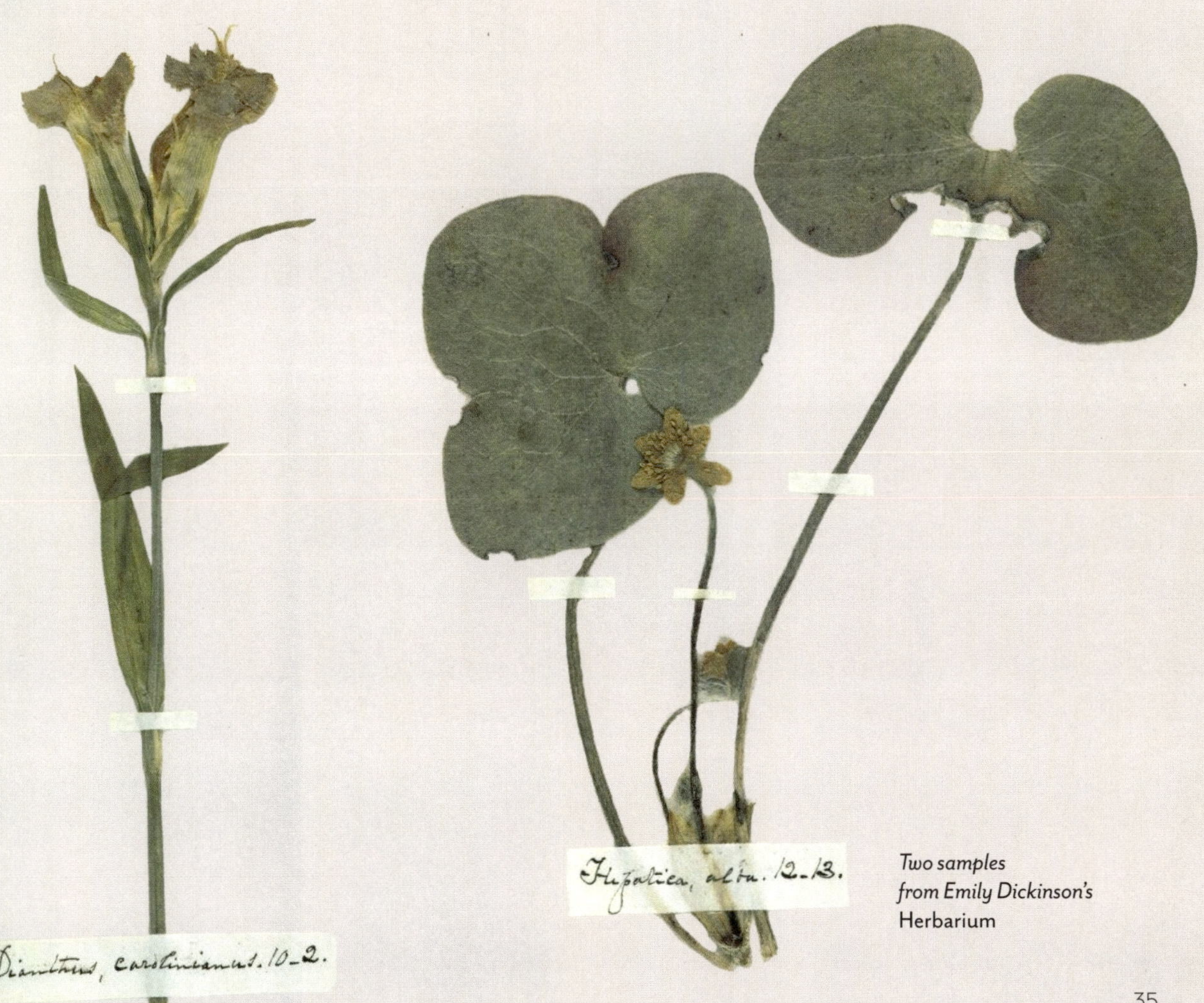

Two samples from Emily Dickinson's Herbarium

Alder Buckthorn

(*Frangula alnus*)

Alder buckthorn, also known as glossy buckthorn or breaking buckthorn, is a tall deciduous shrub that, despite its name, does not have thorns. Both the berries and the pointed, serrated leaves give good results.

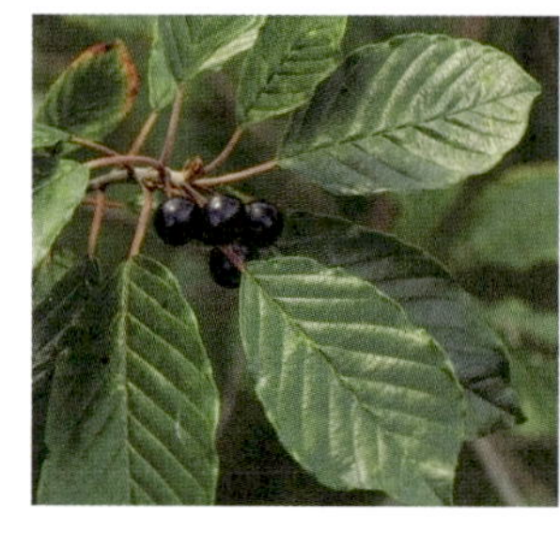

The plummy berries can be simmered with PAS and mixed with gum arabic to make a paste pigment. The bark can be used to make a reddish orange dye by soaking the ground wood in cool water for a few days.

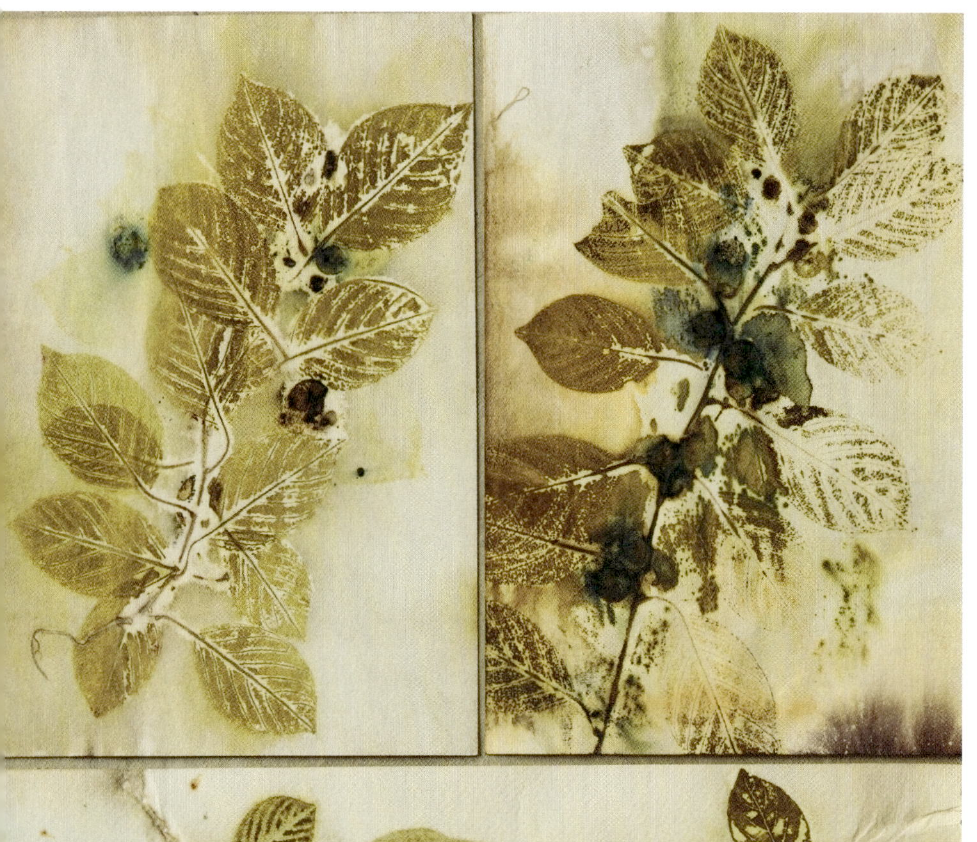

PRINTING NOTES

- The moon side of the leaves imparts a more saturated and more detailed print; the sun side will not offer much color.
- The berries offer a pop of blue to purple coloring. Fresh berries may burst and bleed into the target, which may or may not work to your advantage, depending on what you're hoping for; you may wish to dry them before printing.
- A carrier blanket dye could be made up with the simmered berries and PAS for a plummy background color.

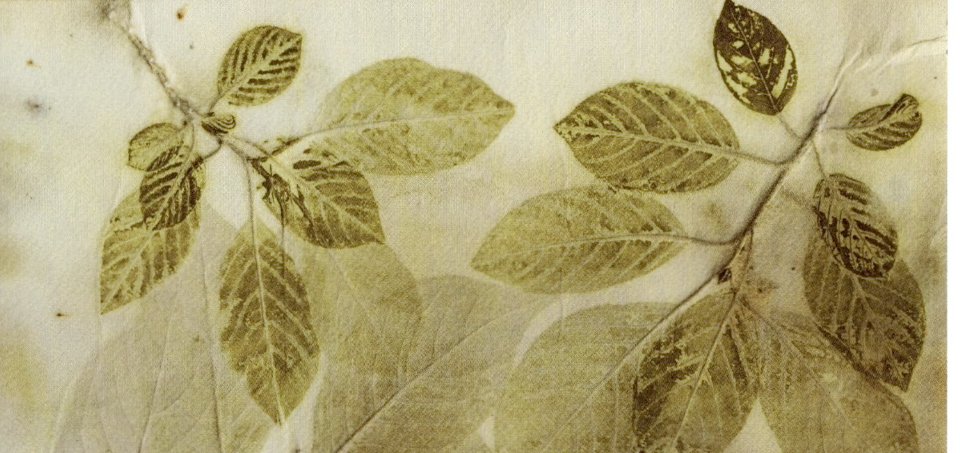

Printed on paper with the dried berries

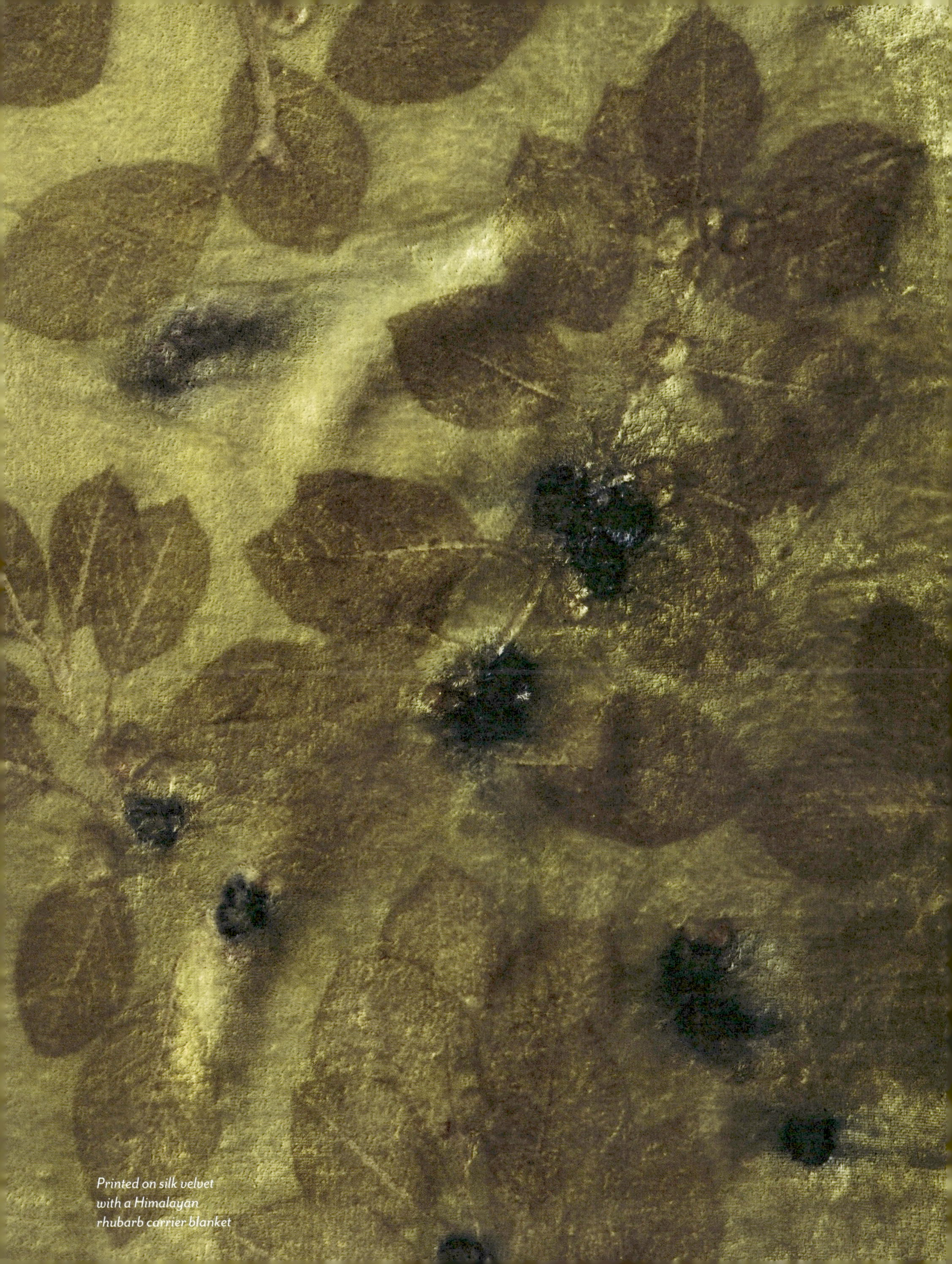

Printed on silk velvet with a Himalayan rhubarb carrier blanket

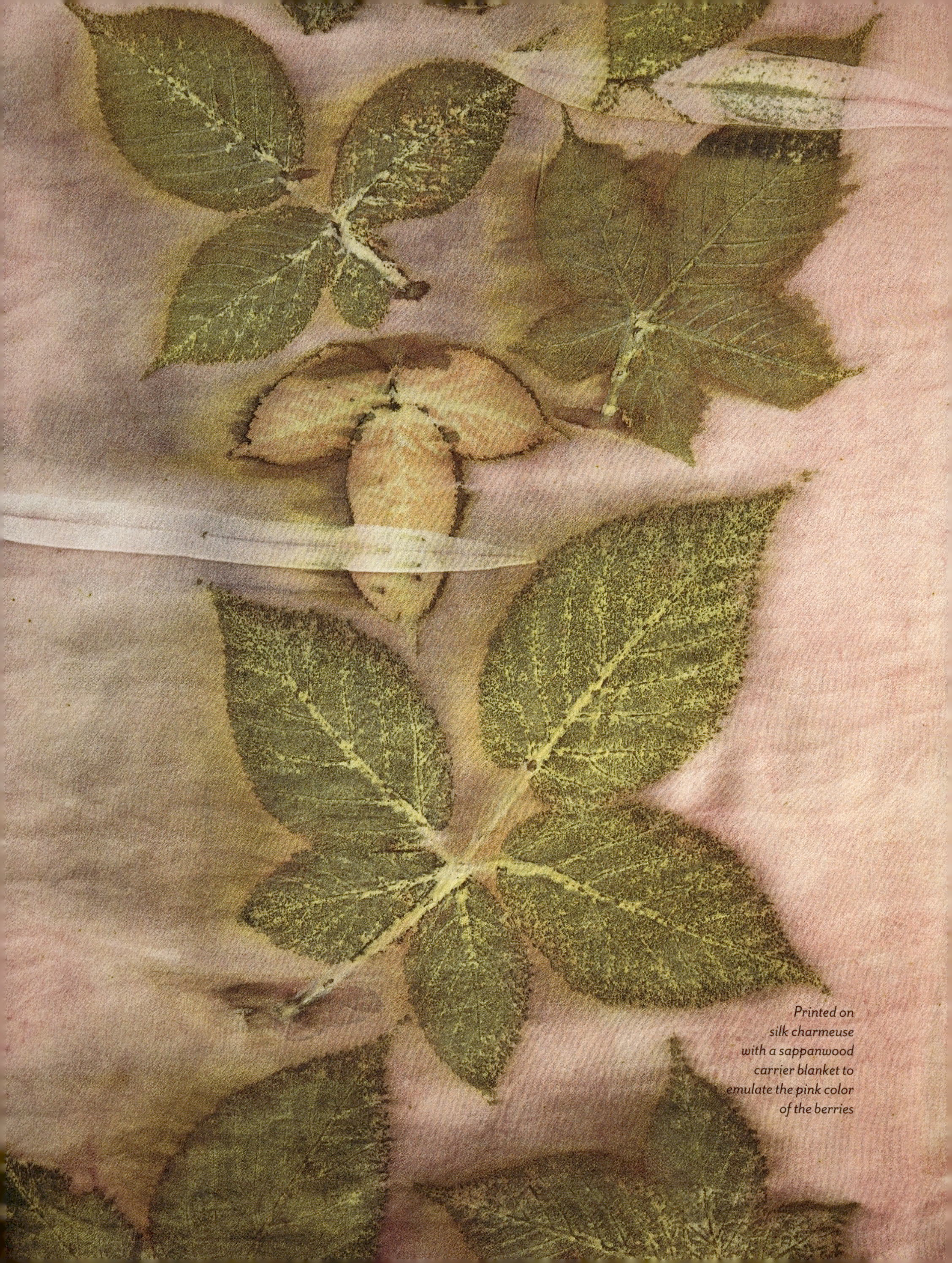

Printed on silk charmeuse with a sappanwood carrier blanket to emulate the pink color of the berries

American Red Raspberry

(Rubus strigosus)

Raspberries thrive in diverse conditions, meaning these plants are readily available for foraging. Raspberry leaves, full of tannins, interact beautifully with the mordants used in this book. These powerful printers give great results. Their hardiness allows for easy preservation, and you can press and dry or freeze them for later use. The flowers are nondescript, but you can use the dried berries for pops of color.

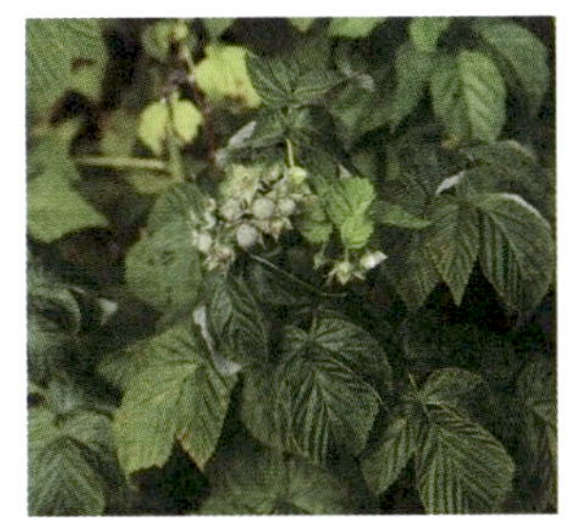

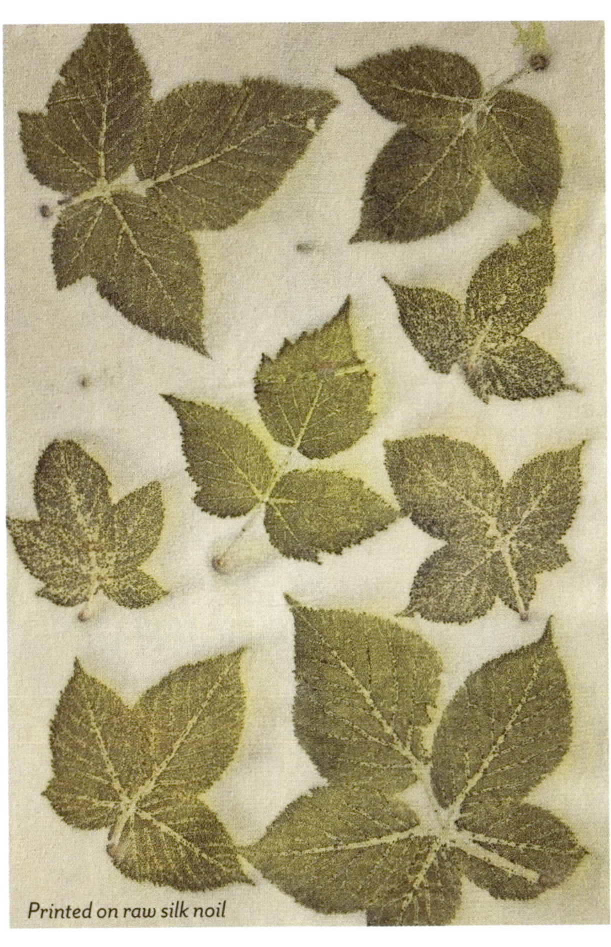

Printed on raw silk noil

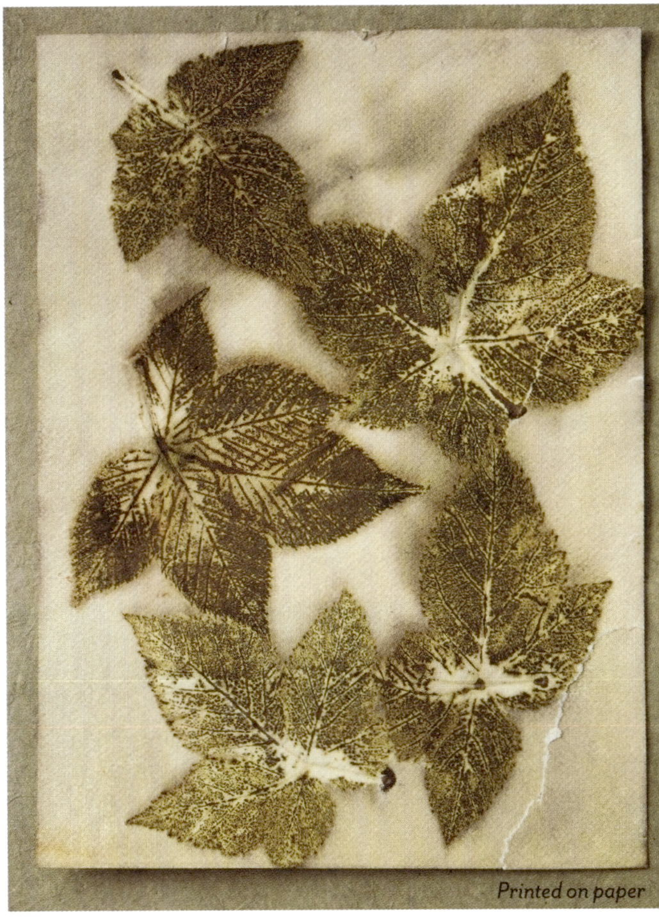

Printed on paper

PRINTING NOTES

- The starlike leaves are pointed with three to five leaflets (occasionally seven, and the youngest bushes will have three), making for interesting dynamics when using a variety of the leaves in printing.
- Both the sun side and moon side will impart color—the moon side leaning blacker, the sun side greener—making this leaf an excellent choice for a mirror-image print.

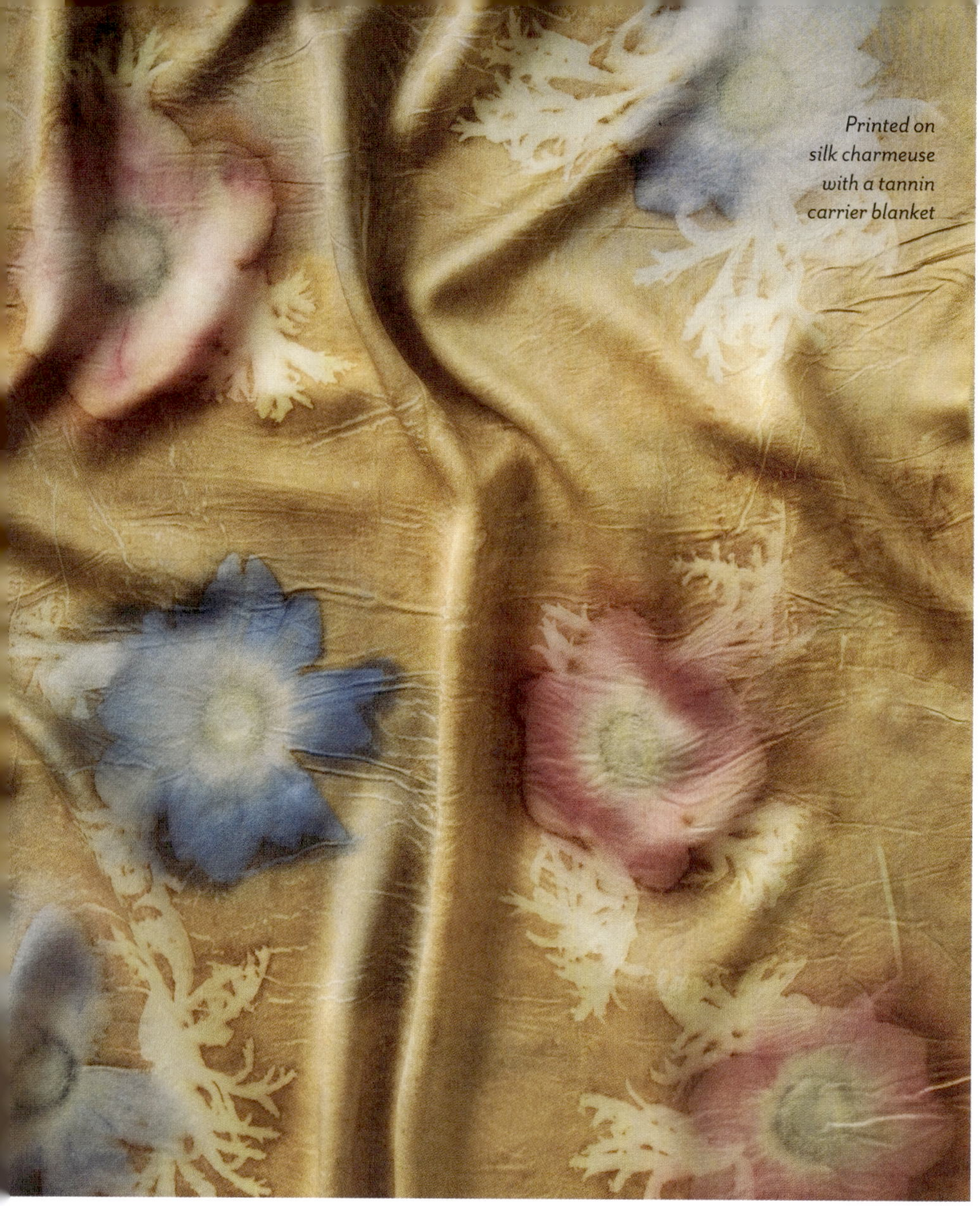

Printed on silk charmeuse with a tannin carrier blanket

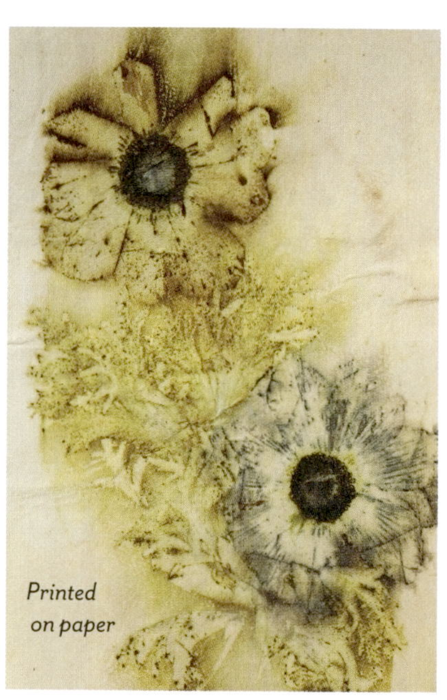

Printed on paper

Anemone

(*Anemone coronaria*)

Also known as the poppy anemone or windflower, *Anemone coronaria* is a member of the Ranunculaceae family, which includes hellebore, delphinium, clematis, and buttercup, all of which may also be used for printing. The magnetic black center of the anemone is surrounded by a crownlike ring of stamens that lend the species its name, *coronaria*. These full blooms are great candidates for drying and pressing. *A. robustissima*, or Japanese anemone, can also be used for printing, both the flowers and leaves.

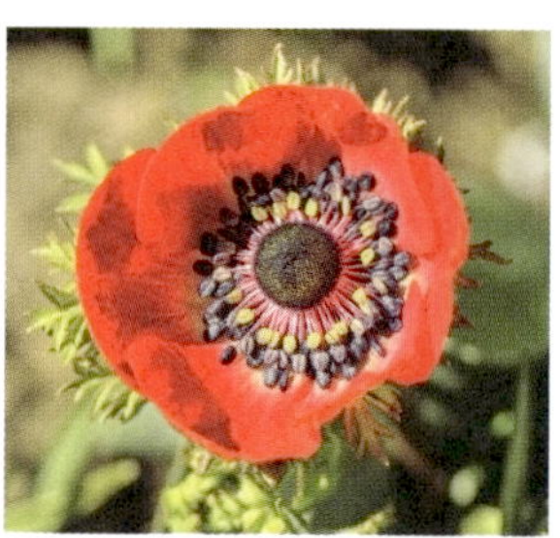

PRINTING NOTES

- Face down, the anemone imparts color from the entire flower, but the back also offers a colorful imprint, minus the darkened center, making them good candidates for a mirror-image print.

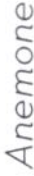

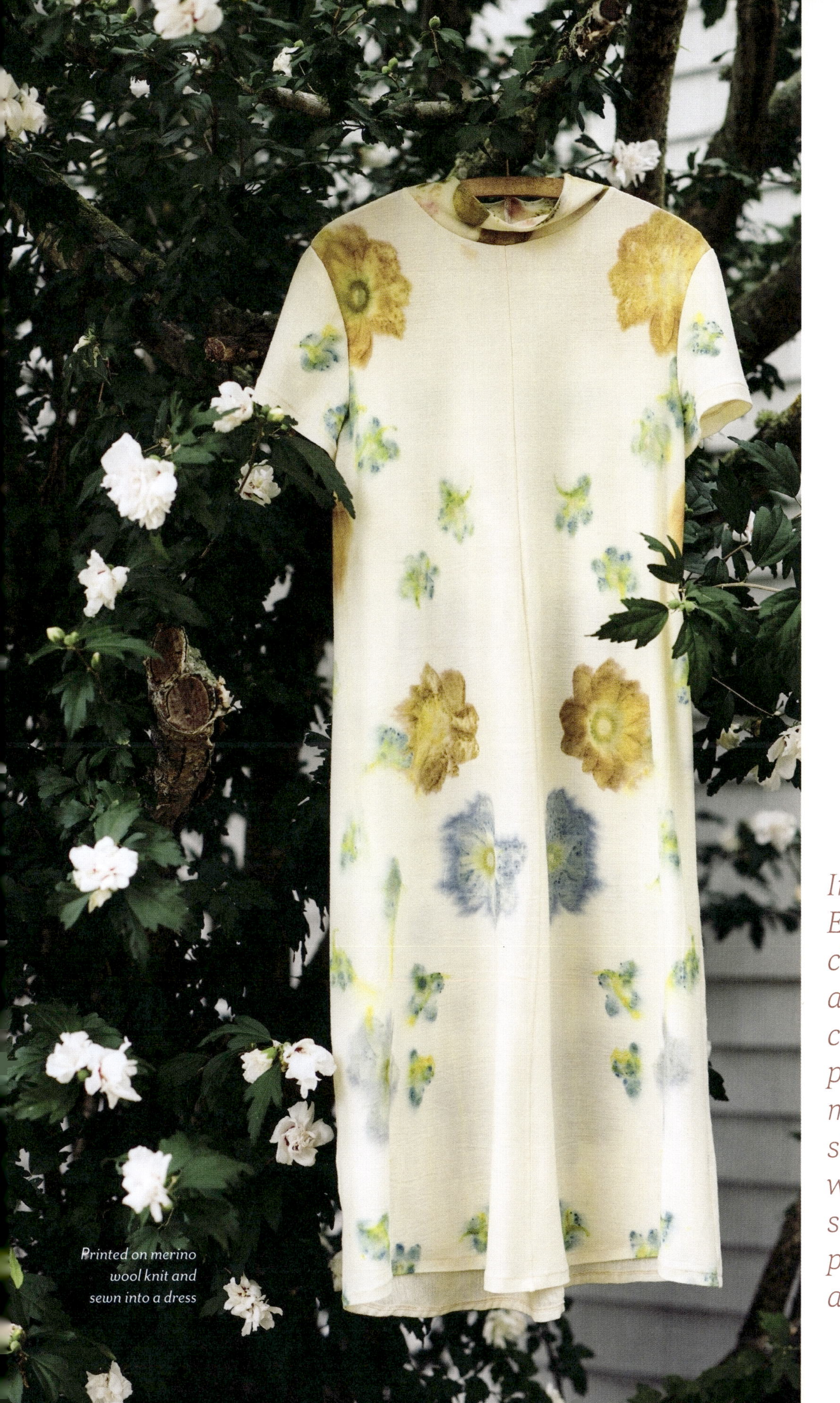

Printed on merino wool knit and sewn into a dress

Irish and English folklore claim that when an anemone contracts its petals, there may be fairies sleeping inside, while others see this more prosaically as a sign of rain.

Bidens

(*Bidens ferulifolia*)

Bidens ferulifolia has delicate fernlike foliage and vibrant blossoms. These annuals or short-lived perennials have prolific blooms of orange, gold, pink, white, or red. *Bidens pilosa*, another varietal that is readily available around the world, also has excellent printing potential. The flowers can be preserved and dried for future use, but I prefer to use them fresh with stalks intact, as the whole stalk prints very well.

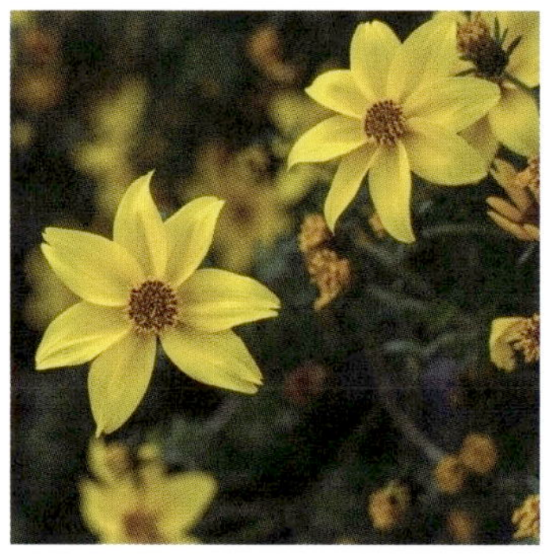

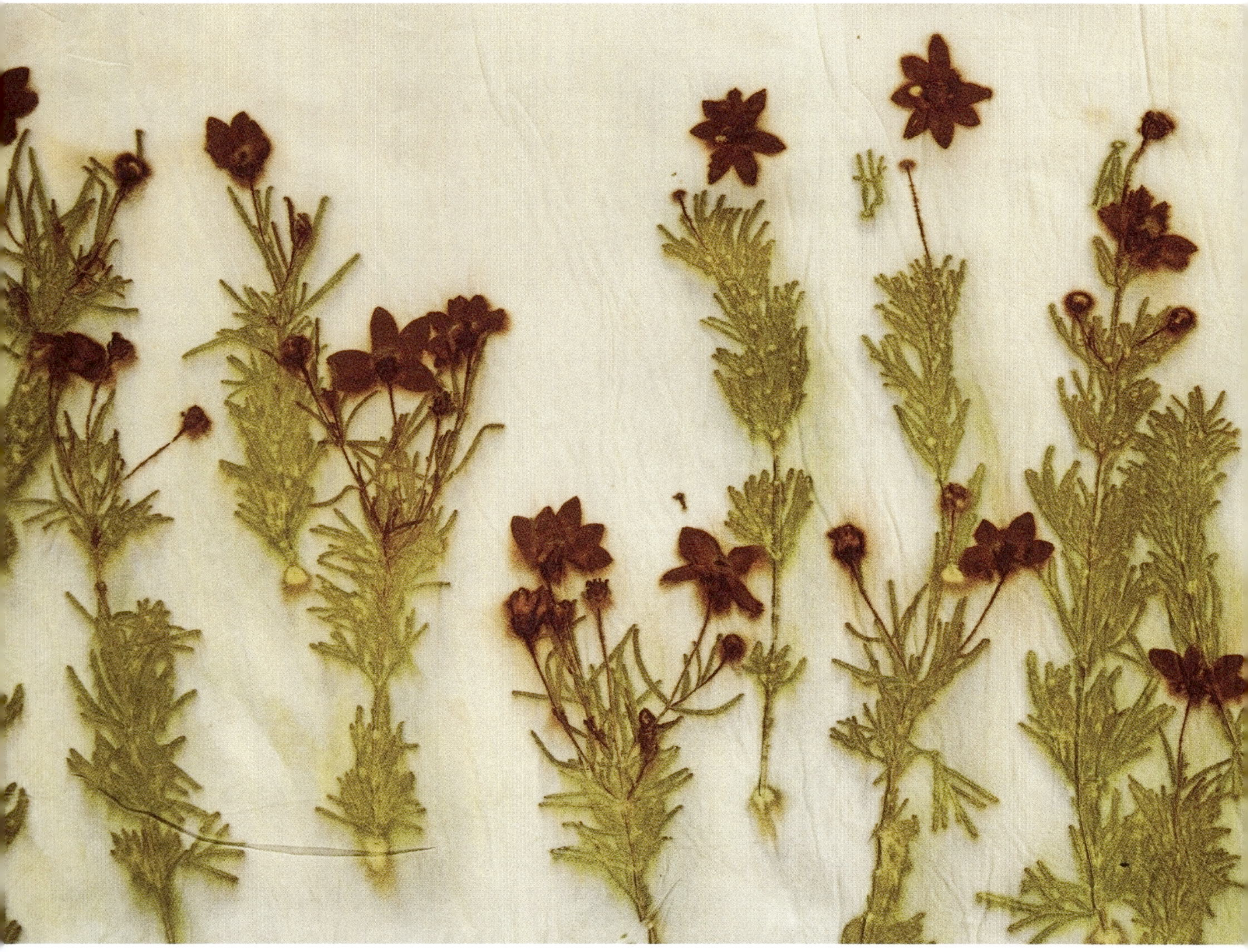

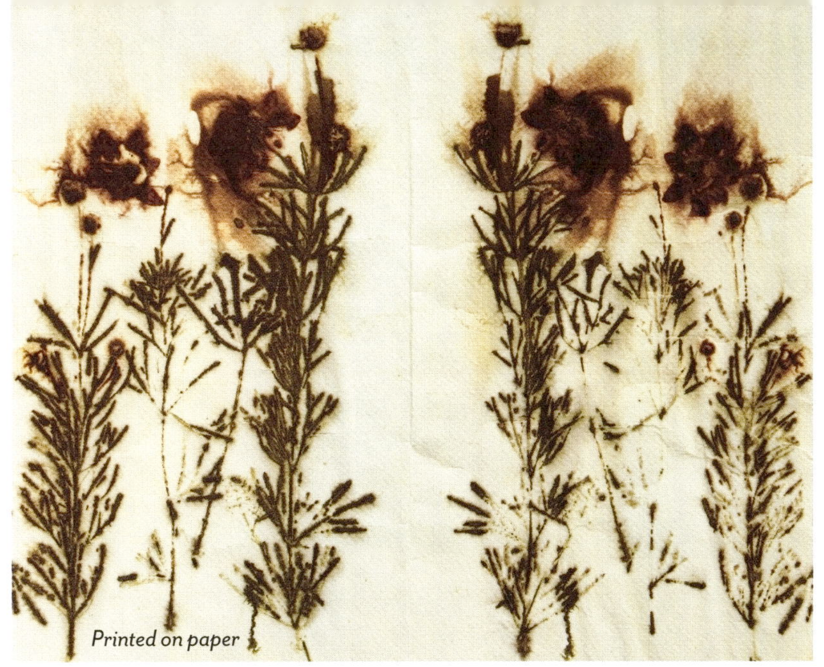

Printed on paper

PRINTING NOTES

- Bidens offer a vibrant touch of color that elevates botanical prints.
- The flowers print best when face down on the target, but the backside will add a saturated pop of color as well, making them ideal flowers for a mirror-image print.
- When iron is used in the mordant, the stalks and leaves provide a dramatic imprint with more intensity.

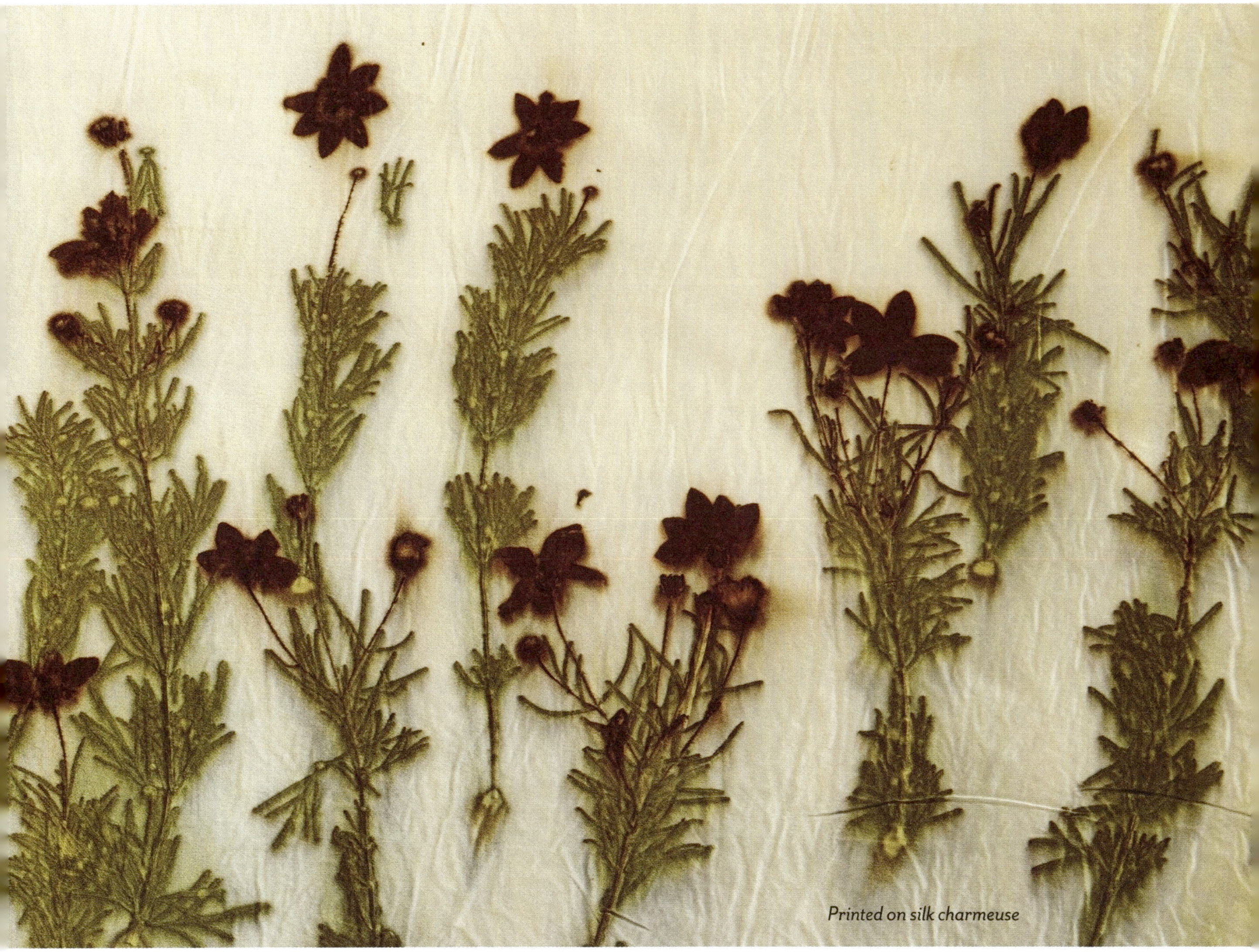

Printed on silk charmeuse

Blue False Indigo

(*Baptisia australis*)

A member of the Fabaceae (legume) family, *Baptisia australis* is a perennial herb used historically by Indigenous peoples of North America for dyeing cloth and making artwork. My mother pointed this herb out to me when I was first beginning to print, and ever since it's been one of my favorite plants for the fresh, spring green color the leaves give.

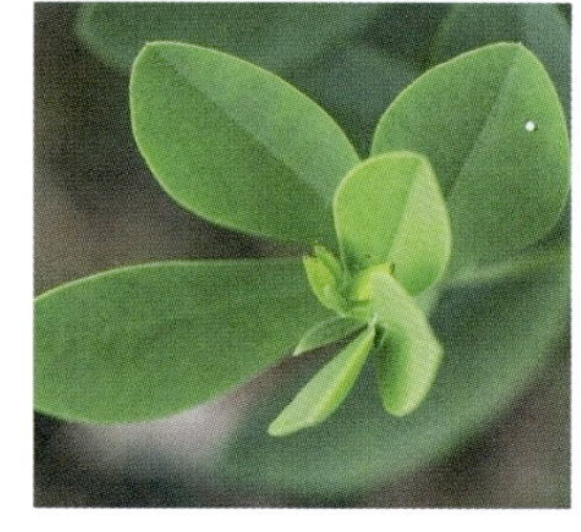

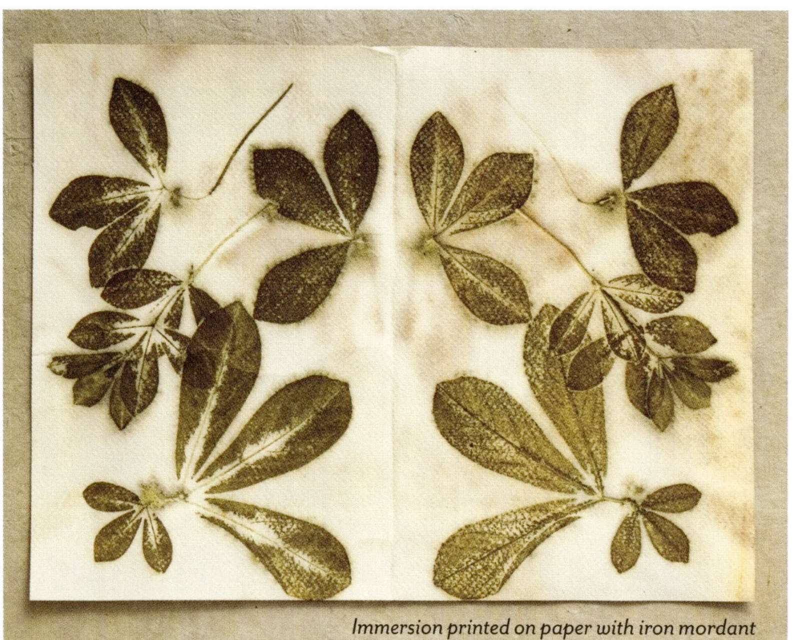

Immersion printed on paper with iron mordant

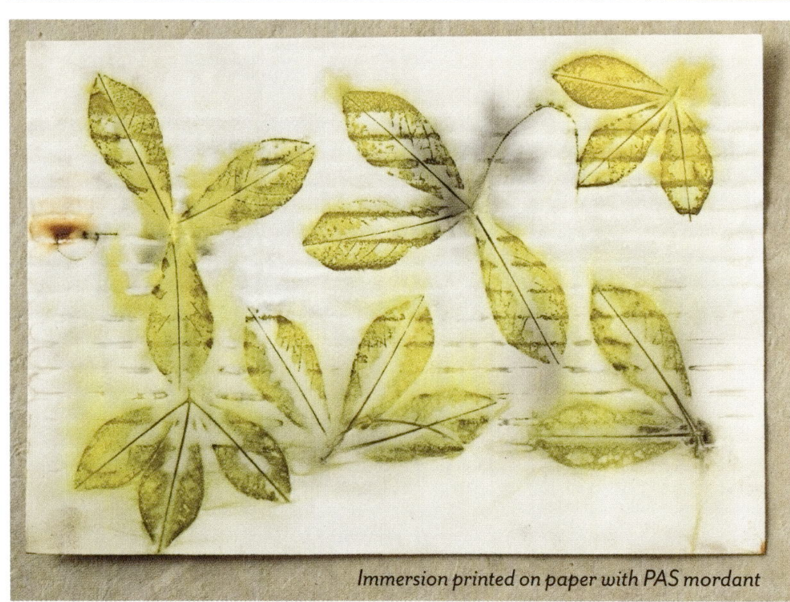

Immersion printed on paper with PAS mordant

PRINTING NOTES

- The leaves are great for printing on a pure white background, as the imprints are packed with pigmentation.
- The leaves can be used on both the sun and moon sides, which adds dimension to a mirror-image print.
- I tend to remove the leaves from the bulky stalk, so they lie flat and enhance the print.
- Use a mordant of PAS, soda ash, and iron to achieve distinctly green prints that are almost perfect in color distribution and can look photorealistic.

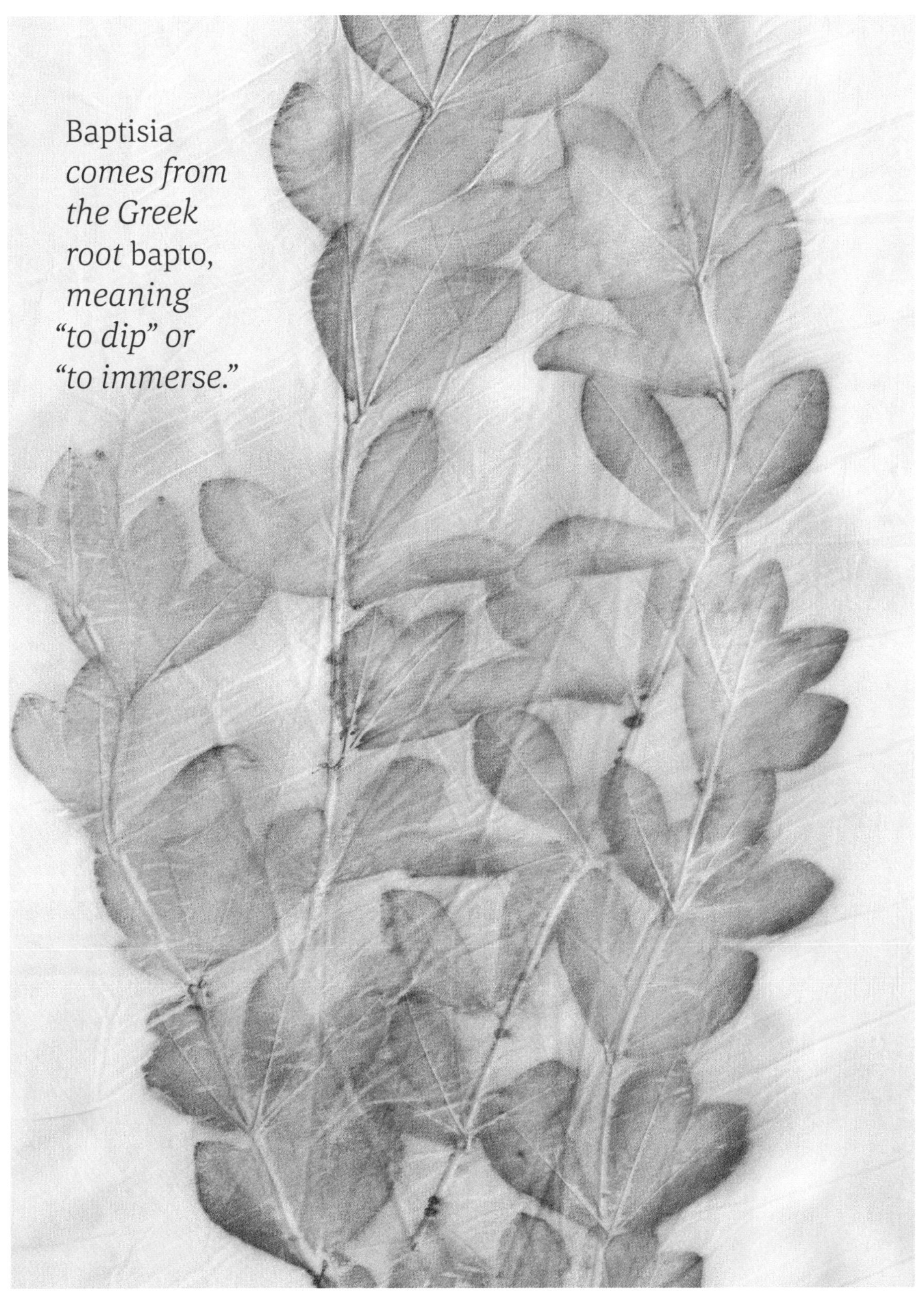

Printed on silk charmeuse with the Fundamental Mordant Bright Outcome recipe

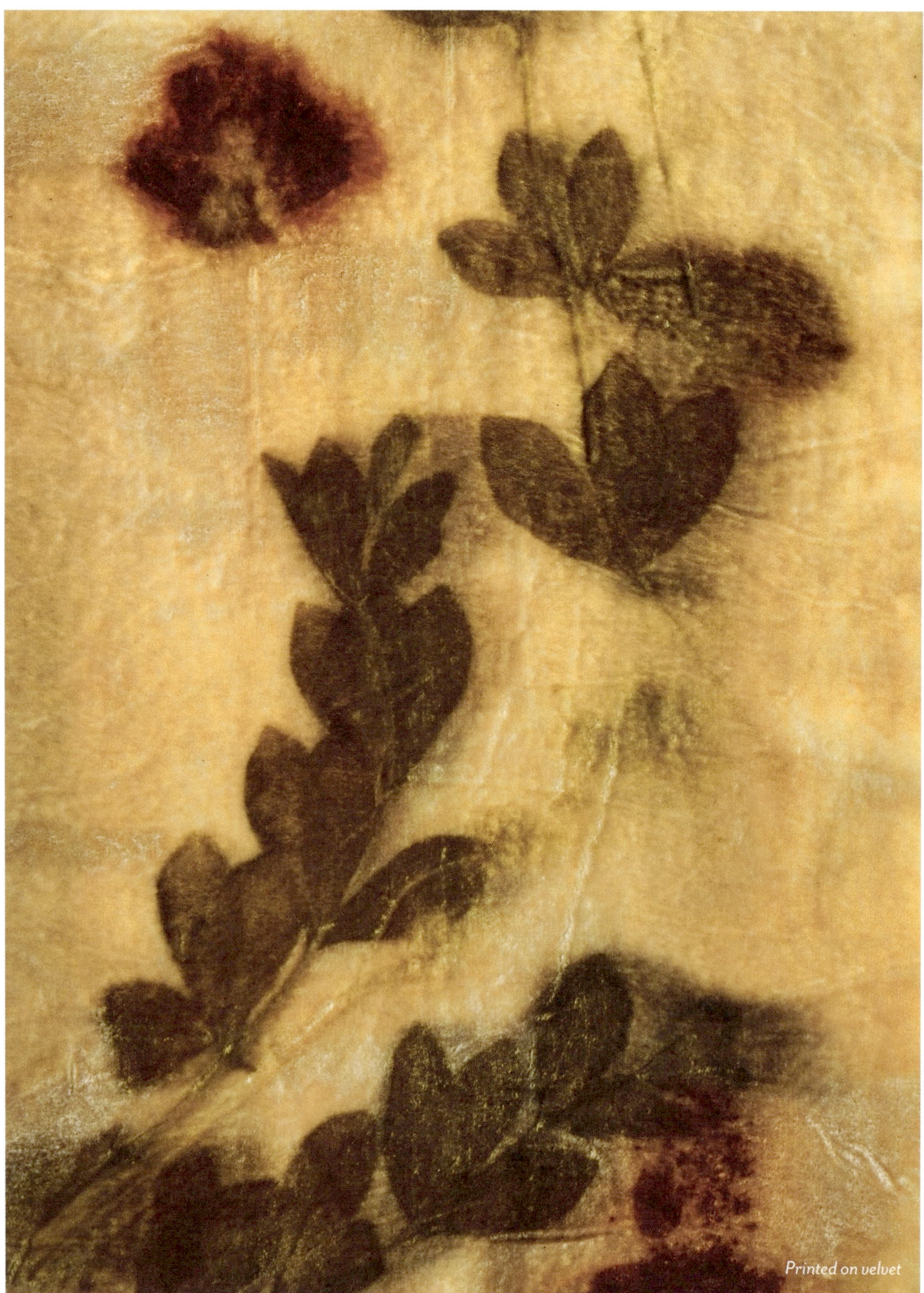

Printed on velvet

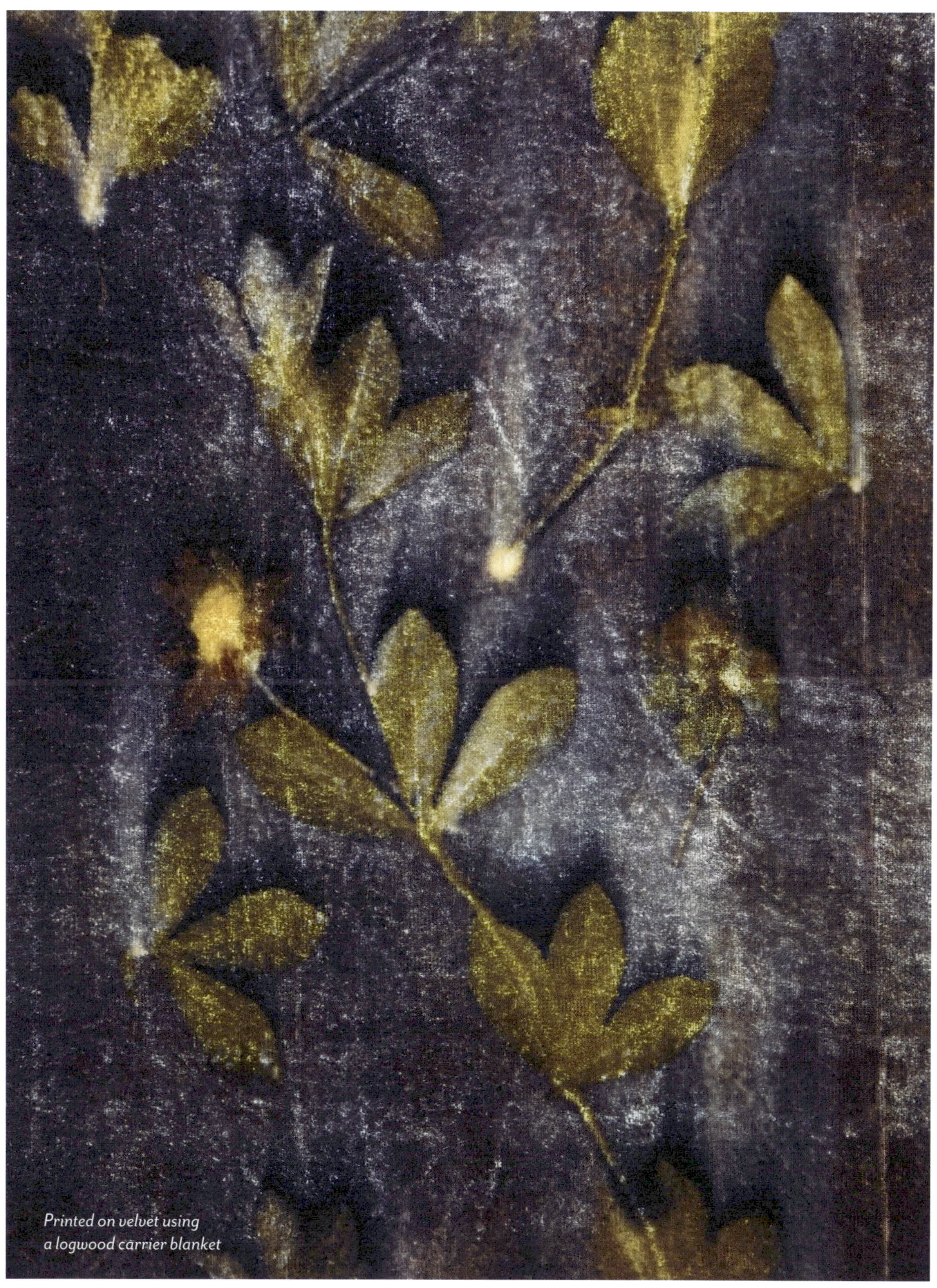
Printed on velvet using a logwood carrier blanket

Butterfly Bush

(Buddleja davidii)

Butterfly bush, also referred to as summer lilac, is a deciduous, drought-resistant shrub with sweetly scented, conical purple flowers. The flowers, leaves, and stems can make for delightful prints. A nice yellow dye, which can be used for a carrier blanket, can be extracted by simmering the petals in water (see below). Drying, pressing, and storing the flowers for later use can enhance the depth of the color.

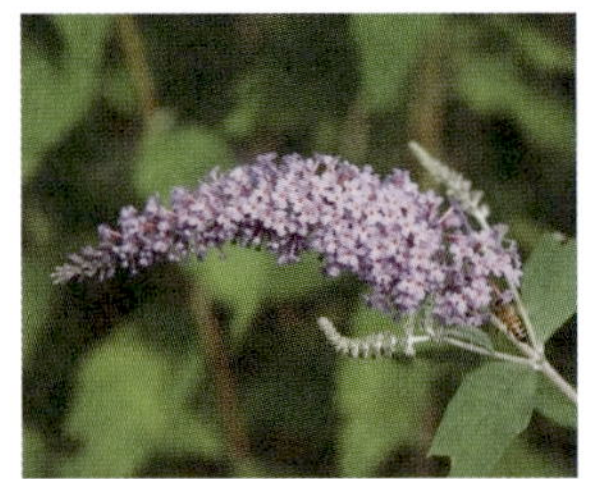

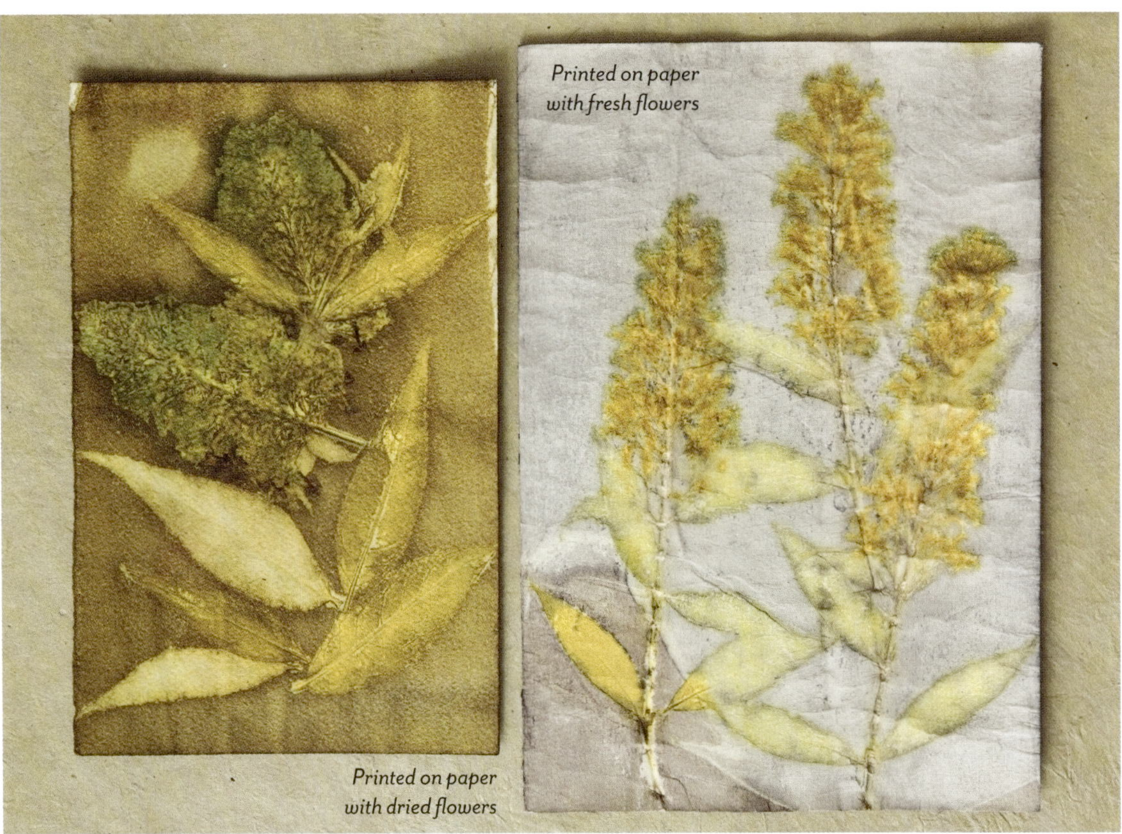

Printed on paper with fresh flowers

Printed on paper with dried flowers

PRINTING NOTES

- To capture the essence of the flower, the fabric or paper should be mordanted with PAS and iron, otherwise a strong contrast won't necessarily be achieved between flower and target.
- The flowers and stalks can be quite bulky. If you'd like, remove some of the petals from the side facing up and sprinkle them into the background of the composition.
- A surprising element is that the purple flowers sometimes print a golden yellow. To enhance this color, use a carrier blanket with a contrasting or darker dye color to add more dimension to the print.
- To extract a dye from the flowers, gently simmer the flower heads in 4 liters (1 gallon) of water for 45 minutes. Allow to steep with the lid on overnight. In the morning, a yellow dye bath should be found.

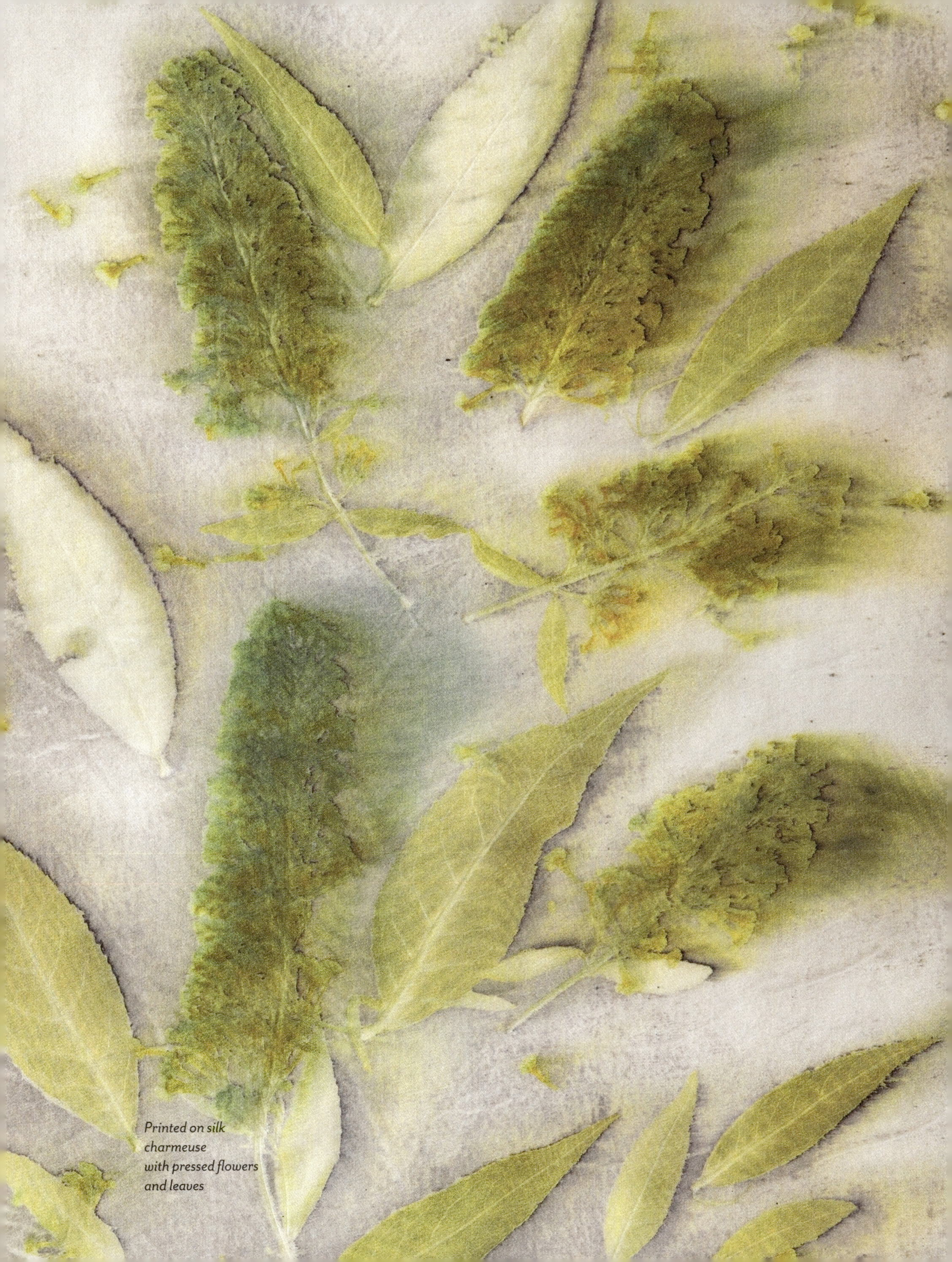

Printed on silk charmeuse with pressed flowers and leaves

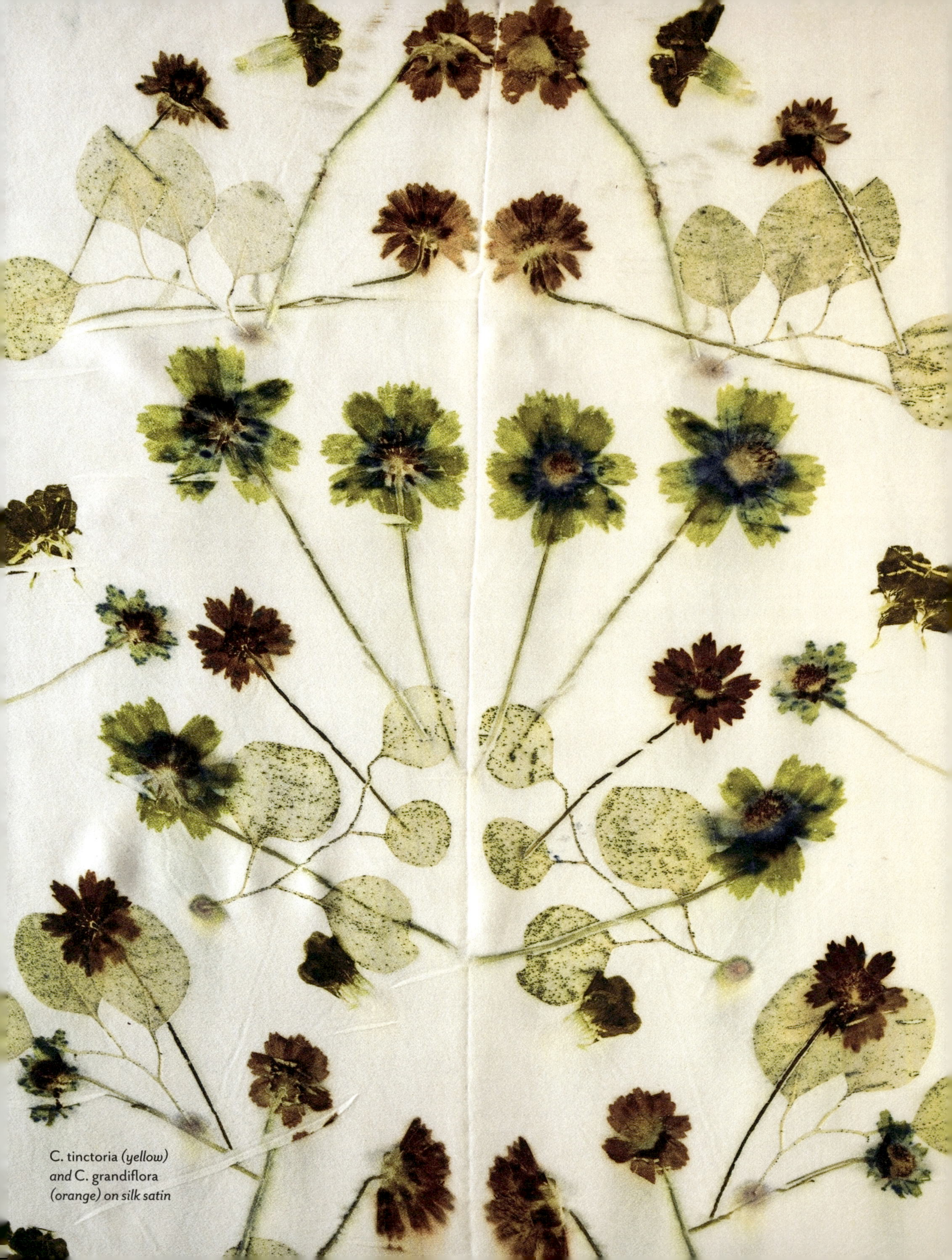

C. tinctoria *(yellow)* *and* C. grandiflora *(orange) on silk satin*

Coreopsis

(*Coreopsis* spp.)

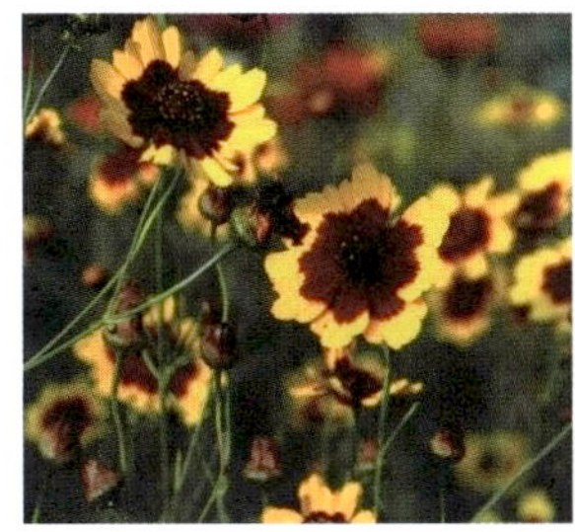

C. tinctoria

Coreopsis is one of the most successful printing flowers I've ever come across, as it offers so much variety. This easy-to-care-for plant adds a ray of sunshine to any garden. Many coreopsis flowers are sunny to golden yellow, but some are a vibrant purple or a striking magenta; they all yield excellent prints. Coreopsis are prolific bloomers; if you can't use them up when fresh, harvest and lay them out to dry, then store them in an airtight container to use for a pop of color in winter. To keep their starburst shape, preserve the flower heads in a flower press or sandwiched between blotting paper and books.

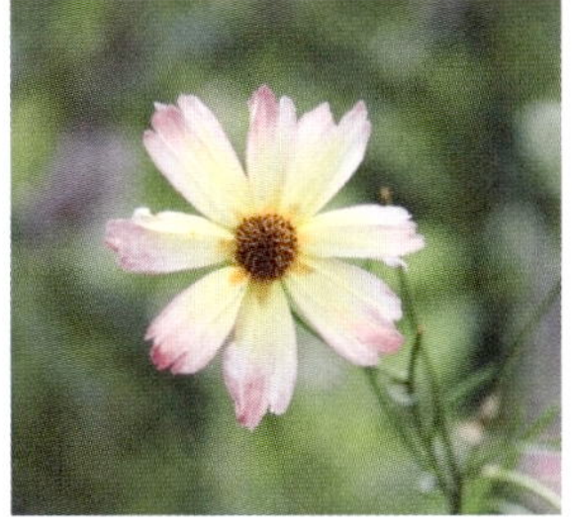

Coreopsis lanceolata *'Sterntaler'*

I grow four varieties: *Coreopsis tinctoria*, known as tickseed or dyer's coreopsis; *C. verticillata*, or whorled tickseed; *C. lanceolata* 'Sterntaler', or lanceleaf coreopsis; and *C. grandiflora* 'Heliot', or large-flowered tickseed.

PRINTING NOTES

- Simply mordanting the fabric in PAS, with a dash of iron and soda ash (as used in the Compound Mordant recipe on page 122), adds depth and expands the range of color.
- Place flowers face down for a photorealistic print, although both sides offer up a full imprint.
- Once flowers have been laid out on the target, I gently hammer the flowers into place using the blunt end of a paint roller. This reduces bulk when rolling the bundle and adds a rich impression at the center.

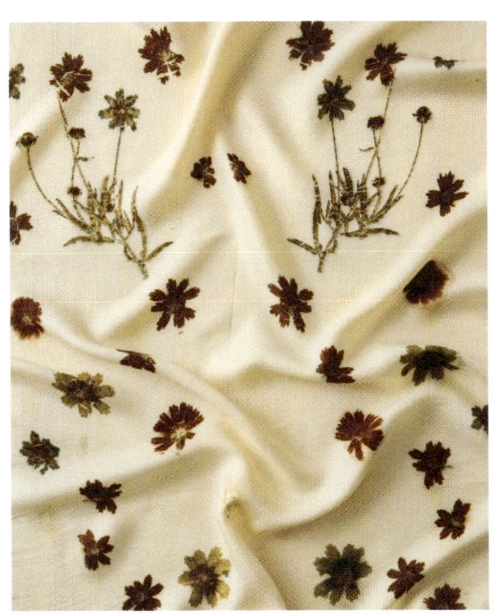

C. lanceolata *'Sterntaler' on silk twill*

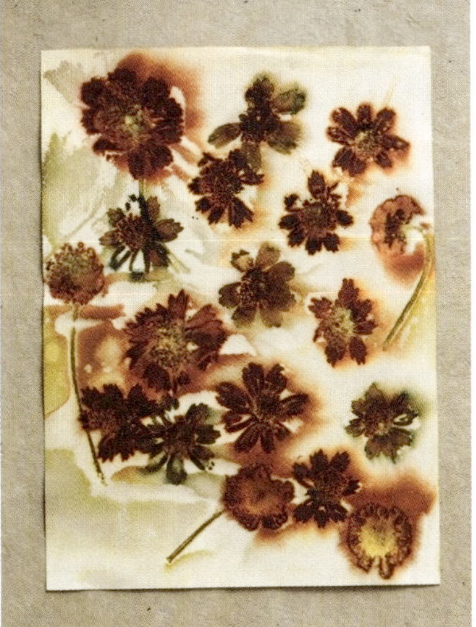

C. grandiflora *'Heliot' on paper*

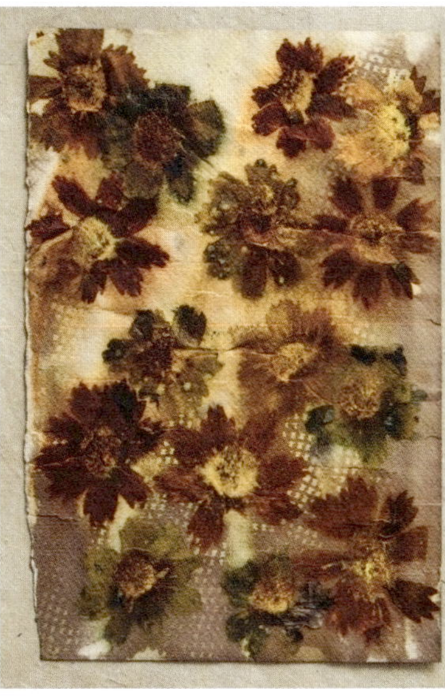

C. lanceolata *'Sterntaler' on paper*

The Zuni people have historically boiled coreopsis flowers to make yellow and red dye for yarn.

Cosmos

(*Cosmos bipinnatus* and *C. sulphureus*)

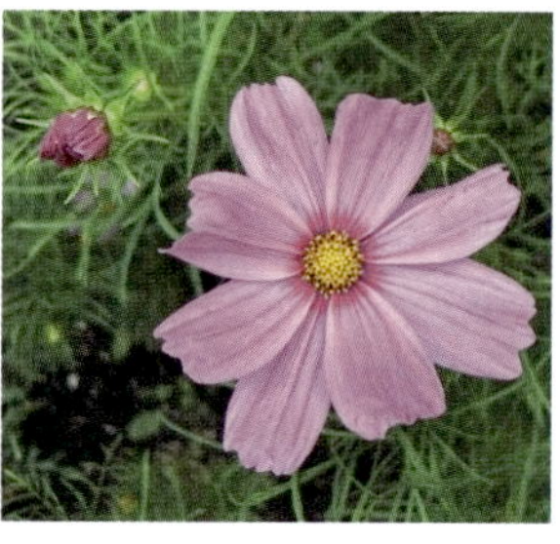

Cosmos, also referred to as Mexican asters, thrive in many regions, bringing color and grace to any garden. The flowers come in a variety of colors, including white, pink, crimson, rose, lavender, purple, orange, and yellow.

Cosmos bipinnatus comes in shades of lavender, mauve, white, and pink. *C. sulphureus*, or sulfur cosmos, is a shining, golden yellow. Both are excellent choices for flower prints. Cosmos are exceptional candidates to be dried, pressed, and stored for future use, but the dried petals are quite delicate.

PRINTING NOTES

- The graceful eight-petaled flowers feature a sunny center that imparts a bold imprint.
- The featherlike bright green leaves and stems are powerful printers and offer a distinctive elegance to a botanical composition.

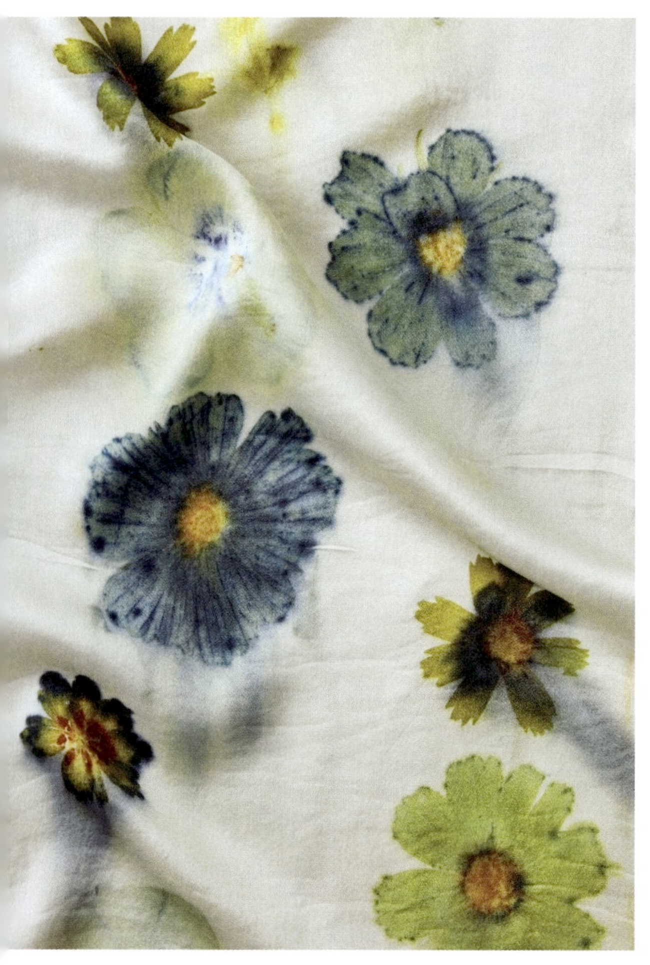

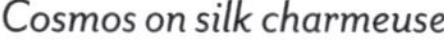

Cosmos on silk charmeuse

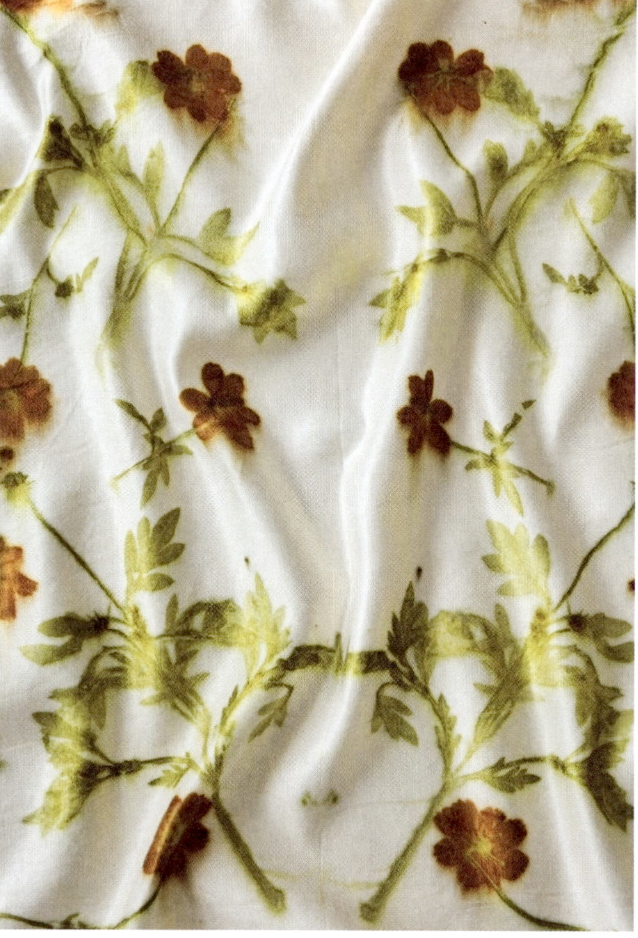

Sulfur cosmos printed on silk hemp

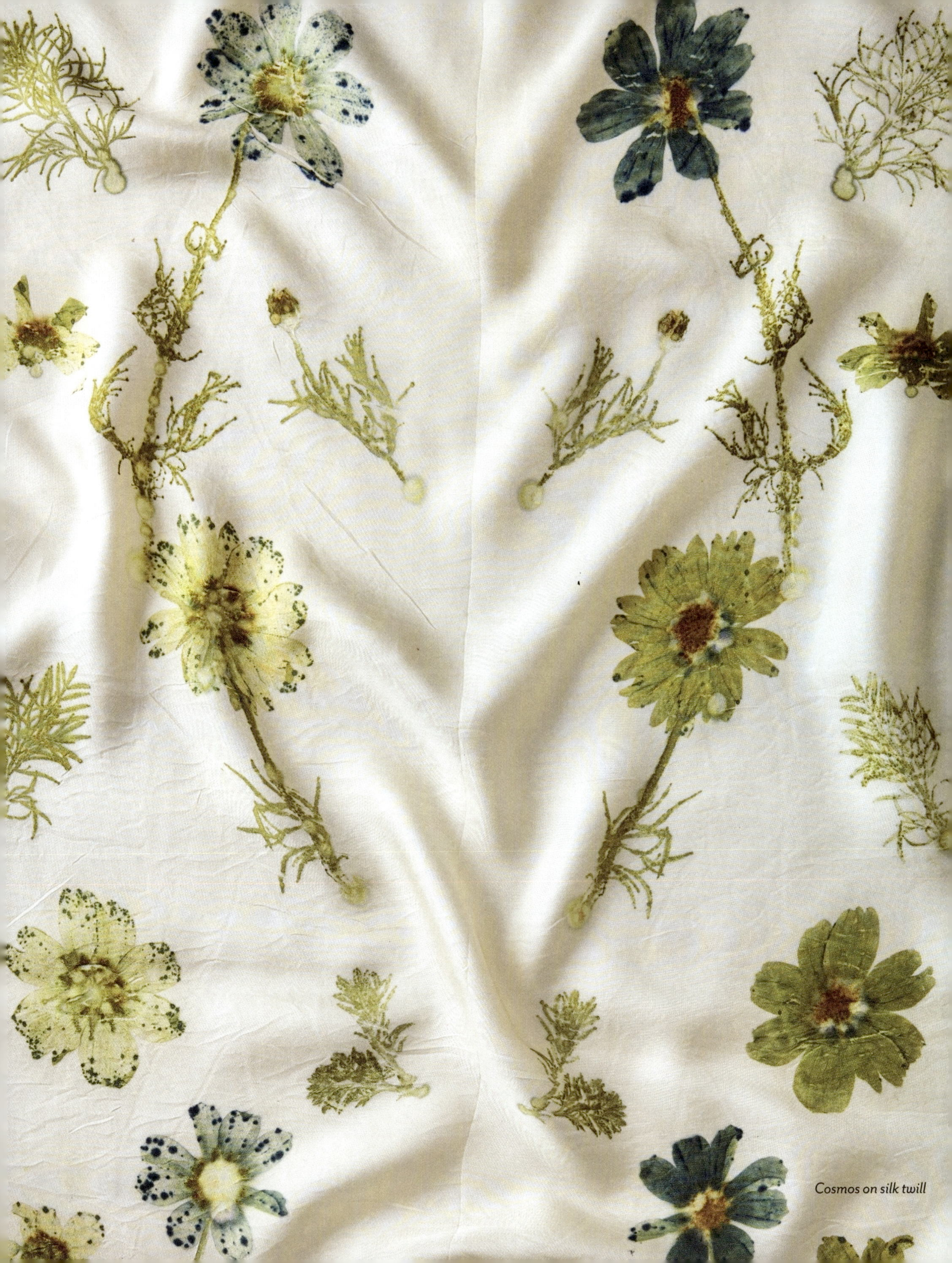

Cosmos on silk twill

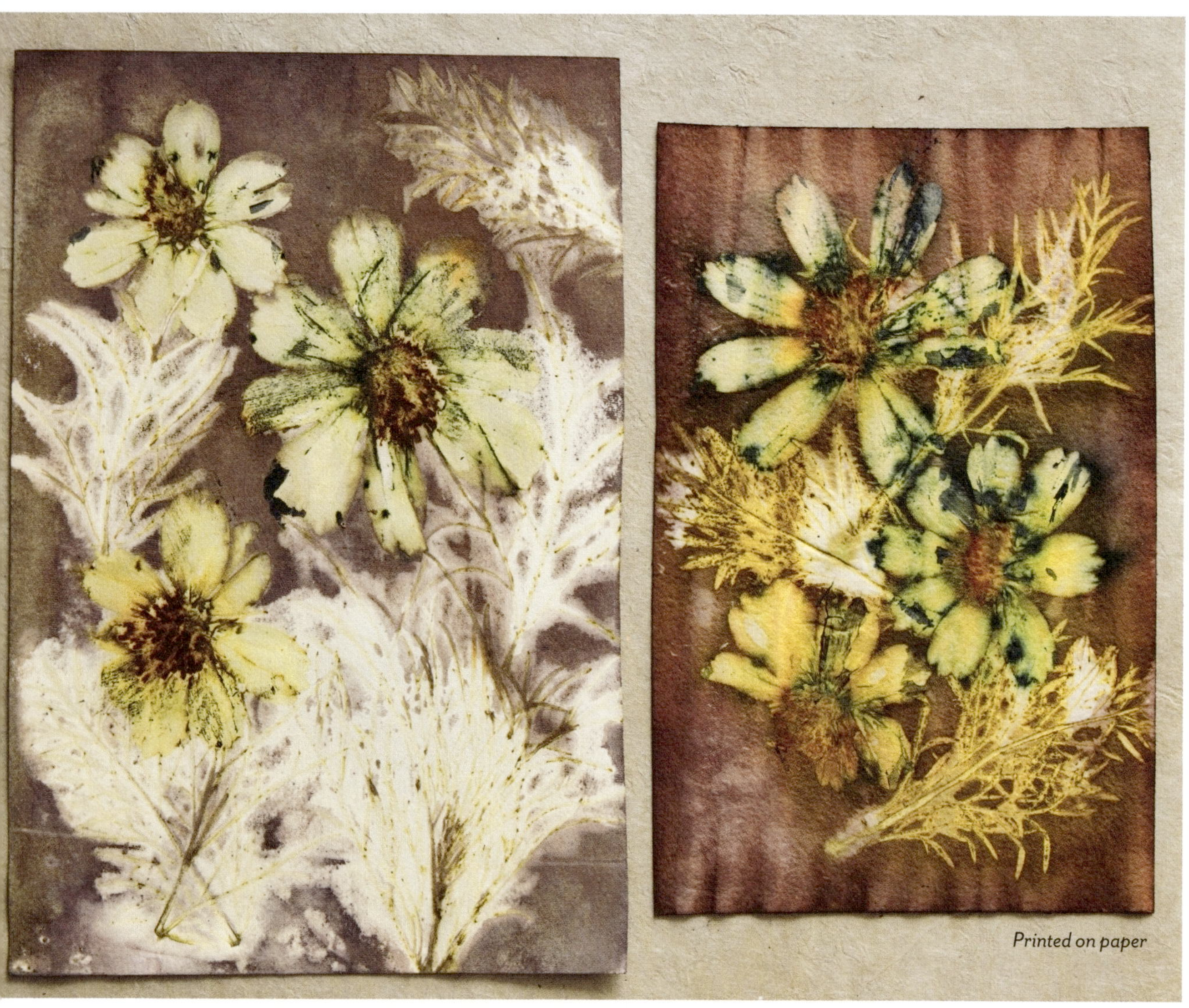

Printed on paper

It is said that the name, derived from the Greek word kosmos, *refers to harmony and balance. Sulfur cosmos was used to make a vibrant orange dye in pre–Columbian America, as evidenced in antique tapestries.*

These examples feature fresh magenta and mauve cosmos, which shift to blue and teal when reacting with the acidic properties of the PAS and iron in the mordant. Using a simple soy milk mordant will impart colors that are truer to the fresh flower.

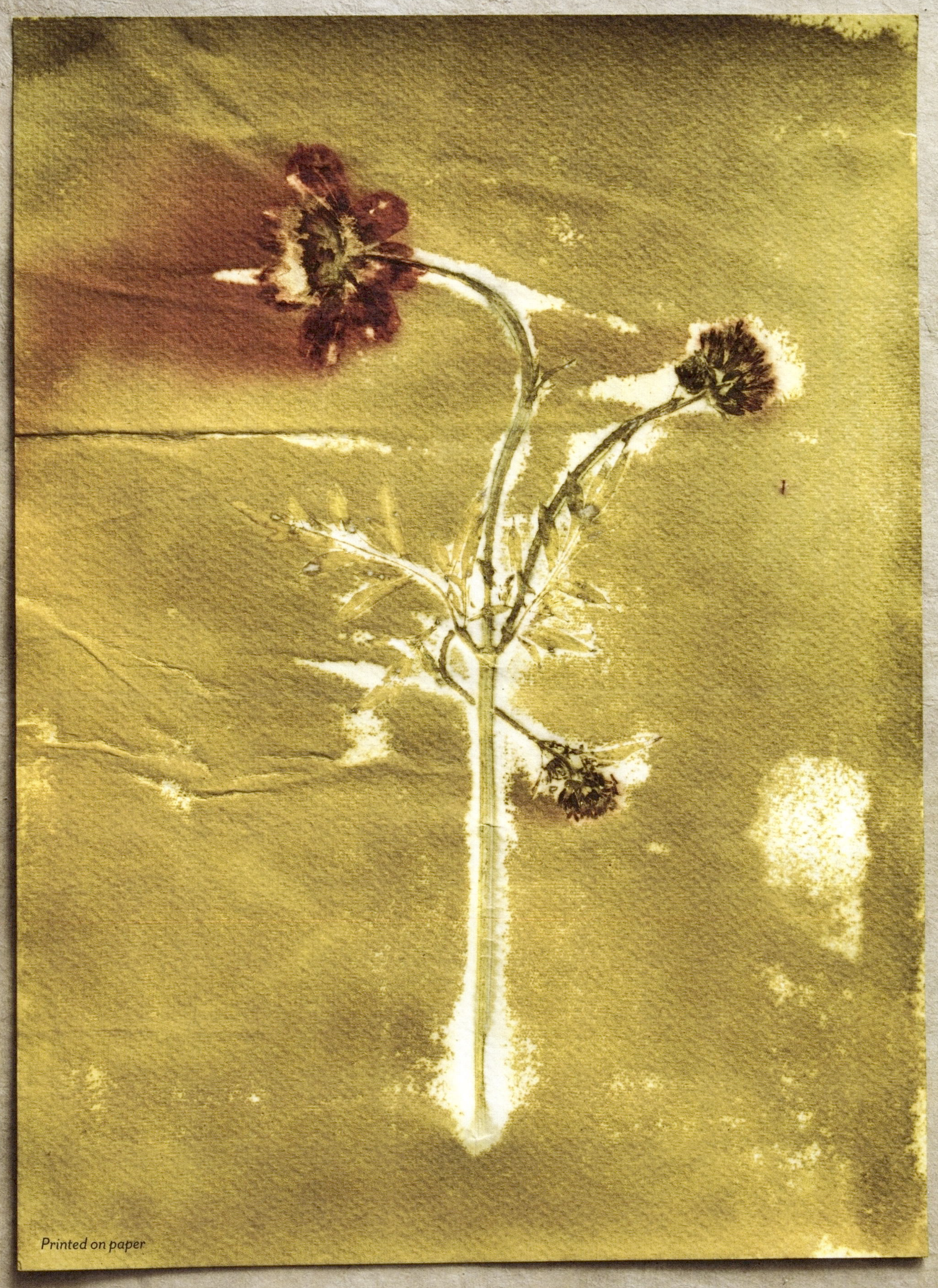

Printed on paper

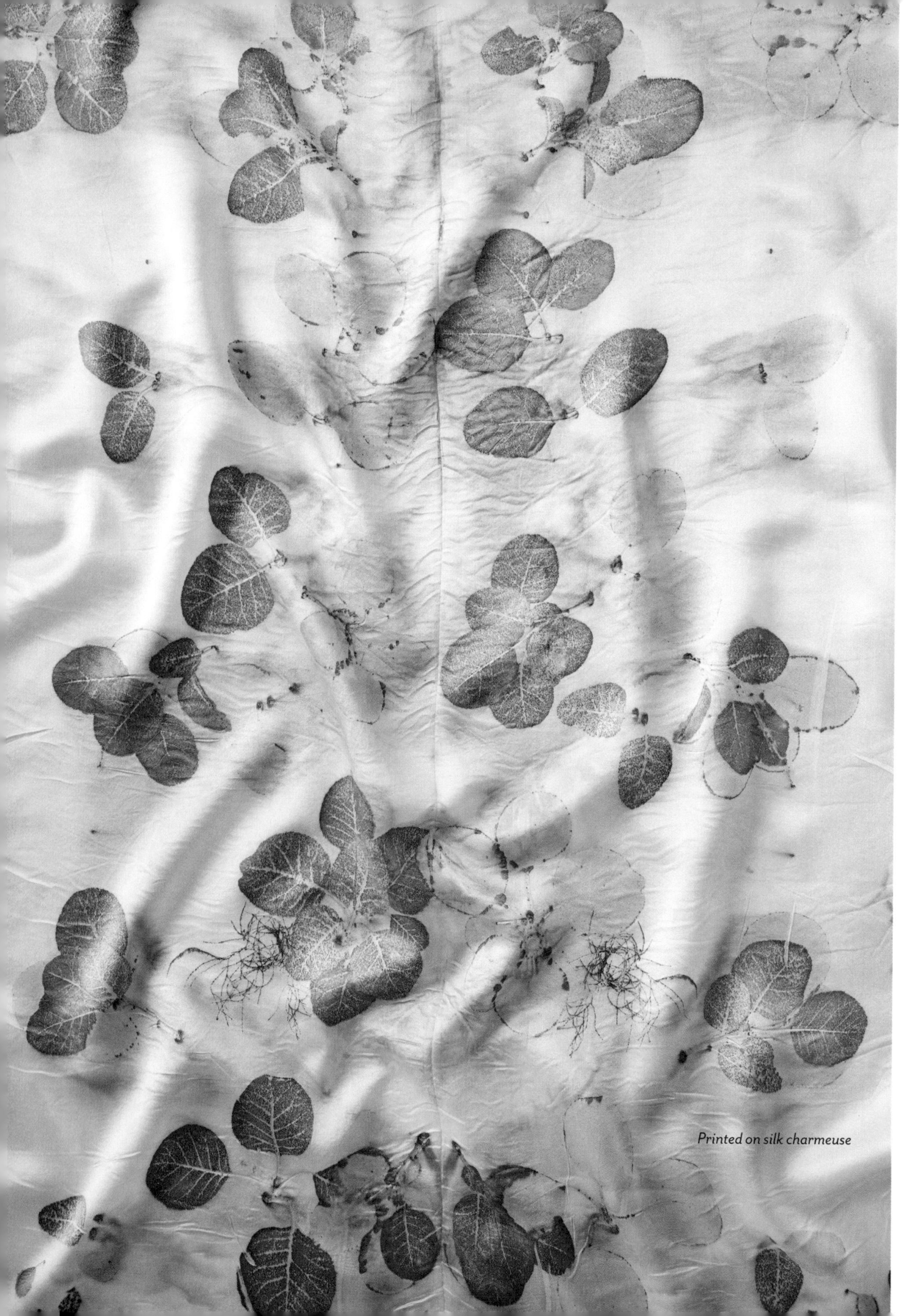

Printed on silk charmeuse

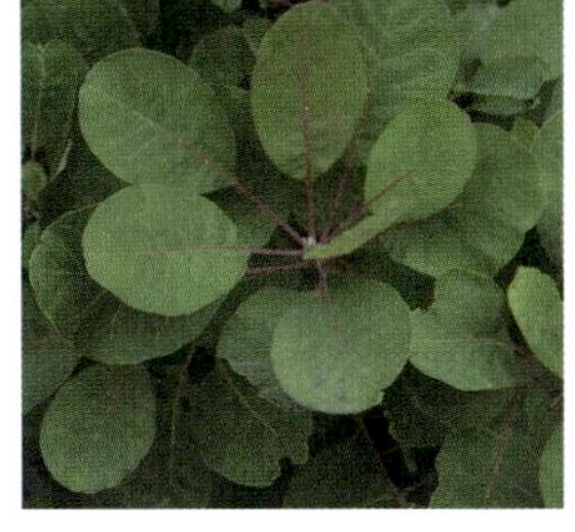

Cotinus

(*Cotinus coggygria*)

Cotinus, also called smoke tree or smoke bush, is named after the puff of smoke the shrub appears to be engulfed in when in bloom. From a distance, its warm pink inflorescences resemble a cloud of smoke against the red wine–colored leaves and range from hues of cream to yellow or red. This deciduous woody shrub (or small tree) has green, purple, or gold leaves that turn a vibrant scarlet in autumn.

Printed on paper

PRINTING NOTES

- The moon side will impart a blue-black coloring with a dark outline when used with a mordant containing iron.
- For a colorful variation, try printing with the leaves on fabric that has been dyed a solid color, such as purple using logwood dye.
- Cotinus leaves are stiff and hardy and do not contain much moisture. You can place them between sheets of paper to preserve them for later use.

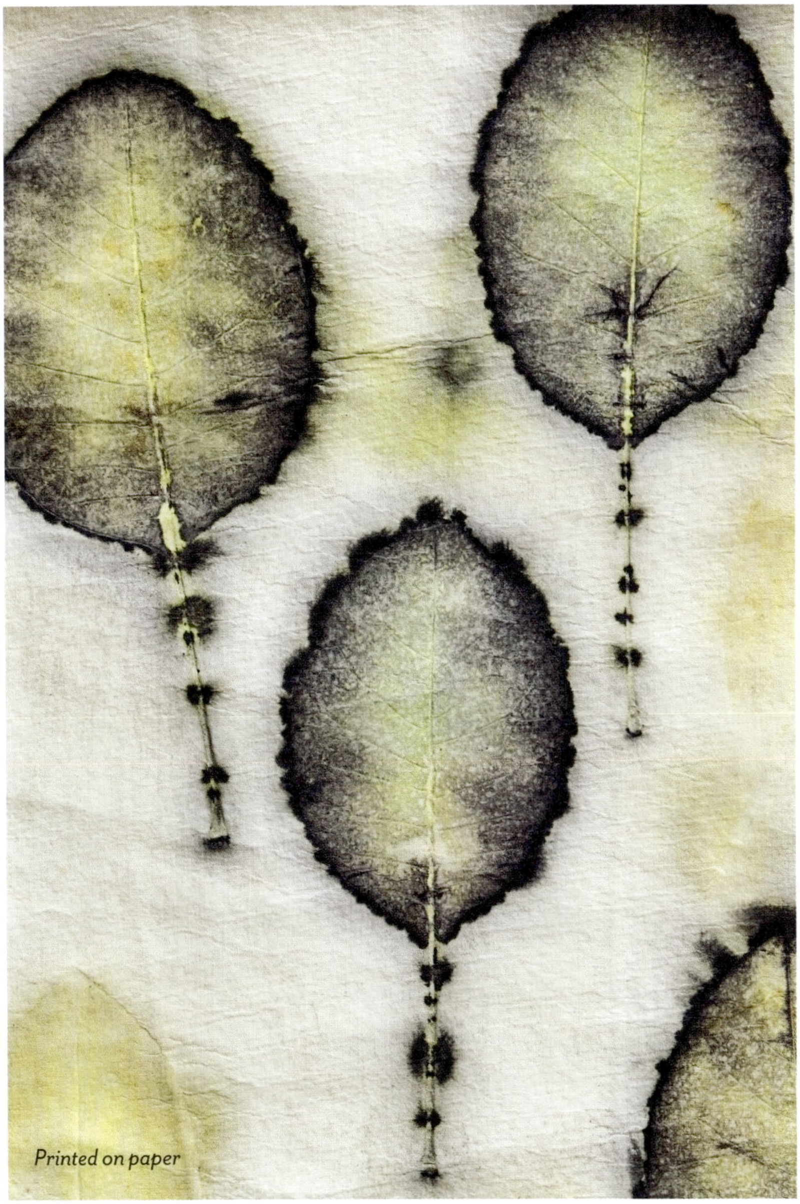

The cotinus bush is rich in phenolic compounds and flavonoids. Both the leaves and bark have been used in traditional Chinese medicine to treat illnesses ranging from bacterial infections and burns to jaundice and hepatitis.

Dahlia

(*Dahlia pinnata*)

Dahlias have earned a place in my heart not only for their beauty on the stem but for the spirit and color they offer in a botanical composition. Their lush, full blooms showcase an impressive spectrum, from fiery reds that command attention to softly glowing yellows that evoke tranquility.

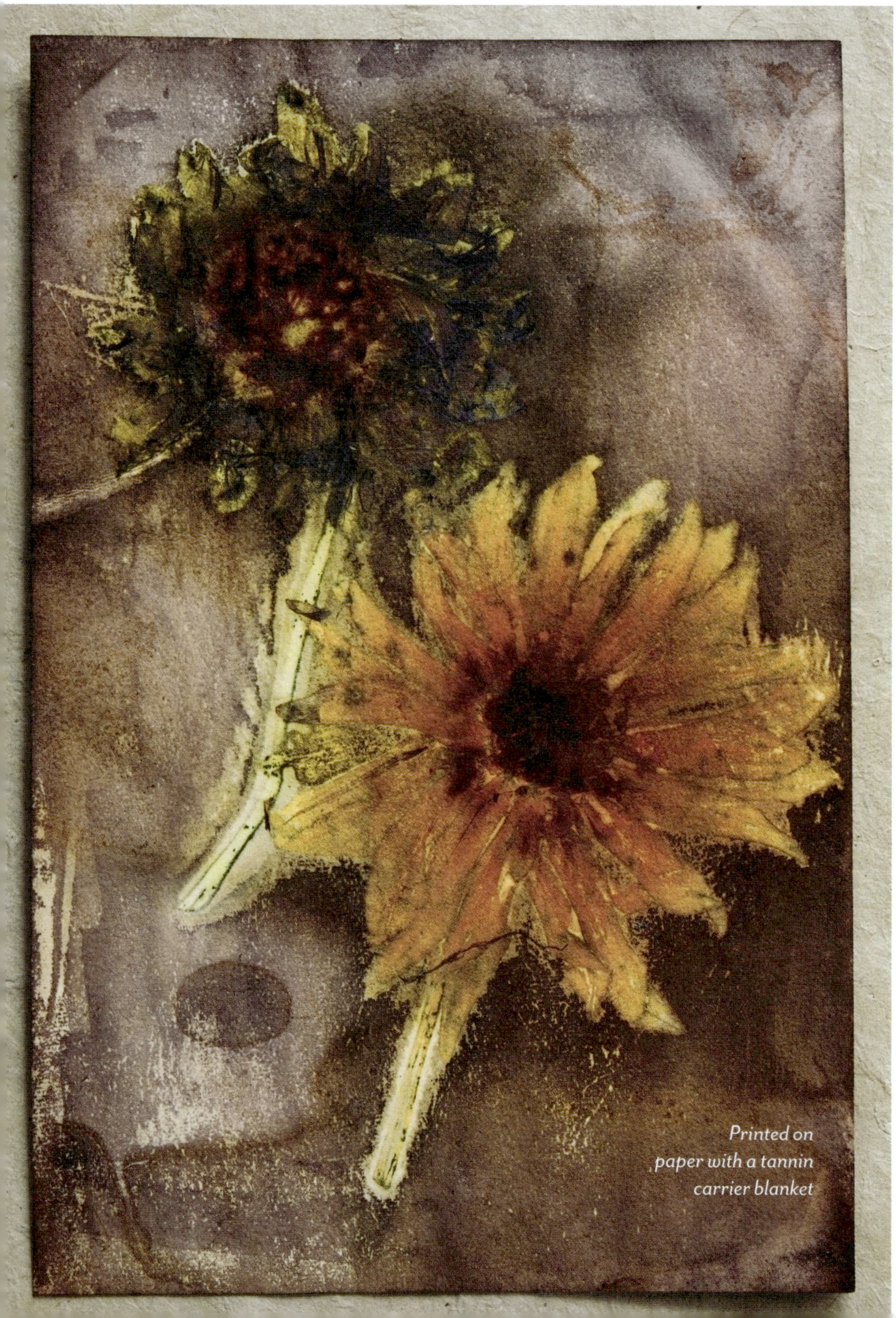

Printed on paper with a tannin carrier blanket

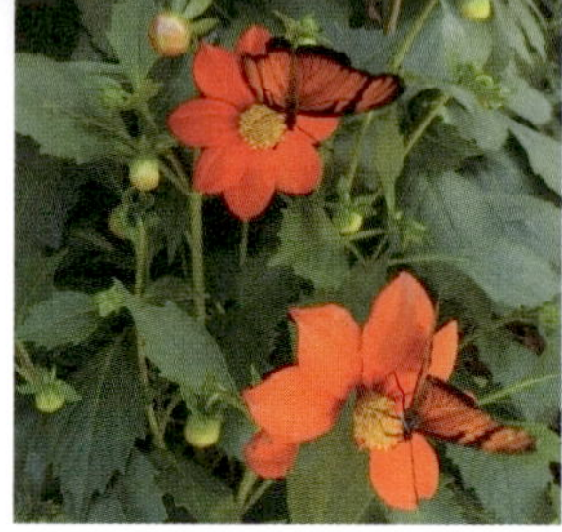

PRINTING NOTES

- My favorites for printing are the bright yellow and hot orange varieties. Any hue but white, or very pale shades, lends a bit of color.
- Dahlias are quite bulky, so I tend to use a cushioning blanket on top of the composition for extra padding when bundling.
- Try to place the flowers in a zigzag pattern so they don't overlap too much when rolling up the bundle—or stick to a more minimal layout such as a single bloom on paper.
- Using a carrier blanket can help you capture the arresting outline of the petals against a contrasting background.
- Dried petals can be broken into smaller pieces for a sprinkle of color when bundle dyeing.

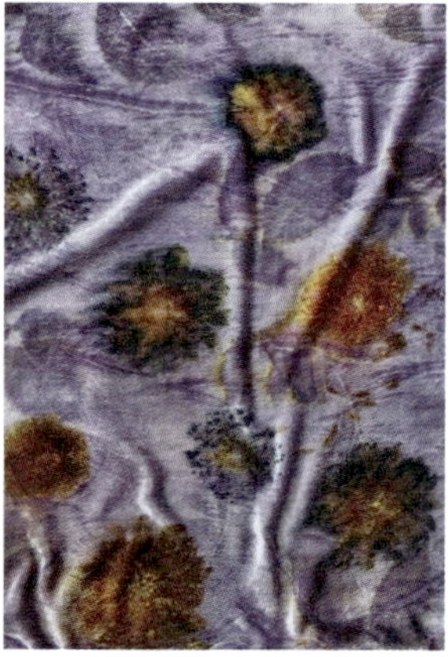

Printed on silk velvet with a logwood carrier blanket

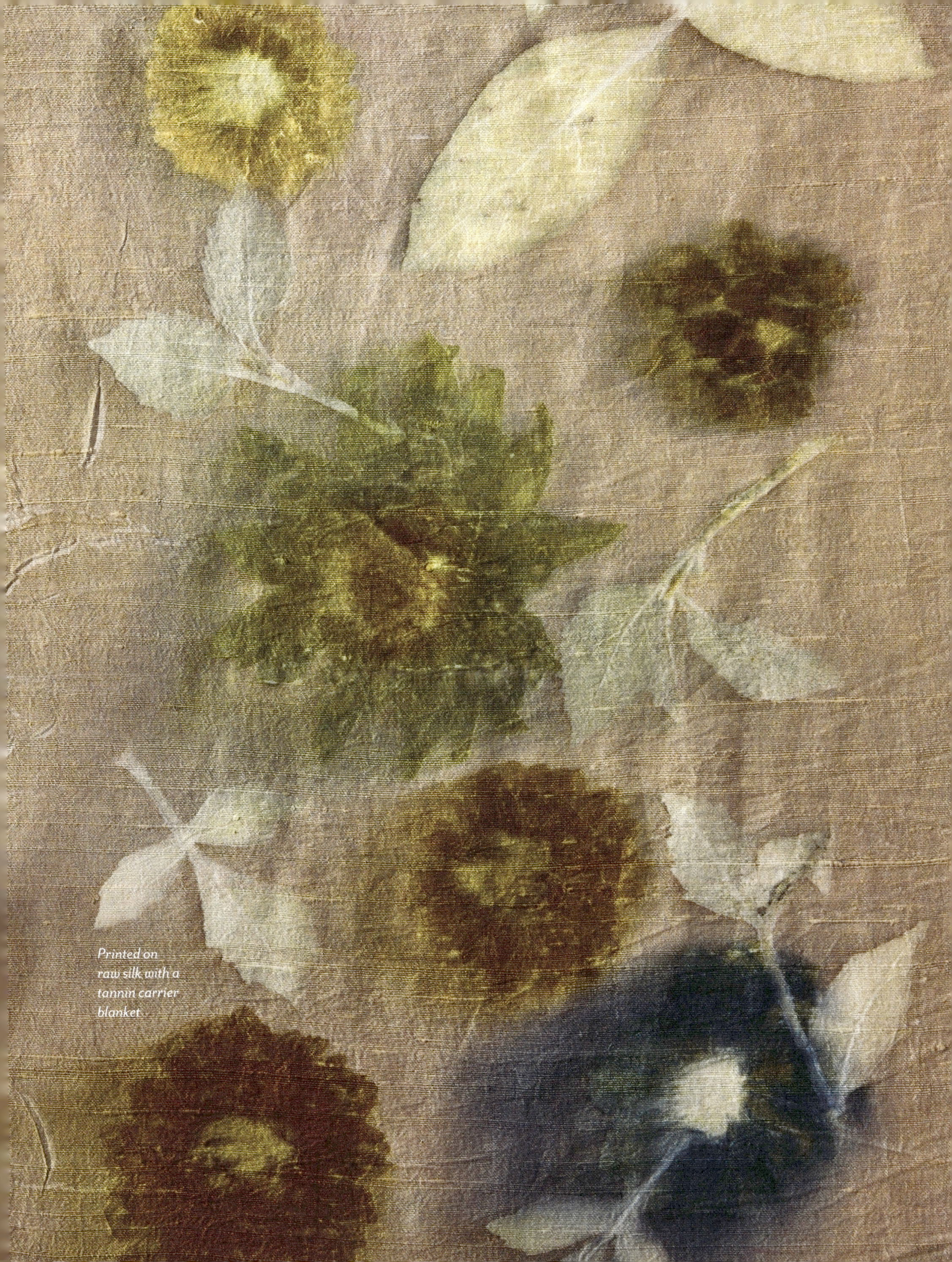

Printed on raw silk with a tannin carrier blanket.

Daylily

(*Hemerocallis fulva*)

Printing with daylilies can be a surprising experience: Eager to coax out the color from these neon orange beauties, I was at first disappointed to see, when using a PAS and iron mordant, that the petals printed a light periwinkle blue due to the acidic nature of the flowers, rather than impart their true orange color. Parts of the flowers also take away, or discharge, some parts of the target. The stems and leaves do not impart much color either, but their elegant curves can make for an alluring design component. The flowers are difficult to preserve and best used fresh.

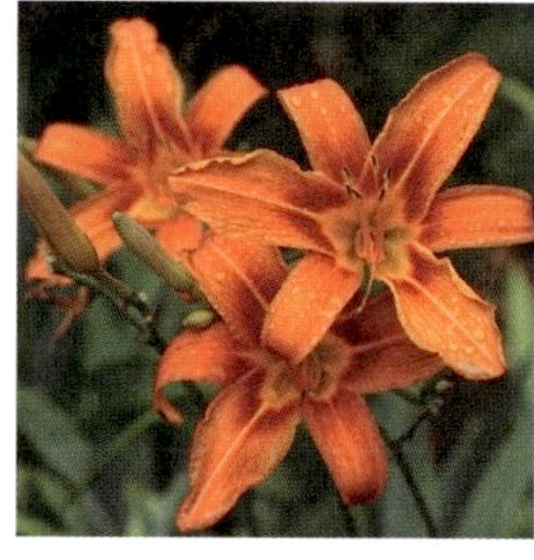

PRINTING NOTES

- To fully capture the essence of these striking flowers, I tend to use a carrier blanket for contrast. To suggest the natural coloring of the flowers, I recommend experimenting with a carrier blanket soaked in an orange dye, such as kamala, turmeric, marigold, or persimmon, as seen in the paper example.
- The flowers are crisp and bulky, so use a blanket to get them as flat as possible when rolling. (A carrier blanket works if you are adding background color, or use a cushioning blanket.) Press a roller over the blanket to further compress the flowers to the target.

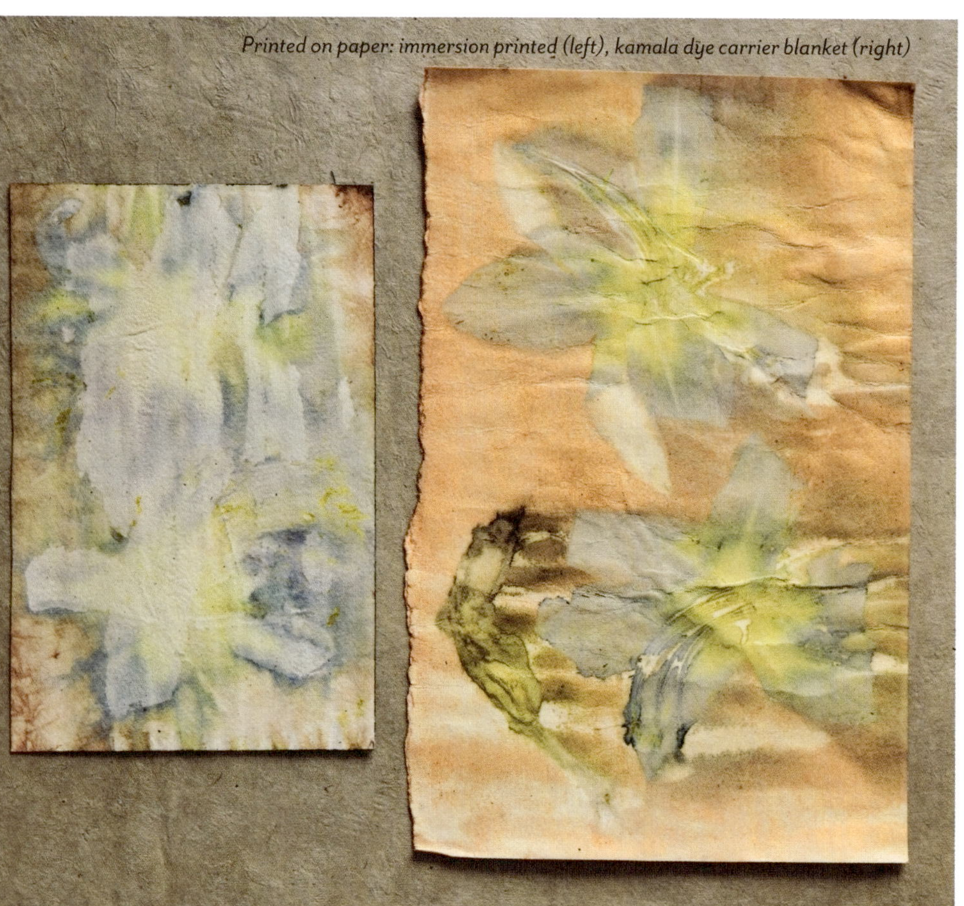

Printed on paper: immersion printed (left), kamala dye carrier blanket (right)

The name Hemerocallis *can be broken into "day" and "beautiful" in Greek.*

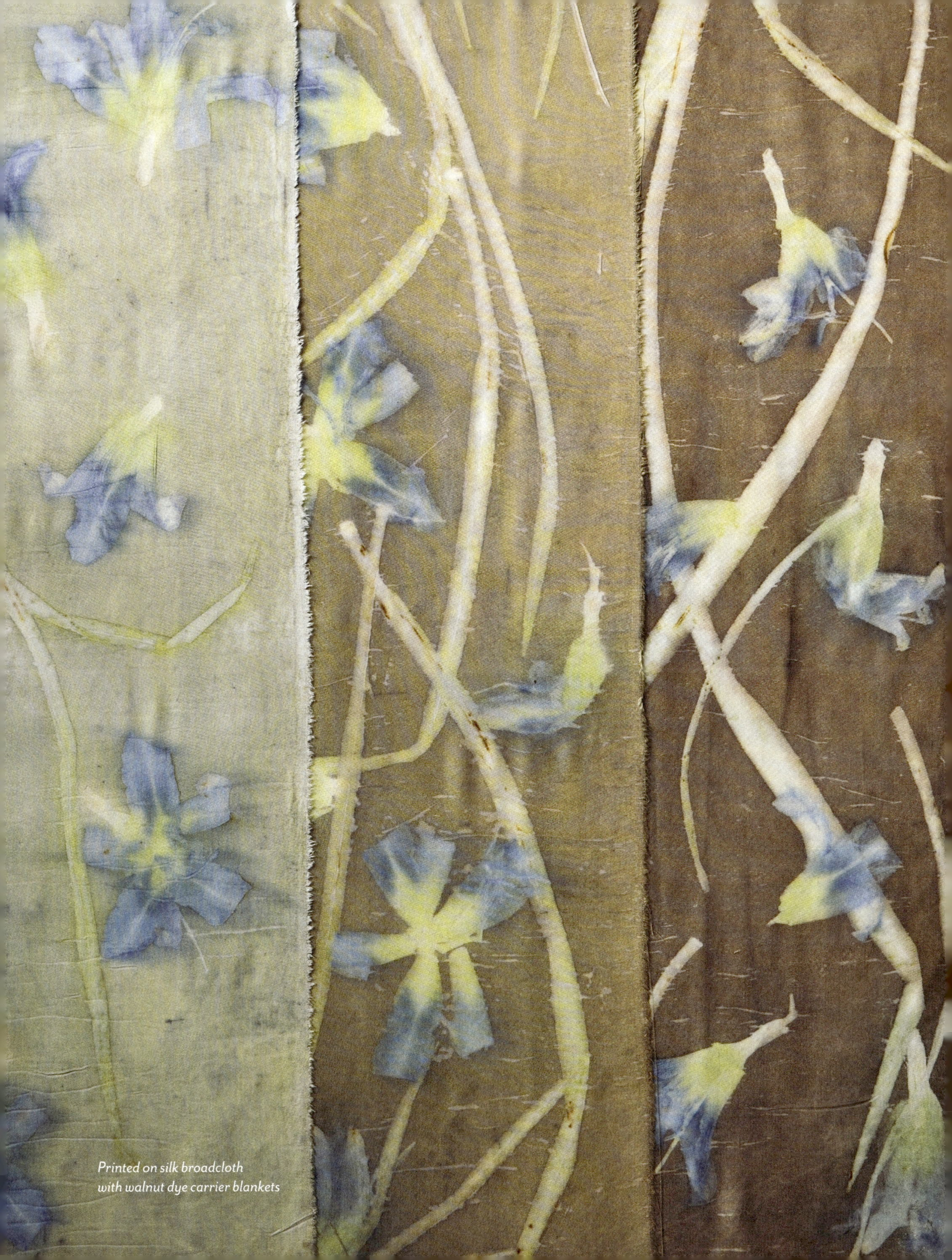

Printed on silk broadcloth with walnut dye carrier blankets

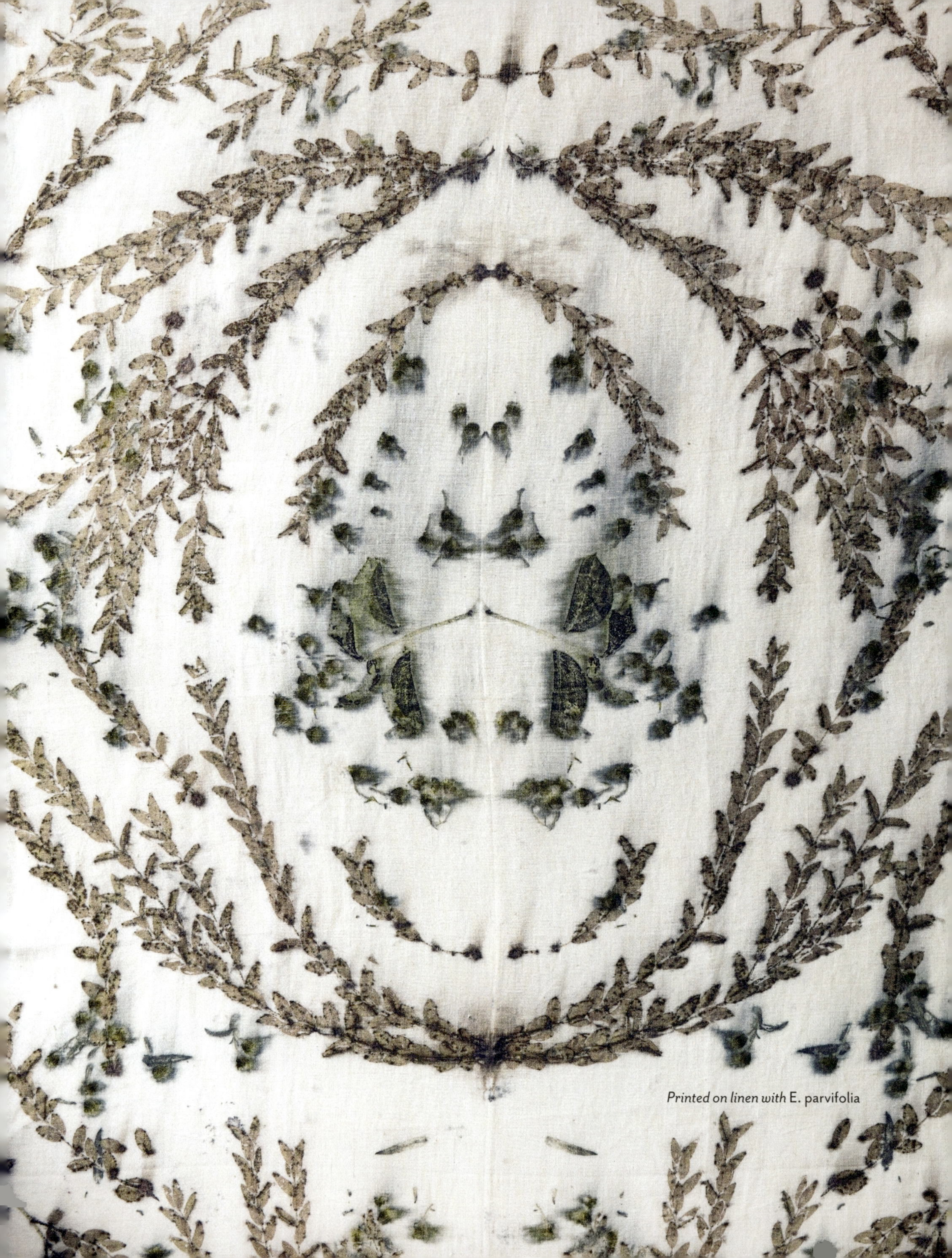

Printed on linen with E. parvifolia

Eucalyptus

Eucalyptus spp. is a versatile plant known for its diverse species and adaptability to various climates. With more than seven hundred species, this botanical wonder can be found in tropical, subtropical, and temperate zones, showcasing an array of leaf shapes and sizes. Rich in tannin, eucalyptus is particularly valuable for printing, as the tannins interact strongly with iron, creating bold imprints. Eucalyptus can be successfully printed with no mordant, although mordanting the target yields more dramatic and longer-lasting results. In regions where it does not grow, try florists or flower markets to source some fresh leaf.

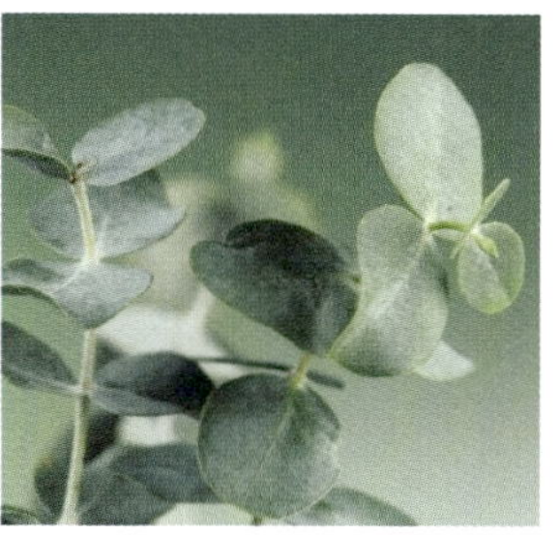

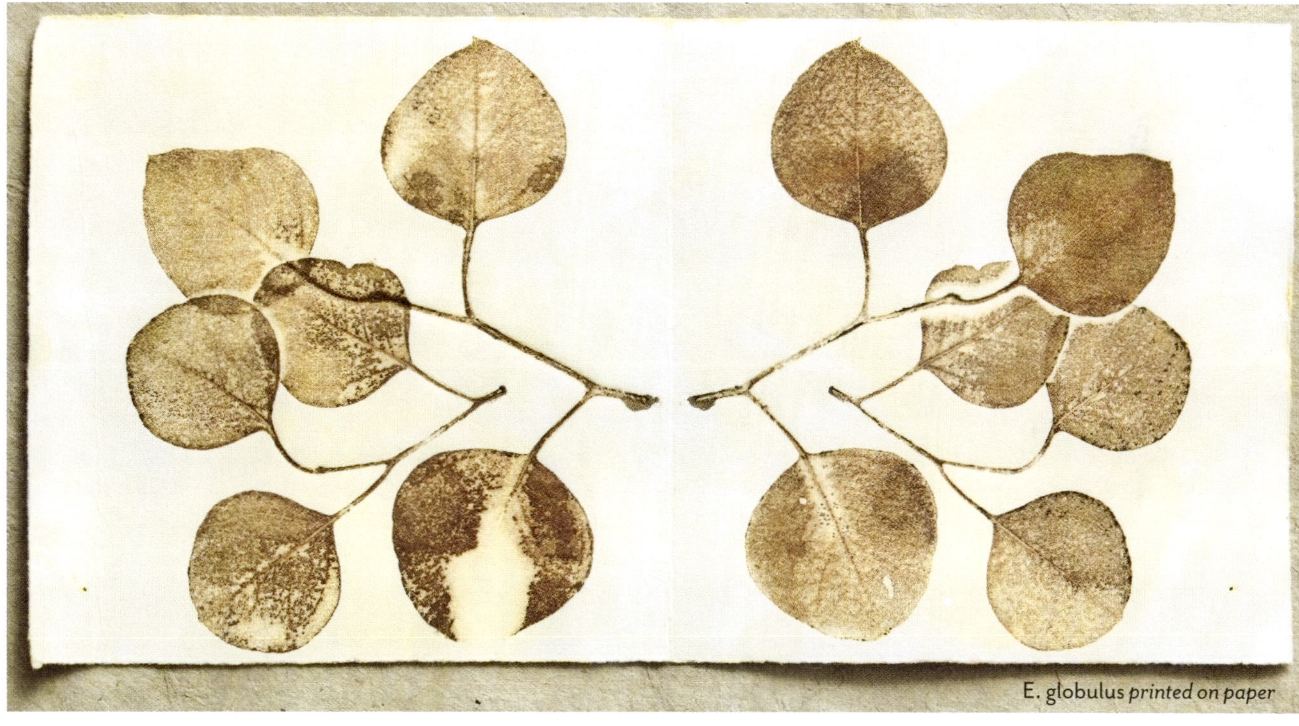

E. globulus *printed on paper*

PRINTING NOTES

- Hardy eucalyptus leaves should be steamed for longer than most other vegetation—for at least 90 minutes to ensure a strong transfer of pigment.
- It is a fine choice for creating bold and dramatic imprints on cellulose fibers such as linen and cotton. With the addition of iron in the mordant, even bolder imprints will occur.
- Eucalyptus leaves print well on both the sun and moon sides.
- When it comes to preserving fresh eucalyptus leaves, freezing is the best bet, as fresh leaves print more fully.
- Soak dried leaves in tepid water overnight to restore some freshness.
- To achieve vibrant orangey red prints, use protein fabrics. Wool generally prints redder than silk. Suggested species for achieving this color are *E. sideroxylon* (red iron bark), *E. cinerea* (silver dollar), *E. polyan-themos* (silver dollar), *E. radiata* (peppermint gum), and *E. populnea* (poplar box).

Eucalyptus *continued*

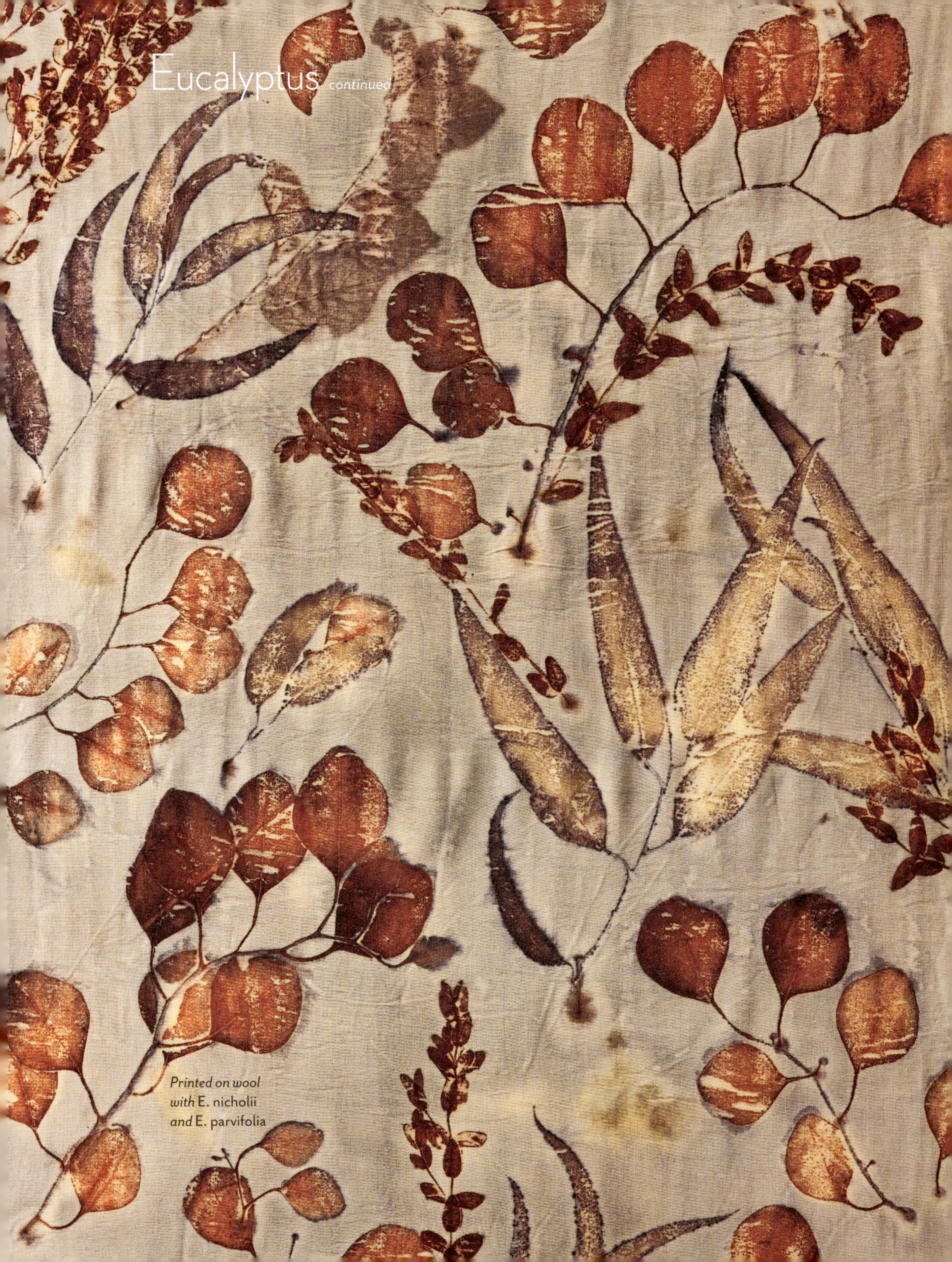

Printed on wool with E. nicholii *and* E. parvifolia

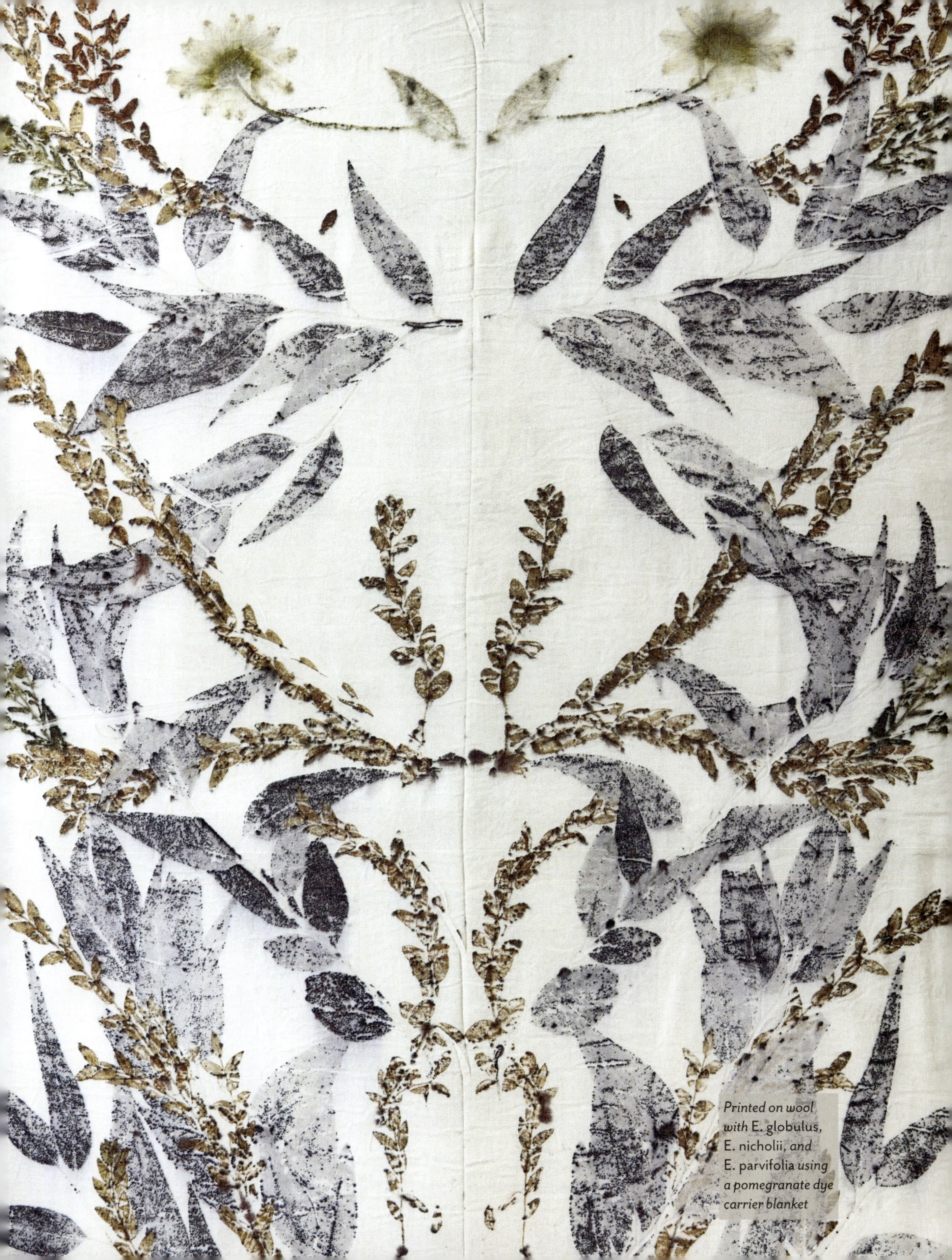

Printed on wool with E. globulus, E. nicholii, *and* E. parvifolia *using a pomegranate dye carrier blanket*

Flowering Dogwood

(*Cornus florida*)

Though the four-part "blooms" resemble flowers, they are actually bracts: extensions of the leaves designed to protect the true flowers nestled within. These bracts surround a central cluster of tough, spiky blooms. The bracts are too delicate to preserve, but the leaves can easily be stored for later use. Because they are quite strong, freezing them with a little bit of water is an effective preservation method.

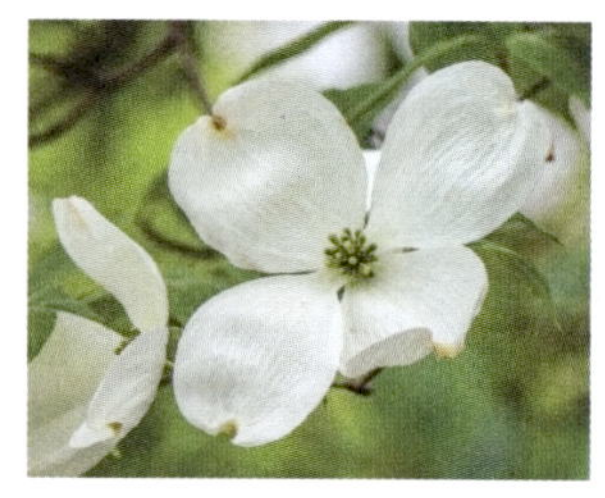

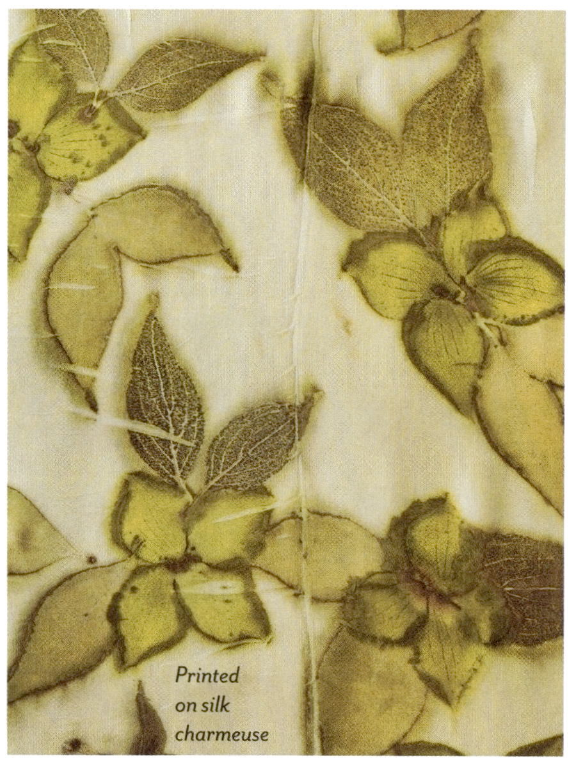

Printed on silk charmeuse

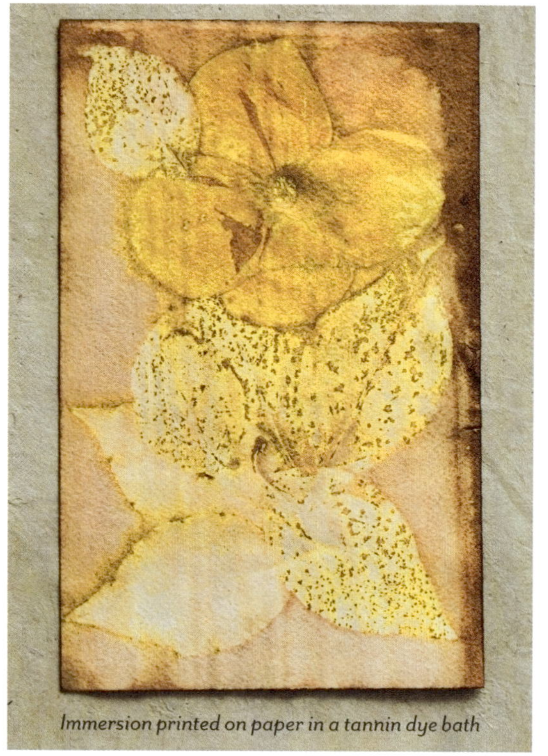

Immersion printed on paper in a tannin dye bath

The inner bark of the dogwood tree is full of tannin, which has traditionally been used as an antiparasitic.

PRINTING NOTES

- Whether white, pink, yellow, or green, the bracts do not offer much color, but their elegant shape can be captured by using a carrier blanket to enhance their outline.
- To achieve a clear print and make the bracts lie flat when bundling, remove the tough flower cluster at the center.
- When iron is used in the mordant, the dark green leaves offer better pigmentation and distinct prints from both sun and moon sides.
- Steam leaves for at least 45 minutes to ensure maximum color transfer.

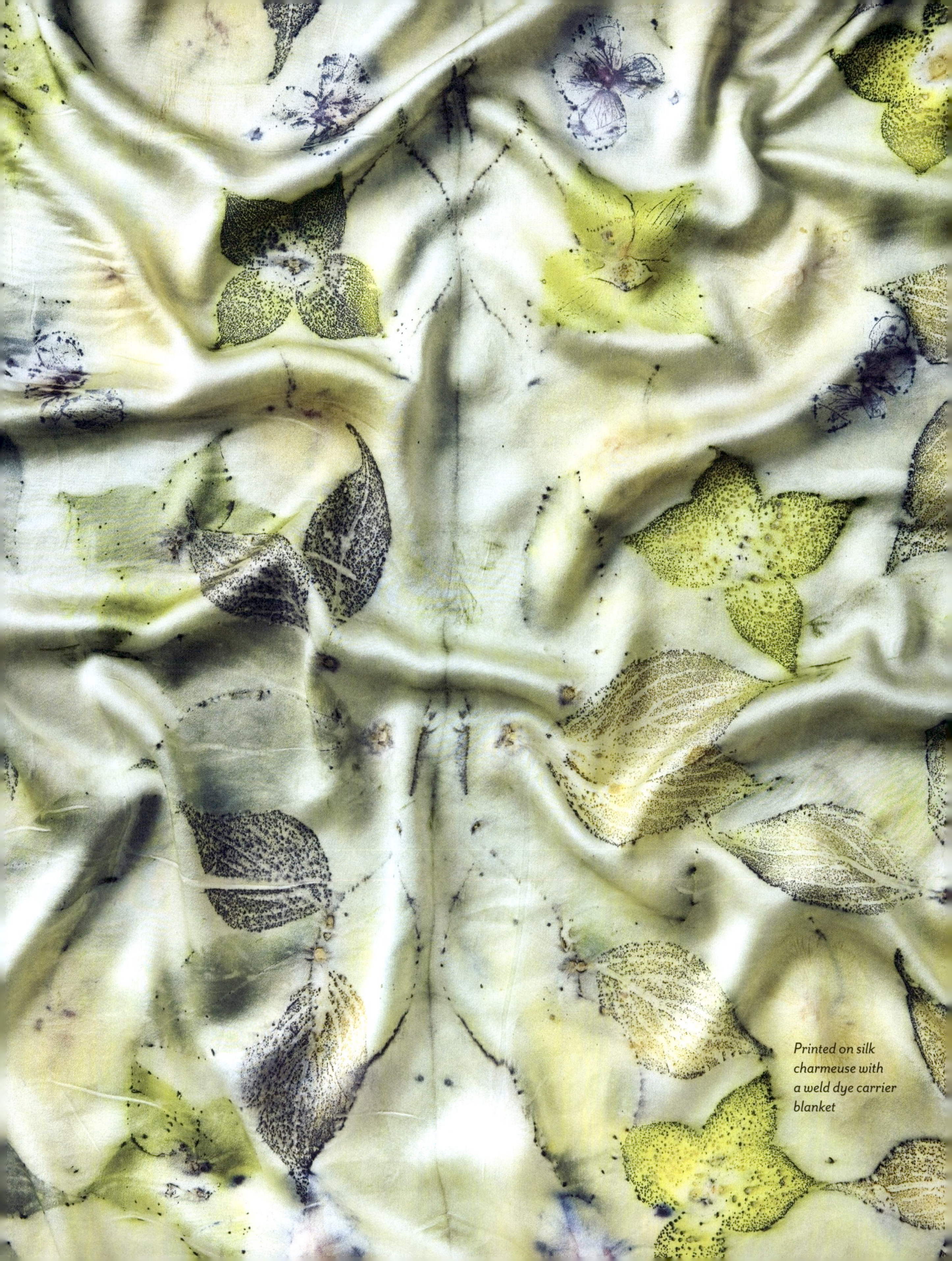

Printed on silk charmeuse with a weld dye carrier blanket

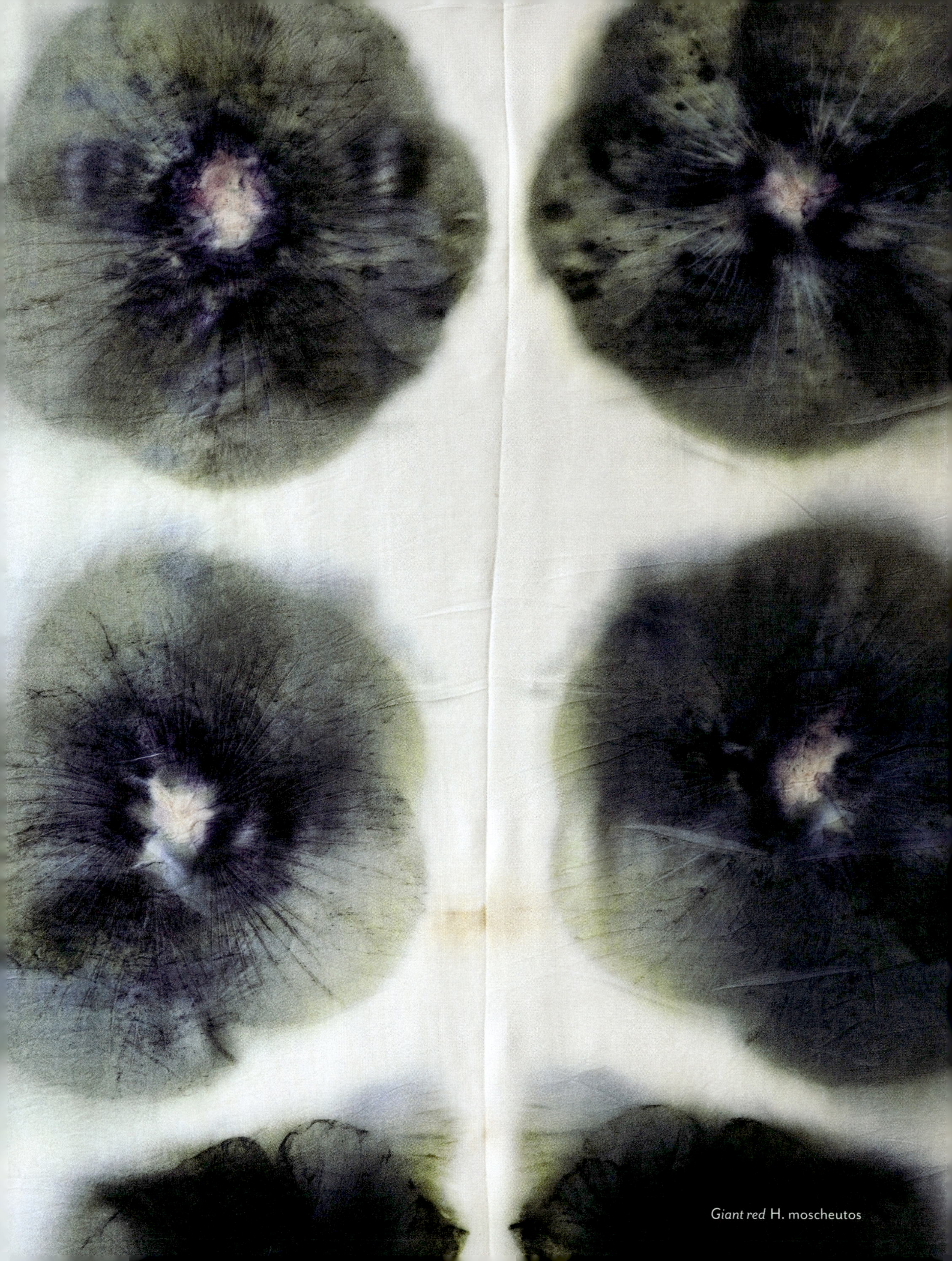

Giant red H. moscheutos

Hibiscus

(*Hibiscus moscheutos*)

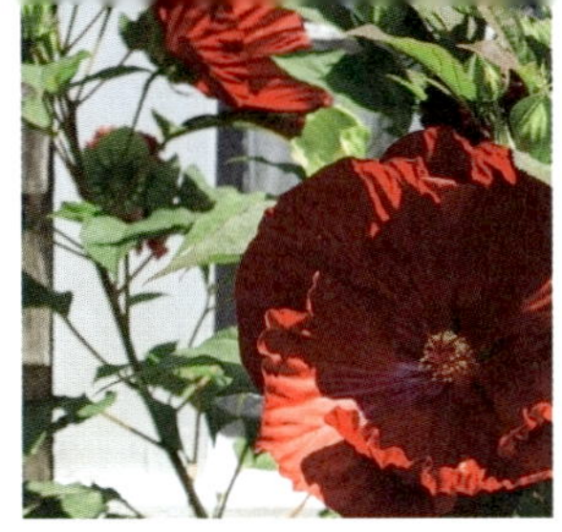

There are hundreds of varieties of hibiscus, some of which thrive in tropical climates and others that flourish in climates as cool as Minnesota. The larger-than-life *Hibiscus moscheutos*, also known as hardy hibiscus or swamp rose mallow, boasts ruffled blooms reaching up to 9 inches in diameter.

It is worth investing in a hibiscus shrub, as these cold-hardy perennials are generous with their blooms and add a sense of tropical flair and awe to any garden.

The flowers come in shades of white, pink, red, or burgundy and bloom from midsummer to early fall. They normally wilt within a day or two, although the succession of blooms can last for weeks. You can preserve blooms in a stack between watercolor or parchment paper and topped with a heavy book. You can set fallen or curled-up blooms to dry and use them for bundle dyeing.

PRINTING NOTES

- Here is an instance where a dark red flower prints blue, whether you use an aluminum mordant with or without iron.
- To achieve a clear print and for the flowers to lie flat when bundling, spread them open, face down on the target, and smooth with a paint roller.
- These flowers print nicely on both sides, making them ideal for a mirror-image print or printing on a white background.
- Steam for 20 to 30 minutes to ensure maximum color transfer but don't go much past that point, as the moisture in the petals can cause the print to bleed.

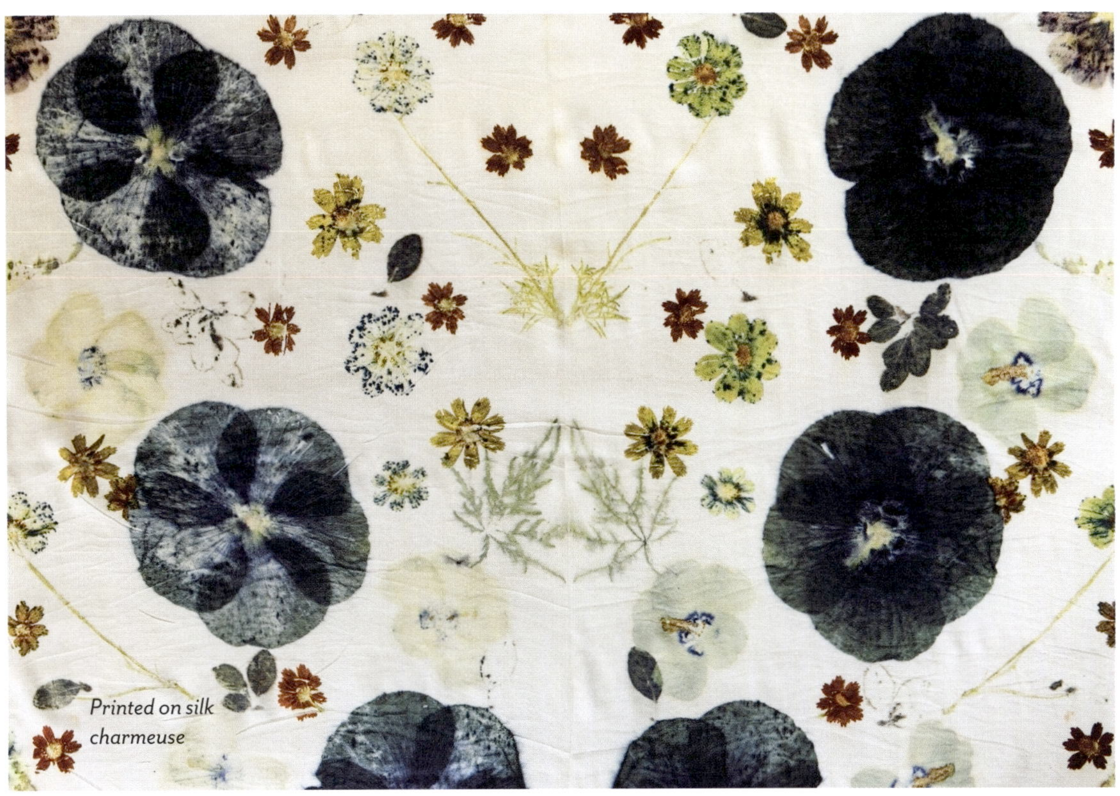

Printed on silk charmeuse

Hibiscus *continued*

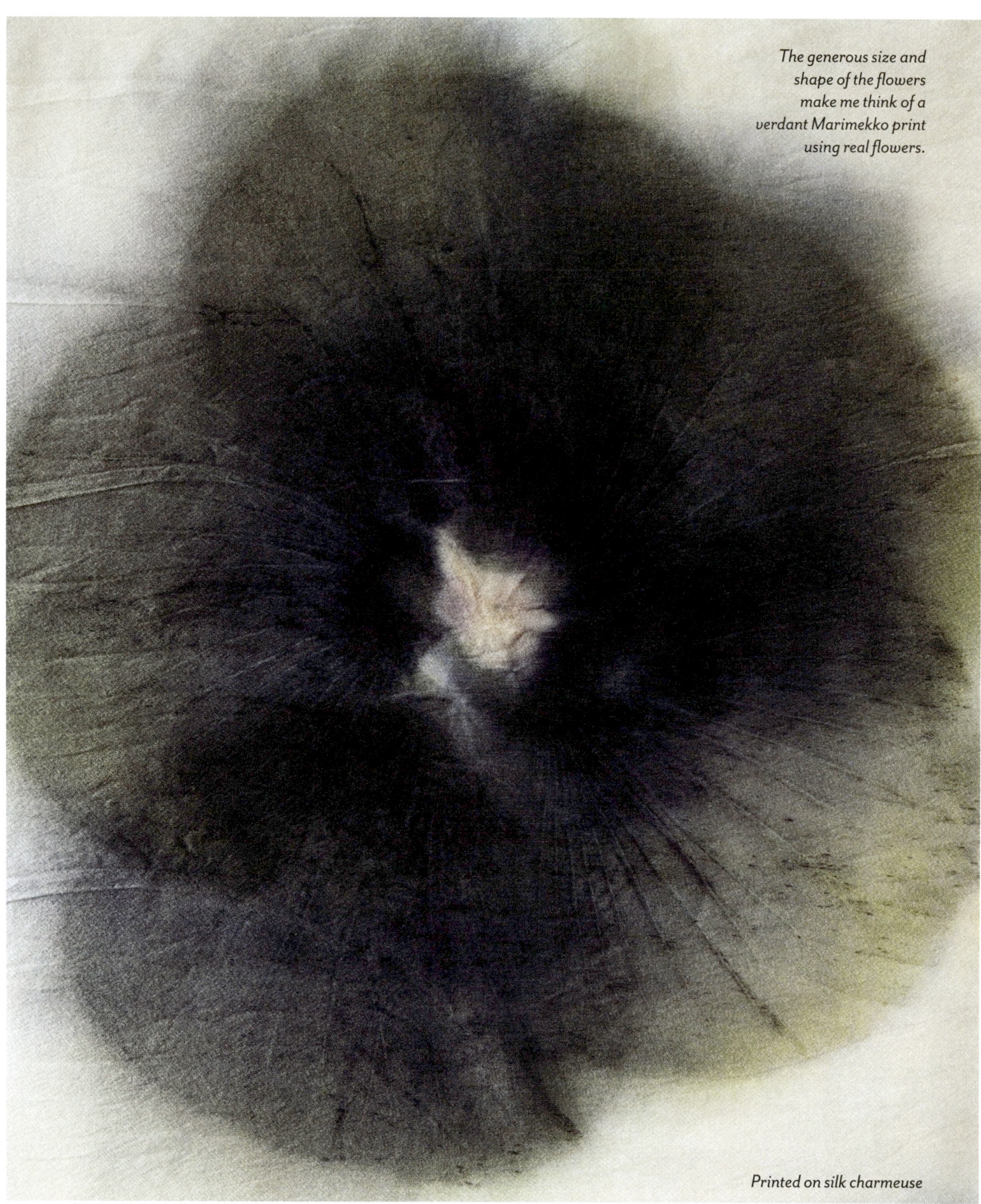

The generous size and shape of the flowers make me think of a verdant Marimekko print using real flowers.

Printed on silk charmeuse

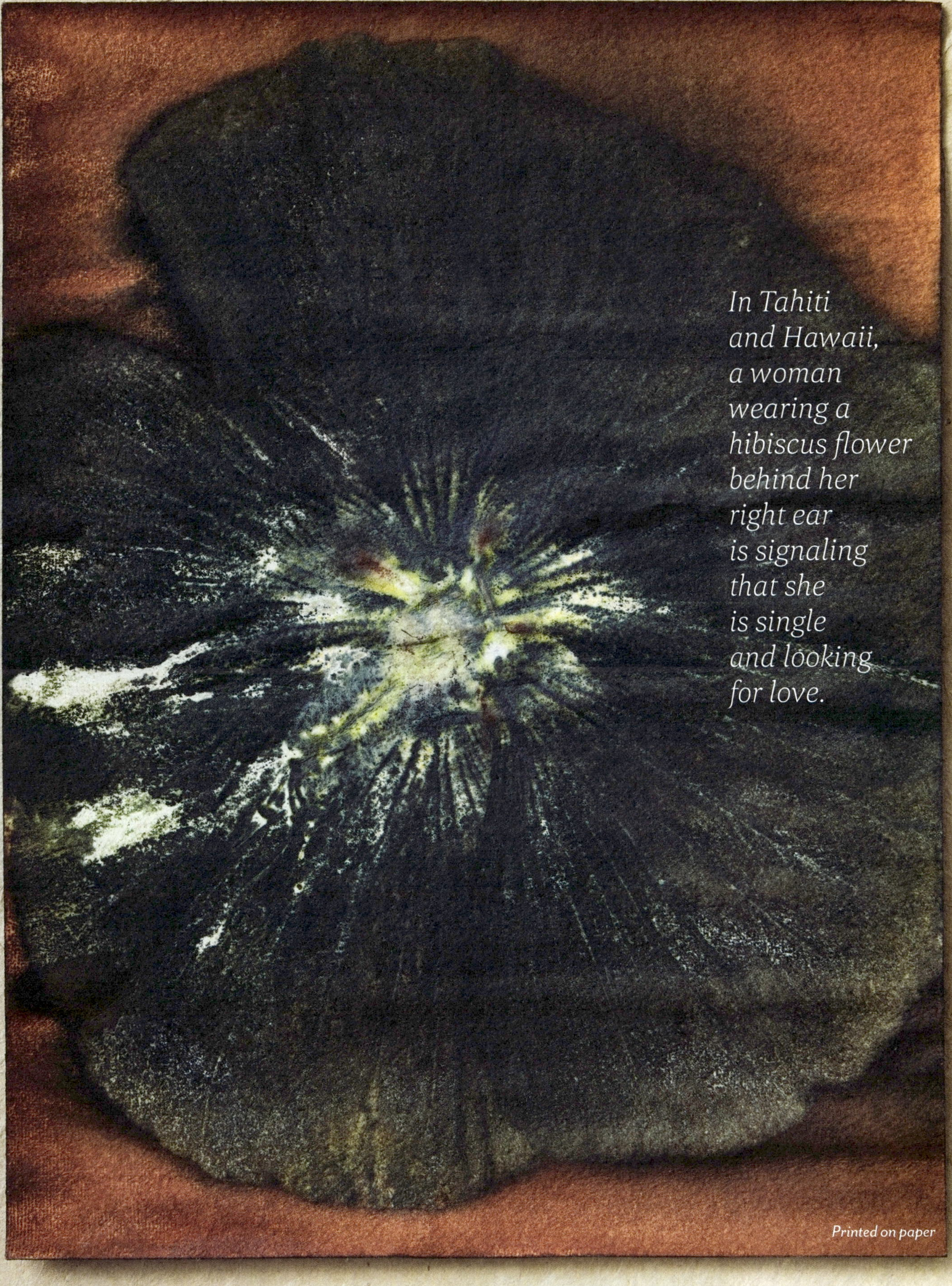

In Tahiti
and Hawaii,
a woman
wearing a
hibiscus flower
behind her
right ear
is signaling
that she
is single
and looking
for love.

Printed on paper

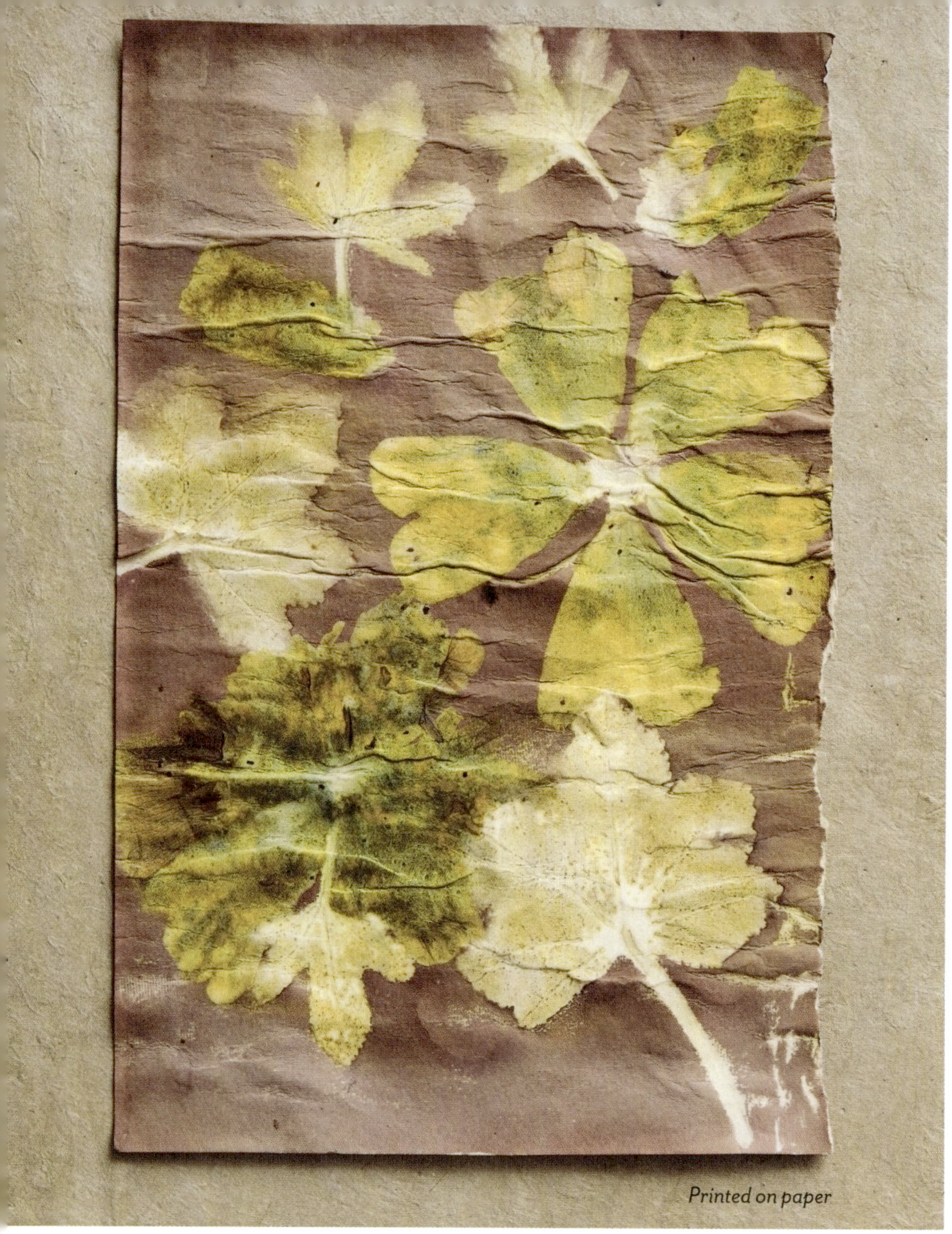

Printed on paper

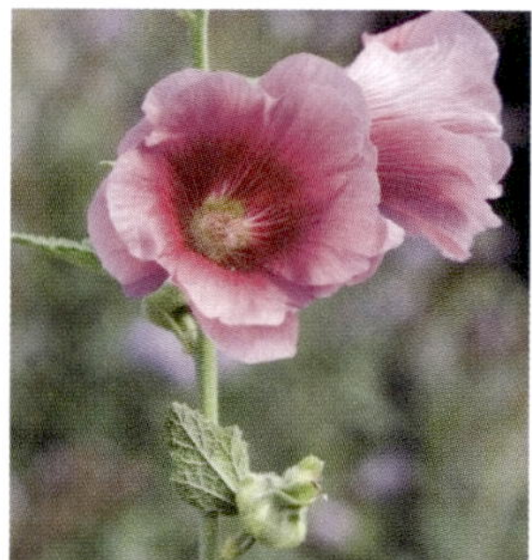

Alcea rosea 'Radiant Rose'

PRINTING NOTES

- Hollyhocks, both fresh and dried, can be powerful printers. The texture of the petals is like velvet, luxurious and soft. It is worth experimenting with the different hues.
- When printing with fresh hollyhock flowers, consider removing the receptacle at the base (where the flower meets the stem), to prevent bulk when bundling.
- The leaves and stems impart a variety of colors and forms—a verdant green on the moon side and a lighter, brighter green on the sun side.

Hollyhock

(*Alcea rosea*)

Hollyhocks, the quintessential cottage garden flower, belong to the Malvaceae family, sharing this lineage with rose of Sharon and hibiscus. Their chiffonlike petals exhibit a delicate texture and can be found in shades of pink, white, purple, eggplant, or yellow. Use them fresh or dried. To preserve the flowers, press them within a flower press, or place them between parchment paper in a heavy book. Leave them for a few days to ensure that excess moisture is removed.

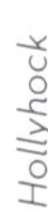

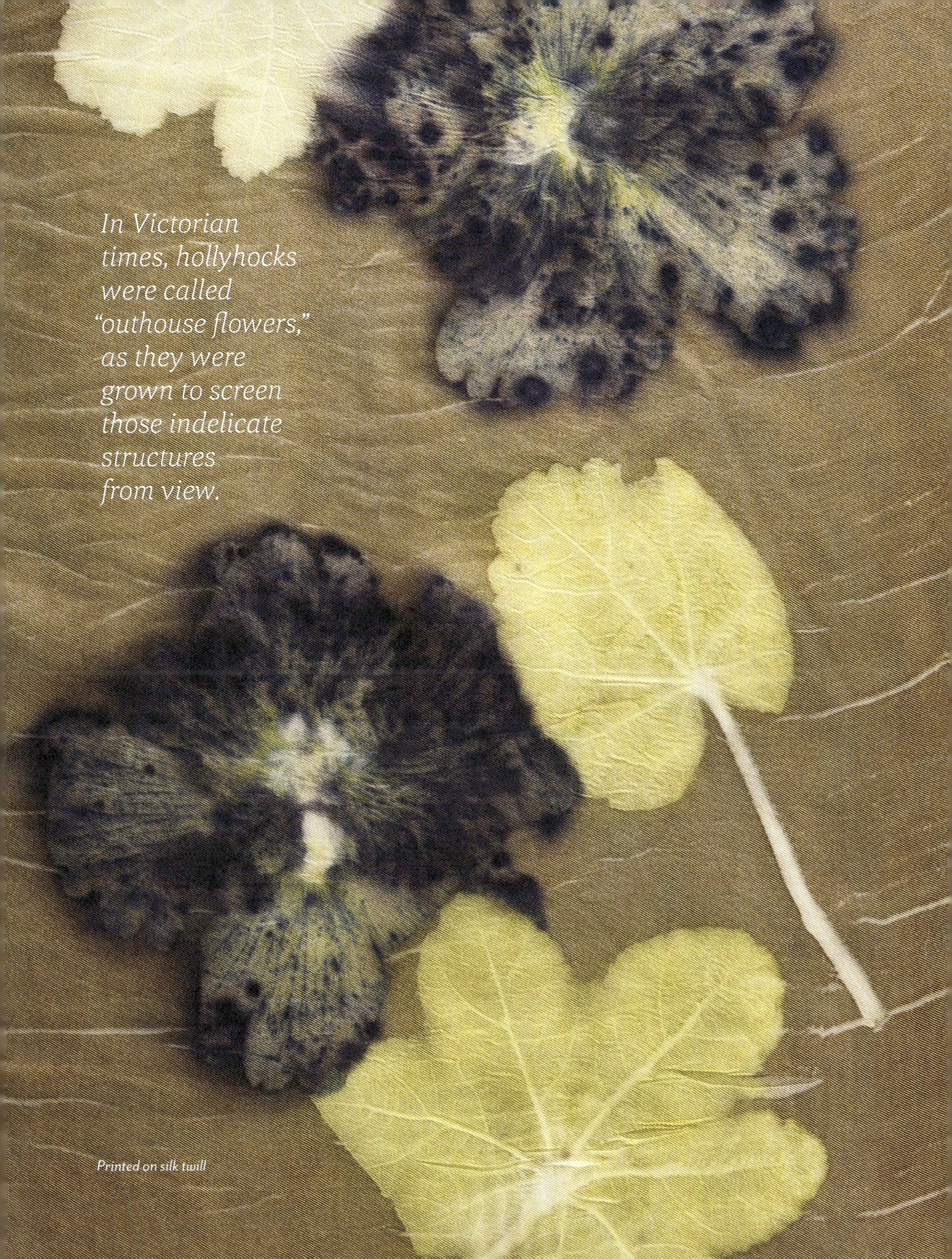

In Victorian times, hollyhocks were called "outhouse flowers," as they were grown to screen those indelicate structures from view.

Printed on silk twill

Horse Chestnut

(*Aesculus hippocastanum*)

The horse chestnut, belonging to the Sapindaceae family, is a large deciduous tree commonly known as the European horse chestnut, buckeye, or conker tree. This species, native to the Balkans, has been widely cultivated and can be found in various temperate regions, including Iceland, New Zealand, Ireland, Norway, and Canada. It is important to distinguish the horse chestnut from the sweet (or Spanish) chestnut, or *Castanea sativa*, which is part of a different family, Fagaceae.

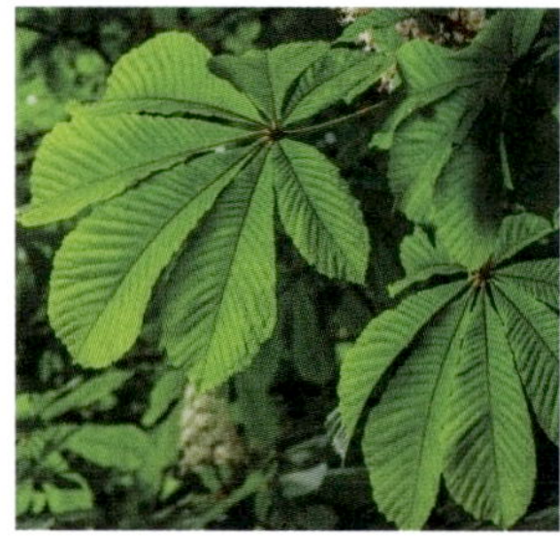

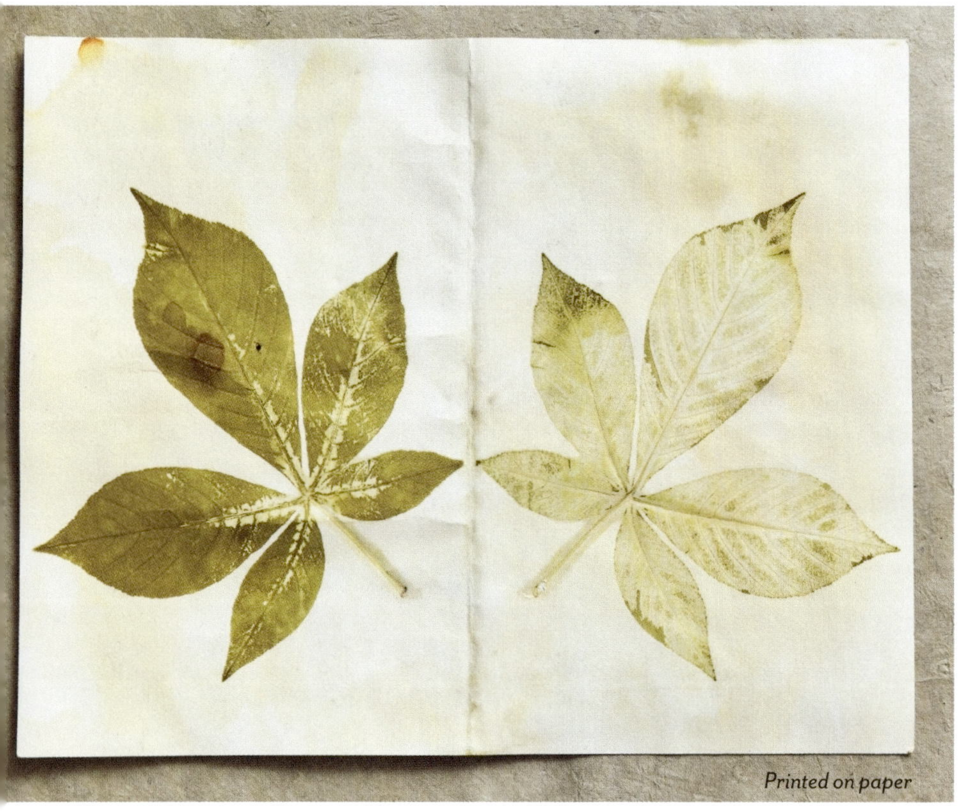

Printed on paper

PRINTING NOTES

- The leaves of the horse chestnut print brilliantly in a true leafy green coloring on both the sun and moon sides when used with a target that has been mordanted with PAS, iron, and soda ash (see the Compound Mordant recipe on page 122).
- The flowers are showy and can be white, pinkish white, or rose red, with a yellow or orange center. They grow in tall spikes called panicles that can be 6 to 14 inches long.
- Each leaf has five leaflets, which are large, deeply textured, and paddle shaped.
- Due to the high levels of tannin within the leaves, these powerful printers can successfully be used on pure white backgrounds and in mirror-image compositions.

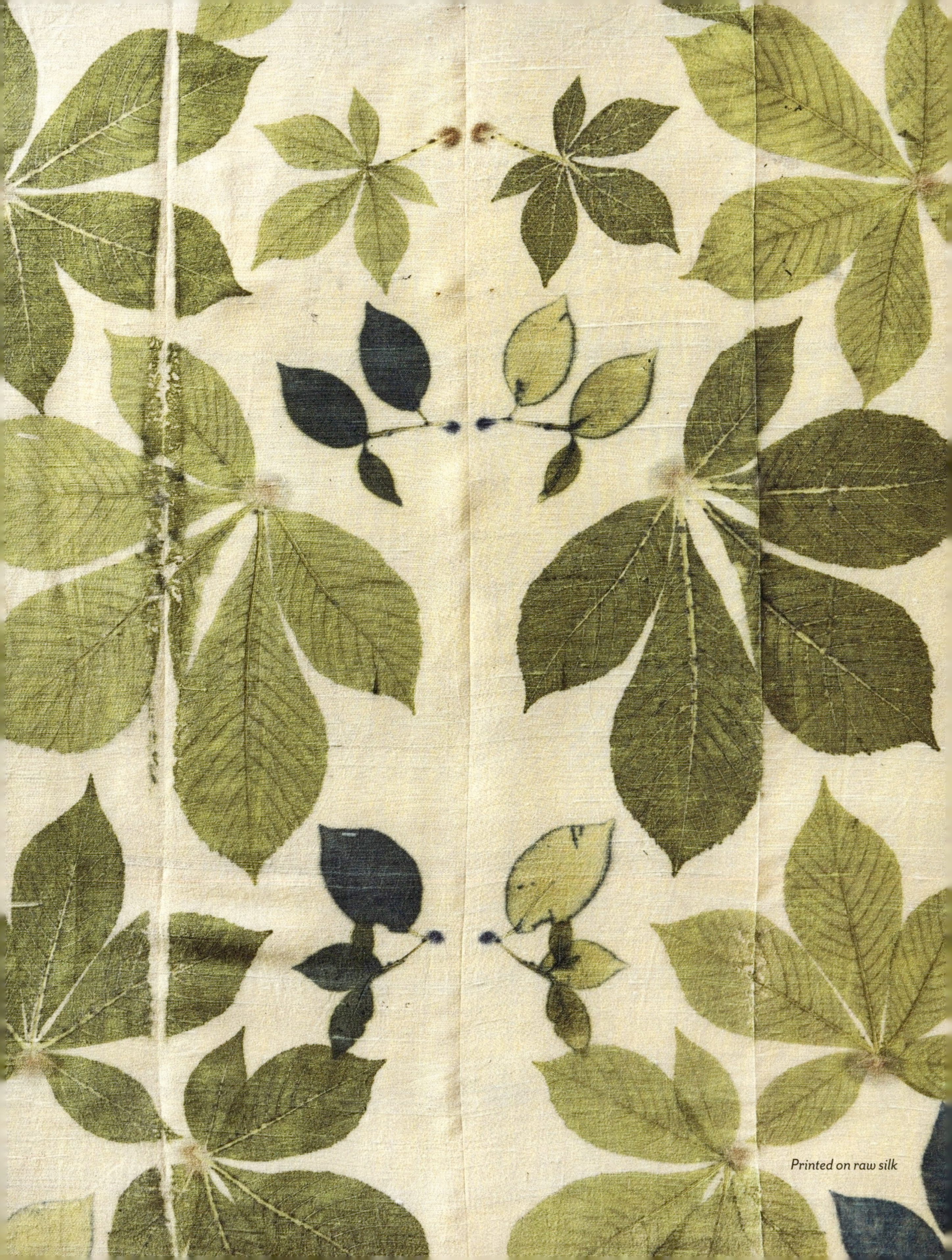

Printed on raw silk

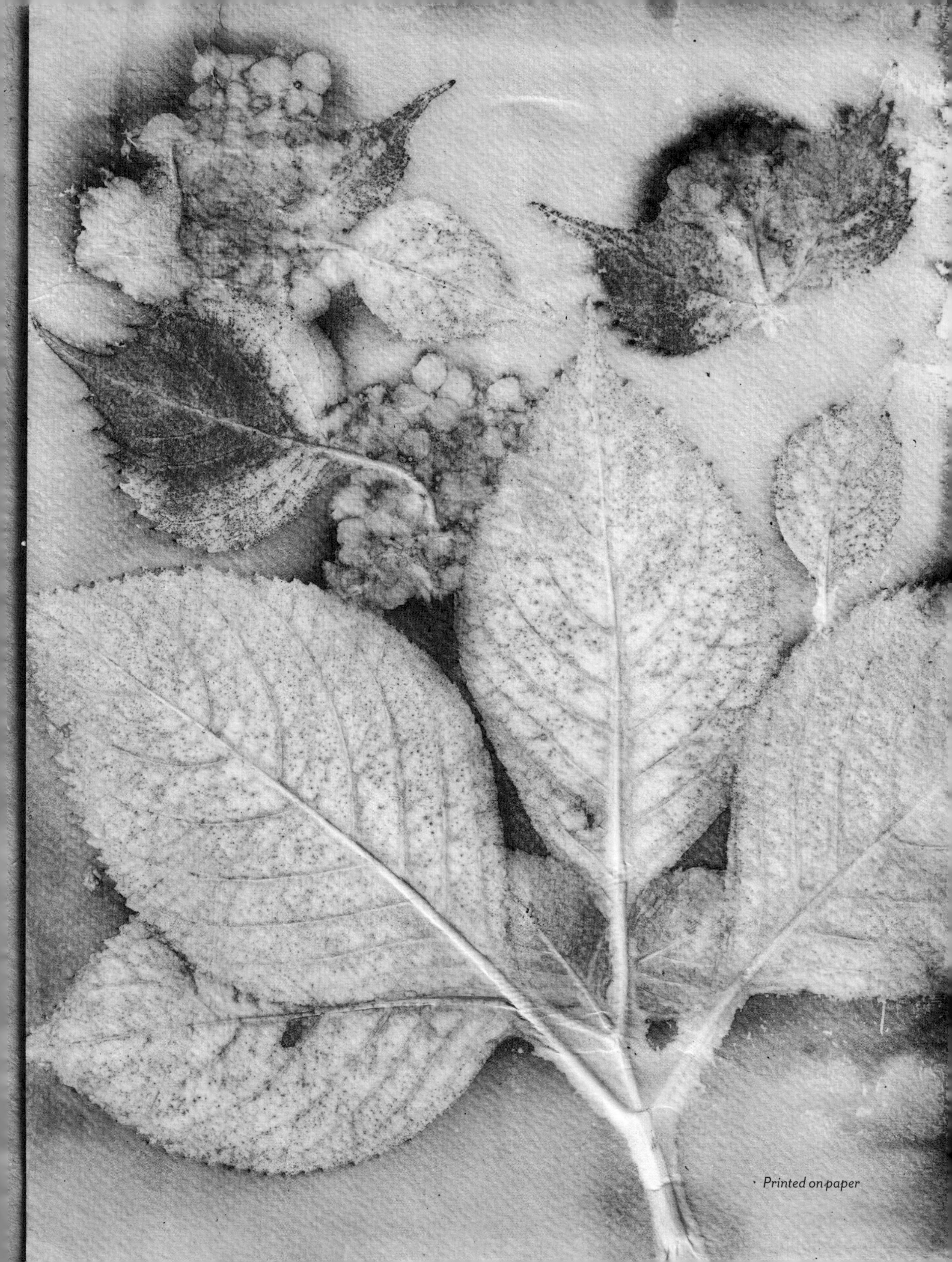

Printed on paper

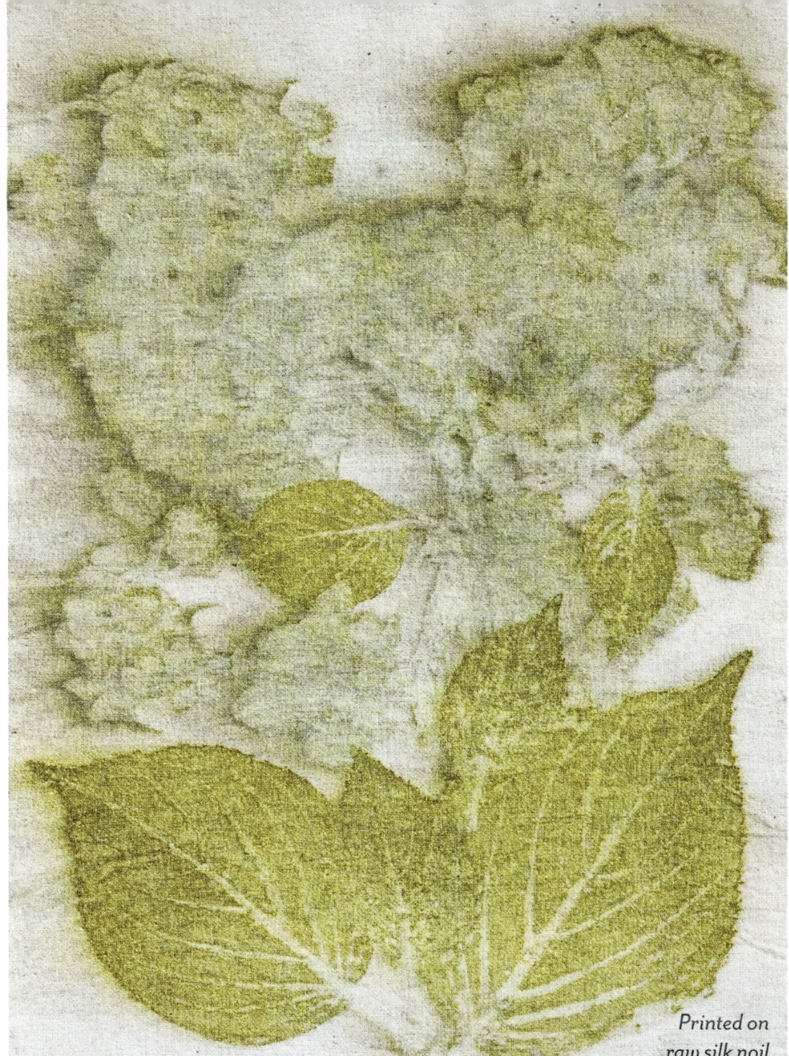

Printed on raw silk noil

PRINTING NOTES

- In the case of the bigleaf hydrangea, both the flowers and the leaves will impart color when used in the botanical printing process.
- These flowers can be used fresh or dried; as for the leaves, fresh is best if you want a pop of green coloring.
- Due to the generous size of the blooms, you may be able to get two or three separate prints from one flower head.
- Carefully divide the bloom into sections and reshape the flowers when laying out your design. Plucking off individual flower clusters and placing them face down can make for an interesting and colorful effect.
- As the stems can be quite inflexible, it's wise to remove them from your composition, but do use the leaves, mimicking their natural arrangement.

Hydrangea

(*Hydrangea macrophylla*)

Hydrangea is a captivating flower known for its unique structure, consisting of sepals, the outer parts of a flower that encase and protect the developing bud before it opens, rather than true petals. This distinctive morphology allows hydrangeas to display an enchanting array of colors, which can shift depending on the pH level of the soil. Acidic soils typically yield vibrant blues, while alkaline conditions bring forth deep pinks and corals.

The flowers can easily be dried by placing them in a vase without water. Alternatively, you can compress the flowers in a press, or de-petal the flowers and dry the bits for bundle dyeing.

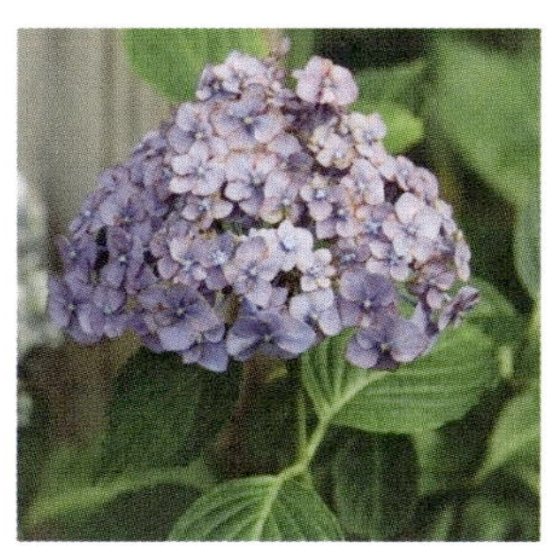

Bigleaf hydrangea

Impatiens

(*Impatiens hawkeri*)

This native of Papua New Guinea and the Solomon Islands was brought to Europe and North America in the late 1800s. My favorite variety is New Guinea impatiens, or *Impatiens hawkeri*, one of the largest varieties in the Balsaminaceae family, which includes a palette of fiery vermilion ('Sunstanding Glowing Scarlet'), fuchsia ('Paradise Rose Flair'), neon pink ('Impacio Lavender Pink'), and yellow ('Spreading Sunpatiens').

These flowers are not ideal candidates for drying and pressing, as they tend to lose their whimsical shape.

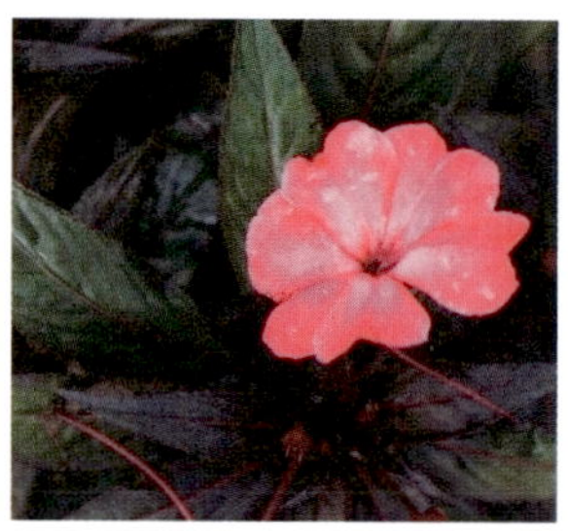

New Guinea impatiens

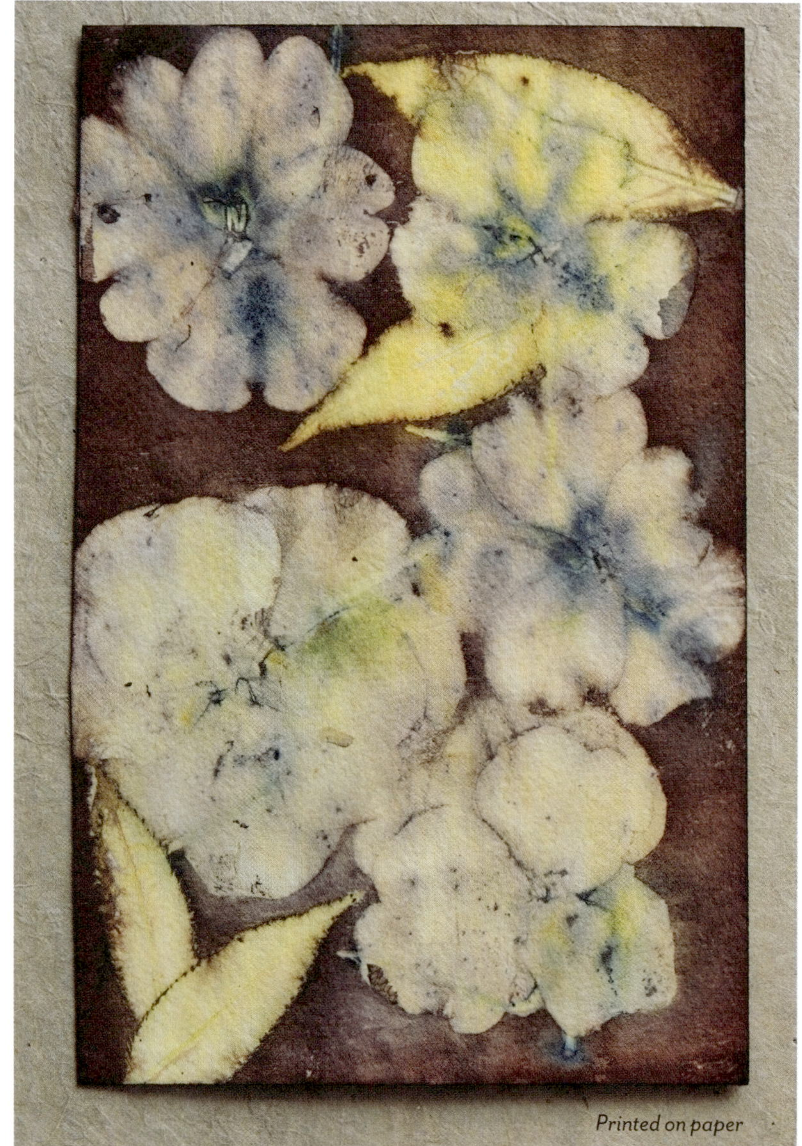

Printed on paper

PRINTING NOTES

- Some pigmentation from the petals can be imbued into the fiber in a dreamy, watercoloresque visual, while the more acidic properties of the flowers may take away color from the area.
- The use of a carrier blanket in the printing process, thus applying a background color and essentially providing an outline around the petals, will result in a more distinct print.
- Keep steaming time between 25 and 30 minutes so as not to overprocess the flowers and lead to bleeds.

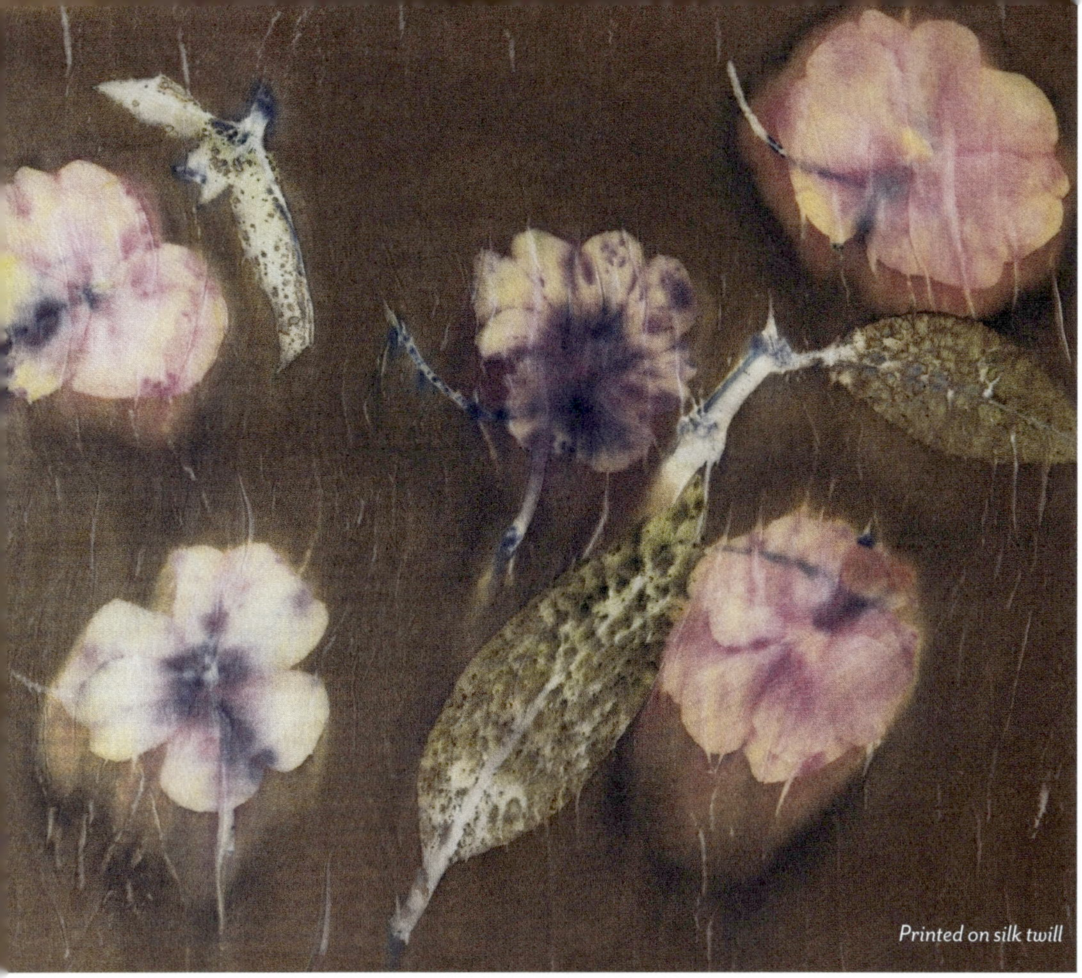

Printed on silk twill

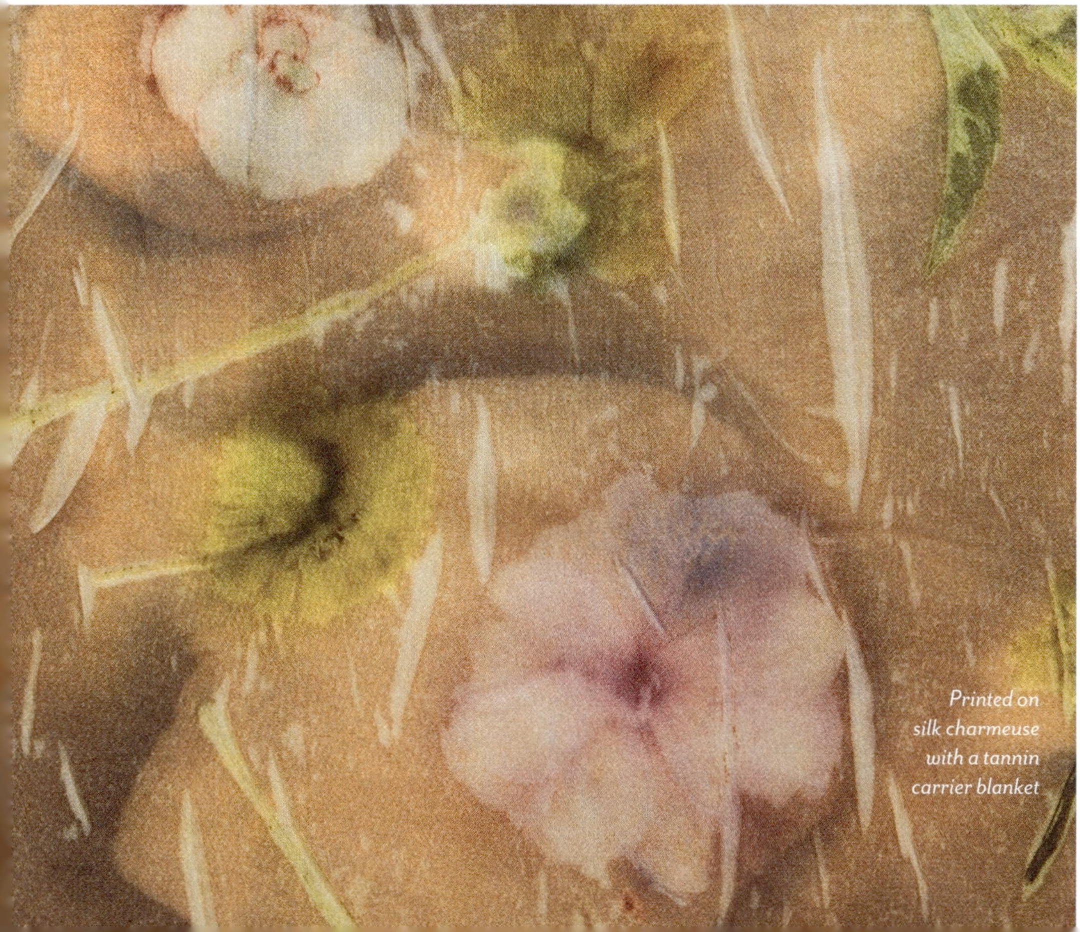

Printed on silk charmeuse with a tannin carrier blanket

The name is derived from the Latin word for "impatient," as the seedpods burst open when ripe, a tendency that also gives these plants the name "touch-me-not."

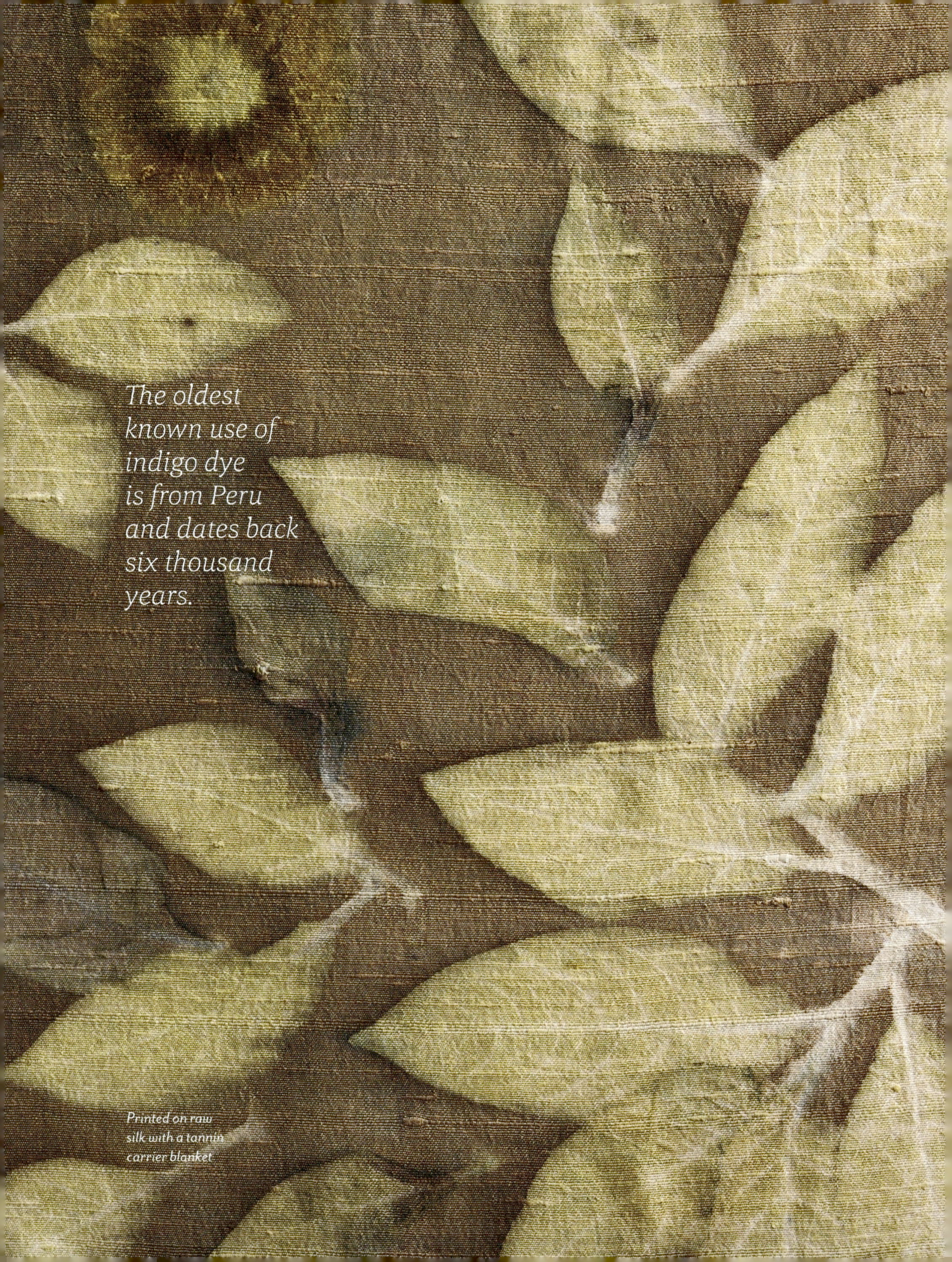

Printed on raw silk with a tannin carrier blanket

Japanese Indigo

(*Persicaria tinctoria*)

Japanese indigo, Chinese indigo, or dyer's knotweed is a traditional dyeing plant cultivated primarily for its leaves, which yield a rich blue dye when processed for an indigo vat. The leaves can be harvested throughout the season. They produce a range of blue, green, and yellow dyes as well as green botanical contact prints.

A gorgeous seafoam green to teal dye can be made by extracting pigment from the fresh leaves of *Persicaria tinctoria* by cold processing the leaves in a blender with cold water. Start with 1 liter (1 quart) of leaves stripped from the stalk and add to a blender. Cover the leaves with water to submerge and blend until the leaves are pulverized. Strain the liquid and use as a dye for protein fibers, immersing the fiber in the dye until the desired color is reached.

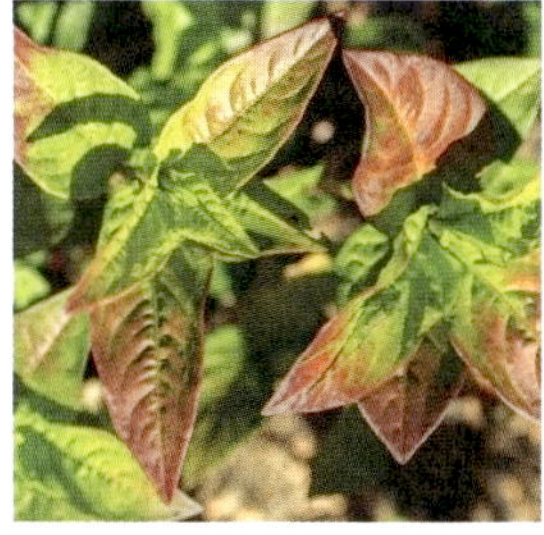

PRINTING NOTES

- While there is not a distinct "indigo blue" imprint from the leaves, some fine coloration and detailing can be captured from the veins of the moon side of the leaves.
- The leaf shape can be emphasized further with the use of a dye-soaked carrier blanket to impart a background color to outline their silhouette.

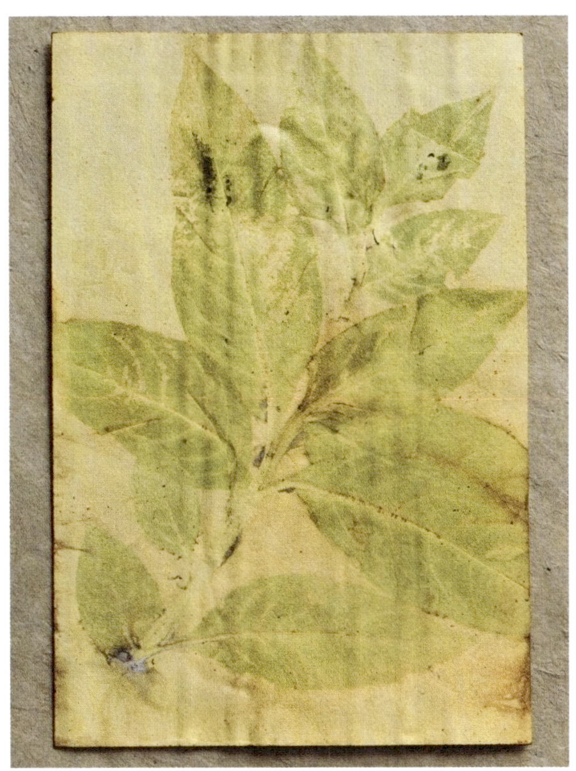

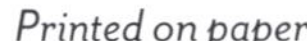

Printed on paper

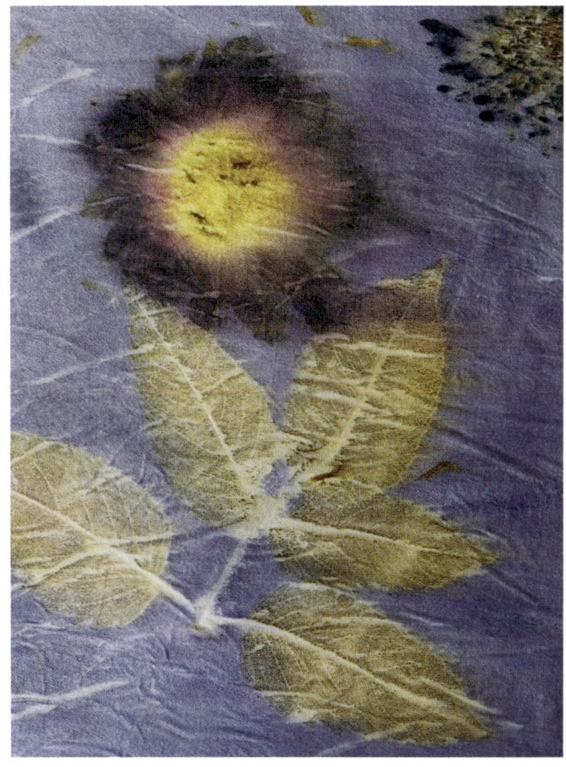

Printed on silk charmeuse

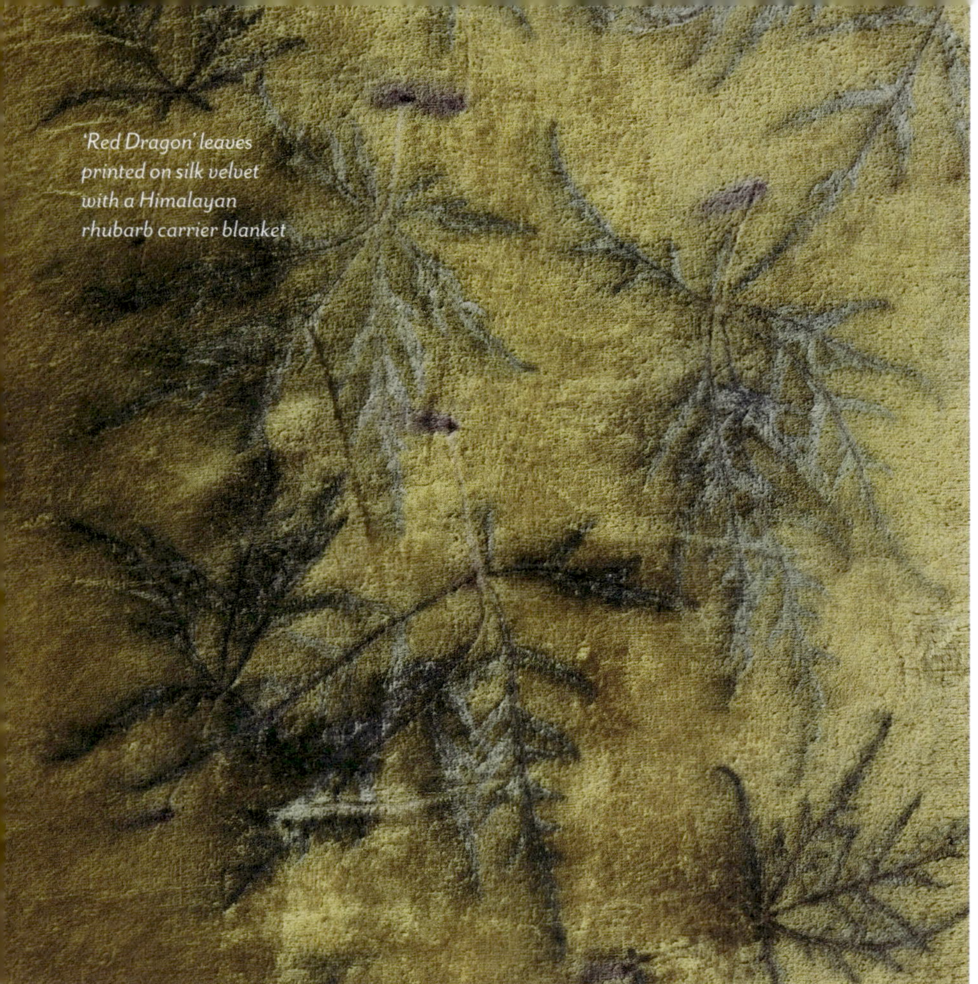
'Red Dragon' leaves printed on silk velvet with a Himalayan rhubarb carrier blanket

PRINTING NOTES

- The leaves can be printed on both the sun and moon sides, each side offering a unique range of coloration from green to pink to red depending on the mordant.
- To capture the distinct outline of these leaves, I use the Compound Mordant recipe (see page 122) to attain imprints ranging from hot pink to red.
- To fully capture the outline of the leaves in detail, a background color can be added to the composition using a carrier blanket soaked in tannin to add more color and depth to the print.
- The leaves can be dried or preserved by freezing and stored for future use.

Japanese Maple

(*Acer palmatum*)

Japanese maples captivate with their vibrant red, tannic leaves, producing prints that reflect their striking colors beautifully. With dozens of cultivars available, each offers a unique aesthetic and appeal. In my yard, the 'Bloodgood' stands out with its deep crimson foliage, while the graceful 'Red Dragon' showcases finely dissected leaves that add a delicate touch to the landscape.

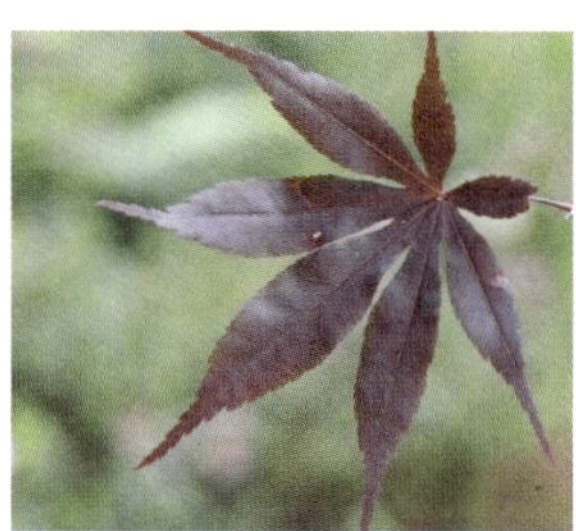
A. palmatum *'Bloodgood'*

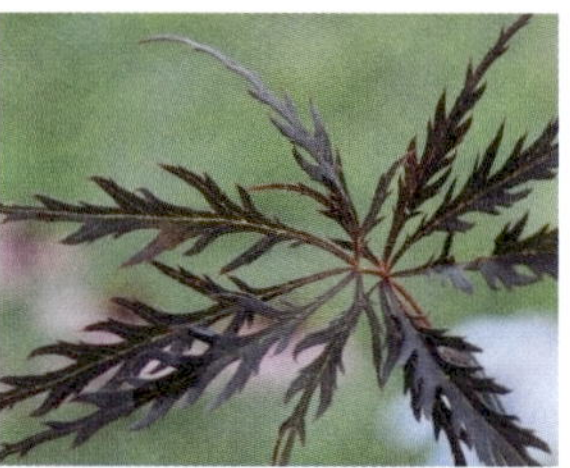
A. palmatum *'Red Dragon'*

The leaves of 'Bloodgood', or smooth Japanese maple, grow in groups of five to nine radially from the center. These leaves are distinctly smooth on the edges and can be dark to neon red.

'Red Dragon' is one of the finest of the lace-leaf weeping umbrella-shaped forms, which present rather sawlike, jagged, intricate edges that print in wonderful detail.

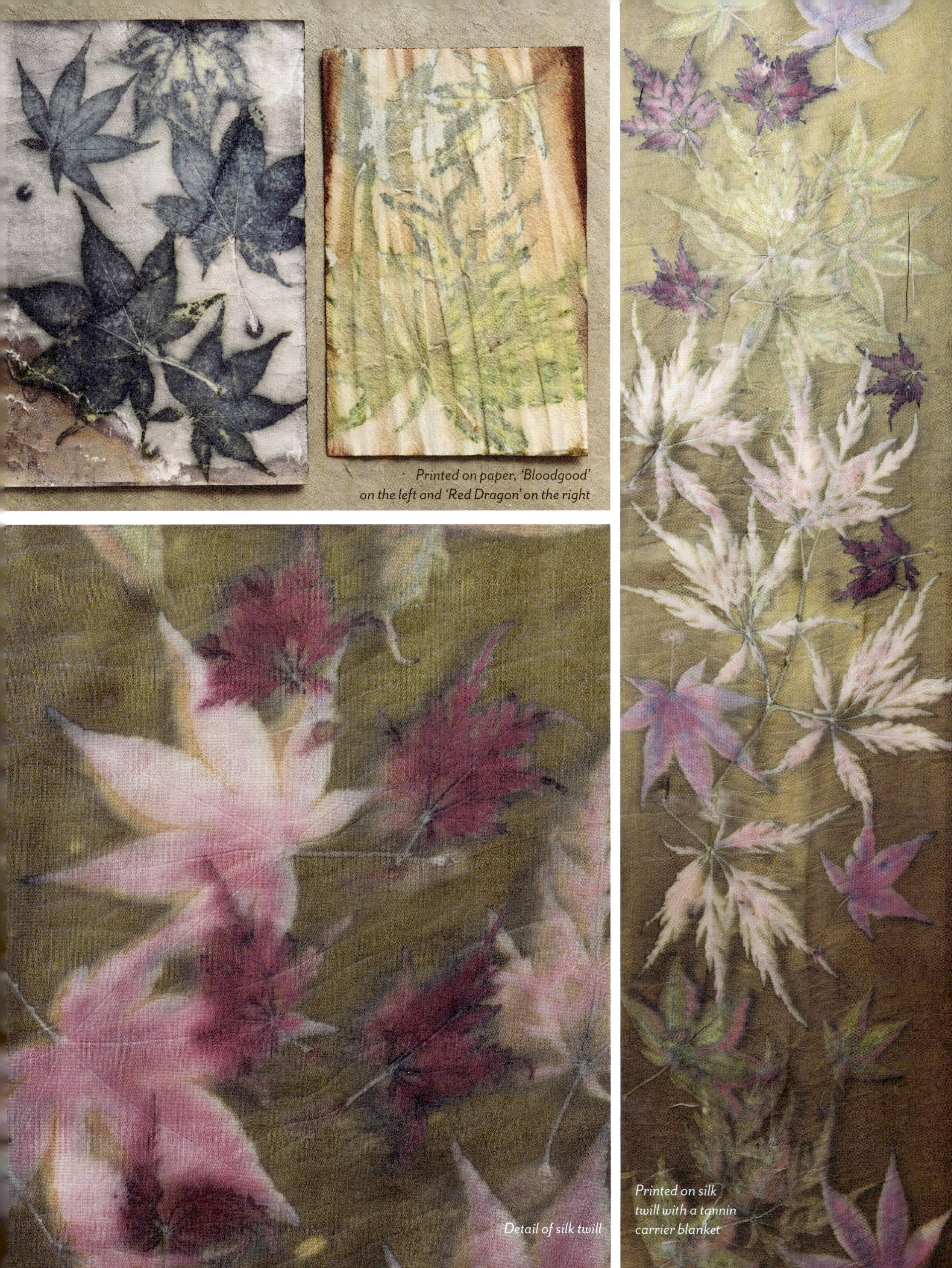

Printed on paper, 'Bloodgood' on the left and 'Red Dragon' on the right

Detail of silk twill

Printed on silk twill with a tannin carrier blanket

Marigold

(*Tagetes* spp.)

With more than 50 species, marigolds showcase a vibrant spectrum of colors including bright yellows, deep oranges, and russet reds. These prolific blooms not only bring stunning beauty to gardens but also dry exceptionally well, making them perfect for future botanical projects. Both fresh and dried marigolds serve as excellent resources for botanical printing, consistently delivering striking color and vibrancy. Additionally, the deep green leaves and stems of the marigold provide a contrast that captures intricate leafy prints, enriching the design.

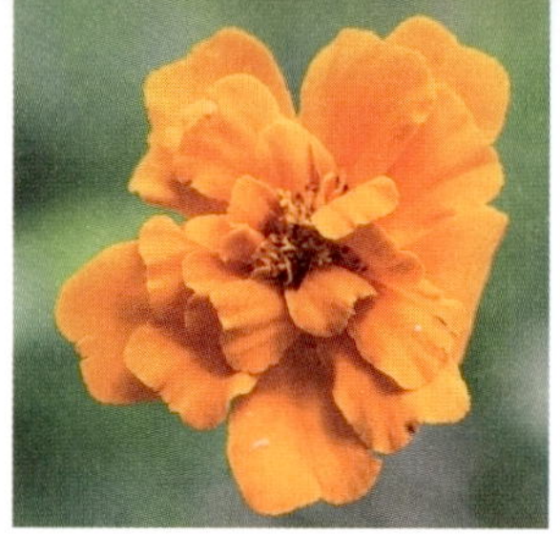

French marigold (T. patula)

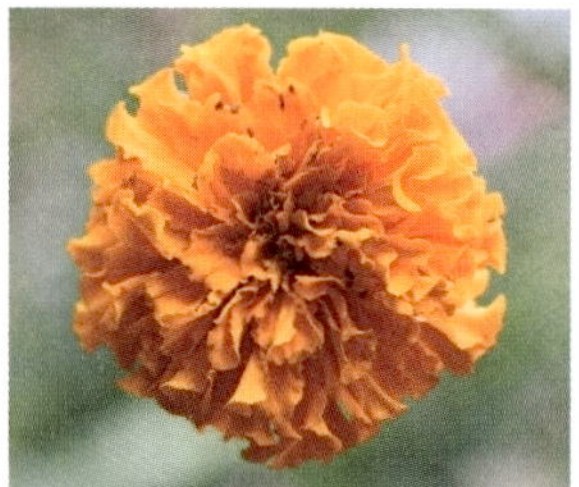

African or Aztec marigold (T. erecta)

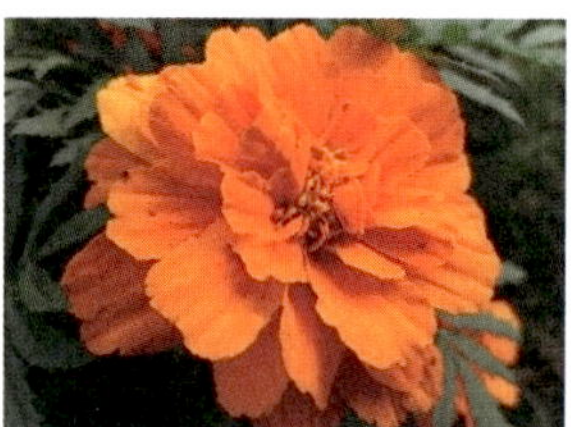

'Safari' marigold (T. patula)

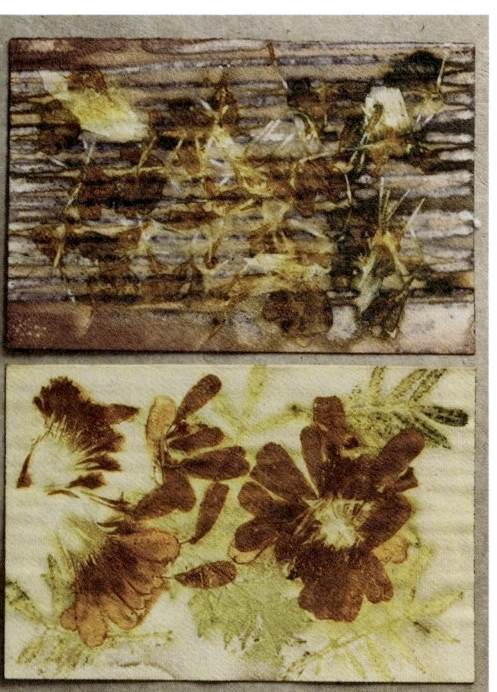

Printed on paper

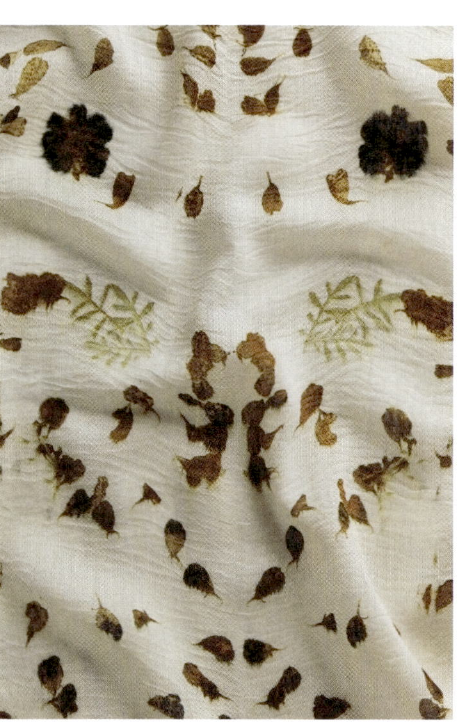

Printed on wool

PRINTING NOTES

- In botanical contact printing, the flowers create glorious pops of neon orange, yellow, gold, red, and brown derived from carotenoid pigment molecules.
- The flower petals print from all sides and can be broken up and sprinkled onto the target for a rain shower of sunny color.
- Break tightly packed flower heads into quarters and lay flat on the target to lessen the bulk when rolling.

In Mexico and parts of Latin America, the marigold, viewed as a gift from the sun god, is used to honor and beckon the dead during Día de los Muertos, or Day of the Dead, celebrations.

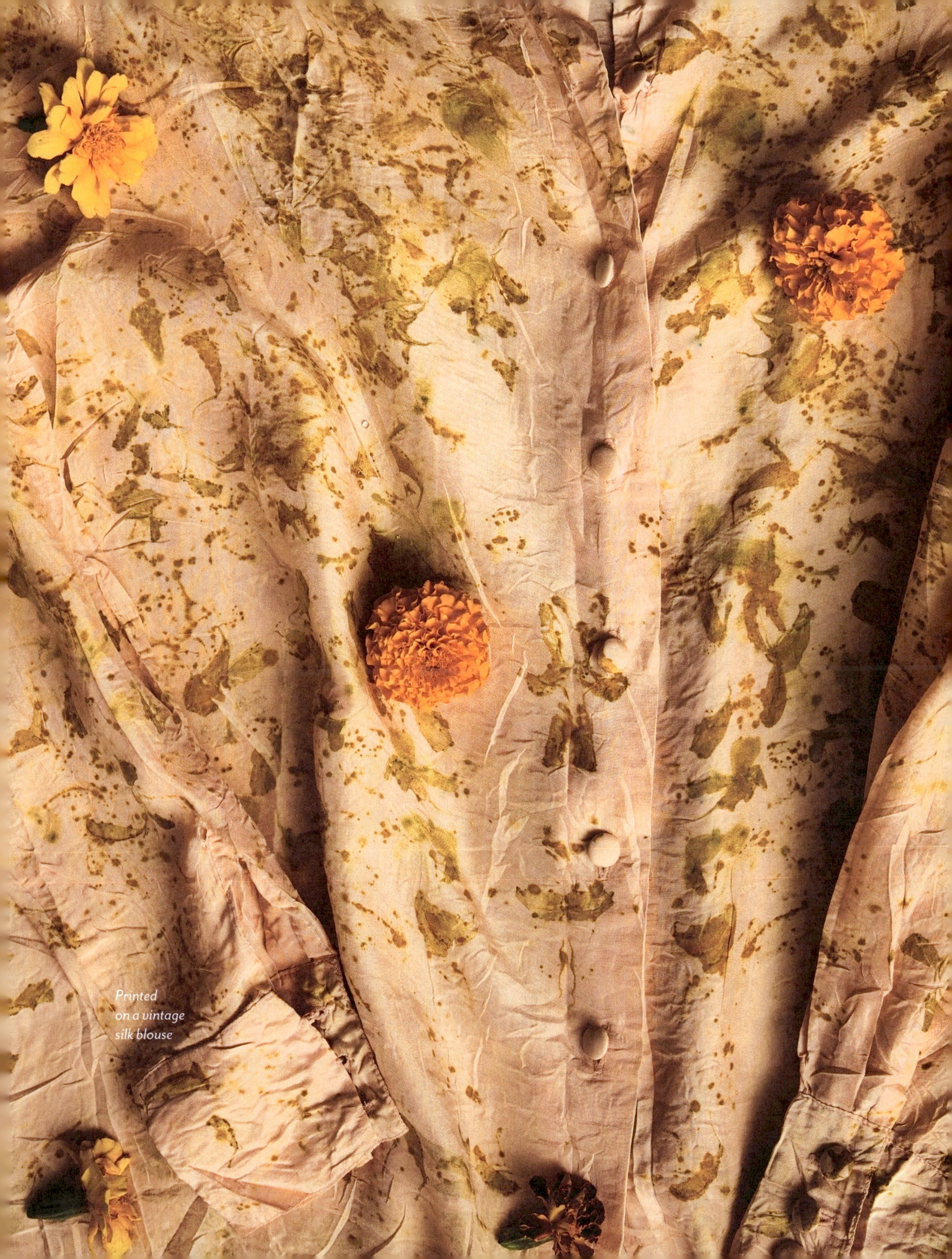

Printed on a vintage silk blouse

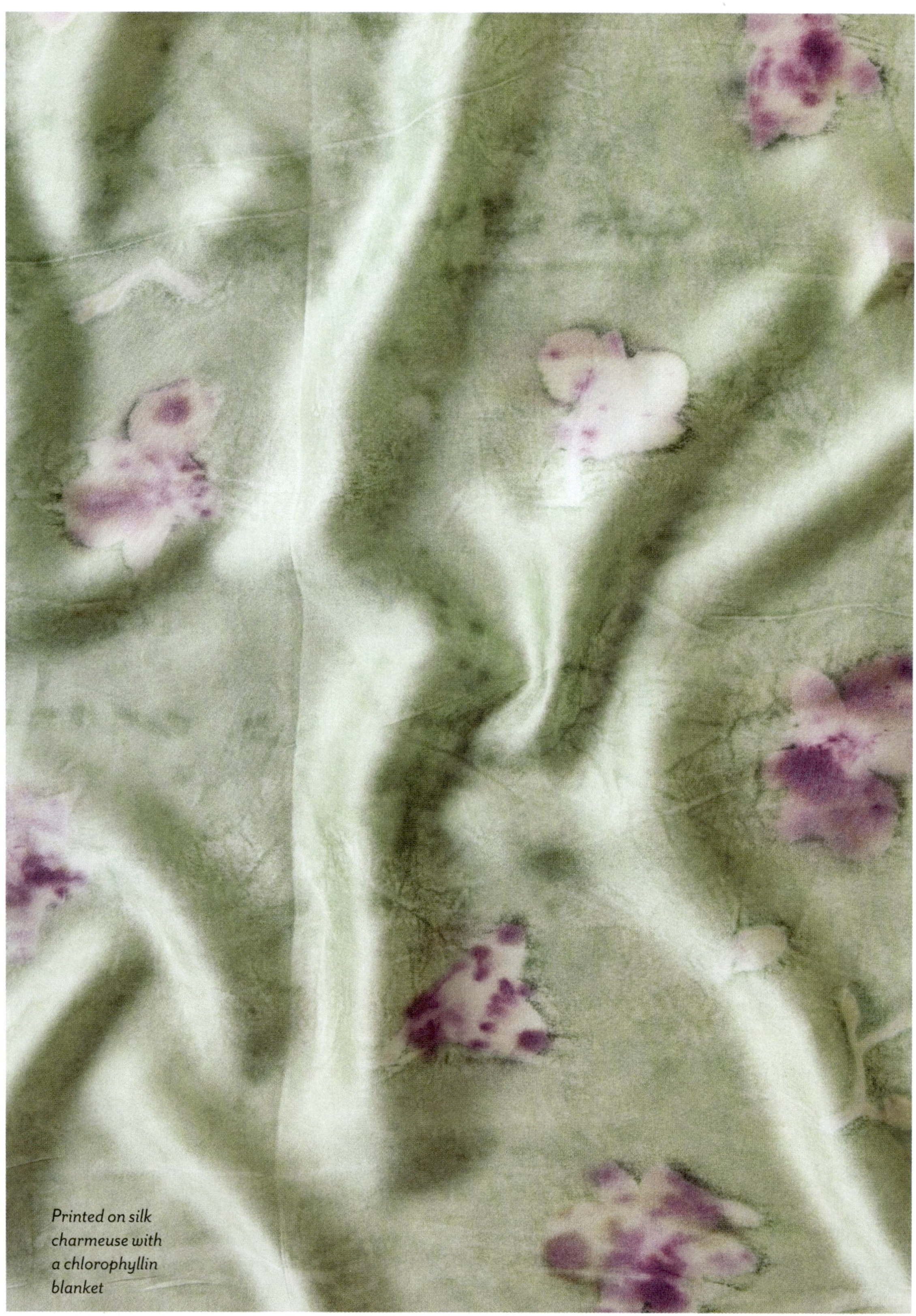
Printed on silk charmeuse with a chlorophyllin blanket

Orchid

(*Dendrobium* spp.)

Orchids have graced this planet since the Jurassic Period and are part of the largest family of flowering plants, Orchidaceae. They grow from the equator to the arctic circle and can be found hanging from trees like acrobats and burrowed in caves.

The blooms can be tiny or large, in almost every color imaginable, and can last for up to six weeks. Some orchids bloom multiple times a year, or even successively. For example, the phalaenopsis orchid, also known as the moth orchid, can bloom for two to six months and up to three times a year once it reaches maturity.

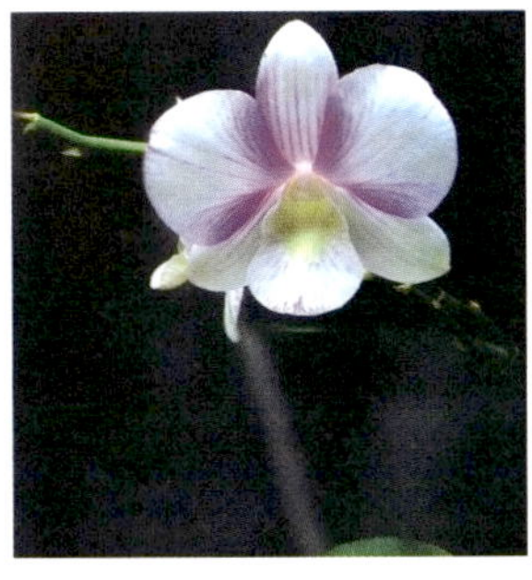

PRINTING NOTES

- The flowers are quite bulky, so it can be helpful to use a cushioning blanket or a carrier blanket when printing. Use a paint roller to flatten the petals for a cleaner imprint.

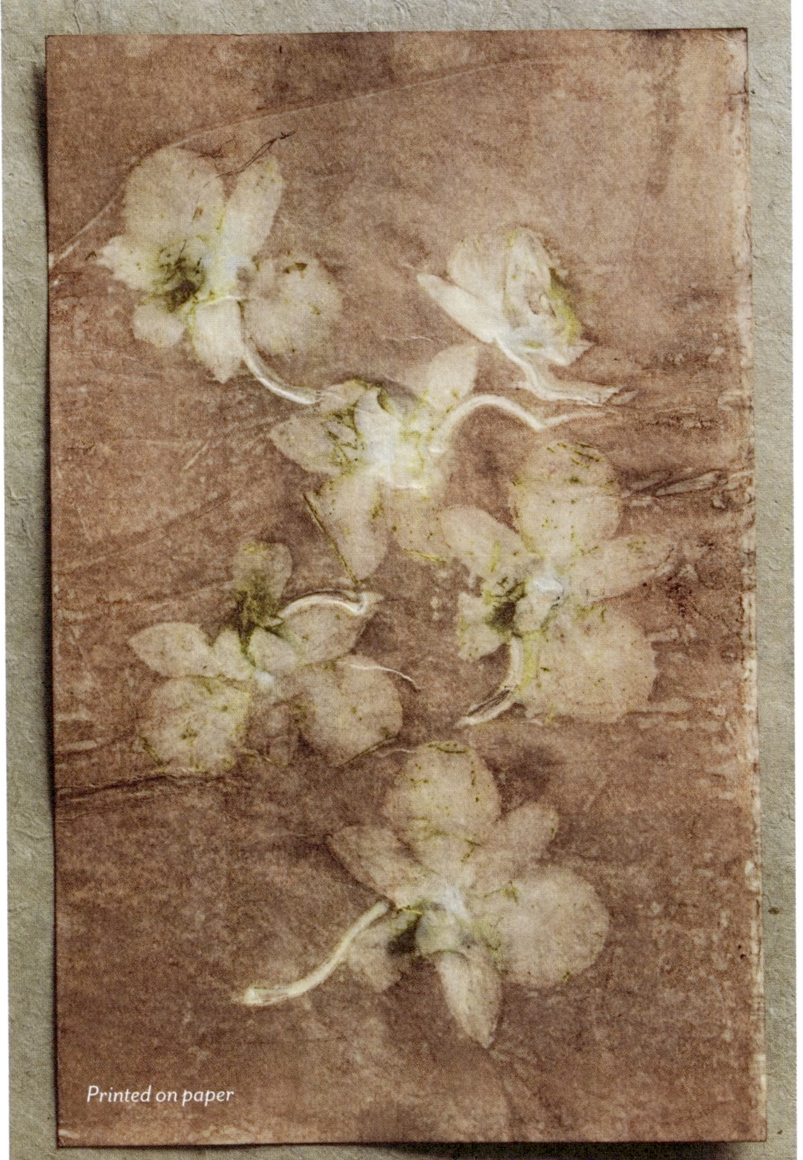

Printed on paper

During the Victorian era, orchid fanciers built conservatories dedicated to orchid cultivation. It was thought that the plants physically reacted to humans—some people viewed them as pets.

Peony

(*Paeonia lactiflora*)

There is no question why artists are drawn to peonies: The intoxicating scent, radiant colors, and delicately ruffled petals reminiscent of silk enliven the senses. The *Paeonia lactiflora* found in my garden, whose lush blooms come in crimson, pink, or white, have spindly bright yellow stamens at the center. The flowers do not impart much color when fresh, but the leaves are tannin-rich and very reliable printers.

When you are pressing blooms for storage, try to splay the petals to reveal the center. Turn them outward and dry flat so that there may be a chance of the bright yellow from the anther, the stringlike center, encountering the fiber when printing. The petals may also be dried and broken into bits for bundle dyeing.

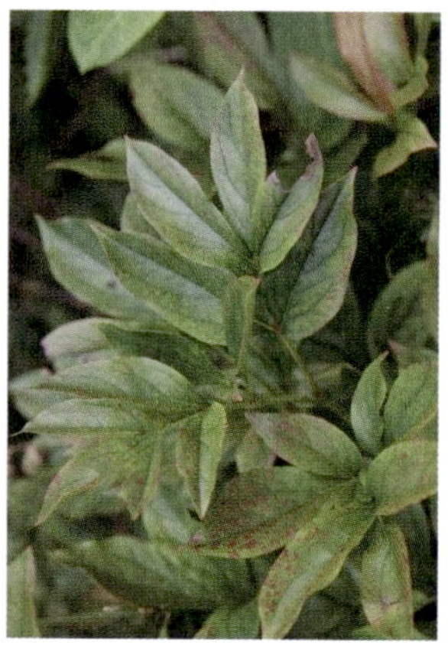

PRINTING NOTES

- The deeply lobed, dark green leaves are packed with tannin and flavonoids. The moon side offers a distinctly dark imprint, almost black in color when printed onto fiber that has been mordanted with iron. The sun side offers more of a green, watercolor-like imprint.
- The dried flowers offer a larger punch of lovely color than do the fresh, which do not offer much coloration.
- The flowers are quite bulky, so it can be helpful to use a cushioning blanket or a carrier blanket when printing. Use a paint roller to flatten the petals for a cleaner imprint.

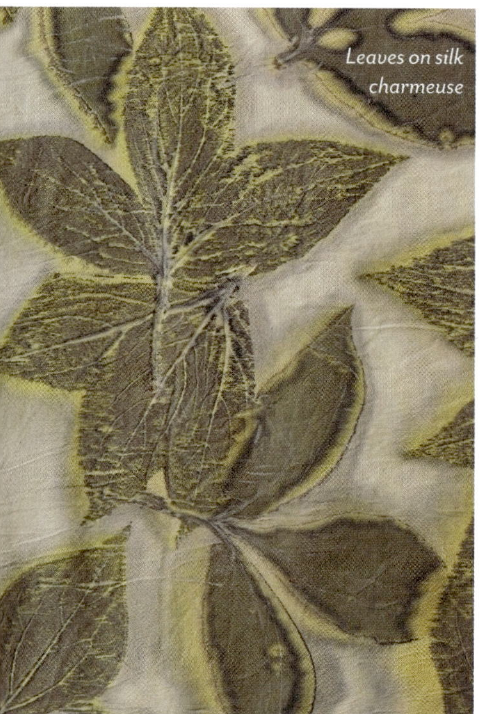

Leaves on silk charmeuse

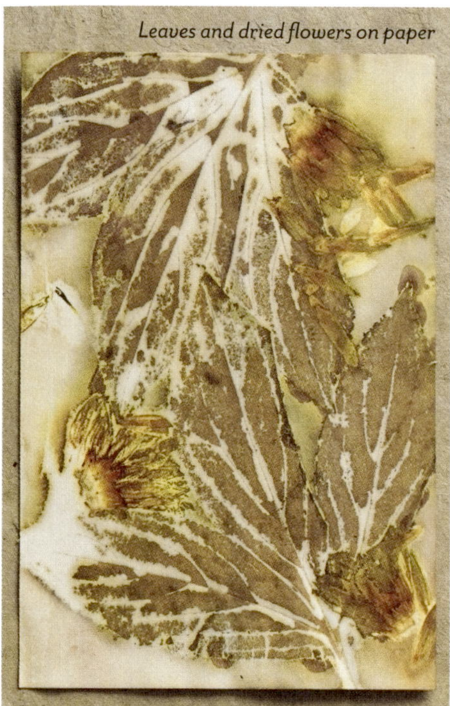

Leaves and dried flowers on paper

Peonies are often mentioned in Greek mythology. When the goddess Paeonia was caught flirting with Apollo, for example, Aphrodite turned her into a red peony.

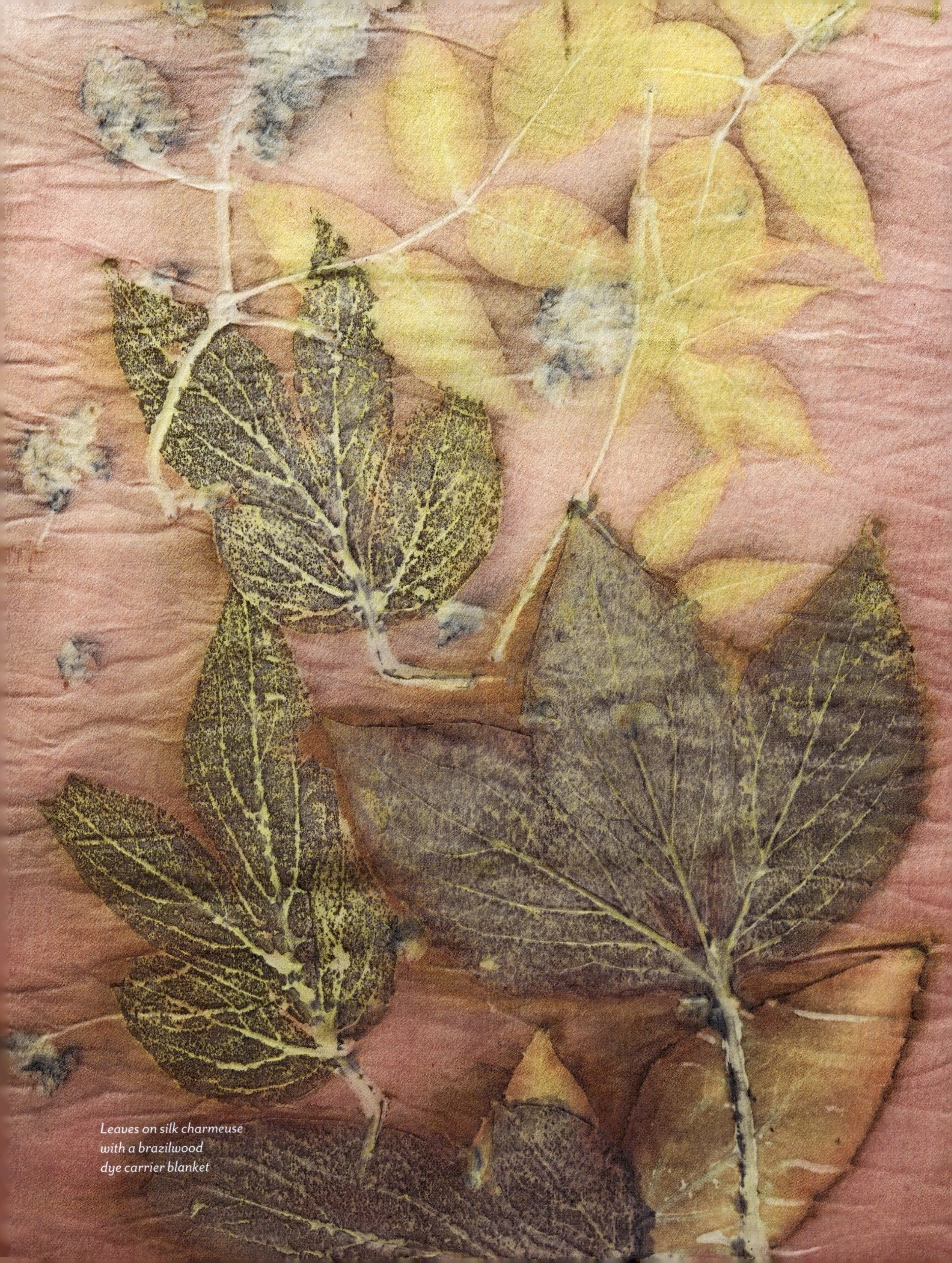

Leaves on silk charmeuse with a brazilwood dye carrier blanket

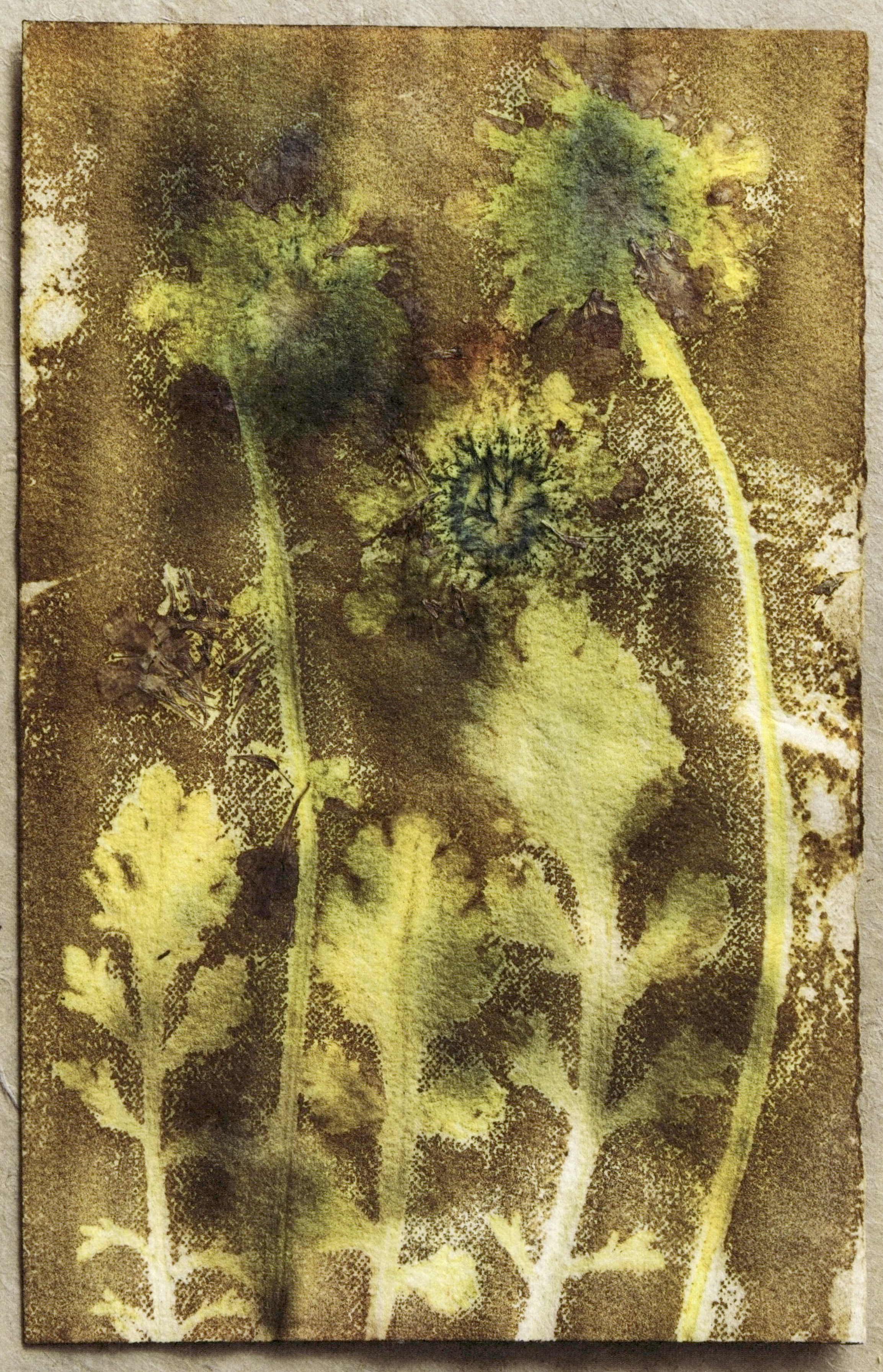

Printed on paper with a tannin carrier blanket

Pincushion Flower

(*Scabiosa* spp.)

Pincushion flowers, also called scabiosa, belong to the Caprifoliaceae family, which includes honeysuckle. Derived from the Latin term *scabiosus*, meaning "itchy," these flowers have a reputation in folk medicine for their use in treating scabies. Native to Africa, Europe, and Asia, *Scabiosa* varieties exhibit a stunning array of colorful hues. Their vibrant pigments make them excellent candidates for printing beautiful and unique imprints on fabrics.

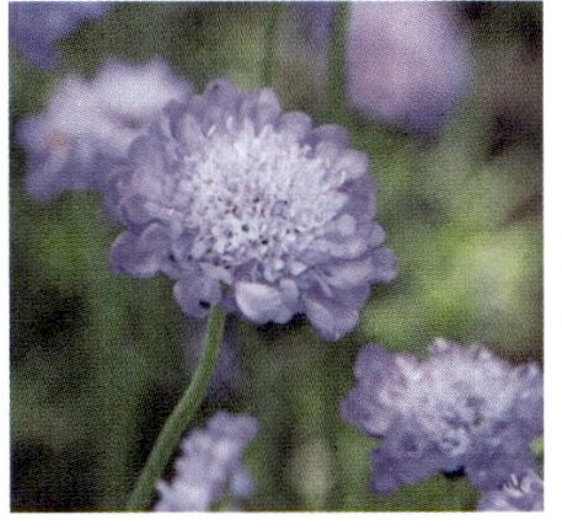

PRINTING NOTES

- Dried dark purple pincushion flowers offer a punch of concentrated blues and teals.
- The fresh flowers and leaves also yield colorful results, their silhouettes brought to life when outlined by a contrasting carrier blanket.

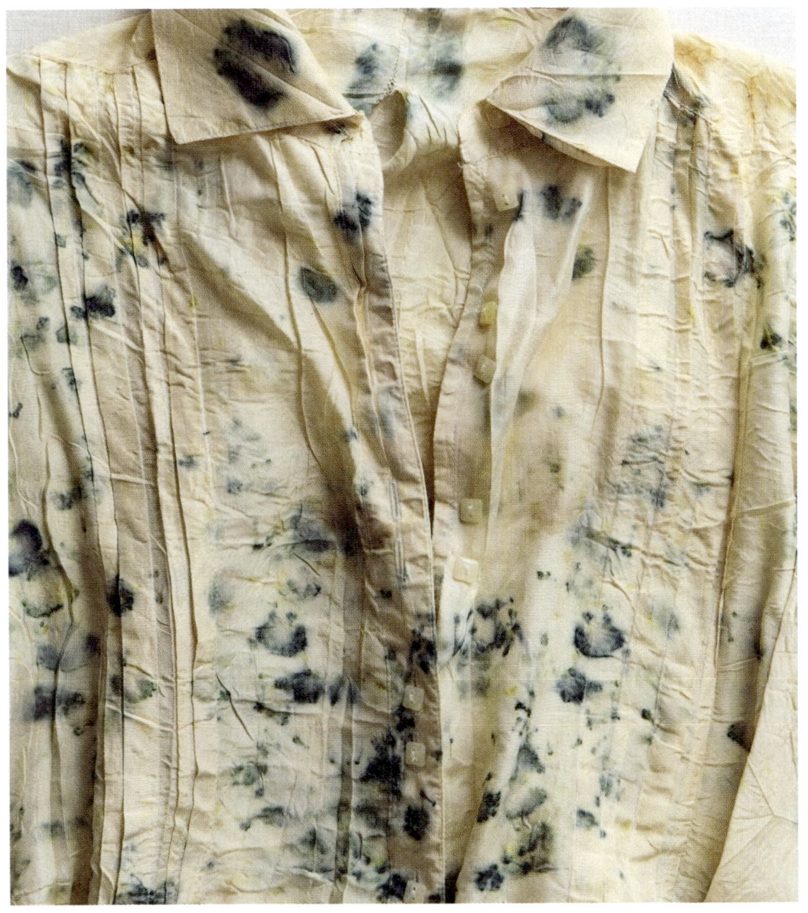

A handful of dried purple pincushion flowers were scattered over a vintage silk blouse to create an abstract botanical motif using the bundle dyeing technique (page 140).

In flower language, scabiosa represents sad love. S. atropurpurea, *or sweet scabious, has dark flowers that symbolize death or widowhood. This connection has led to the plant being called mourning bride and mournful widow, adding a touch of sadness to its lovely appearance.*

Purple Leaf Plum

(*Prunus cerasifera*)

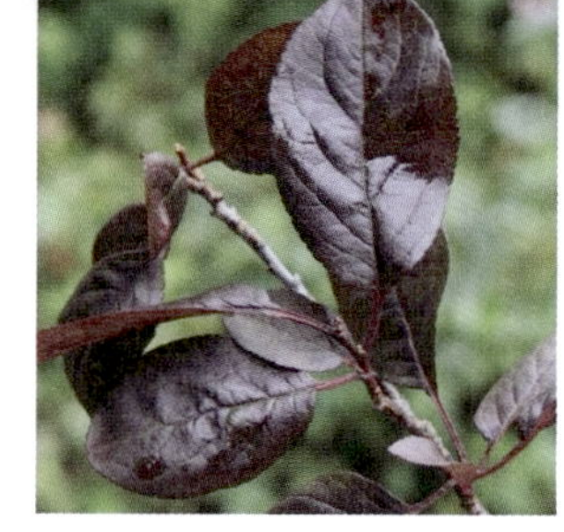

Purple leaf plum, also known as cherry plum and myrobalan plum, is a worthy addition to any botanical dye garden. The plum-hued leaves produce stunning results due to the elevated level of tannins; they imbue the target with colors ranging from teal to aqua. The flowers are worth experimenting with, too, if you catch them in early spring. Fresh leaves can be dried or preserved by freezing and stored for later use.

Purple leaf plum is part of the rose family, which includes roses, blackberry, pear, and crabapple—their leaves may also be used for printing.

PRINTING NOTES

- Both sides of the leaves are worth using. The moon side offers a swoon-worthy teal when used in combination with PAS and iron.
- Detach the leaves from the harder, inflexible branches so they can lie flat on the target, making them easier to roll up.

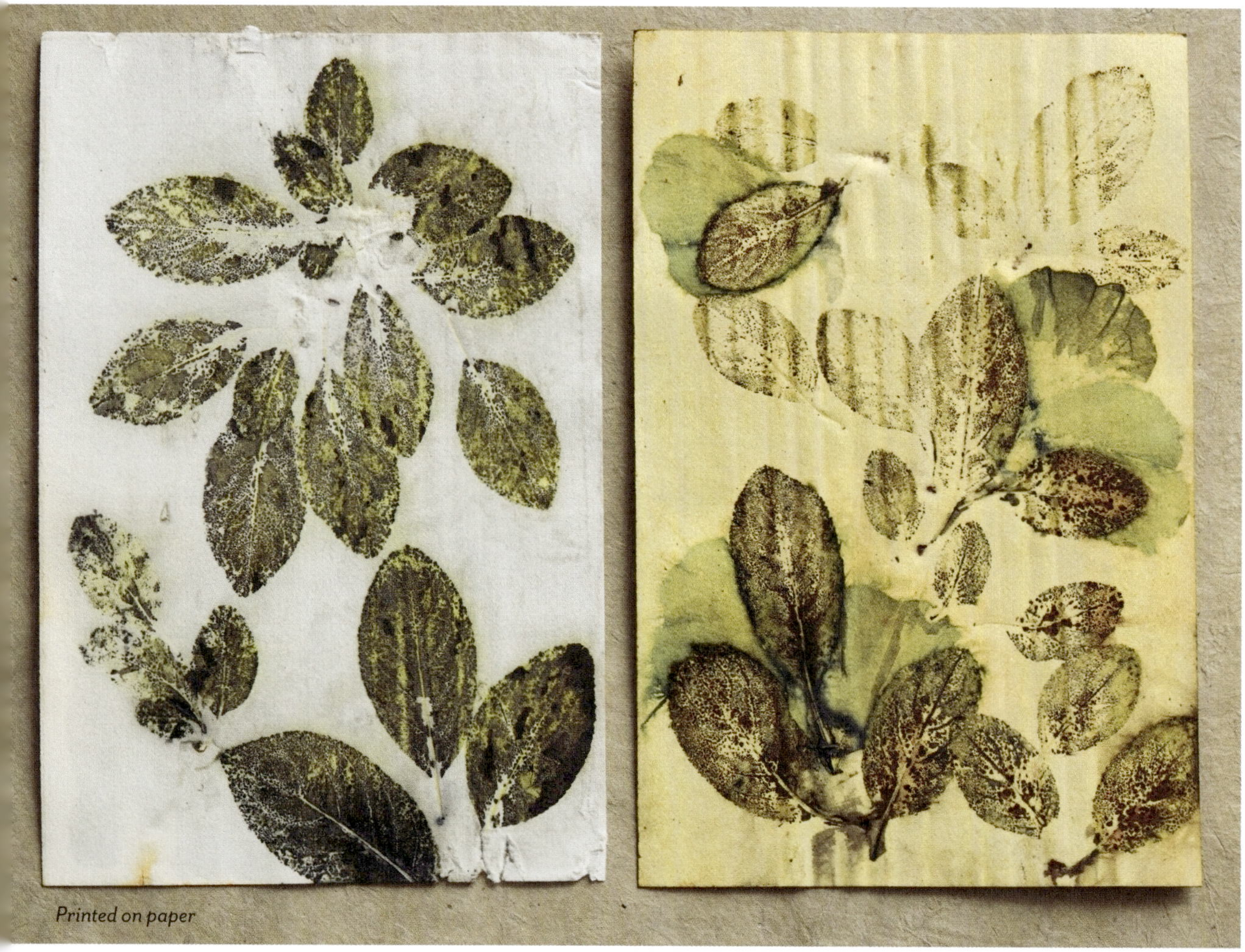

Printed on paper

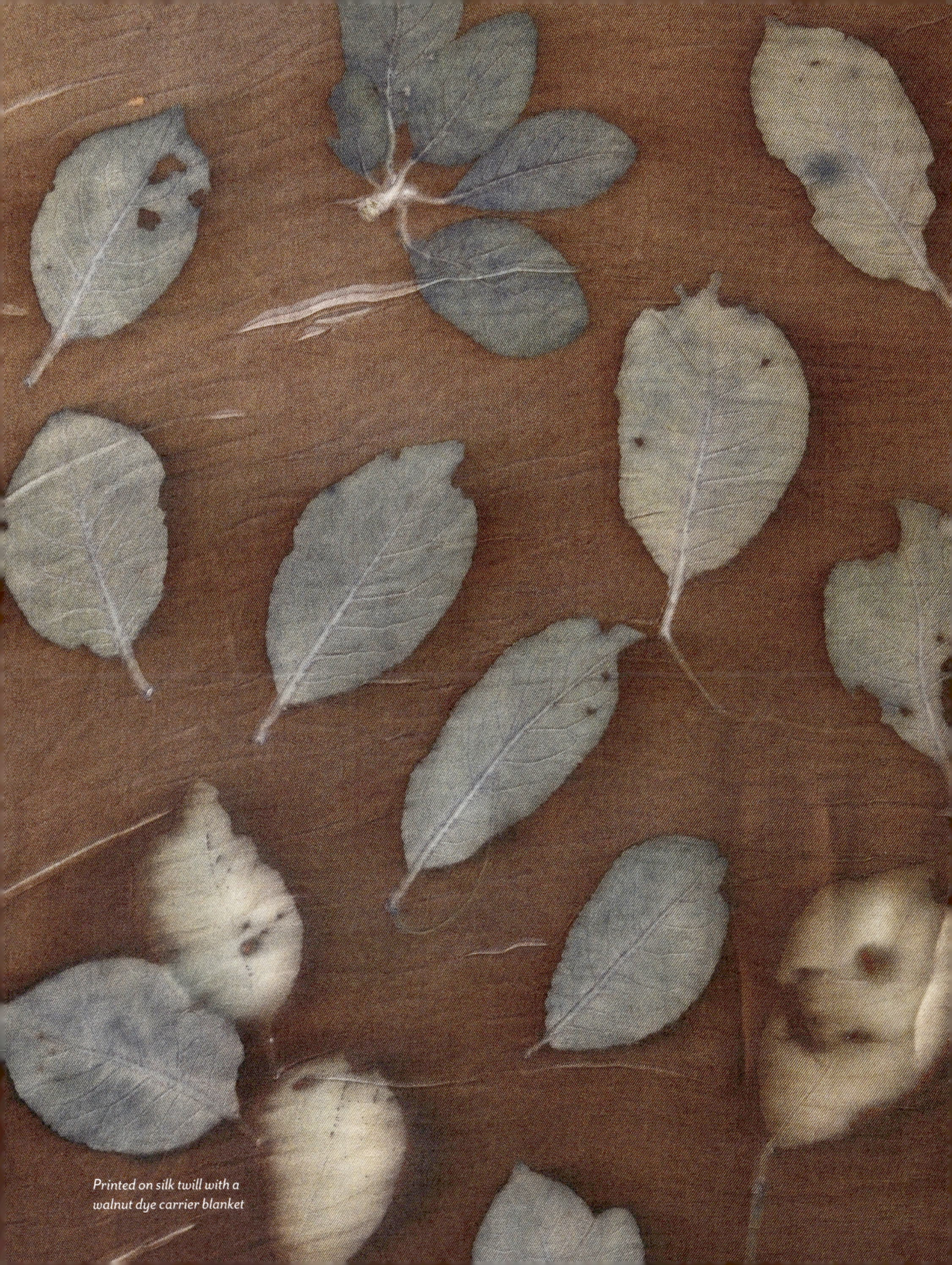

Printed on silk twill with a walnut dye carrier blanket

Purple Leaf Plum *continued*

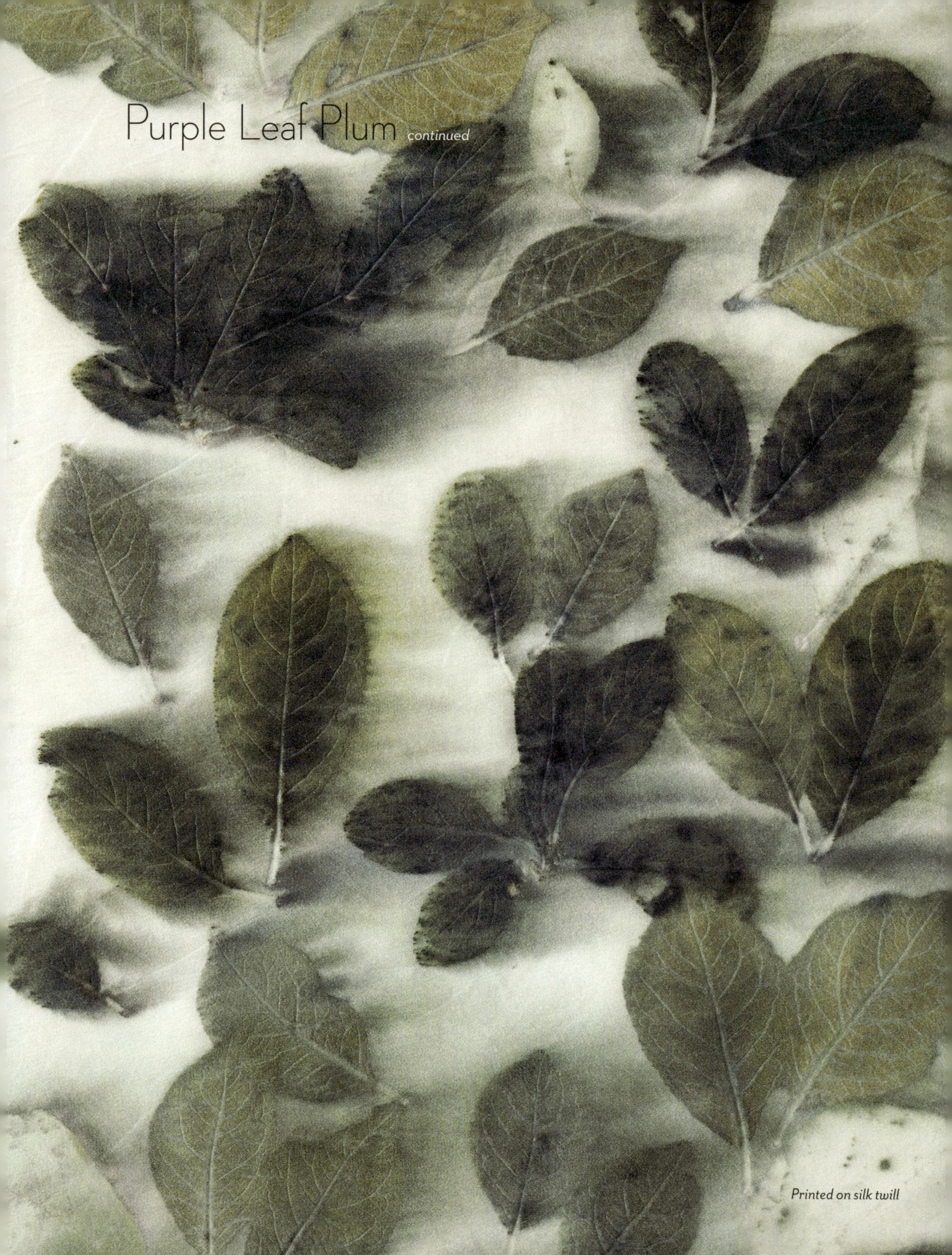

Printed on silk twill

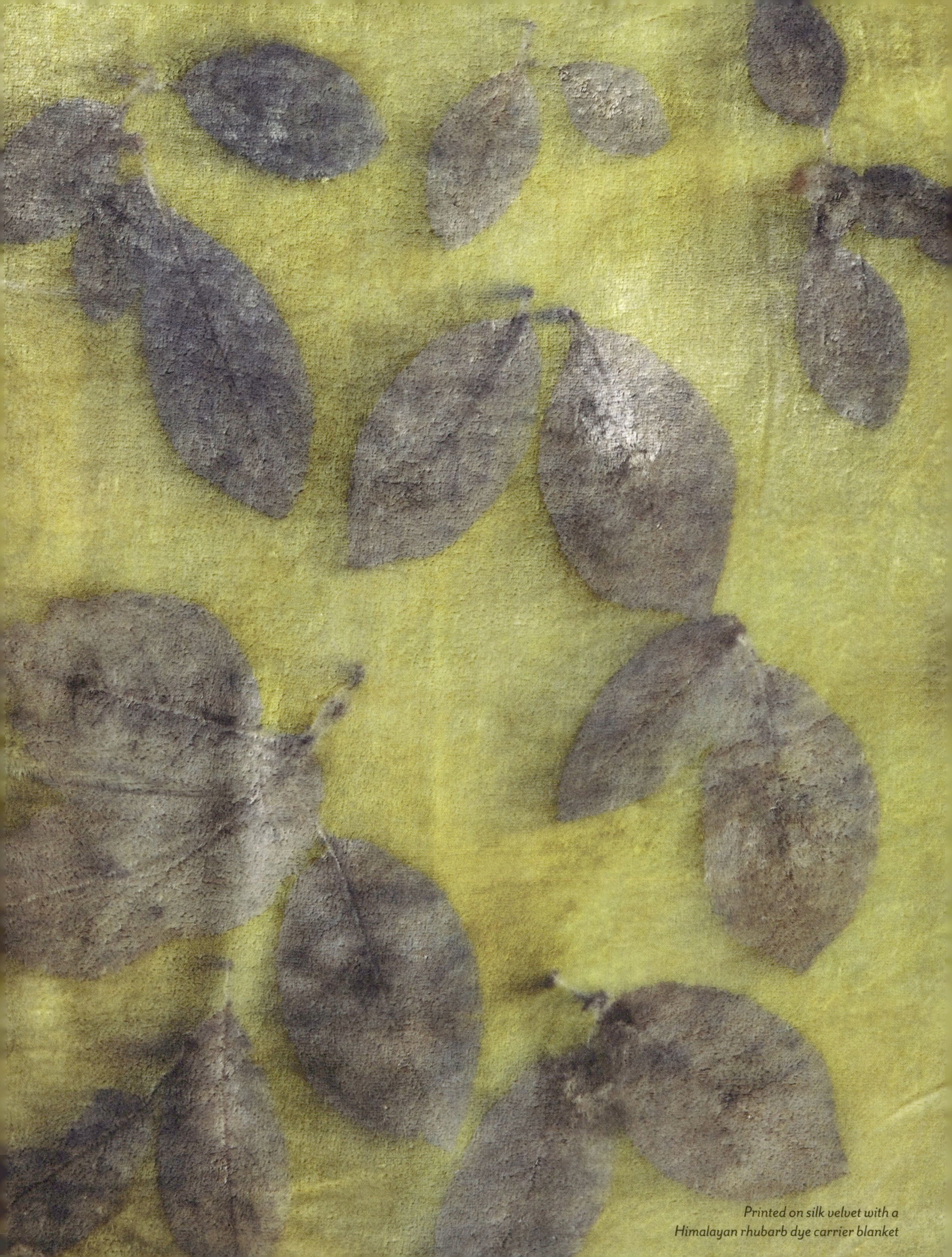

Printed on silk velvet with a Himalayan rhubarb dye carrier blanket

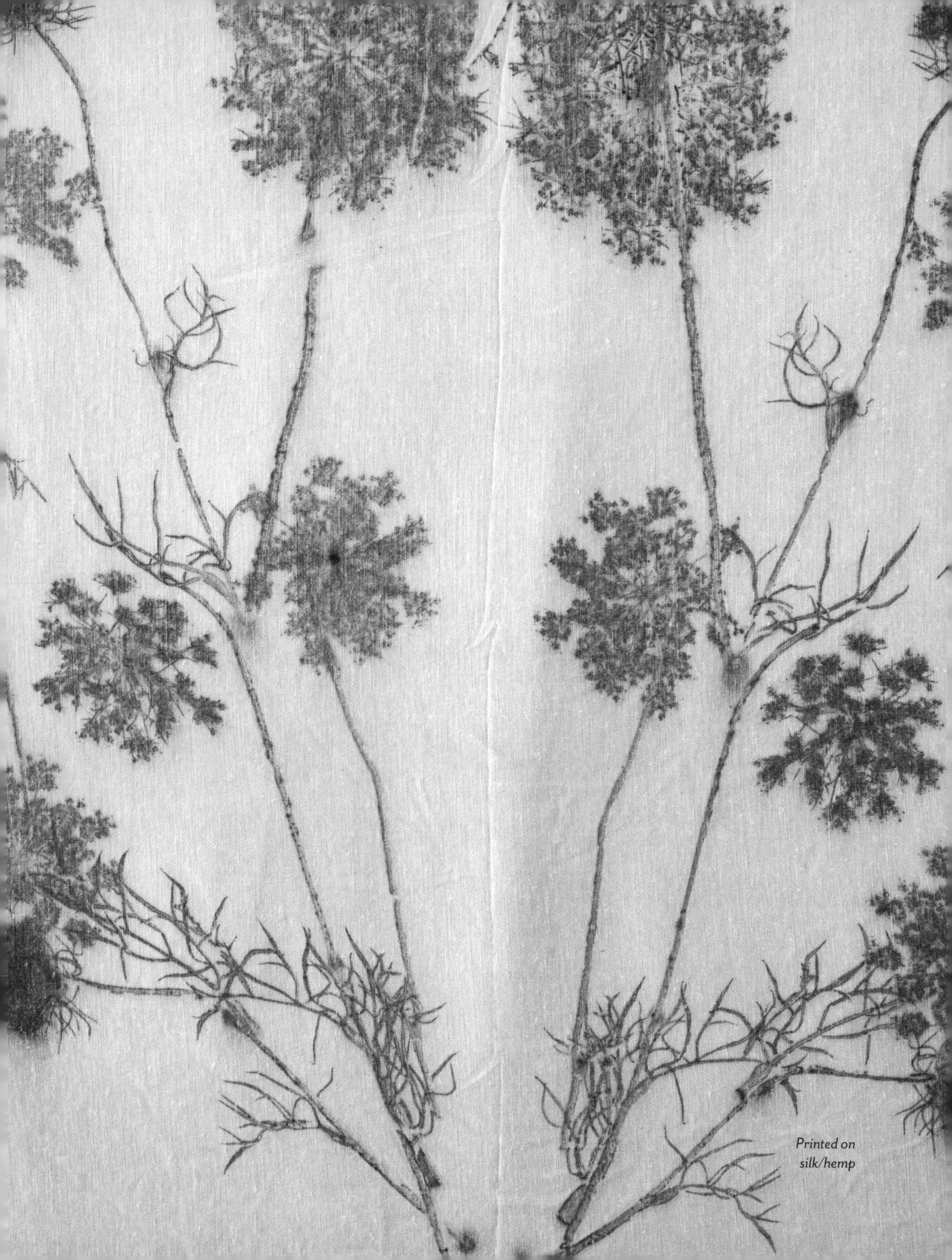
Printed on silk/hemp

Queen Anne's Lace

(*Daucus carota*)

Queen Anne's lace, commonly known as wild carrot, is an enchanting flowering plant that thrives along roadsides and in open fields from early spring to late fall. This plant showcases clusters of delicate, white, flat-topped flowers, known as umbels, which are made up of thousands of tiny blossoms. At the center of these clusters lies a purplish dot that often resembles an insect, a clever adaptation that scientists think may help attract pollinators.

While it may be mistaken for poison hemlock due to its similar habitat, Queen Anne's lace can be easily identified by its hairy stalk and smaller stature, typically reaching no more than 3 feet in height.

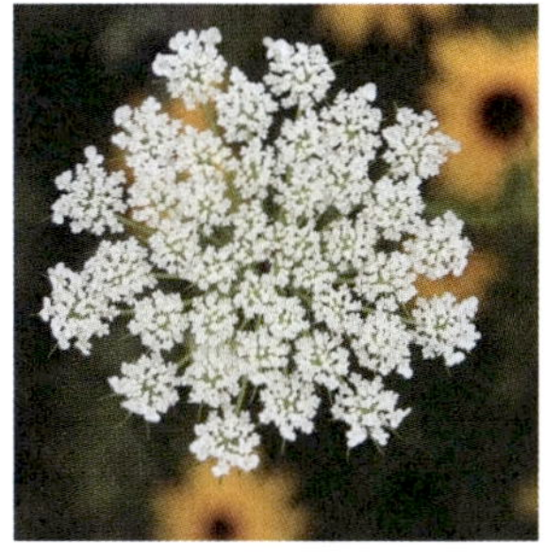

PRINTING NOTES

- Use the entire plant to beautiful effect. The stem, leaves, and flowers offer up a spindly olive-hued print.
- To achieve a bolder, more dramatic imprint, use iron in the mordant recipe.
- By removing the stem and using just the flower heads, the lacelike disks can create a starburst motif.

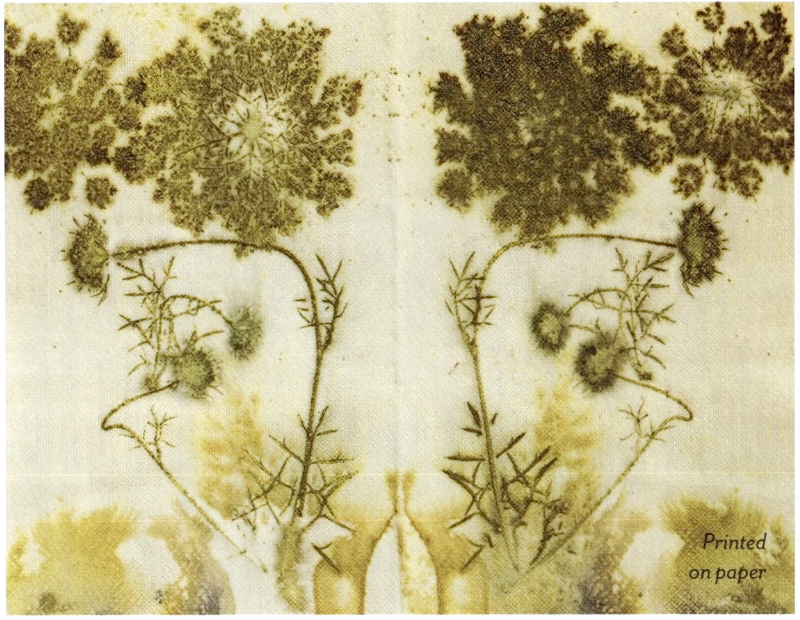

Printed on paper

Queen Anne II is purported to have challenged her ladies-in-waiting to create lace as beautiful as the flower. The flower remained unmatched, earning it the name "living lace" and showing nature's timeless charm compared to human art.

Rose

(*Rosa* spp.)

Beloved for their intoxicating fragrance and vibrant colors, roses are a valuable resource in botanical printing. While the flowers print best when dried, the leaves of various rose types, particularly long-stemmed varieties, are rich in tannins and offer excellent potential for creating stunning prints. I adore the leaves of the beach plum rose (*Rosa rugosa*), which are abundant in both tannin and pigmentation. For optimal results, fresh leaves are ideal; they can be preserved effectively, however, by freezing them in a small amount of water.

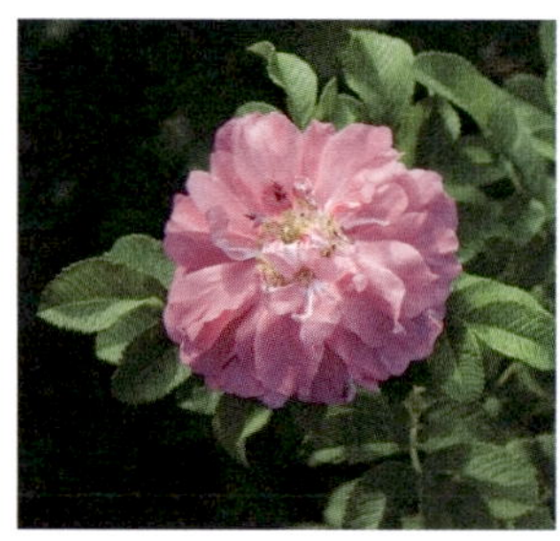

R. rugosa

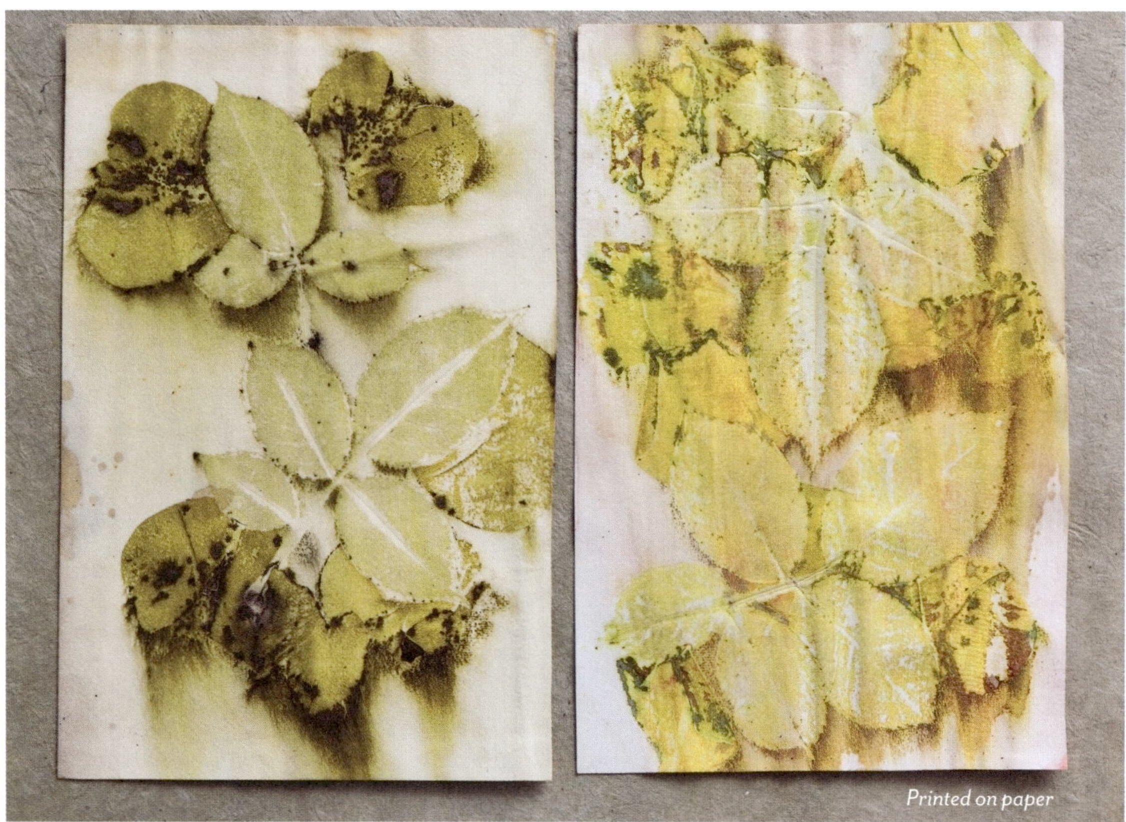

Printed on paper

PRINTING NOTES

- Dried rose flowers print best—use clusters of red, pink, or purple petals to make powerful, concentrated prints. Fresh petals impart little color.
- Both sides of rose leaves offer lovely coloring; the sun side prints more green, the moon side more black.
- Add color to your composition by using a carrier blanket that is reminiscent of the flower color; for example, using brazilwood for a bright pink.

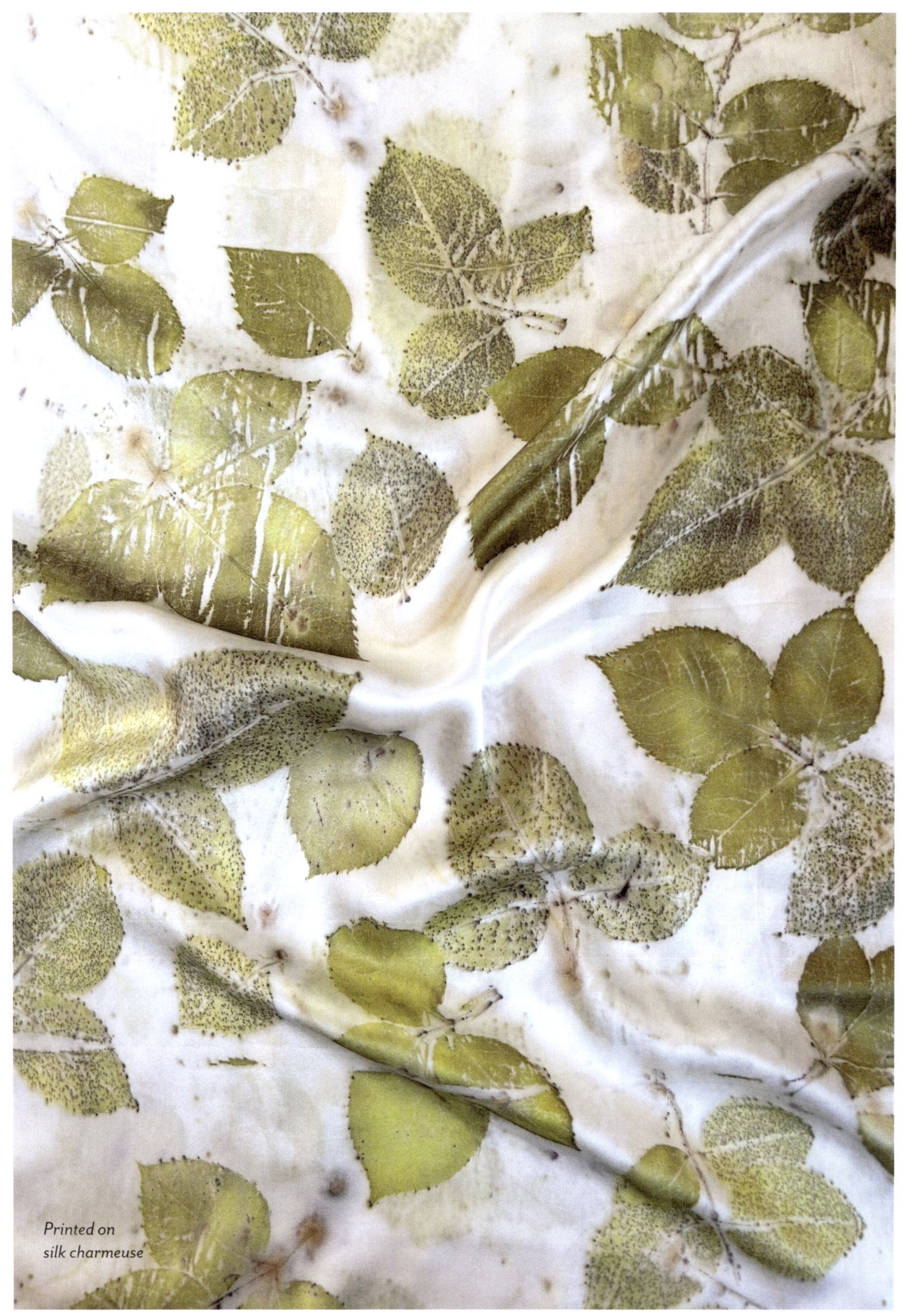
Printed on
silk charmeuse

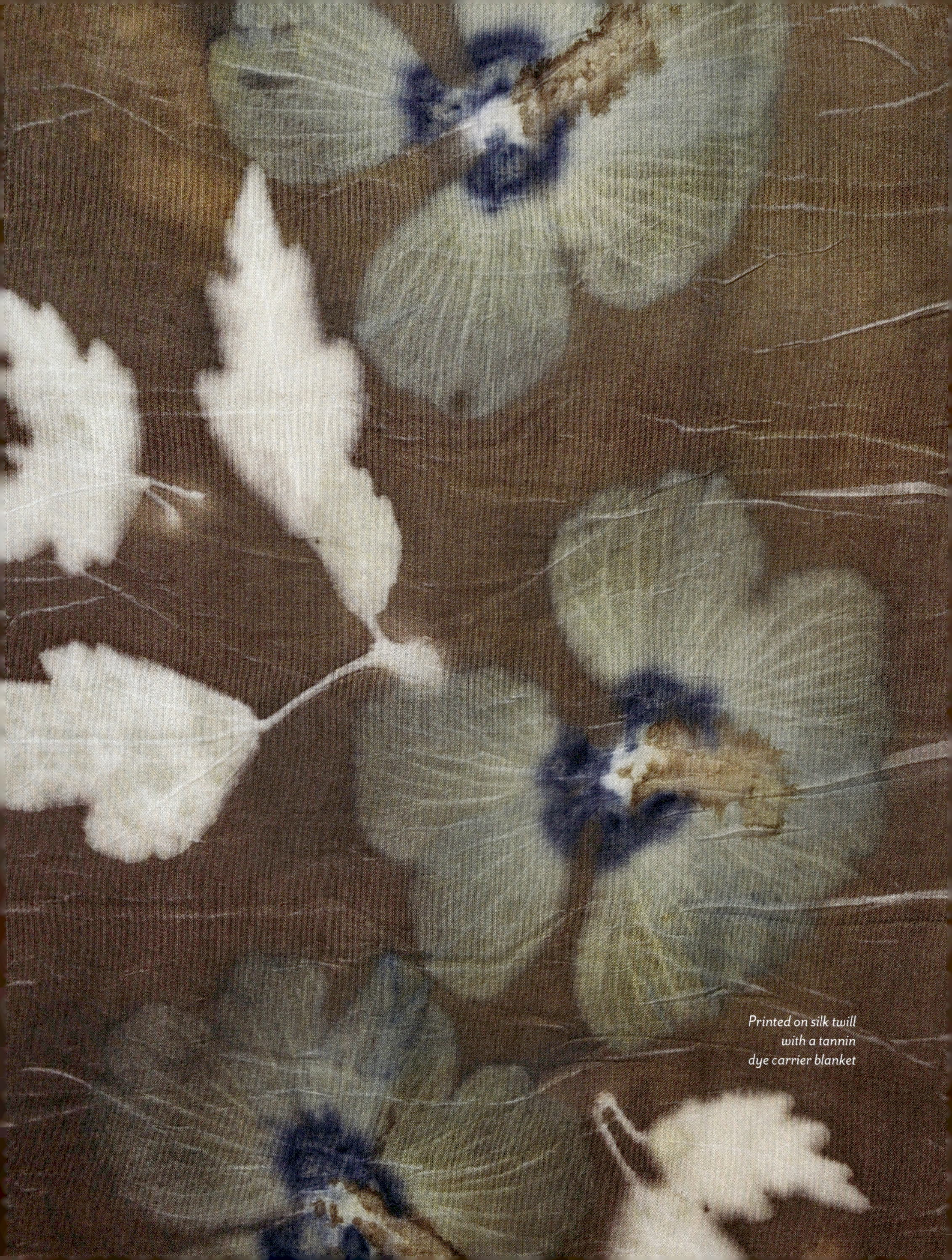

Printed on silk twill with a tannin dye carrier blanket

Rose of Sharon

(*Hibiscus syriacus*)

One of my favorite flowers for printing, the rose of Sharon, also called rose mallow or althea, is a prolific bloomer that can produce flowers from June through September in North America. Part of the Malvaceae, or mallow, family, the rose of Sharon is a relative of the hollyhock. Each bloom is fleeting, typically lasting only a day, making it essential to act quickly. For optimal use, gather the flowers when they are fully open. The anthocyanin-rich petals offer a unique opportunity to achieve a range of light blues, while a seafoam green can be captured from the 'Blue Chiffon' variety.

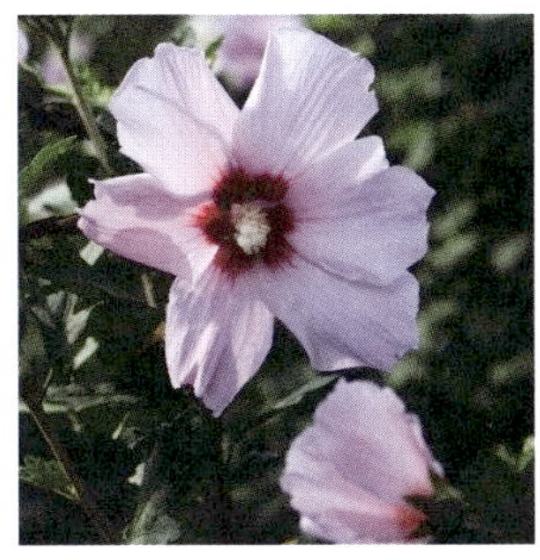

I grow 'Purple Pillar' for its lavender-colored flowers that present a bright splash of deep magenta in the center.

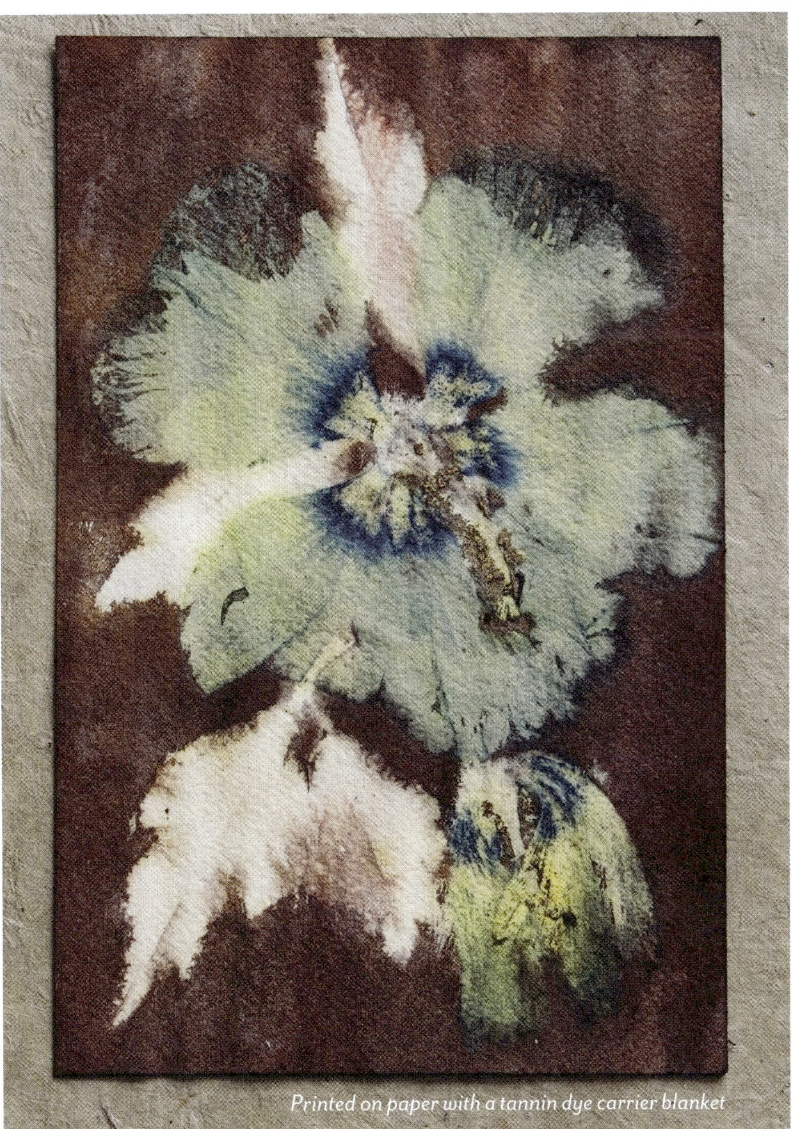

Printed on paper with a tannin dye carrier blanket

PRINTING NOTES

- The leaves are jagged and palmately veined. While they do not contain much tannin or impart significant color when steamed, their shape is interesting to incorporate into a design. Try using a carrier blanket soaked in dark color dye to capture their outline.
- The five-petaled flowers can be placed face down onto fabric or paper. Remove the receptacle, or tough green base, to reduce bulk when bundling or pressing in paper. The saturated stamen will add color and shape.
- Fallen blooms usually curl back into a tightly wrapped cone, which can make for an interesting print as well. Or you can carefully reopen the petals and lay the bloom flat to print.
- The delicate petals can be easily torn or overprocessed, so keep steaming to a maximum of 45 minutes.

Staghorn Sumac

(*Rhus typhina*)

I used staghorn sumac in one of my first experiments with mesmerizing results, and I have created countless prints with it since. I knew artist India Flint reliably used eucalyptus leaves to get a nice leafy imprint, so imagine my surprise when I got such striking impressions with these tannin-packed leaves!

Except for the roots, each part of staghorn sumac can be used as natural dye and mordant. The plant contains high amounts of tannins and can be added to dye baths to increase fastness.

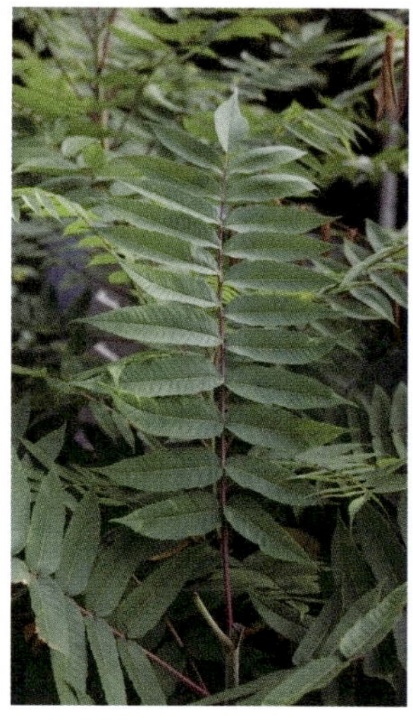

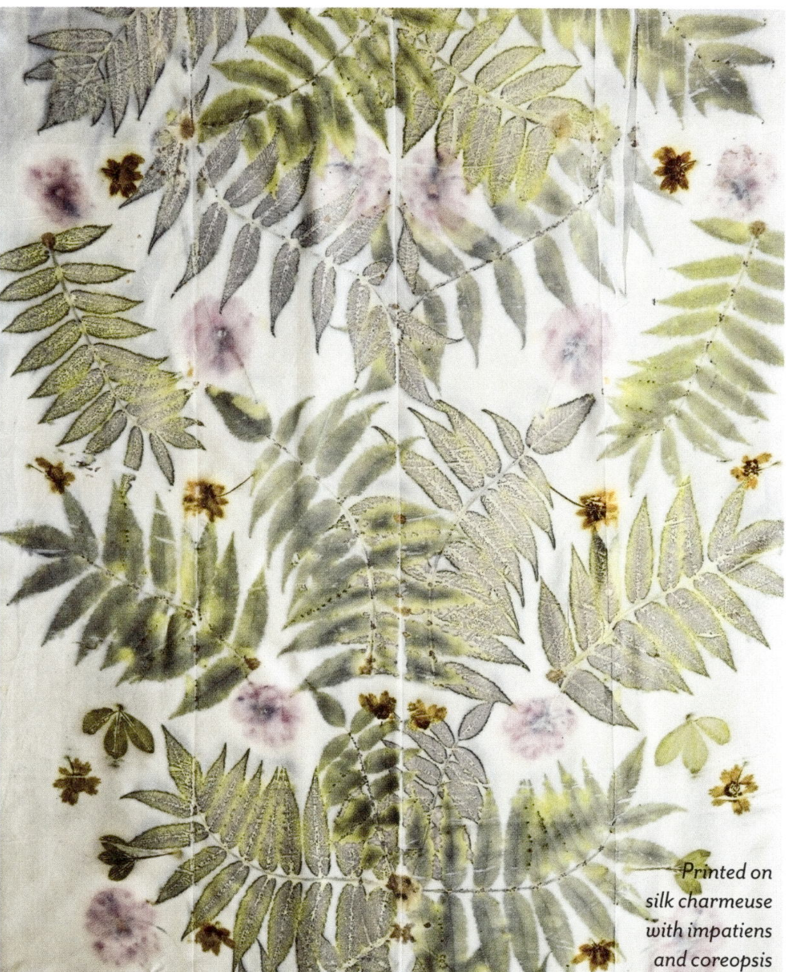

Printed on silk charmeuse with impatiens and coreopsis

PRINTING NOTES

- The branches are excellent for large-scale botanical prints, as you can arrange entire stalks to create movement and grace in a composition. The stems are flexible enough to roll into a tight bundle.
- Both sides of the leaves may be used effectively. The moon side depicts a blacker imprint and the sun side a greener one.
- The fuzzy pink fruit produces a pop of fluorescent pink.

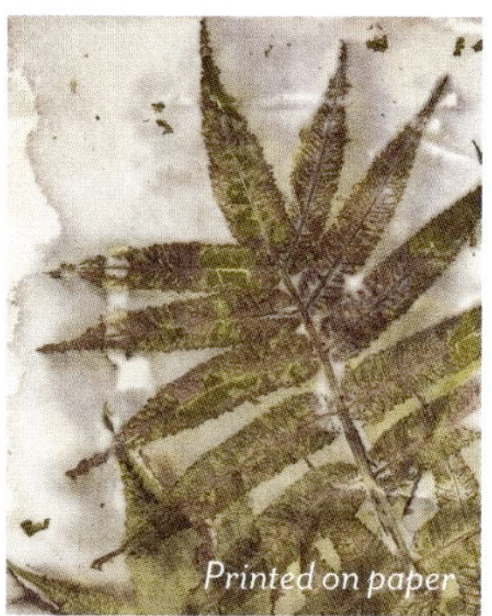

Printed on paper

Historically, Indigenous peoples of North America have used staghorn berries to make a healing concoction similar to lemonade.

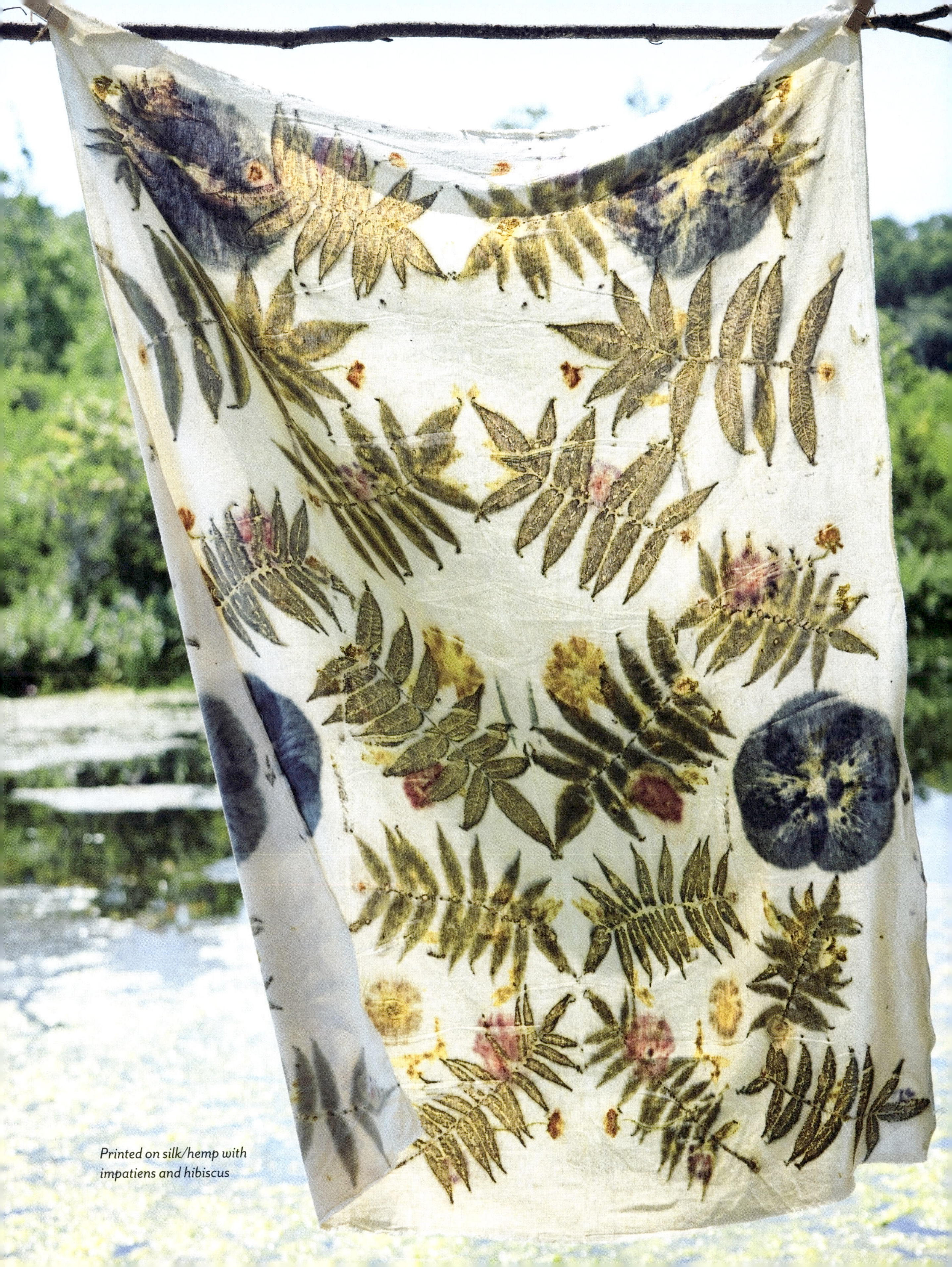

Printed on silk/hemp with impatiens and hibiscus

Wild Geranium

(*Geranium maculatum*)

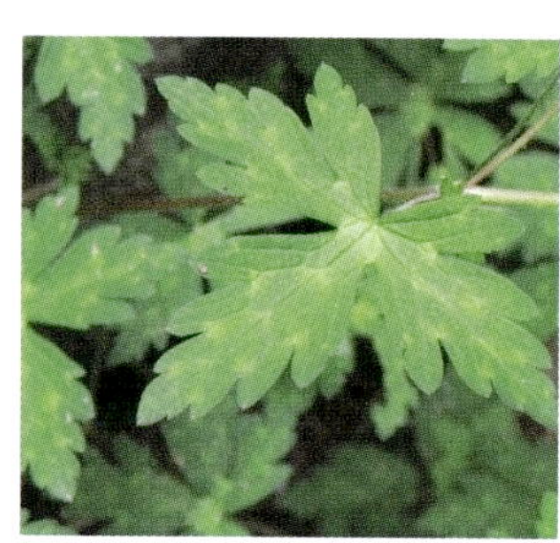

Wild geranium is often referred to as alum root, alum bloom, cranesbill, spotted cranesbill, wild cranesbill, spotted geranium, or wood geranium. These hardy perennials have attractive fuzzy leaves that showcase a profusion of delicate flowers in shades ranging from pure white or pale pink to rose, magenta, violet, blue, and purple.

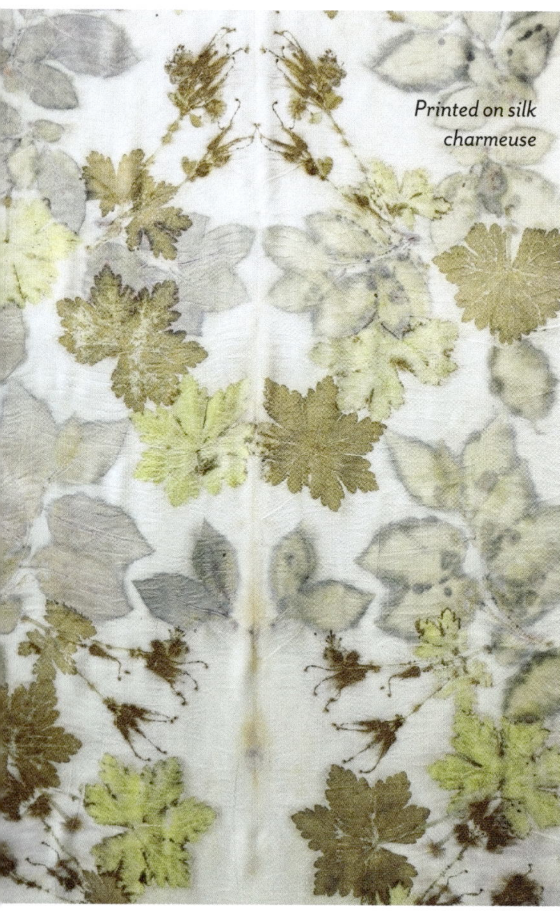

Printed on silk charmeuse

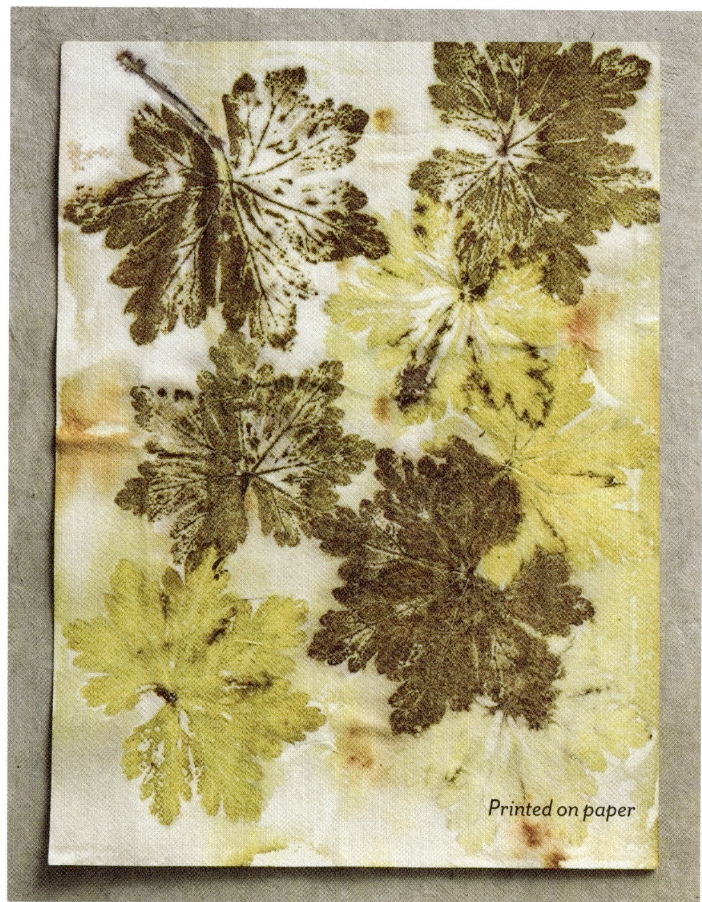

Printed on paper

PRINTING NOTES

- The flowers offer some color but not at the same level of saturation as others; the quality is more watercolor-like and can show up in spots.
- The leaves are more valuable for printing: Both the sun and moon sides print brilliantly, so they are good candidates for creating a mirror-image print.
- In the examples, I used a carrier blanket soaked in cutch extract for a golden background color that offers a distinct contrast to the outline and natural coloring of the leaves.

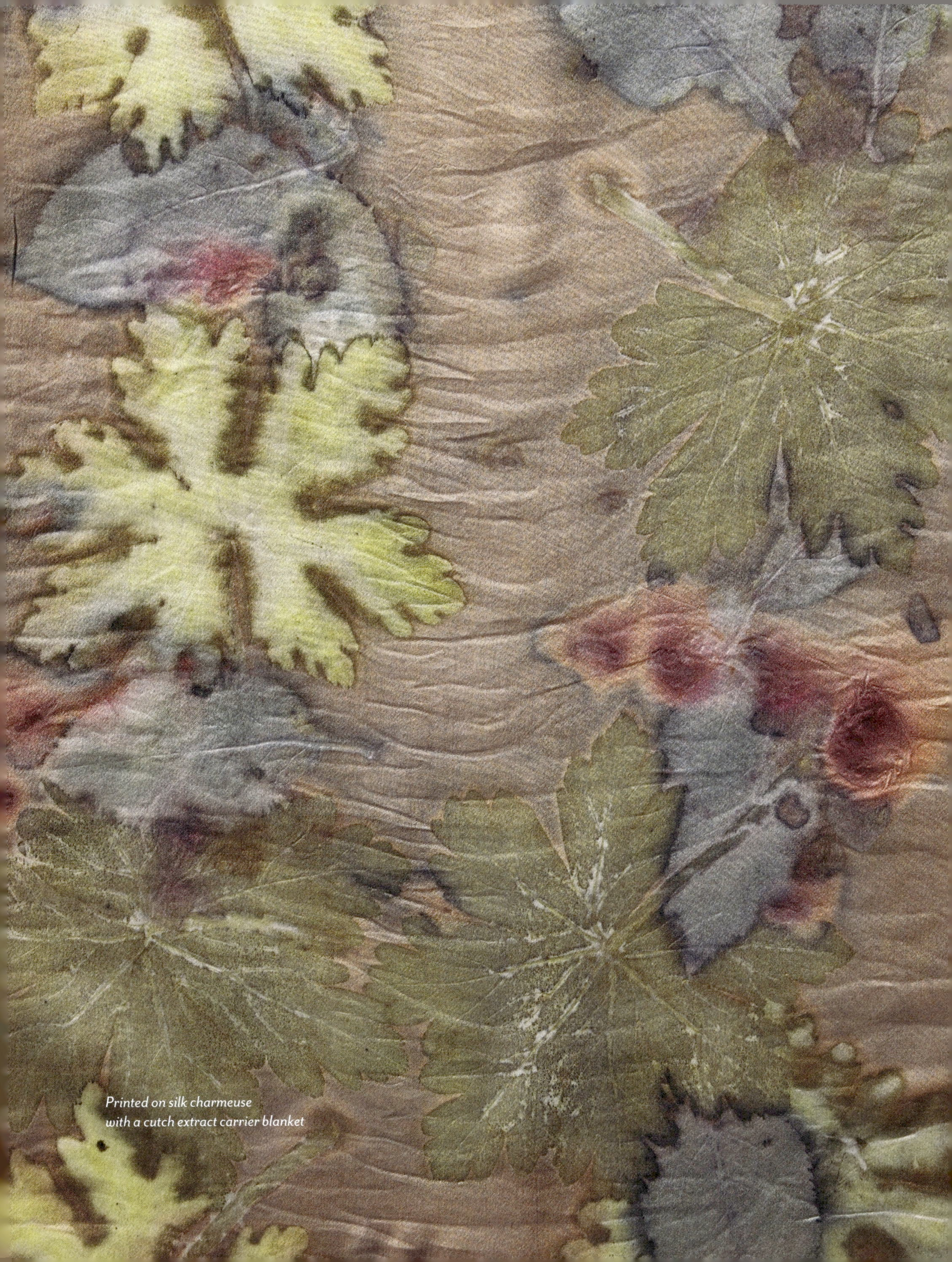

Printed on silk charmeuse with a cutch extract carrier blanket

BLUE FALSE INDIGO

JAPANESE MAPLE

SUMAC

PURPLE LEAF PLUM

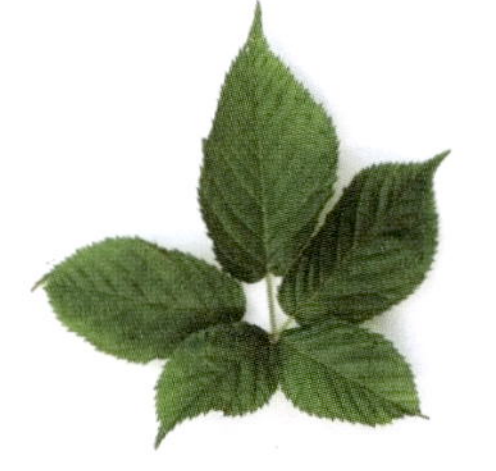

RASPBERRY

Other Plants to Experiment With

LEAVES

- Apple (*Malus domestica*)
- Bamboo (*Arundinaria* spp.)
- Birch (*Betula papyrifera*)
- Blackberry (*Rubus fruticosus*)
- Cannabis (*Cannabis sativa, C. indica*)
- Carrot (*Daucus carota* subsp. *sativus*)
- Castor (*Ricinus communis*)
- Catalpa (*Catalpa speciosa*)
- Catmint (*Nepeta × faassenii*)
- Chaste tree (*Vitex agnus-castus*)
- Chenille plant (*Acalypha hispida*)
- Cherry (*Prunus* spp.)
- Chestnut (*Castanea sativa*)
- Chocolate vine (*Akebia quinata*)
- Coral vine (*Antigonon leptopus*)
- Dyer's broom (*Genista tinctoria*)
- Elder (*Sambucus nigra, S. canadensis*)
- Fig (*Ficus carica*)
- Fountain grass (*Pennisetum polystachion* and others)
- Ginkgo (*Ginkgo biloba*)
- Grape (*Vitis riparia*)
- Grevillea (*Grevillea banksii*)
- Ironweed (*Vernonia fasciculata*)
- Mimosa (*Mimosa* spp.)
- Oak (*Quercus* spp.)
- Pecan (*Carya illinoinensis*)
- Peruvian pepper tree (*Schinus molle*)
- Purple basil (*Ocimum basilicum*)
- Rangoon creeper (*Combretum indicum*)
- Saint John's wort (*Hypericum* spp.)
- She-oak (*Casuarina* spp.)
- Strawberry (*Fragaria* spp.)
- Sweetgum (*Liquidambar styraciflua*)
- Teak (*Tectona grandis*)
- Virginia creeper (*Parthenocissus quinquefolia*)
- Walnut (*Juglans* spp.)
- Willow (*Salix* spp.)

FLOWERS

- African violet (*Streptocarpus ionanthus*)
- African or Aztec marigold (*Tagetes erecta*)
- Amaranth (*Amaranthus* spp.)
- Butterfly pea flower (*Clitoria ternatea*)
- Catmint (*Nepeta × faassenii*)
- Columbine (*Aquilegia* spp.)
- Chrysanthemum (*Chrysanthemum* spp.)
- Crown daisy (*Glebionis coronaria*)
- Dyer's marguerite (*Anthemis tinctoria*)
- Jerusalem artichoke (*Helianthus tuberosus*)
- Lilac (*Syringa* spp.)
- Mexican marigold (*Tagetes lucida*)
- Pansy (*Viola* spp.)
- Passionfruit (*Passiflora edulis*)
- Purple sand cherry (*Prunus × cistena*)
- Safflower (*Carthamus tinctorius*)
- Saskatoon Berry (*Amelanchier alnifolia*)
- Serviceberry (*Amelanchier arborea, A. laevis, A. canadensis*)
- Signet marigold (*Tagetes tenuifolia*)
- Sumac berries (*Rhus coriaria*)
- Sunflower (*Helianthus* spp.)
- Tiger lily (*Lilium lancifolium*)
- Tulip (*Tulipa* spp.)
- Zinnia (*Zinnia angustifolia*)

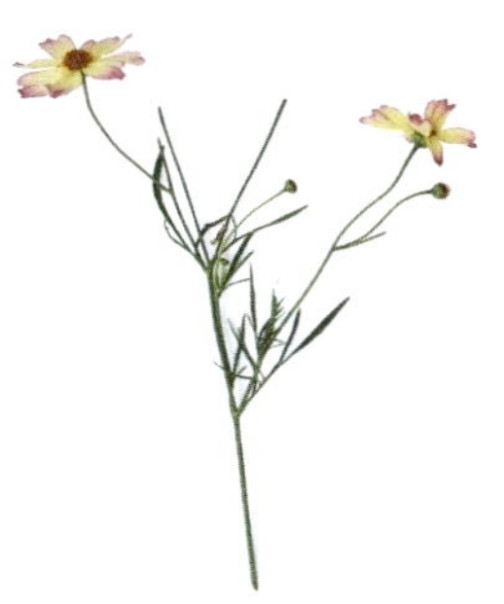
COREOPSIS

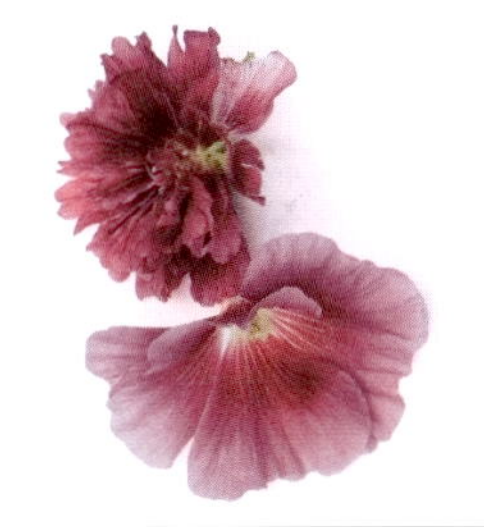
HOLLYHOCK

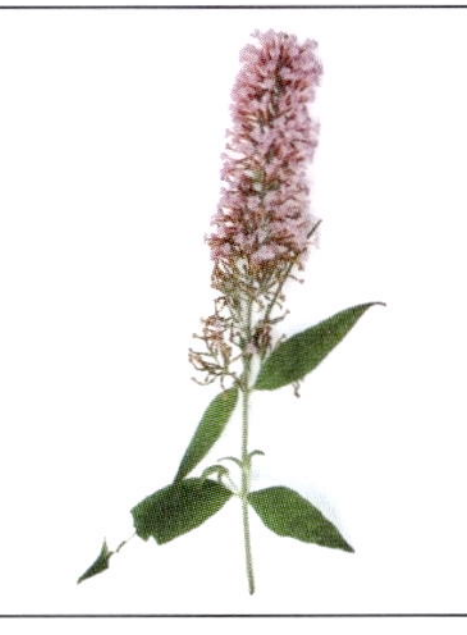
BUTTERFLY BUSH

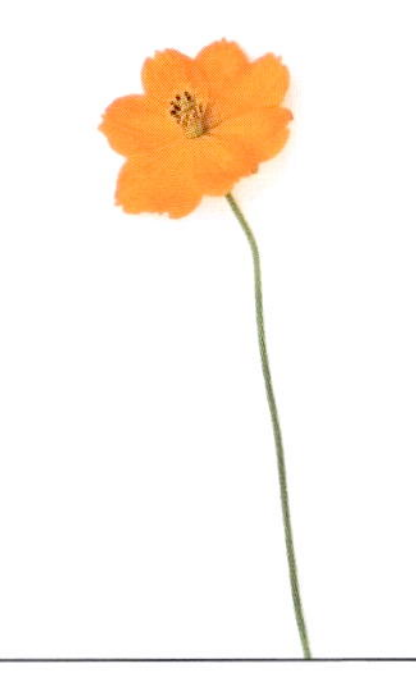
COSMOS

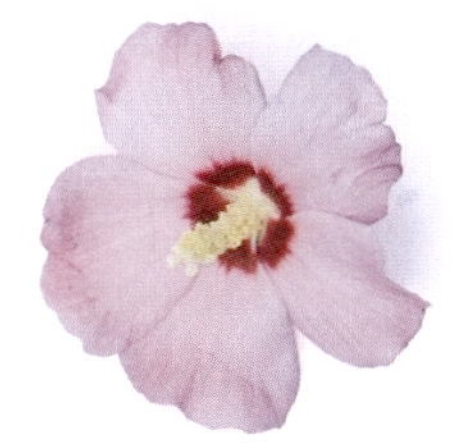
ROSE OF SHARON

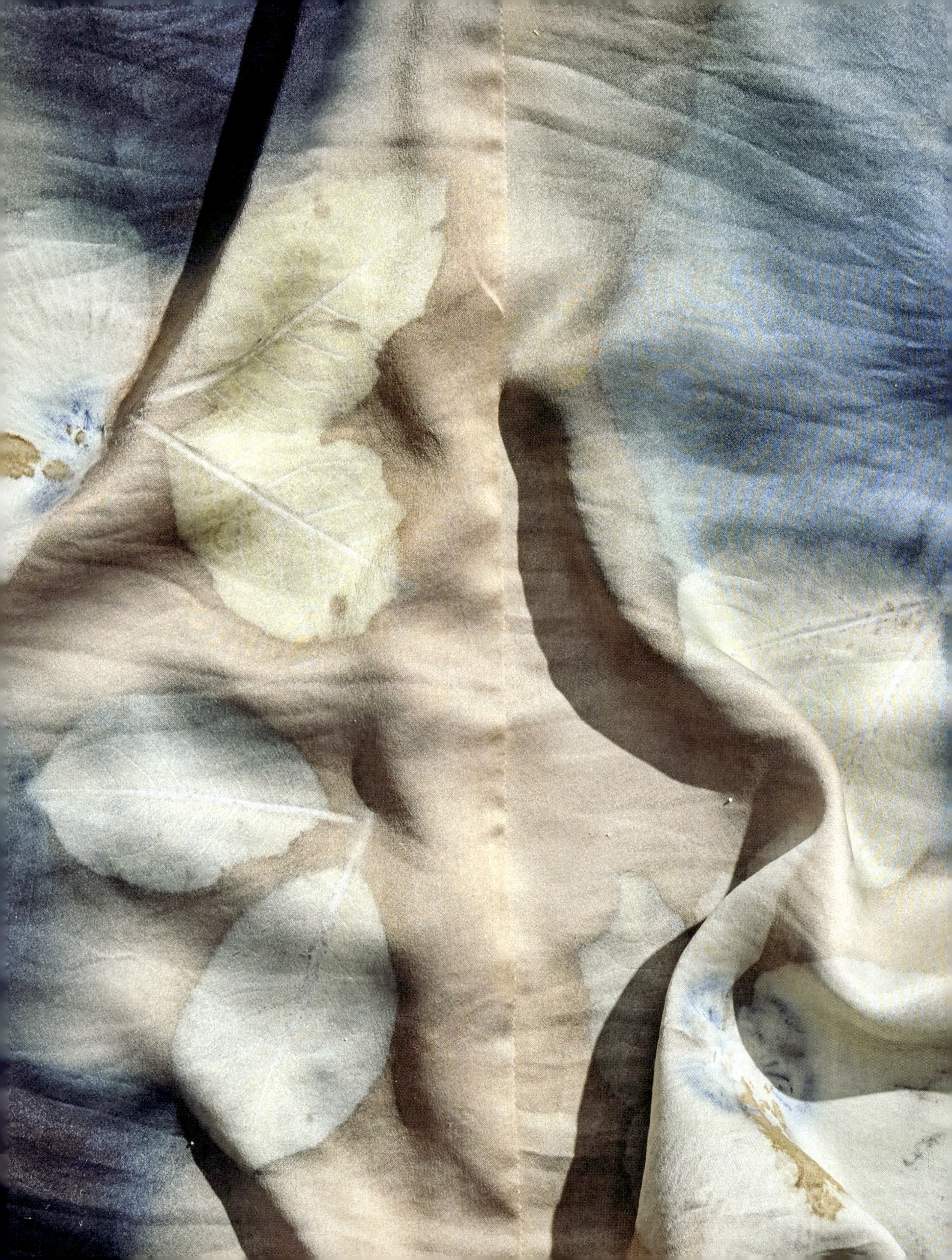

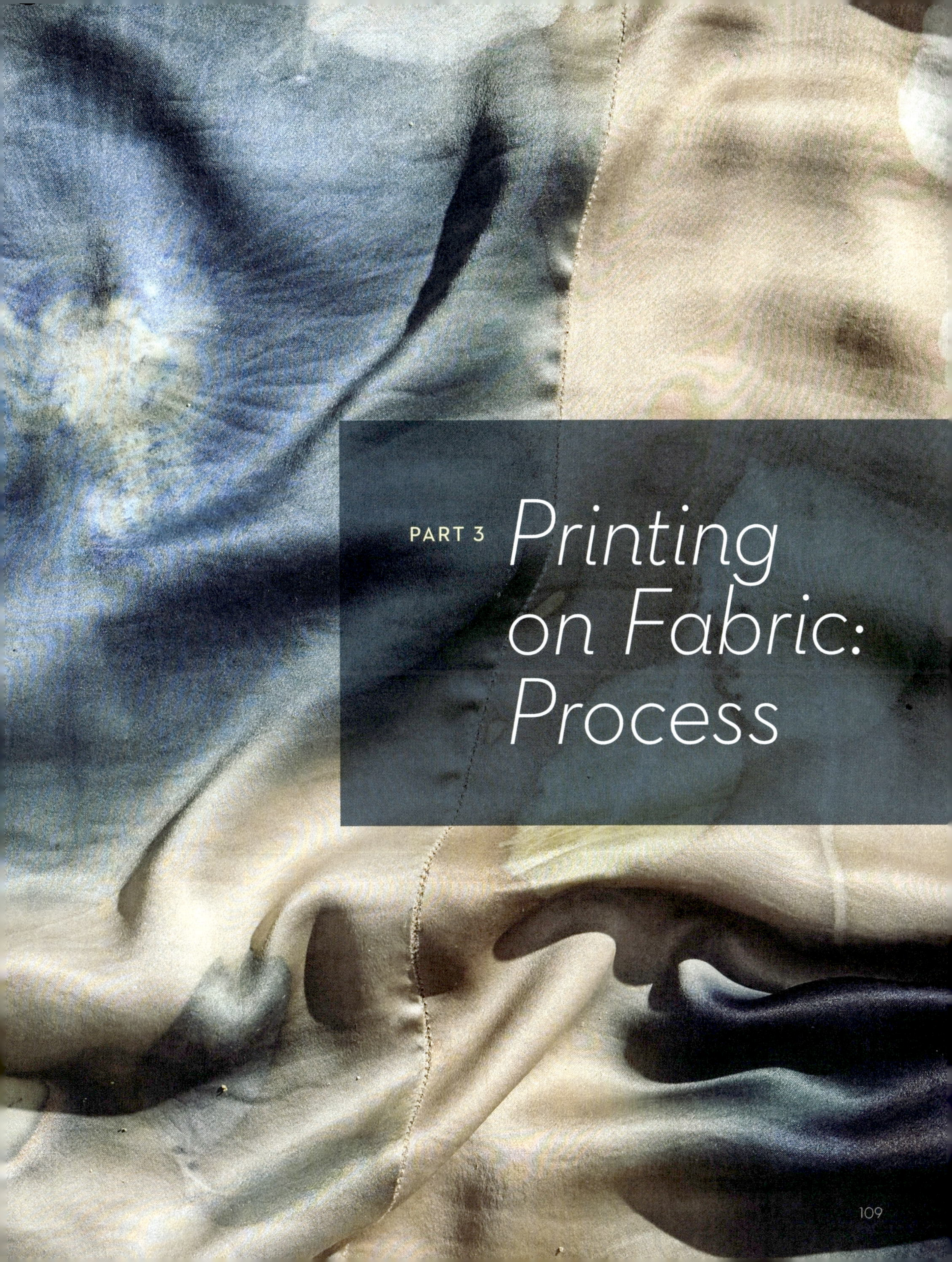

PART 3

Printing on Fabric: Process

The charm of botanical printing lies in the delightful reveal—the careful unwrapping of beautifully transformed bundles that tell nature's intricate story. My journey has been filled with numerous challenges, each one contributing to my growth and helping me improve my techniques. While exploring the most thoughtful ways to prepare fabric and use various mordants, I've come to realize the immense value of both patience and attention to the minutest of details. This section offers tips and insights to ensure a joyful and successful process for those practiced in the art as well as those just starting out.

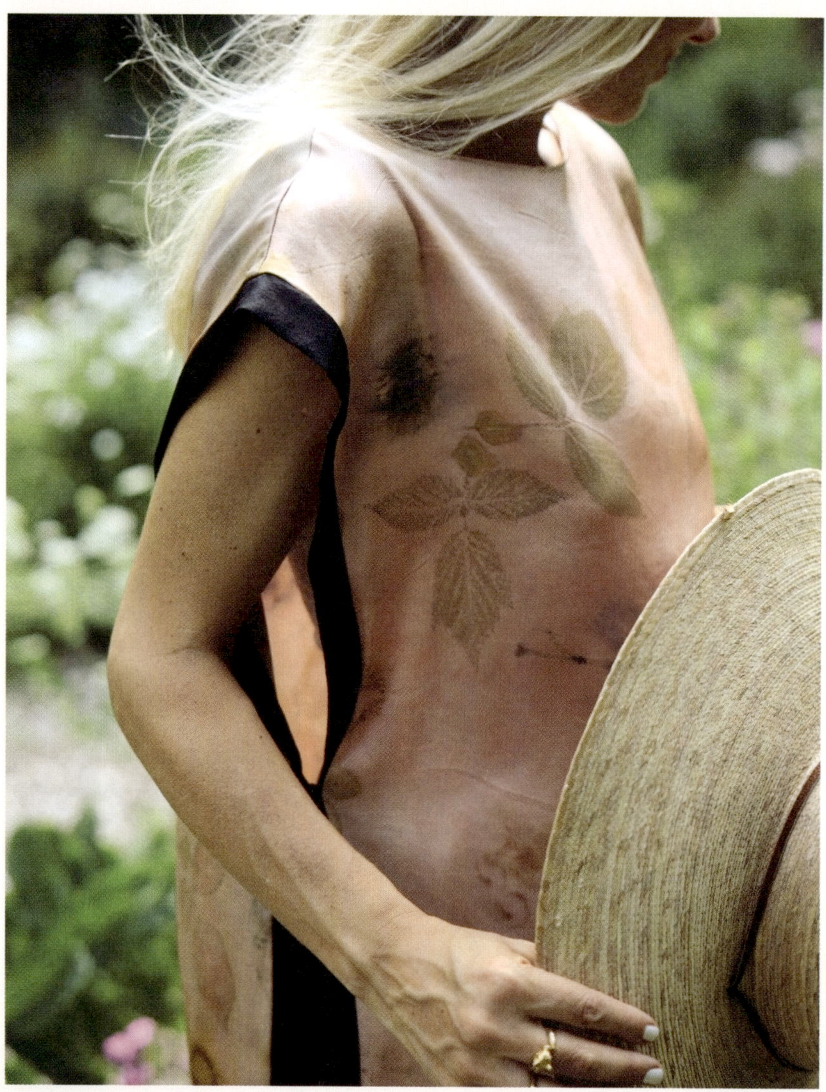

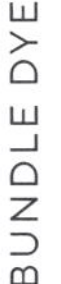

BUNDLE DYED

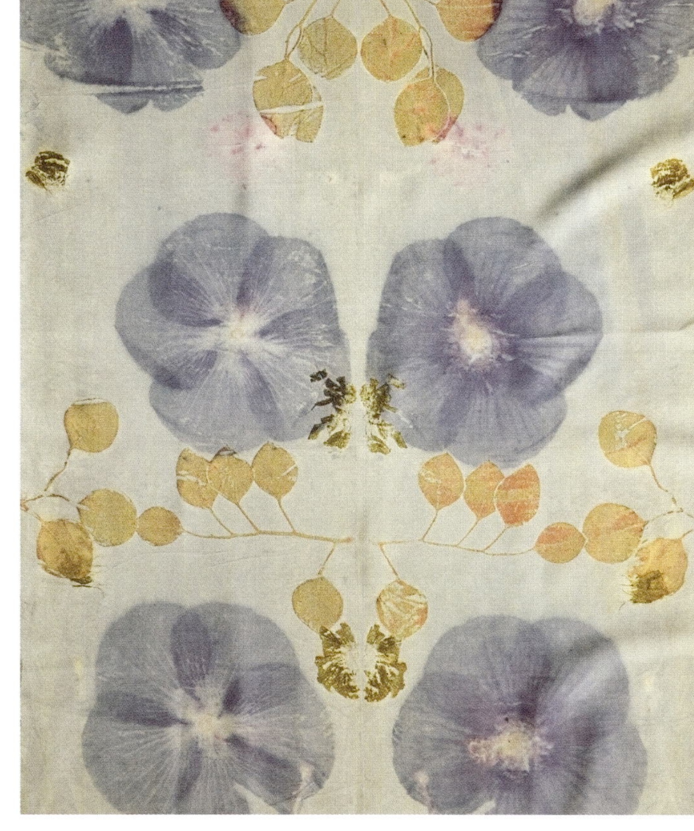

MIRROR IMAGE

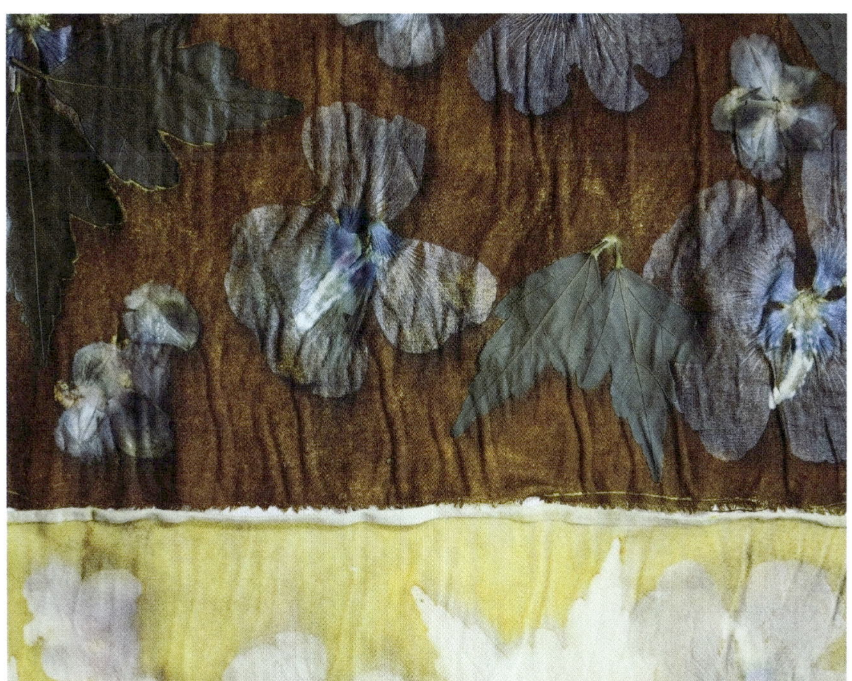

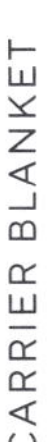

CARRIER BLANKET

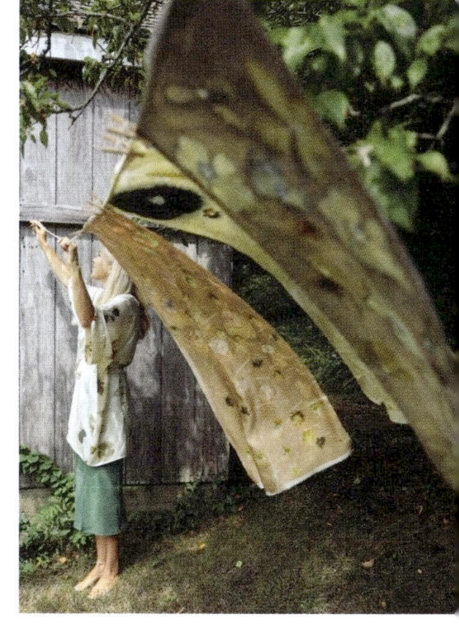

Choosing Textiles

It may not come as a complete surprise that botanical dyes form better bonds with natural fibers than with synthetic ones. Natural fibers fall into two categories: protein and cellulose.

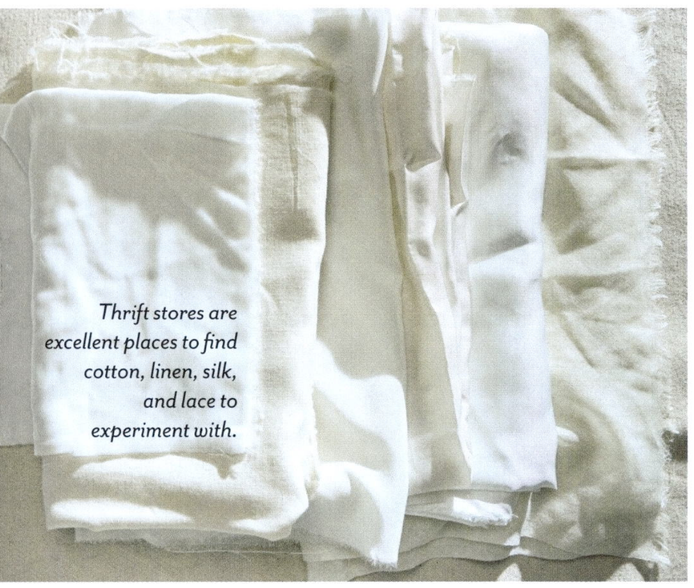

Thrift stores are excellent places to find cotton, linen, silk, and lace to experiment with.

Protein fibers, such as silk, cashmere, and wool, come from animals. These fibers take color brilliantly and produce some of the most vibrant results possible. It's important to note that these superior fabrics can be more costly and may not be the best for experimenting. Consider holding off until you've practiced a given process a few times.

Cellulose fibers come from plants: cotton, linen, hemp, ramie, bamboo, pina, viscose, Tencel, and paper, among others. Cellulose fabrics may take up the plant pigment in a slightly more watercolor-like fashion than protein fibers, with softer hues that are also beautiful. Don't forget that these fabrics must be scoured before using.

The realm of natural fibers is full of luscious possibilities, and I suggest experimenting with as many different ones as you can. There are many options for obtaining certified organic, sustainable, regenerative, or fair-trade fabrics from reliable suppliers around the world. For your first experiments, I highly recommend using cotton, linen, silk, and wool remnants or small swatches.

Synthetic fibers, such as polyester and nylon, aren't nearly as cooperative when it comes to retaining mordant salts and/or botanical pigmentation as natural fibers. I don't recommend experimenting with them.

Semi-synthetic fibers comprise both synthetic and natural components derived from plants (e.g., cellulose from eucalyptus, bamboo, beech, and spruce) but require extensive chemical processing to create fiber. Some of these fibers—rayon blends, silk/velvet, cotton/viscose knit—successfully take up both mordants and botanical pigmentation.

WEIGHING THE FIBER

The amount of mordant you need is based on the dry weight of fiber (WOF) to be mordanted. Before wetting out or scouring your target, weigh it dry and make a note. The following recipes are based on a WOF of 250 grams (½ pound). If you have less than 250 grams of fabric, you can save the excess mordant for later. If the weight exceeds 250 grams, each ingredient in the recipe can be doubled, allowing you to mordant 500 grams (1 pound) of fiber.

You can streamline the process by mordanting large quantities of fabric at one time. Once fabric has been mordanted, it stays that way forever and just needs to be wetted out again before printing on it.

Wetting Out the Target

"Wetting out" is the process of soaking fabric in water prior to scouring or printing. This initial soaking step allows the fibers to open up and release more dirt, oil, and pectin, ensuring both a successful scour and the even distribution of mordant to fiber. Wetting out is useful with cellulose fibers and particularly helpful with vintage linens. It is not necessary for protein fibers or when printing on paper. When it comes time for printing, however, the fabric and paper must be damp and not dry.

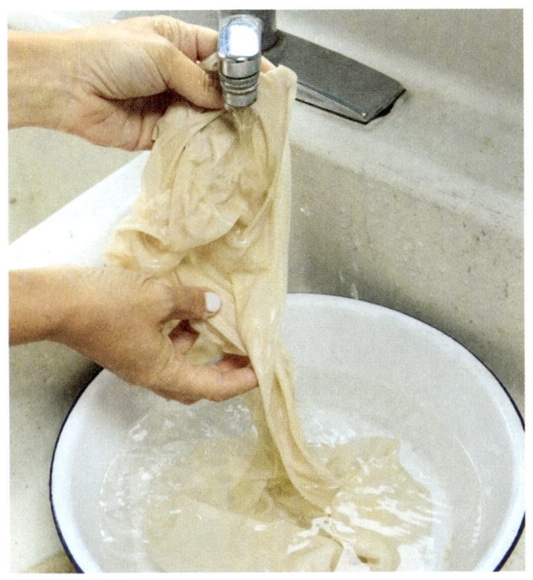

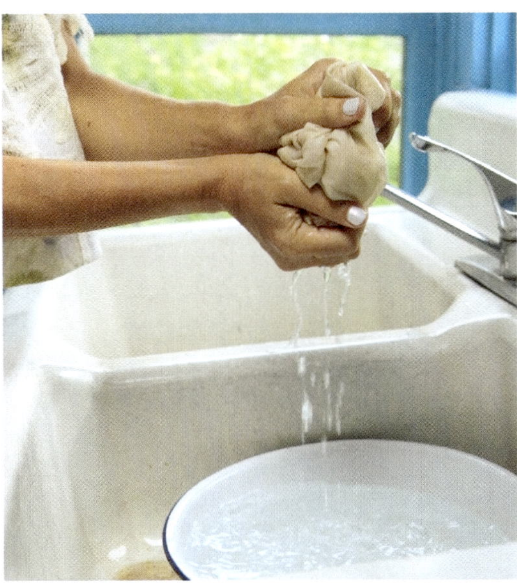

1 Before scouring, fill a large bucket with water and about ⅛ teaspoon of pH-neutral soap. Put the target in the bucket and add as much water as is necessary in order to submerge it.

2 Knead the fabric in the bucket for a few minutes to distribute the soap, then allow it to soak for 2 hours minimum. Wool, raw silk noil, and some types of cellulose textiles can take some time to become fully saturated with water. You can leave the target in the water until you move on to the next step: scouring.

3 When ready, wring out the target over the bucket and transfer to a scouring pot or clean empty vessel.

WETTING OUT MORDANTED FABRIC

Before printing, if your mordanted fabric is dry, you can either dip it in a bucket of water or run it under the tap to wet it. Gently wring out and hang on a line or lay on a clean surface to allow the fabric to partially dry, so it is damp but not dripping with water—if it is too wet, the prints might bleed when steaming, but too dry and the prints won't transfer.

If the fabric gets too dry while decorating, use water from a spray bottle to dampen the fabric.

Scouring the Target

Scouring (washing) prepares the fabric to accept the mordant and plant pigment. It is essential to scour cellulose fibers in order to remove stubborn barriers, including dirt, grease, sizing (starches and polymers that strengthen the fiber), and pectin, which prevent uniform absorption and color distribution.

While it is not critical to scour protein fibers (i.e., from animals), it is usually a good idea to do so. Raw silk contains sericin, a coating from the cocoon of the silkworm, and wool contains dirt and lanolin, all of which can interfere with even dyeing and printing. Vintage linens can hold dirt and buildup within the fabric.

New fabrics labeled as "ready for dyeing" or "ready to dye" or "prepared for dyeing" do not need to be scoured, but they should be wetted out before mordanting.

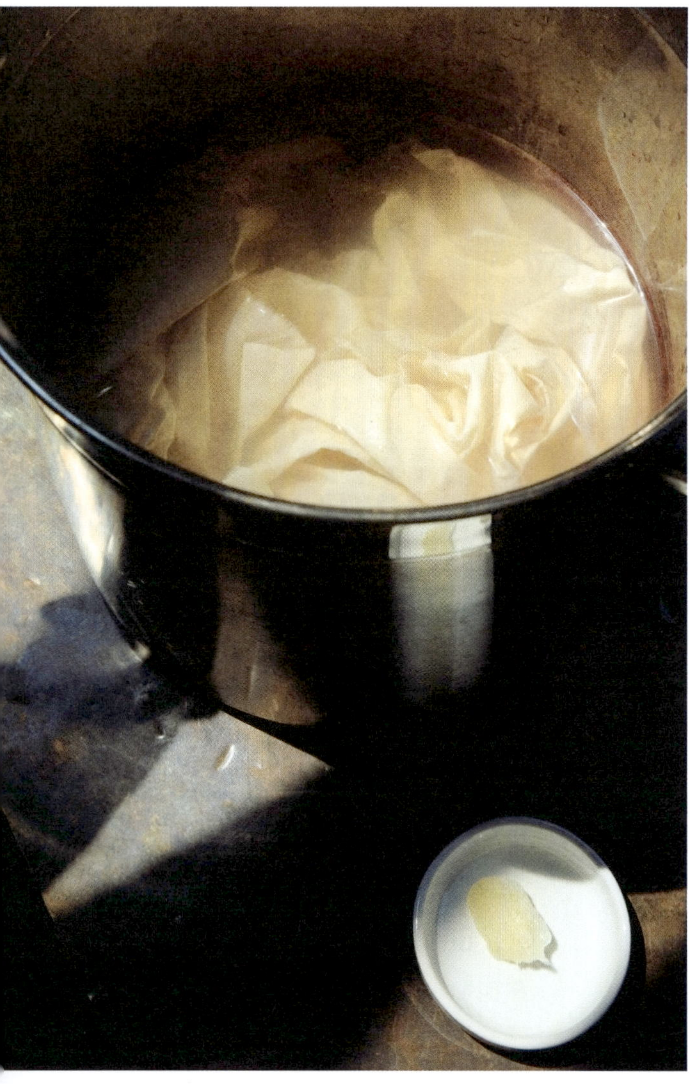

MATERIALS

- Aluminum pot large enough to hold your target immersed in water
- Water (tap is recommended)
- Whisk
- Measuring spoons
- Synthrapol or Liquid Scour (for cellulose fibers)
- Soda ash (for cellulose fibers)
- Orvus Paste Soap (for protein fibers)
- Large spoon or stick for stirring the pot
- Heat source
- Tongs
- Bucket or bowl large enough to hold your target

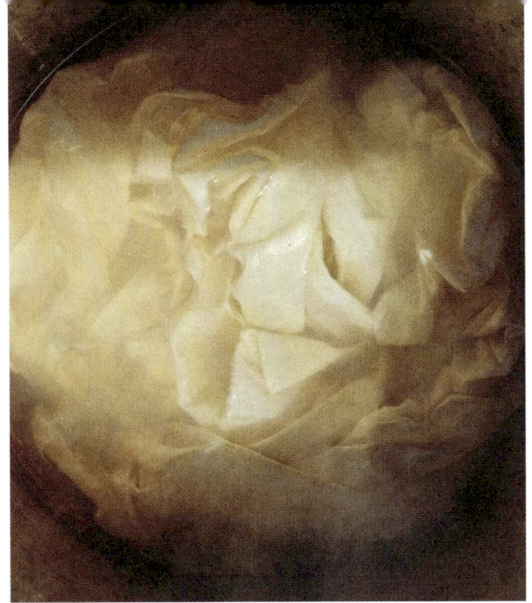

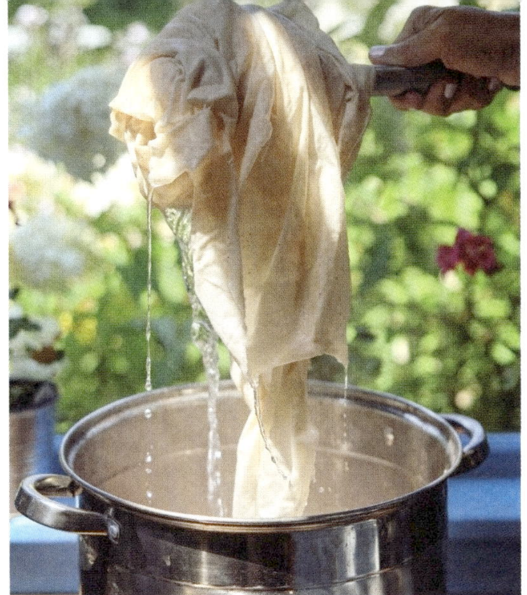

FOR CELLULOSE FIBERS

This is a batch recipe for scouring up to 250 grams (½ pound) of cellulose fabric. You can double the recipe to scour up to 500 grams (1 pound) of fabric.

1. Partially fill the pot with water. Add 5 milliliters (1 teaspoon) Synthrapol or Liquid Scour and 10 grams (2 teaspoons) soda ash and whisk until dissolved.

2. Put the fabric in the pot and add more water to fully submerge it. Occasionally stir and agitate the goods to ensure movement and full saturation.

3. Bring the water to a gentle simmer, around 185°F (85°C), and hold it for 1 hour. The water should be murky when the time is up.

4. Turn off the heat. Allow the fabric to cool in the pot until it reaches a safe temperature for handling. Using tongs, remove the fabric from the pot, place it in the bucket, and rinse under cool running water or plunge into a bucket of cool water. Wring out and hang to dry.

FOR PROTEIN FIBERS

This is a batch recipe for scouring up to 250 grams (½ pound) of protein fabric. You can double the recipe to scour up to 500 grams (1 pound) of fabric.

1. Partially fill the pot with water. Add 2.5 milliliters (½ teaspoon) of Orvus Paste Soap and whisk until dissolved.

2. Put the fabric in the pot and add enough water to fully submerge it. Occasionally stir and agitate the goods to ensure movement and full saturation.

3. Bring the water to around 140°F (60°C) and hold it for 1 hour without letting it reach a simmer. The water should be murky.

4. Turn off the heat. Allow the fabric to cool in the pot until it reaches a safe temperature for handling. Using tongs, remove the fabric from the pot, place it in the bucket, and rinse under cool running water for a few seconds or plunge into a bucket of cool water. Wring out and hang to dry.

Mordanting

Mordanting is the process of soaking your target, be it fabric or paper, prior to printing, in a solution of metallic salts; this increases the capacity of the fibers to accept pigmentation and makes color last longer. Mordanted fabric can be stored for a long time before being used; it simply needs to be wetted out with water before printing.

After years of experimentation, I rely primarily on two distinct mordanting methods, each with variations for specific outcomes. The following formulas use combinations of nontoxic (in small doses) ingredients that bond to both cellulose and protein fibers to create colorful results. My intent is to streamline a rather complex process full of variables and offer a solid foundation you can build from; this way, you'll have the freedom to be creative and have fun while meeting certain expectations.

None of these recipes require a heat source. They can be made with room-temperature tap water (or rainwater) or, when called for, distilled white vinegar. The variations in results occur by altering the amounts of each ingredient or by changing the type of aluminum in the recipe. I call these two recipes the Fundamental Mordant and the Compound Mordant. Here are examples of the effects produced by each.

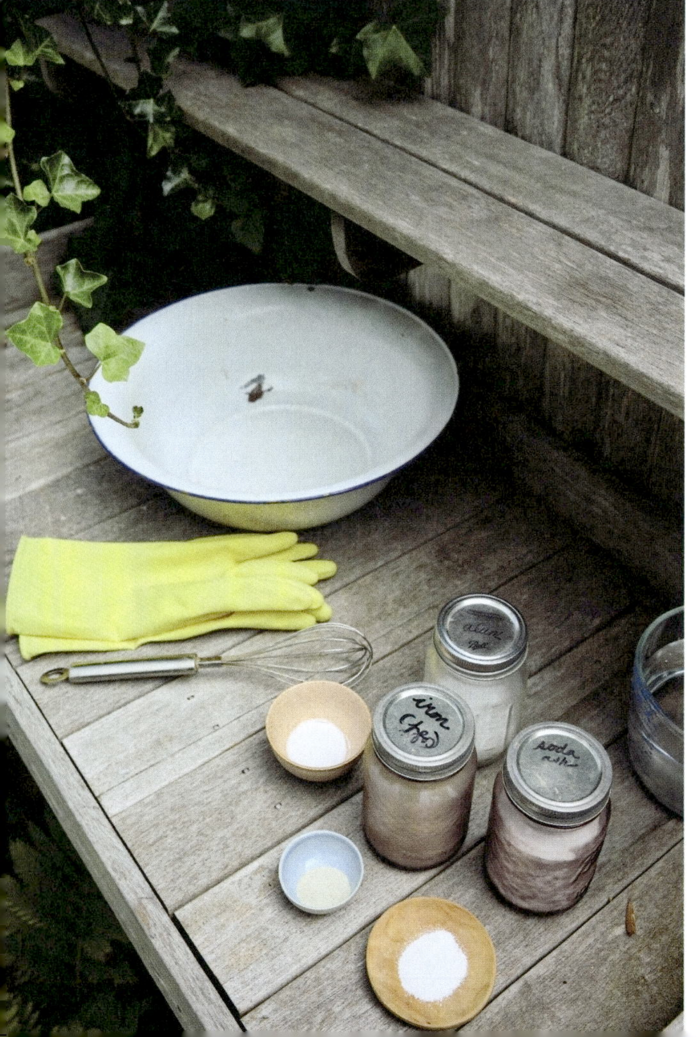

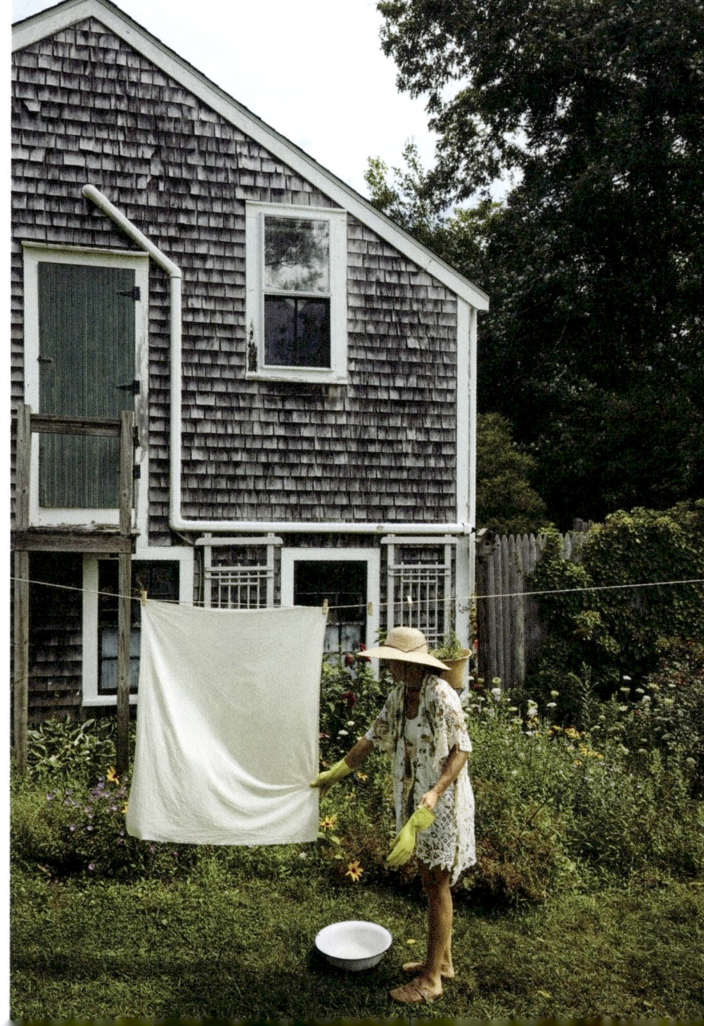

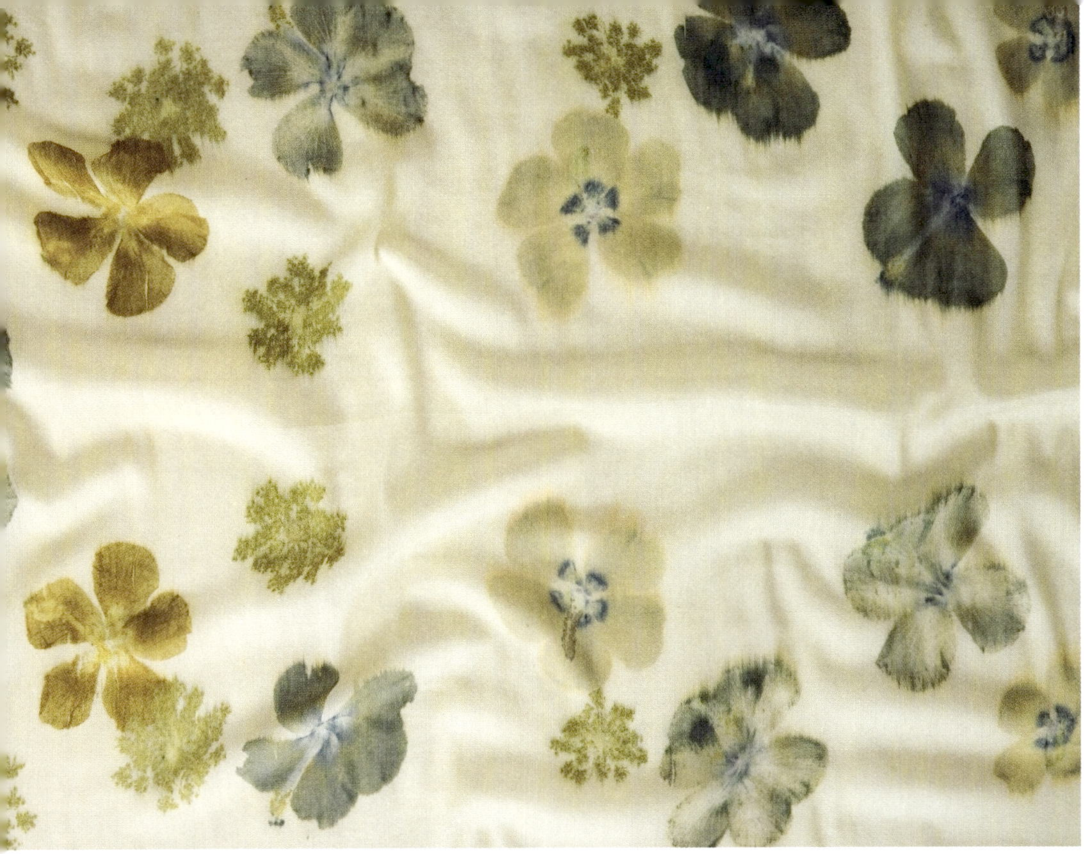

top:
The Fundamental Mordant Recipe: *rose of Sharon, hibiscus, and Queen Anne's lace printed on silk/wool*

bottom left:
The Compound Mordant Dark Outcome: *Queen Anne's lace printed on silk/hemp*

bottom right:
The Compound Mordant Bright Outcome: *sulfur cosmos printed on silk/hemp*

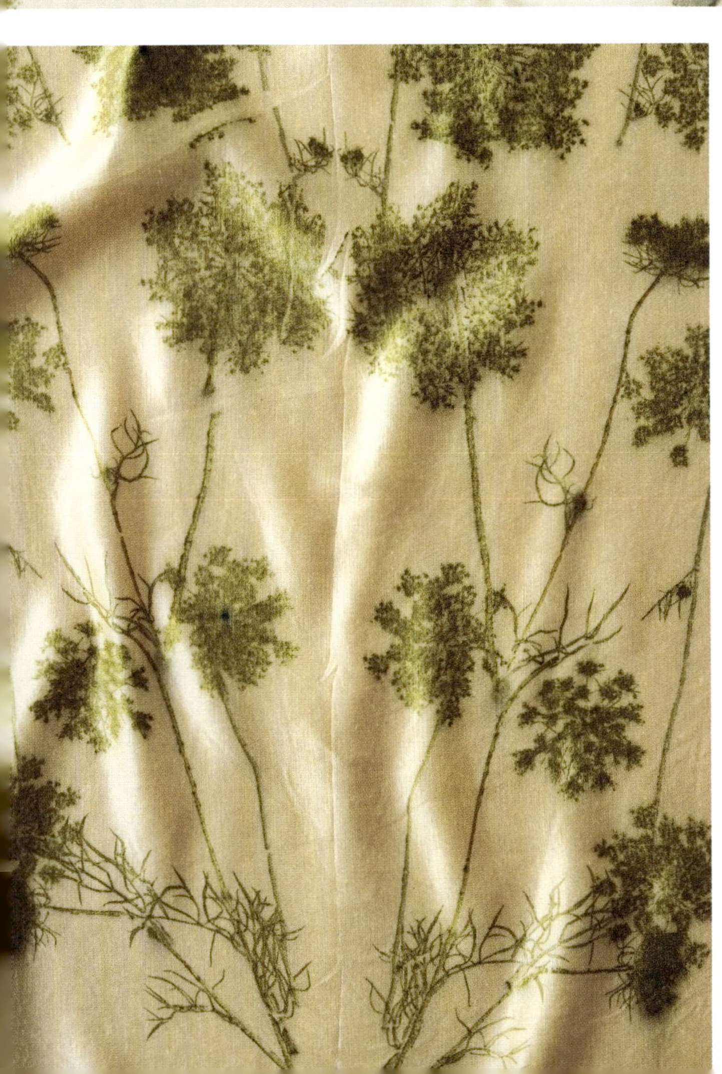

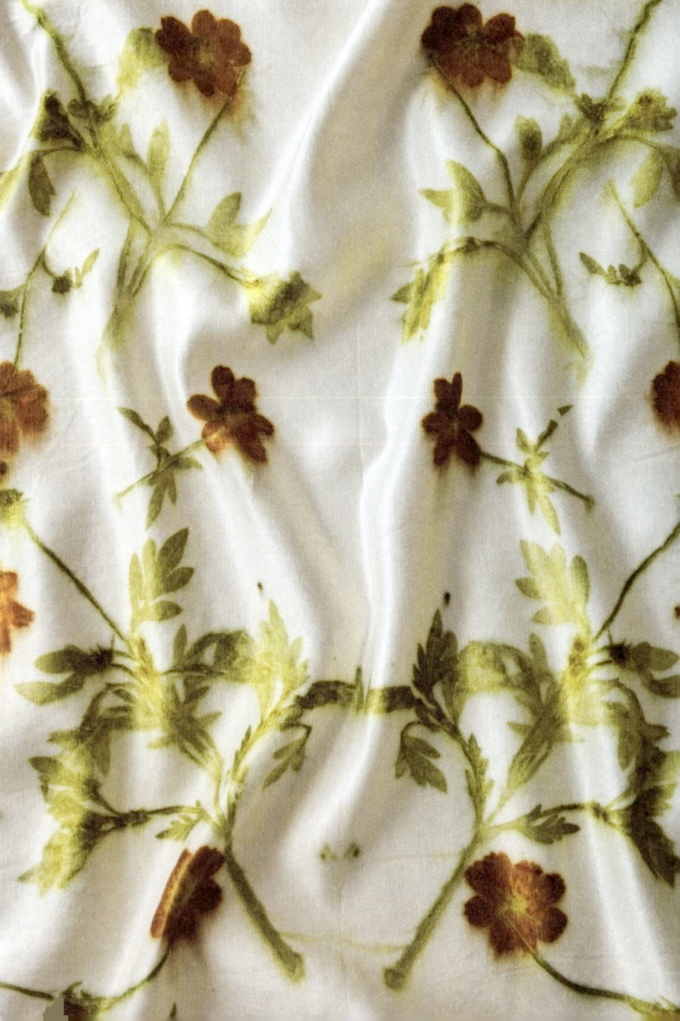

THE FUNDAMENTAL MORDANT RECIPE

This is the simplest mordanting method in this book and is suitable for both cellulose and protein fibers. Use this recipe for creating prints with a pure white background and expect saturated imprints and bright bursts of color.

This batch recipe can mordant up to 250 grams (½ pound) of fiber: Make a note of how much your fabric weighs when dry before making the mordant. Aluminum triformate is not always readily available. If necessary, you may substitute it with 50 grams of potassium aluminum sulfate. After mordanting 250 grams of fiber with the batch recipe, the batch should be considered exhausted, and a new batch should be created.

This recipe offers the option of doing a ferrous sulfate dip directly before printing. Use this step if printing with leaves or if you wish to create darkened or less saturated imprints from vegetation.

MATERIALS

- Target fabric
- Mask and gloves
- Small vessel for weighing aluminum triformate
- Precision scale
- 10 grams aluminum triformate
- Whisk
- Clean 5- to 12-gallon plastic bucket for wetting out and mordanting
- Measuring cup

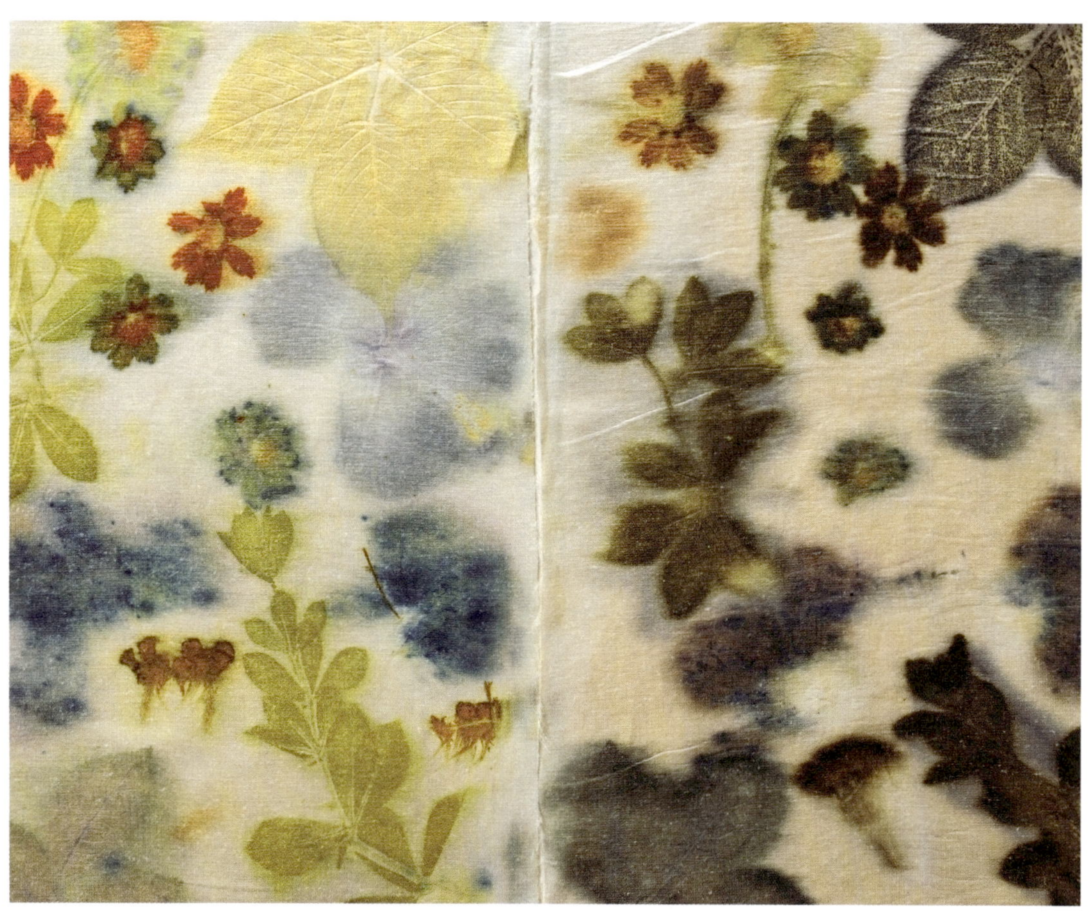

Both of these samples were mordanted using the Fundamental Mordant recipe, which provides bright, saturated colors. The sample on the right was then dipped in ferrous sulfate, which adds contrast and gives darker imprints.

STEPS

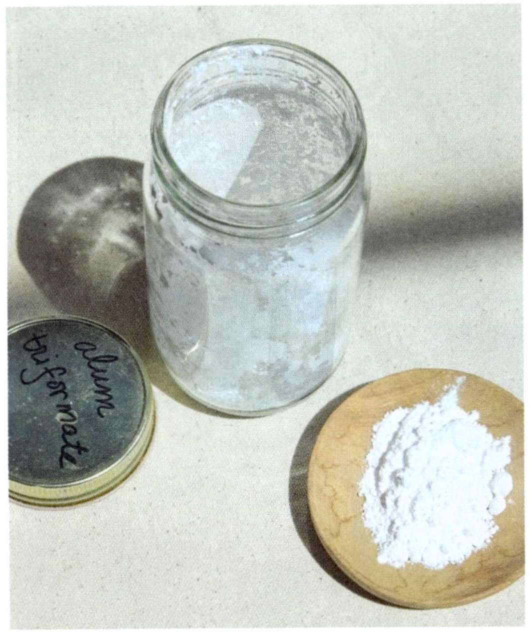

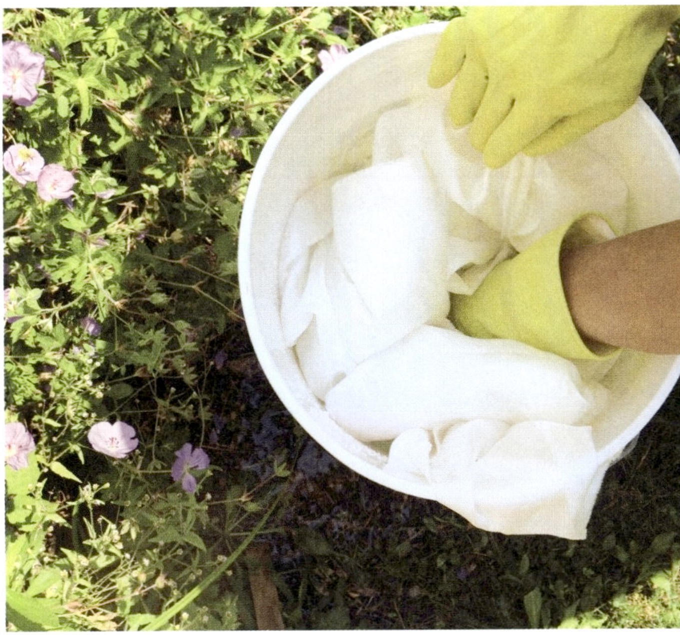

1 **Wet out the fabric** for printing by following the steps on page 113. Wearing a mask, place the small vessel onto the scale and press "tare" to bring the weight to zero. Weigh out the aluminum triformate. Remove the vessel from the scale, add a bit of warm (not hot) water, and whisk until the powder is completely dissolved.

2 **Add the liquid** to the bucket, then add about 4 liters (1 gallon) of water and stir with the whisk. The water should be clear with a slightly blueish tint. Wearing gloves, add the target textiles to the bucket and work them into the mordant for a few moments. If necessary, add more water—enough to allow the fabric to move freely and be completely submerged.

3 **Allow the fabric to soak** for at least 8 hours in the mordant. It can soak for days without going bad if it is lidded and kept out of heat and sun. After the allotted time, gently wring out the fabric and rinse well using cool water. At this point, you can hang the fabric to dry and store it for later projects. If you are ready to print, move on to decorating the target or prepare a ferrous sulfate bath if desired.

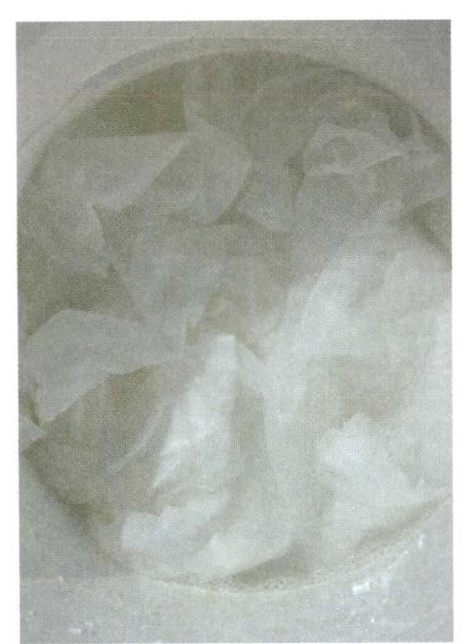

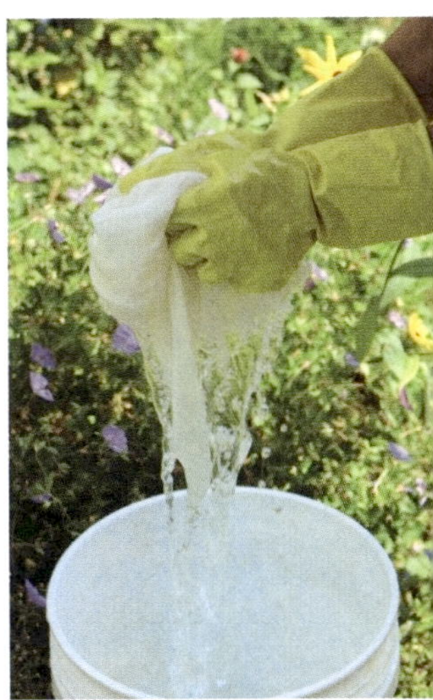

Variation: Ferrous Sulfate Bath for Dark Outcome

Ferrous sulfate, or iron, is a mighty ingredient, and a little bit goes a very long way. Too much iron can damage silk and wool, so measure it carefully. Add the target to an iron bath immediately before printing because iron oxidizes rapidly in water and can add unwanted yellowing to the textile.

The amount of iron should be between 1 and 2.5 percent of the WOF. Use around 1 percent ferrous sulfate for more saturated results or go up to 2.5 percent for darker results.
For 100 grams of fiber, the calculation is 100 grams of fiber × 1 percent iron = 1 gram of iron.
For each 100 grams of fiber, use 2 liters (½ gallon) of cold water.

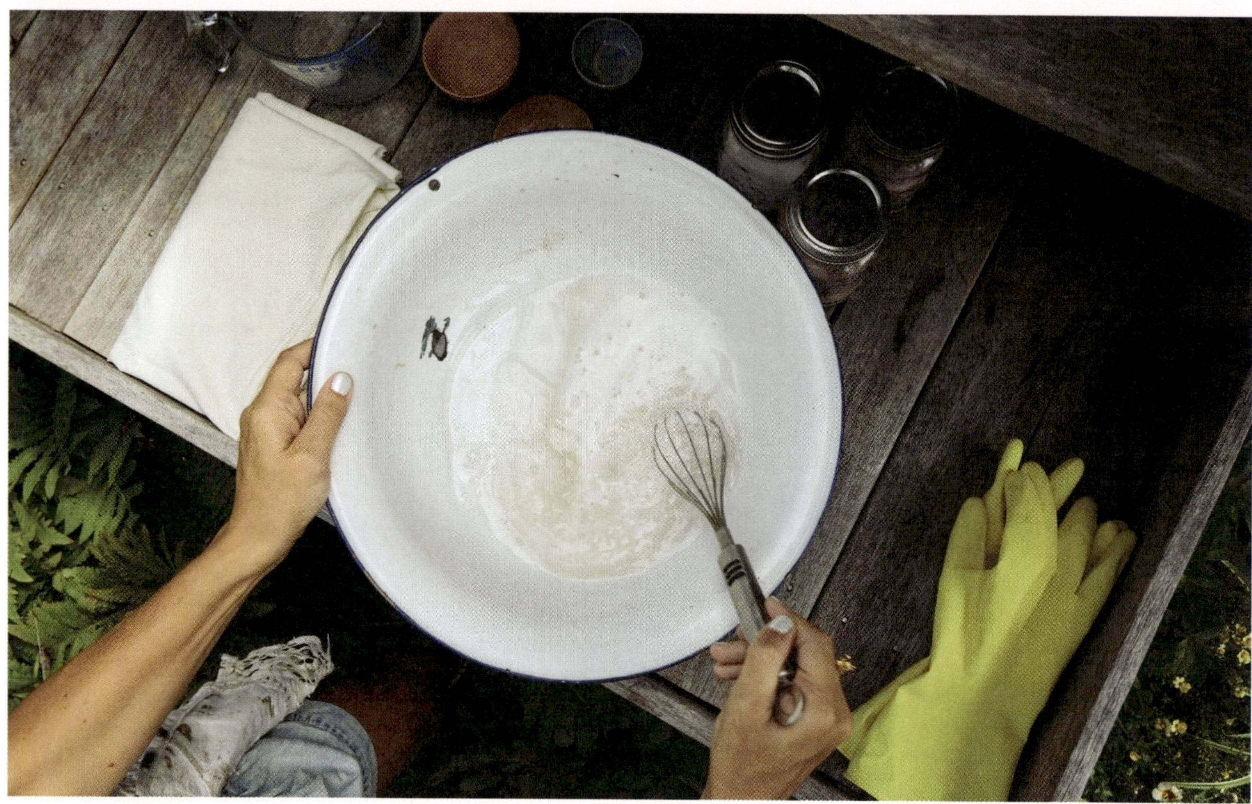

MATERIALS

- Mask and gloves
- Precision scale
- 1–2.5 grams ferrous sulfate (or more, based on WOF)
- Plastic or stainless steel mixing vessel
- 2 liters (½ gallon) cold tap water
- Whisk or spoon

STEPS

1 **Wearing a mask,** weigh out the ferrous sulfate and add to the mixing vessel. Add the water and whisk until the powder is fully dissolved—this may take a minute or so.

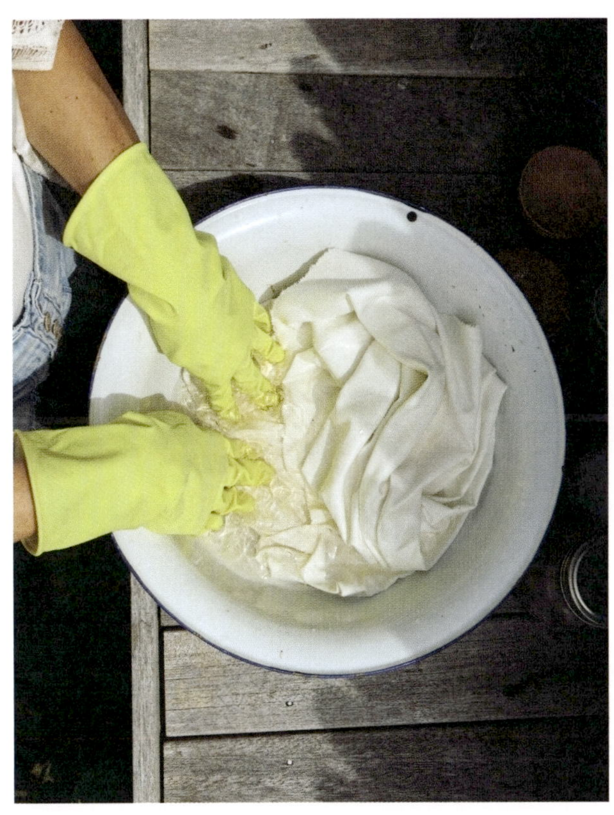

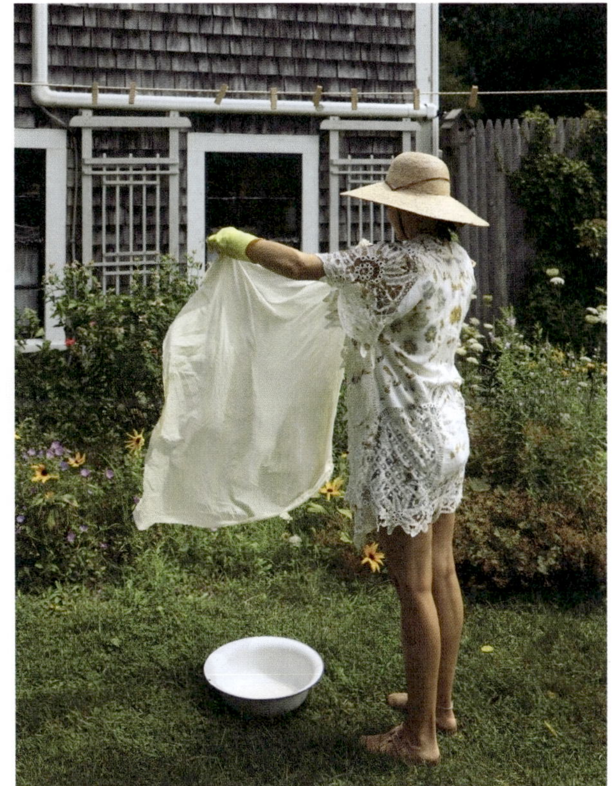

2 **Wearing gloves,** immerse the target in the solution and work it with your hands for about 15 seconds.

3 **Gently wring out** the target and allow it to dry slightly on a rack or line; it should be damp, not dripping wet, when you lay it on your printing surface to decorate with botanicals. After a few minutes, the leftover iron water will begin to oxidize and turn yellow and can be rinsed down the drain.

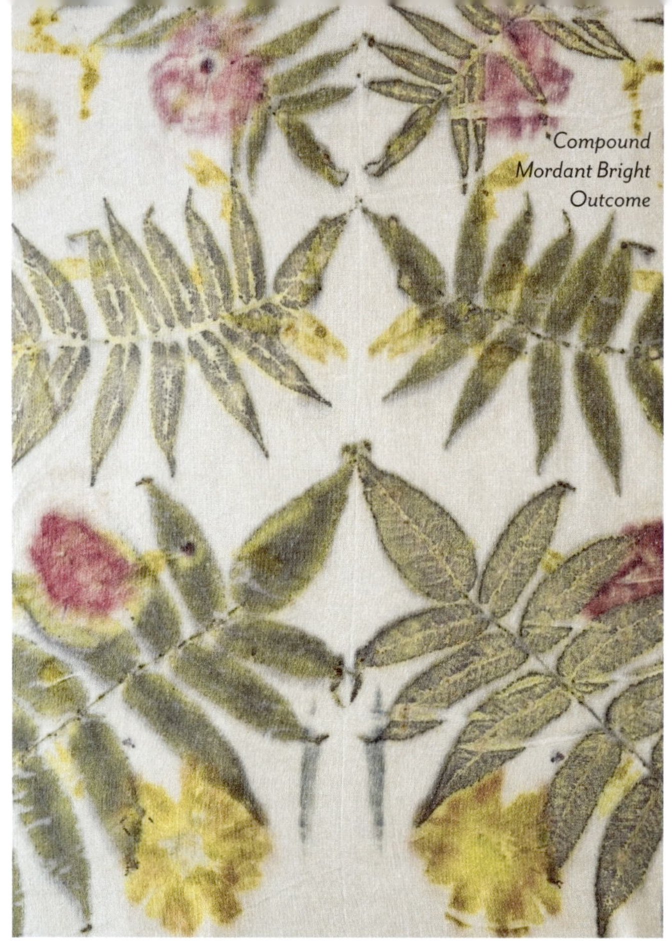

Compound Mordant Bright Outcome

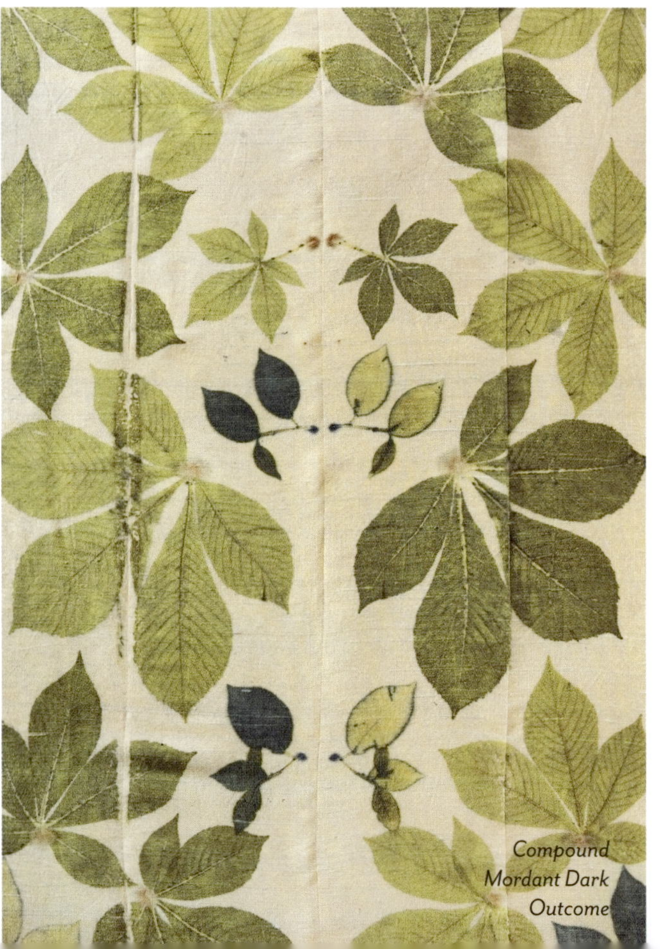

Compound Mordant Dark Outcome

THE COMPOUND MORDANT RECIPE

This compound mordant is suitable for protein and cellulose fibers. It is made with three ingredients—potassium aluminum sulfate (PAS), ferrous sulfate, and soda ash—mixed with distilled white vinegar. This recipe was adapted from chemist and botanist Michel Garcia's recipe for natural dyeing featured in the DVD *Colors of Provence Using Sustainable Methods*. Here, in place of calcium hydroxide (which can cause yellowing to the target fabric), use soda ash. With this recipe, the fabric is not wetted out but added to the solution dry and then allowed to fully dry again; this lets the vinegar evaporate and strengthens the bond of mordant to fiber. The last step is to bathe the fabric in an oatmeal bath to further ensure the metallic bond.

This batch recipe can mordant up to 250 grams (½ pound) of fiber; make a note of how much your fabric weighs when dry before making the mordant. After mordanting 250 grams of fiber with the batch recipe, the batch should be considered exhausted and a new batch created.

The compound mordant can be made in two ways, depending on the desired outcome: bright or dark. Use the bright outcome variation for vibrant and natural coloring and the dark outcome variation for a darker, bolder effect. Both variations can be used to print vegetation on a white background, but they can also be used to create intensely colored compositions when combined with carrier blankets (see Technique 3, page 152).

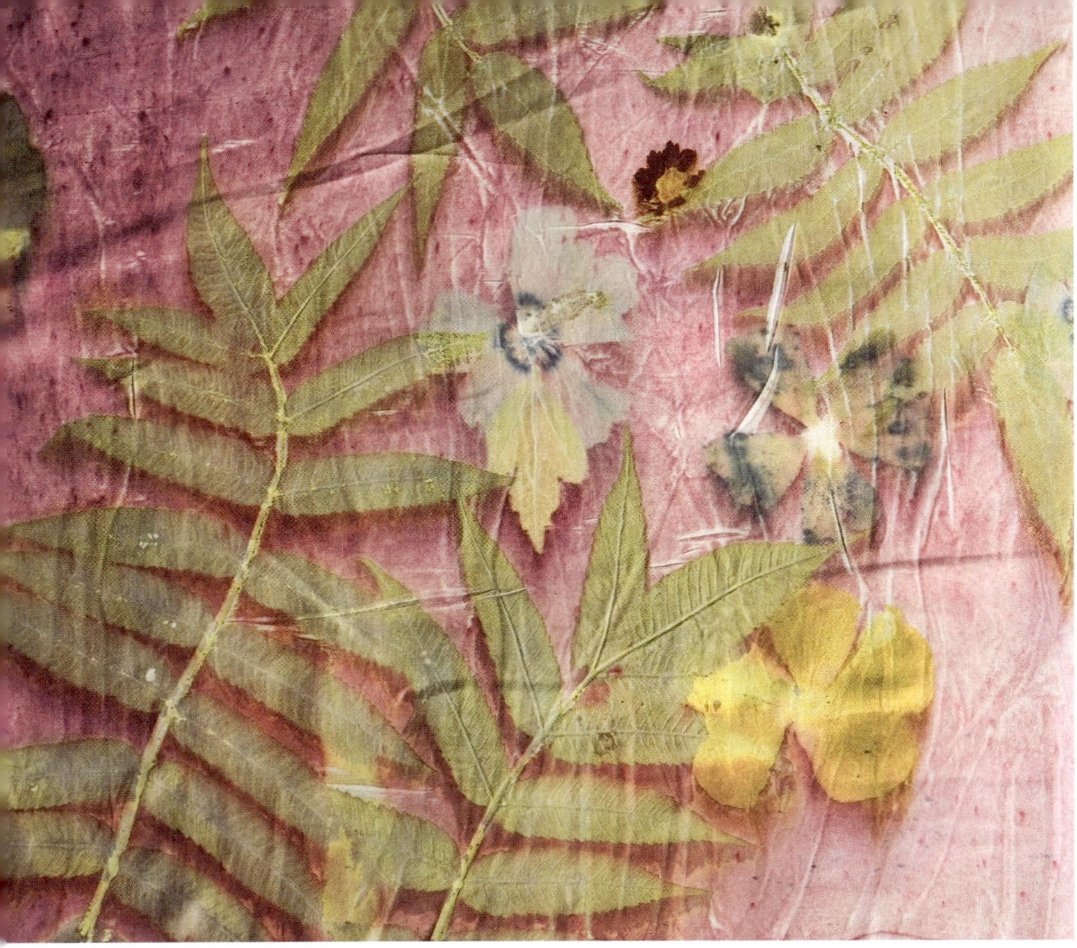

To create a composition with a bright and colorful background from a carrier blanket, use the Bright Outcome recipe and the colorful carrier blanket option in Technique 3 *(see page 156).*

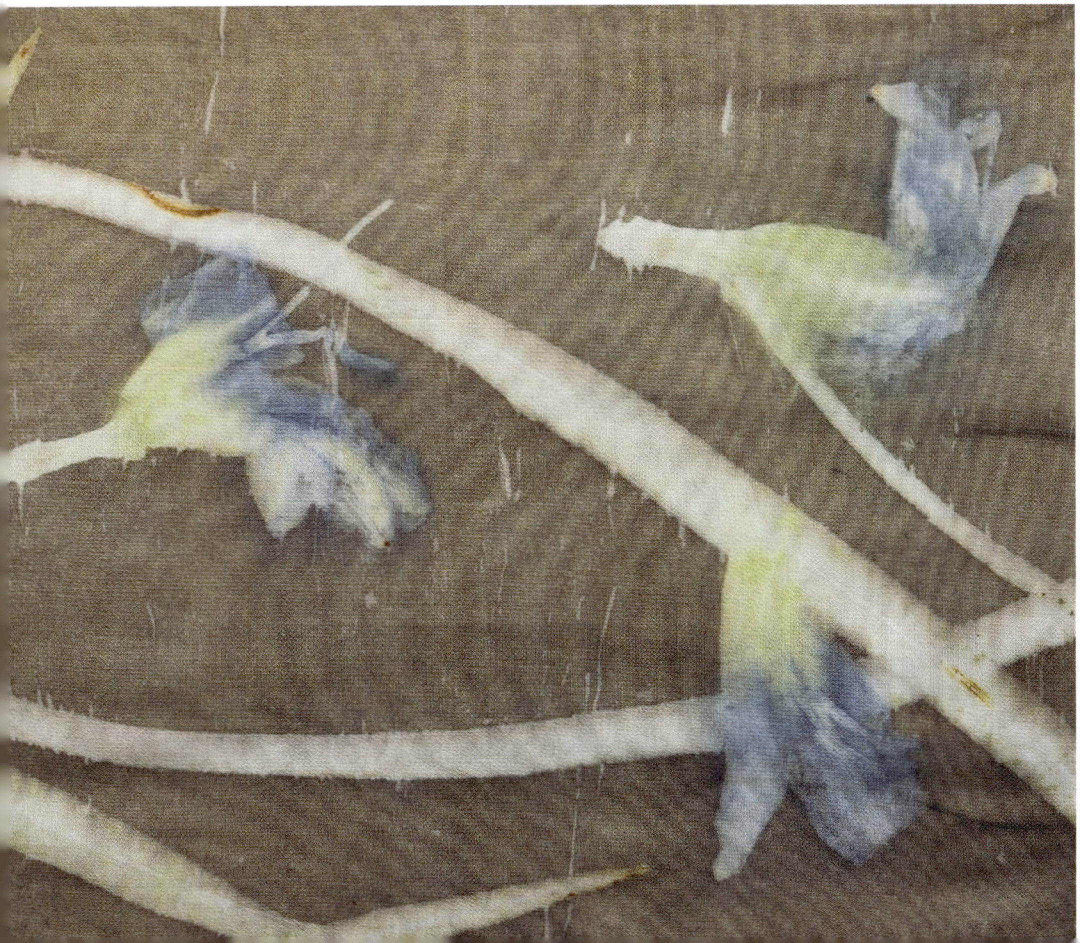

To create a composition with a compellingly dark background from a carrier blanket, use the Dark Outcome recipe and the dark carrier blanket option in Technique 3 *(see page 157).*

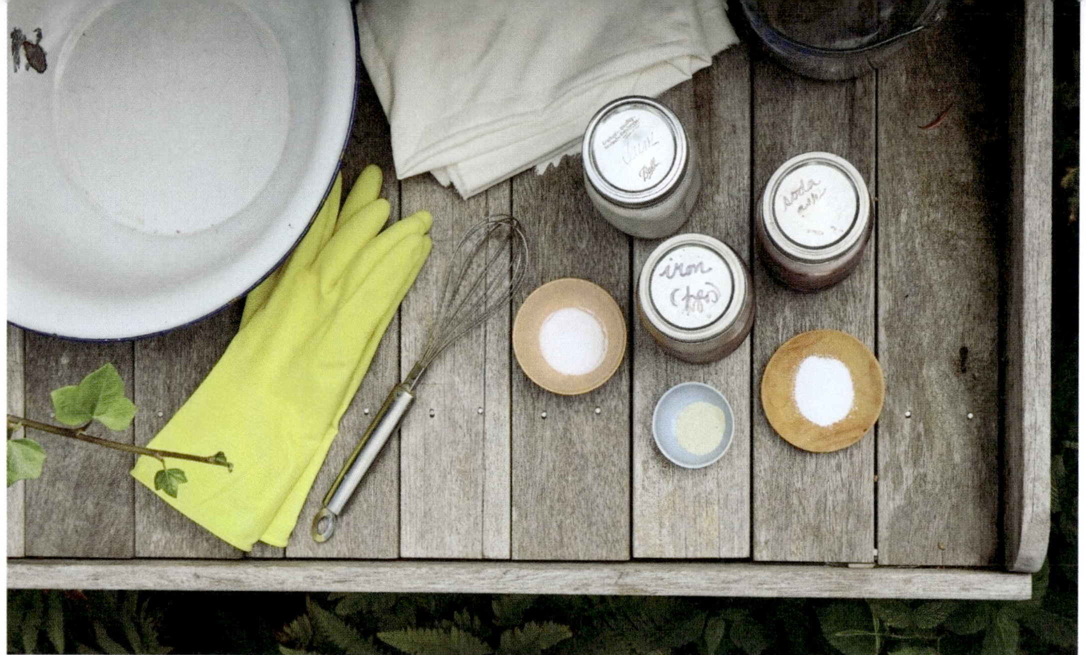

THE COMPOUND MORDANT RECIPE

MATERIALS

- Mask
- Precision scale
- Measuring cup
- Plastic or stainless steel mixing vessel
- Whisk
- Gloves
- Target fabric

TO MORDANT 250 GRAMS (½ POUND) OF FIBER

- 50 grams potassium aluminum sulfate (PAS)
- ½ liter (½ quart) distilled white vinegar

Ferrous Sulfate

- Bright Outcome: 1–2 grams
- Dark Outcome: 5-10 grams

Soda Ash

- Bright Outcome: 25 grams
- Dark Outcome: 30 grams

STEPS

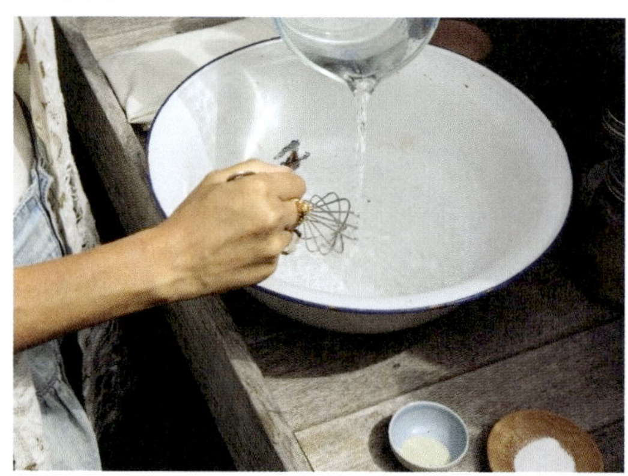

1 **Wearing a mask,** measure the PAS and add it to the vessel. Add the vinegar and whisk until the PAS is completely dissolved.

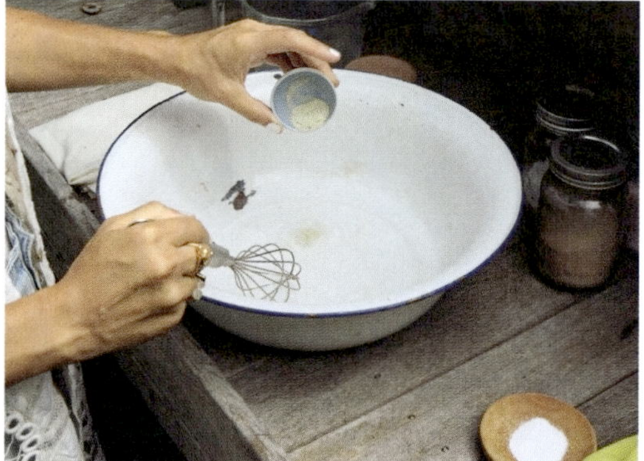

2 **Add the ferrous sulfate** to the vessel and whisk until completely dissolved. All particles must be fully dissolved before adding the soda ash to prevent the mordant from becoming murky or discolored.

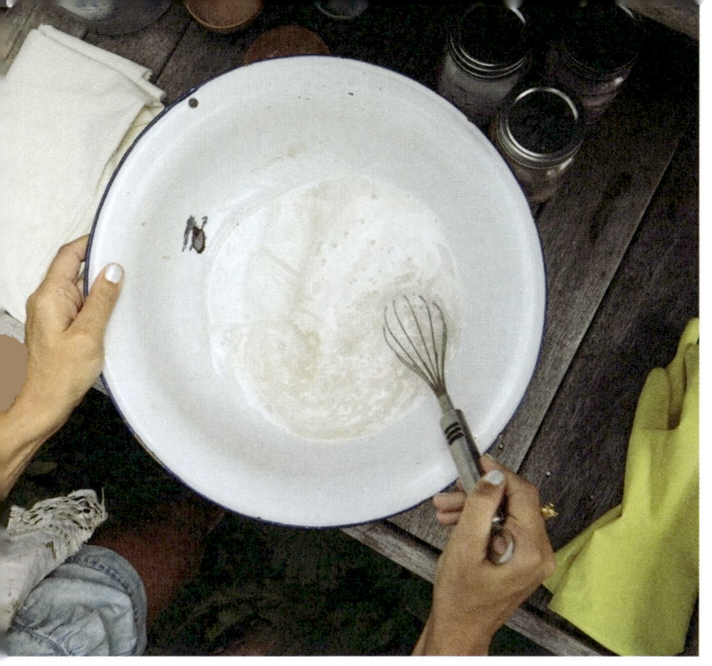

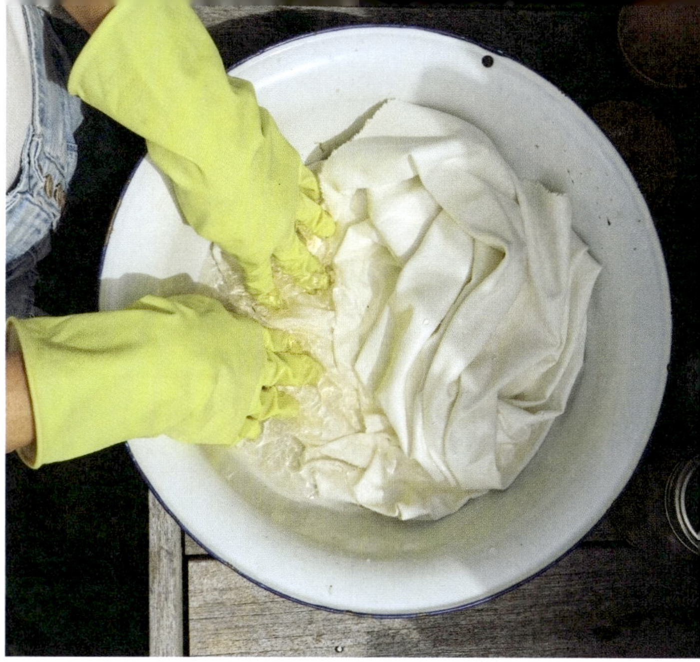

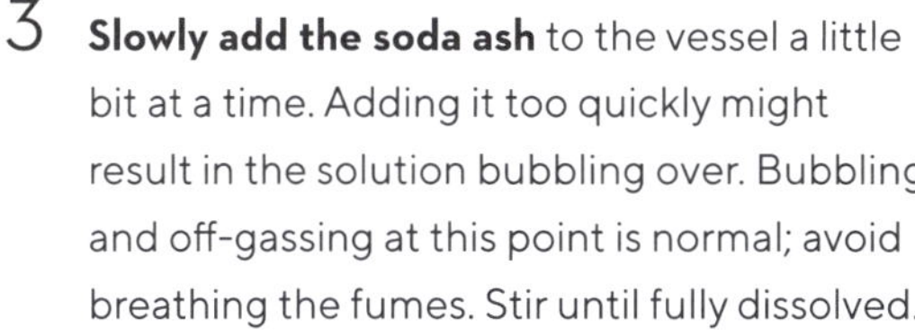

3 **Slowly add the soda ash** to the vessel a little bit at a time. Adding it too quickly might result in the solution bubbling over. Bubbling and off-gassing at this point is normal; avoid breathing the fumes. Stir until fully dissolved.

4 **Wearing gloves,** add the dry fabric to the solution and work into the mordant for 1 to 2 minutes.

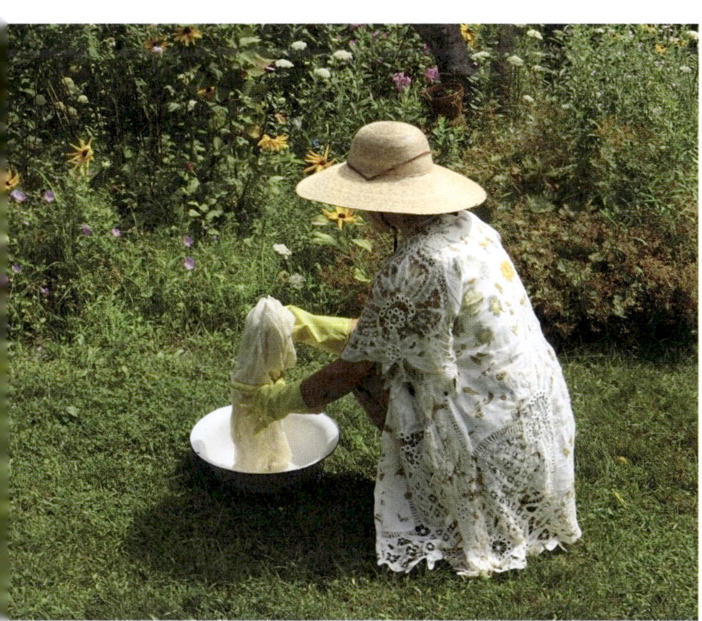

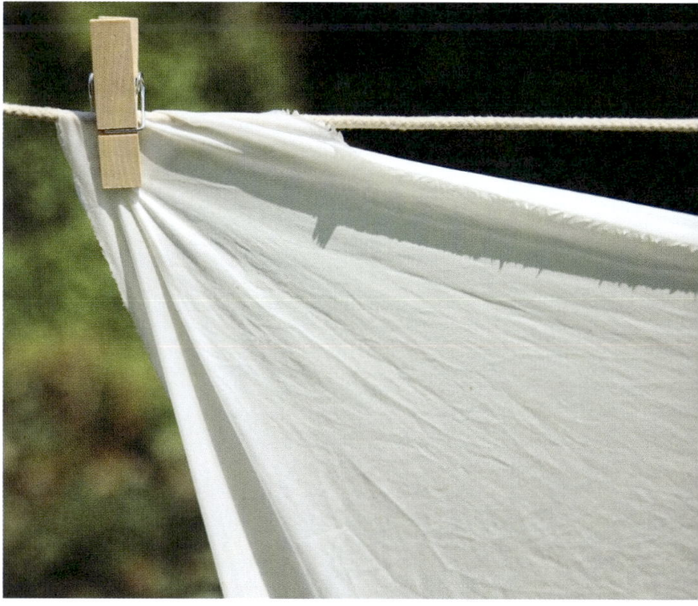

5 **Remove the saturated fabric** from the mordant and gently wring it out over the vessel, being careful to preserve any excess liquid.

6 **Fasten the fabric** to a clothesline or drying rack with clothespins. Pin it corner to corner with no folds or overlaps, pulling the fabric taut so that the mordant fully coats the fibers. If the fabric is folded onto itself, streaking can result.

THE COMPOUND MORDANT RECIPE *continued*

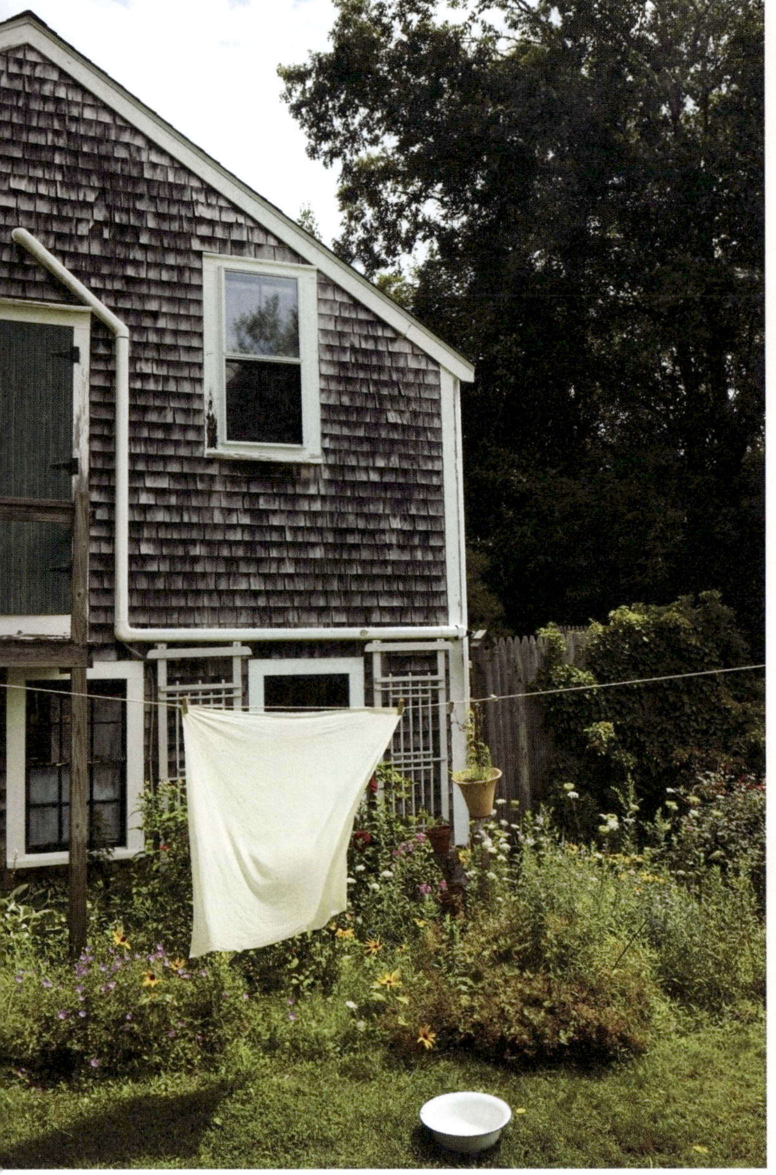

RECIPE BY WEIGHT OF FIBER (WOF)

If you wish to make a batch of mordant specific to the actual weight of your fabric, you can weigh your fabric dry, take a note of it, and follow this equation:

FOR BRIGHT OUTCOME

- 20% weight of fiber (WOF) in potassium aluminum sulfate (PAS)
- 0.2–0.5% WOF in ferrous sulfate
- 5% WOF in soda ash

FOR DARK OUTCOME

- 20% WOF in PAS
- 2–3% WOF in ferrous sulfate
- 6% WOF in soda ash

If your fabric weighs 100 grams, the measurements would be as follows:

100 grams of dry fabric
× 20 percent potassium aluminum sulfate
= 20 grams potassium aluminum sulfate, and so forth.

7 **When the fabric has dried** completely, it will be stiff and coated in a light powder of mordant. As soon as possible, soak it in the oatmeal bath solution according to the instructions on the facing page. This step is important to ensure that all stray mordant powders are rinsed away; it also helps the mordant bite onto the fiber and stay.

Fixing the Compound Mordant with an Oatmeal Bath

Complete this step after mordanting fiber in one of the Compound Mordant recipes. The bath helps remove any stray mordant molecules left on the fibers from the mordanting process and strengthens the bond of metallic salts to fiber, enhancing the quality of the print.

This solution can be used to fix more fiber. Store covered in a cool, dry place for up to three days. If bubbles or mold form or it begins to smell, dispose of the batch.

MATERIALS

- 1 cup (80 grams) oatmeal or wheat bran
- Square of cheesecloth or other fine-mesh fabric, or a nylon stocking, large enough to contain the oatmeal in a bundle
- String
- Medium bowl
- Vessel large enough to hold the target

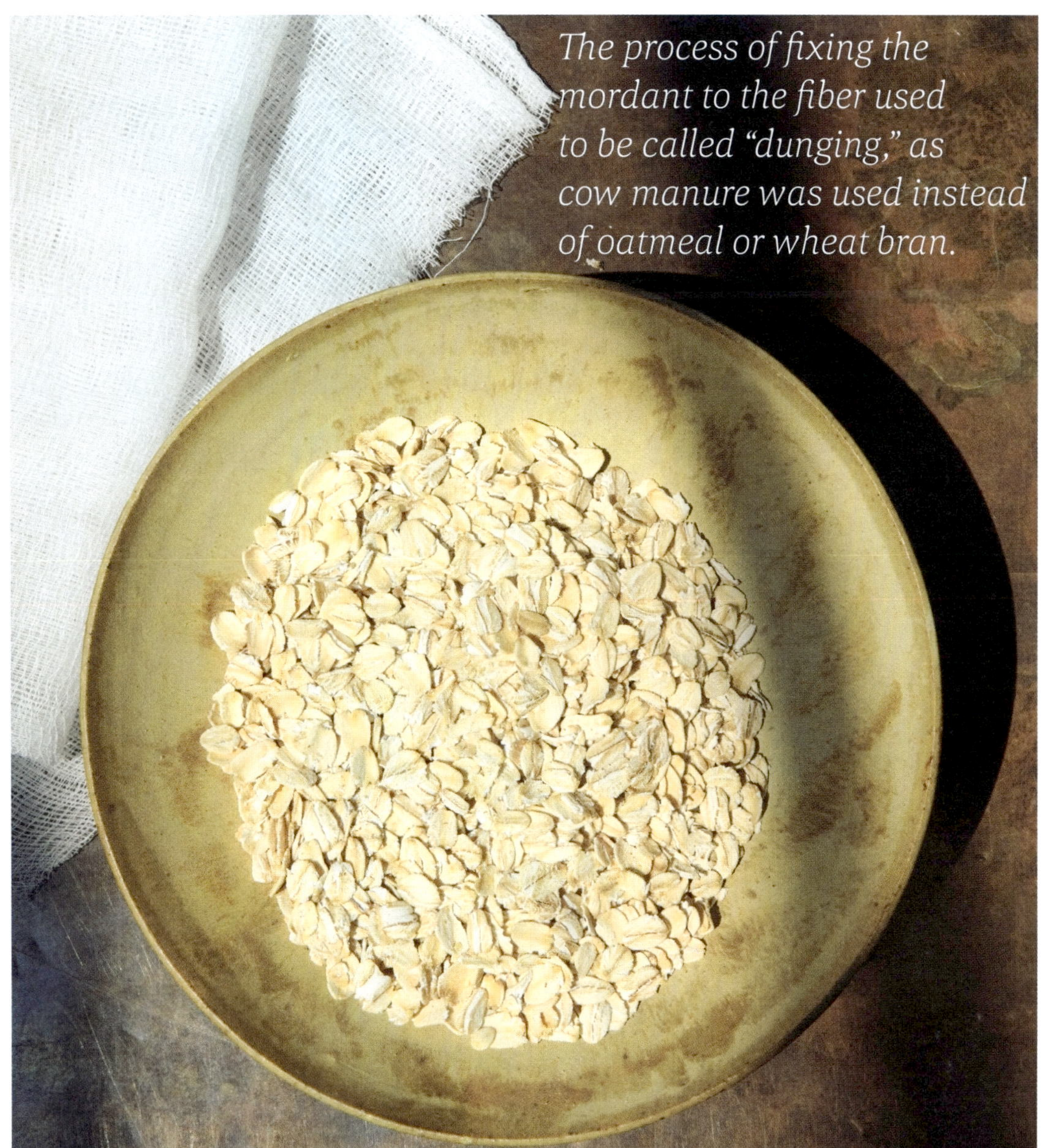

The process of fixing the mordant to the fiber used to be called "dunging," as cow manure was used instead of oatmeal or wheat bran.

OATMEAL BATH *continued*

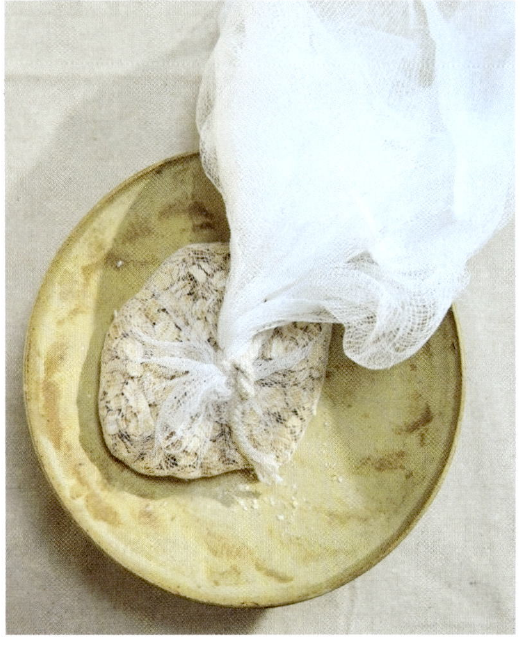

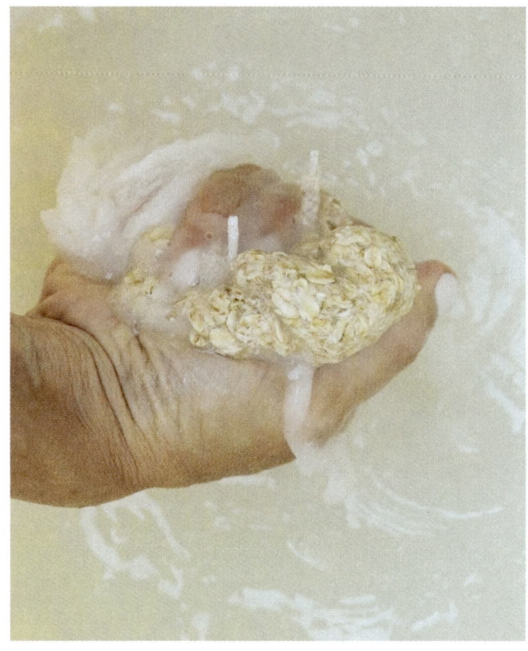

STEPS

1 **Place the oatmeal** into the cheesecloth square and tie it into a bundle. Fill the bowl with about 2 liters (½ gallon) of warm water and place the bundle into the bowl.

2 **Work the bundle** in the water with your hands for a few minutes, until the oatmeal is saturated, then let it steep for 15 to 20 minutes, or until the solution turns milky. Remove the bundle and discard it.

3 **Pour the solution** into the vessel and add enough cold or room-temperature water to fully submerge the target. Add the target to the vessel and work it with your hands to agitate the bath, then let soak for 5 to 10 minutes. Remove the target from the bath and rinse with tap water or plunge into a bucket of water to wash off stray particles. Gently wring out the target until it is damp, not dripping. You can print with it at this point or hang it to dry for later use.

SOY MILK AS MORDANT AND FIXER

Soy milk has historically been used as a pretreatment ingredient in indigo dyeing practices in Japan and is still used in the making of botanical printing pastes and as part of the mordanting process for cellulose fibers. The soy protein in the milk acts as a binder and improves colorfastness on targets that are not protein rich. Protein fibers, such as silk and wool, form a natural bond with botanical pigments and mordants, but cellulose fibers, such as cotton and paper, lack protein and can be more difficult to saturate with plant-derived color. A soy milk bath adds a layer of protein to the cellulose fiber, potentially making for more colorful prints when used in combination with the Compound Mordant recipe (see page 122).

While this step is not crucial, it is worth mentioning in case one wishes to experiment with enhanced mordant processes. Some people prefer to only use soy milk as mordant for fabric and paper, and while the results might not be as colorfast as the metallic-based mordants in this book, it is a safer and simpler option, especially for children, that eliminates potentially harmful inhalation of the mordant powders.

RECIPE: Soy Milk Bath for Cellulose Fibers
This bath can be completed after mordanting cellulose fabrics with either the Fundamental or Compound Mordant recipe, to add a protein-rich component to the target. Alternatively, it can be used alone as a simple mordant for cellulose fibers. The color- and washfastness might not be as long lasting as a metallic mordant if the bath is used without mordanting. Use unflavored, unsweetened soy milk, preferably organic.

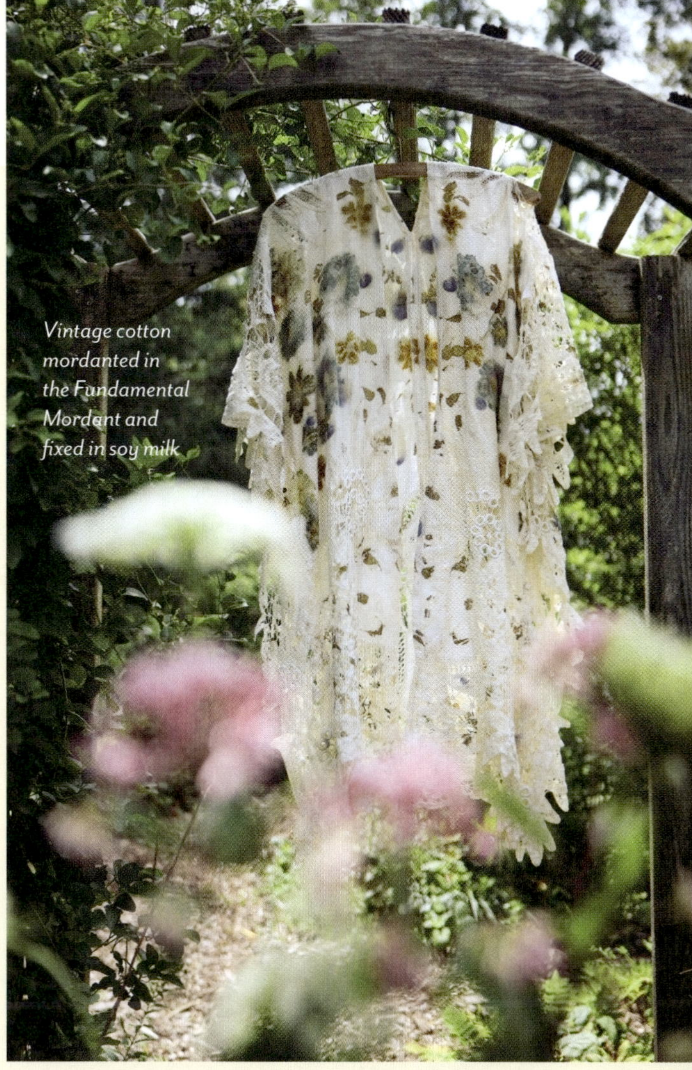

Vintage cotton mordanted in the Fundamental Mordant and fixed in soy milk

1. **Place 1 liter (1 quart)** of soy milk into a bucket and top off with enough water to allow the fibers to be submerged and move freely.
2. **Add the wetted-out fibers** to the bucket, check the water level to ensure the fabric can move freely, and let soak for 12 hours.
3. **Gently agitate** and stir the mixture from time to time.
4. **After 12 hours,** remove the fiber from the soy milk bath and wring out over the bucket. Hang to dry completely. When fully dry, rinse well, and the item is ready to print. Alternatively, you can allow to dry and then store for future printing.

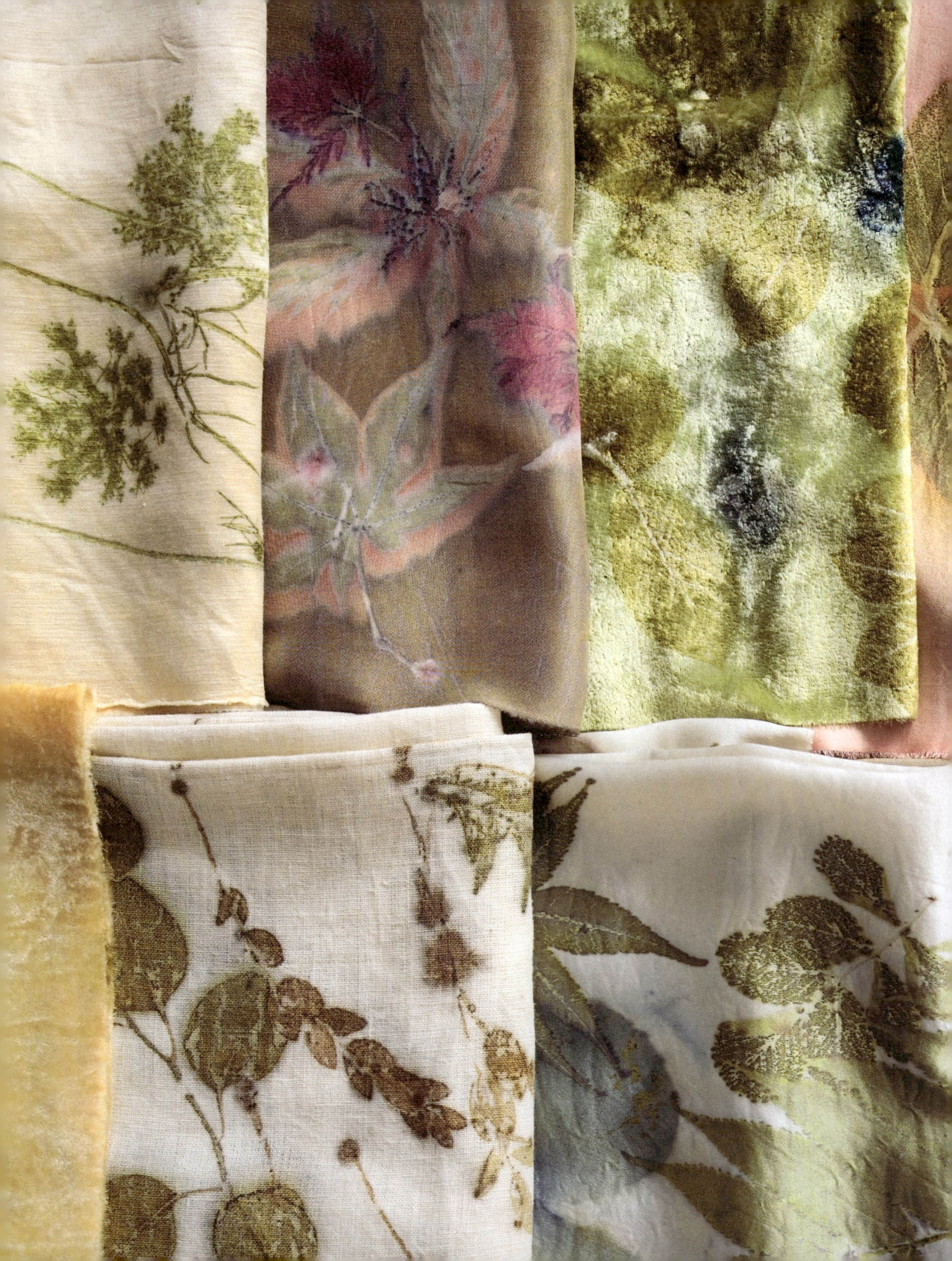

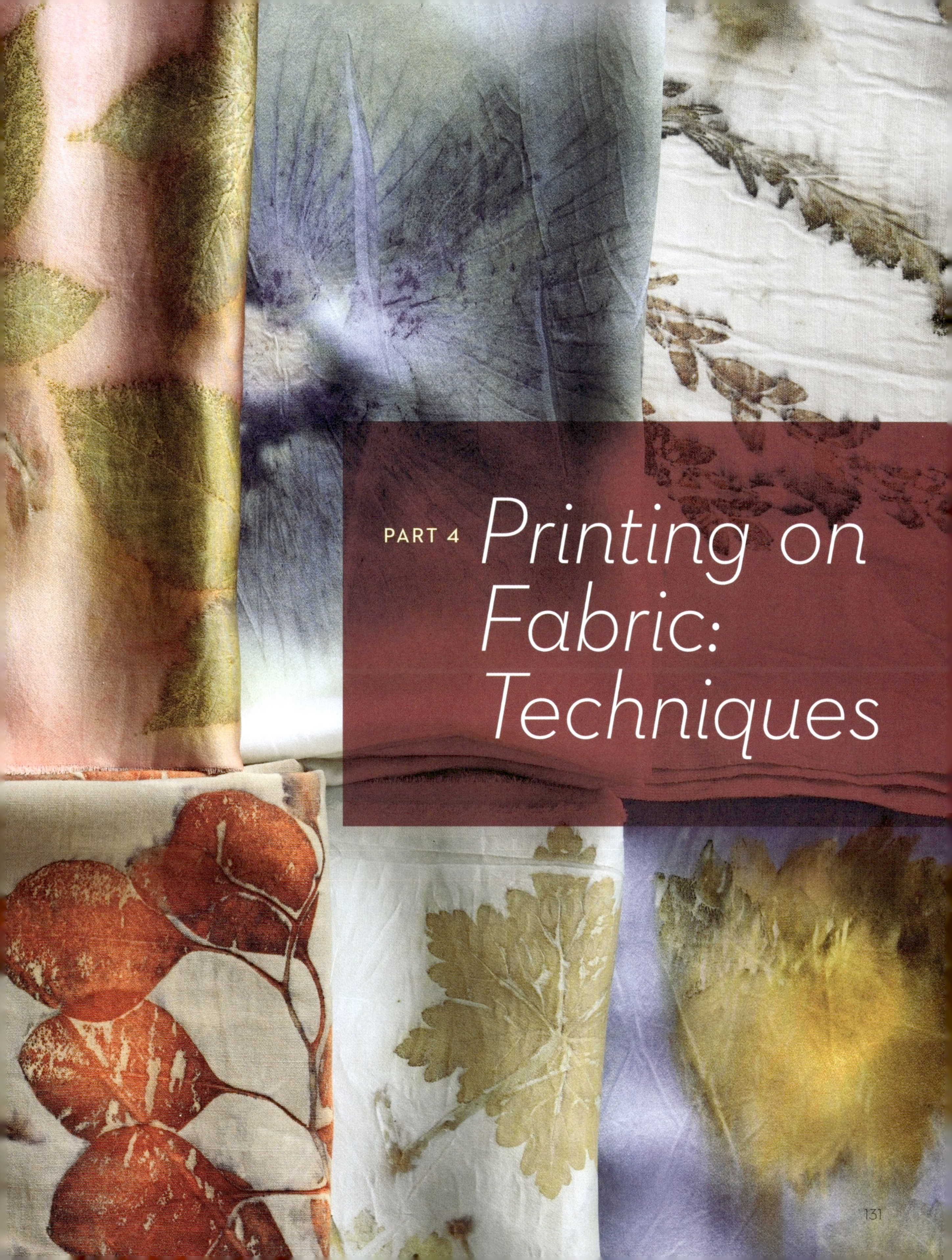

PART 4

Printing on Fabric: Techniques

Once your fabric has been mordanted, you can use a variety of methods to print on it with botanicals. These techniques, though distinct, share a fundamental approach: They all rely on the interaction between the plant material, the mordant, and the steaming process to create one-of-a-kind prints. The four techniques outlined in this section are well-established practices that produce consistent, beautiful results. Each method provides a unique opportunity to explore how different plants react, giving you the freedom to experiment and discover new possibilities in your botanical printing projects.

Technique 1: Bundle dyeing (page 140) is the simplest method for creating colorful prints brimming with variety. In this technique, you layer leaves and flowers onto the fabric, roll it tightly, and then tie it for the steaming or boiling process. The heat and moisture help transfer the pigments onto the fiber, resulting in intricate patterns and vibrant colors.

Technique 2: Mirror-image printing (page 147) allows you to take advantage of both sides of vegetation to create a symmetrical composition. By placing leaves and flowers onto the fabric and folding the opposite side over it, you can achieve a striking mirrored effect. This method emphasizes the fine details of the botanical motifs, creating a beautiful, balanced print.

Technique 3: Using a carrier blanket (page 152) allows you to impart a background color to the target fabric while simultaneously transferring botanical prints. By layering your vegetation between a dye-soaked carrier blanket and the target, you can create an intricate tapestry of color and design. This technique is especially effective for adding depth and contrast to your finished piece.

Technique 4: Printing on clothing (page 160) is a practical technique for renewing stained or vintage garments. By carefully applying botanical imprints, you can effectively cover imperfections or create entirely new designs. This method not only revitalizes old clothing but also offers a unique way to express your personal style using your favorite natural elements.

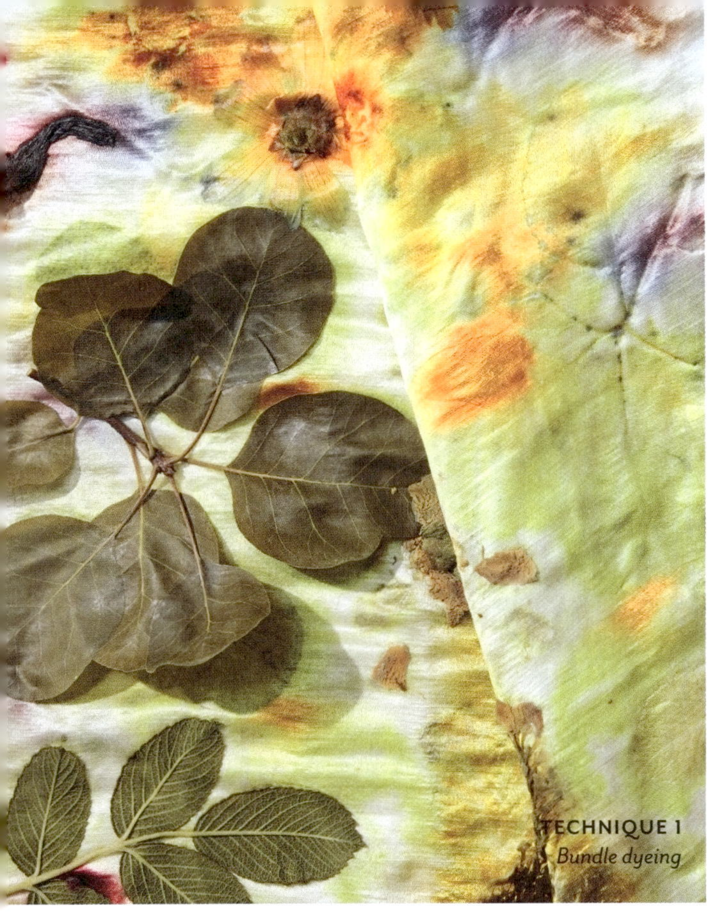

TECHNIQUE 1
Bundle dyeing

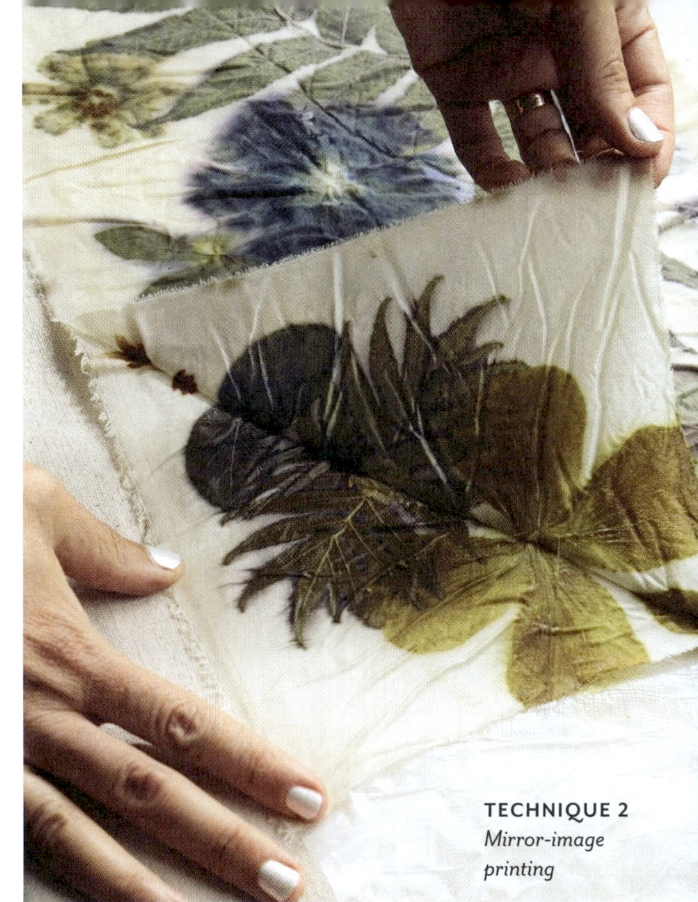

TECHNIQUE 2
Mirror-image printing

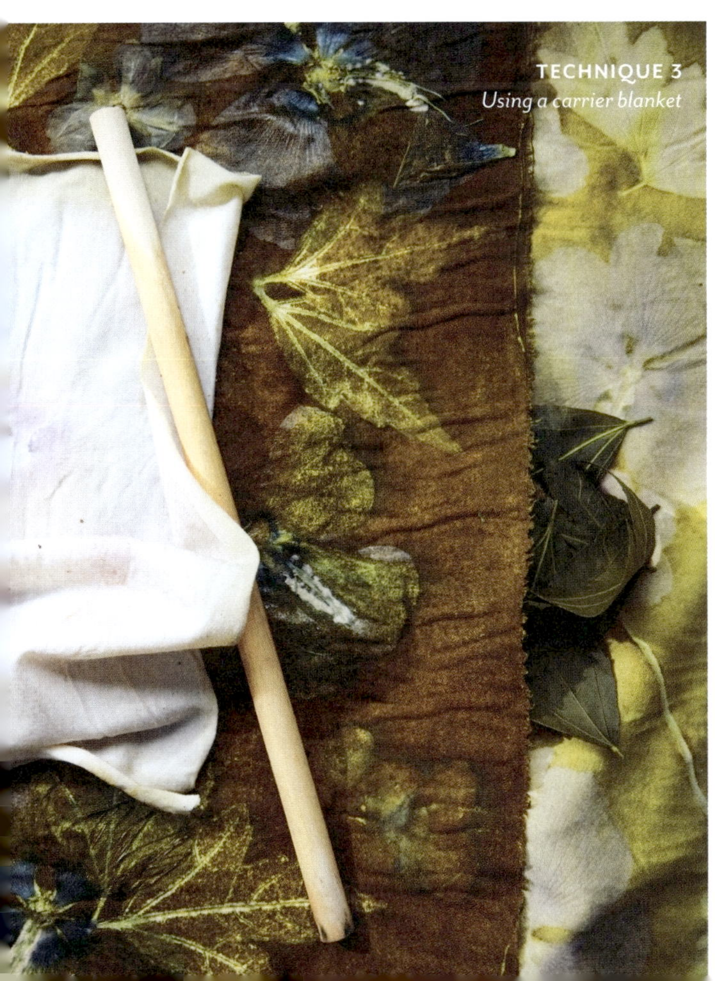

TECHNIQUE 3
Using a carrier blanket

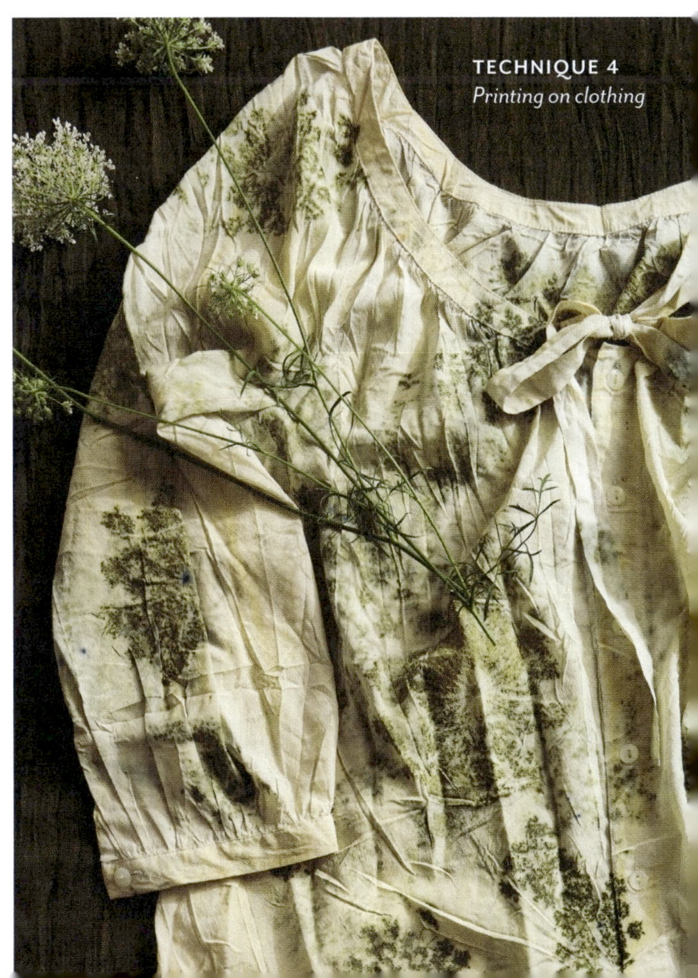

TECHNIQUE 4
Printing on clothing

Using a Barrier

A barrier is a layer of a nonporous material that is placed on top of and rolled within a botanical print to prevent plant matter from bleeding through the backside of the target. Without a barrier, the plant matter on the front of the target, or on the top, encounters the back of the target when one rolls up a bundle, creating many repeats and bits and spurts of color, known as "ghost prints," or bleeds. When bundle dyeing on fabric, these repeats are embraced and used to one's advantage, as the goal is to create an allover repetitive abstract print. When printing on paper, if the diameter of the dowel is wide enough (such as a 28-ounce tin can) to prevent the paper from overlapping itself, you do not need a barrier.

In order to achieve crisp imprints from vegetation on a pure white background without any unwanted areas of coloring, use a barrier. A barrier is necessary when printing a composition with a carrier blanket (see page 152). Without one, the liquid from the blanket will be absorbed from the backside of the fabric, thus saturating the area where the plant matter should print without added color. Materials normally utilized are reusable painter's plastic, parchment paper, or a layer of thick fabric that is not very absorbent yet impenetrable, such as canvas.

A barrier layer, usually plastic, prevents pigments from seeping through when the target is bundled.

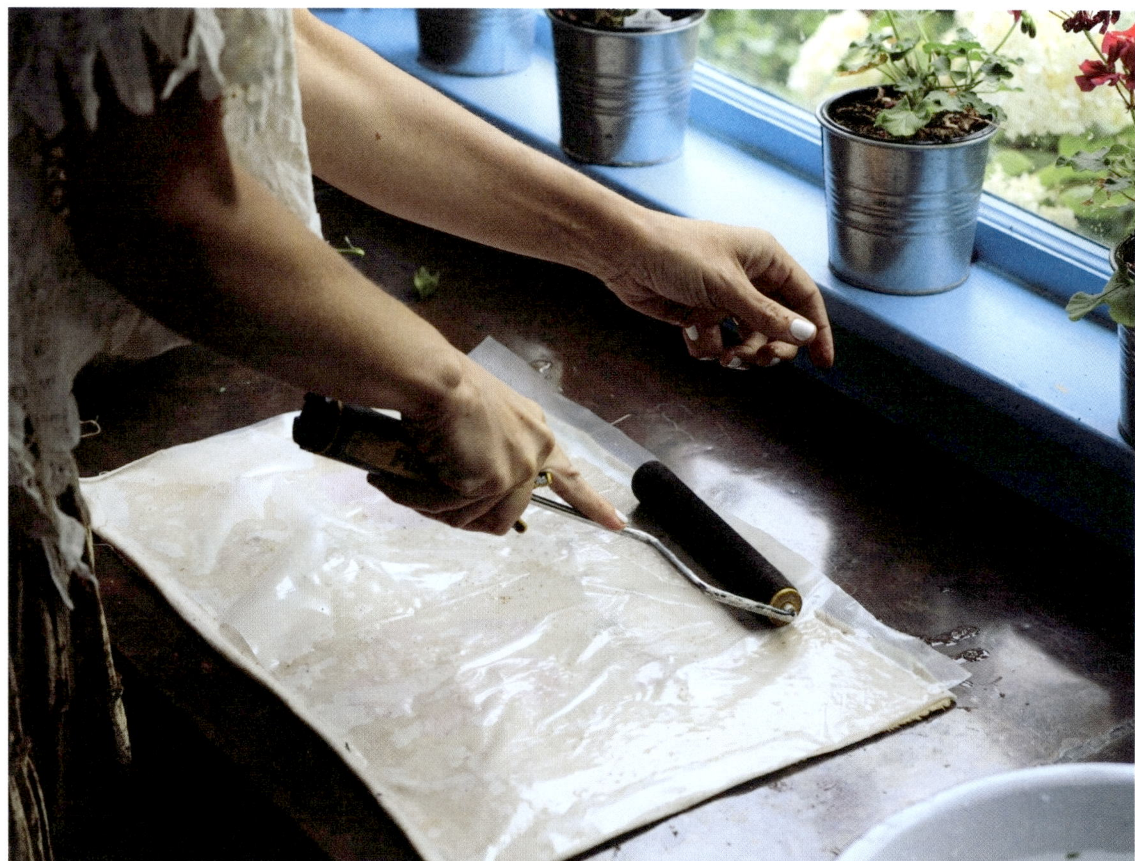

Using a Cushioning Blanket

A cushioning blanket is an optional layer of fabric used when rolling the target around a dowel. This additional layer helps make direct contact between target and vegetation. A cushioning blanket may aid to fill in the negative space around bulky stems, stamen, bark, receptacles, and so on. I prefer to use fabric that has some stretch and body, such as a thick knit jersey or French terry.

Use a cushioning blanket when creating a single-layer print without a fold or carrier blanket. When using a cushioning blanket, my preferred layout for making a bundle is the following: barrier, target, vegetation, cushioning blanket, then roll. This piece of cloth should be damp, not dripping, when placed on the target. It can be washed and reused.

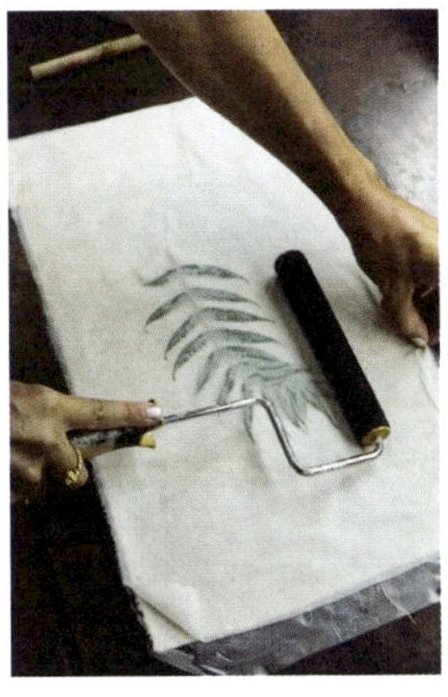

A cushioning blanket helps the botanical material make better contact with the target, creating crisper and more detailed prints.

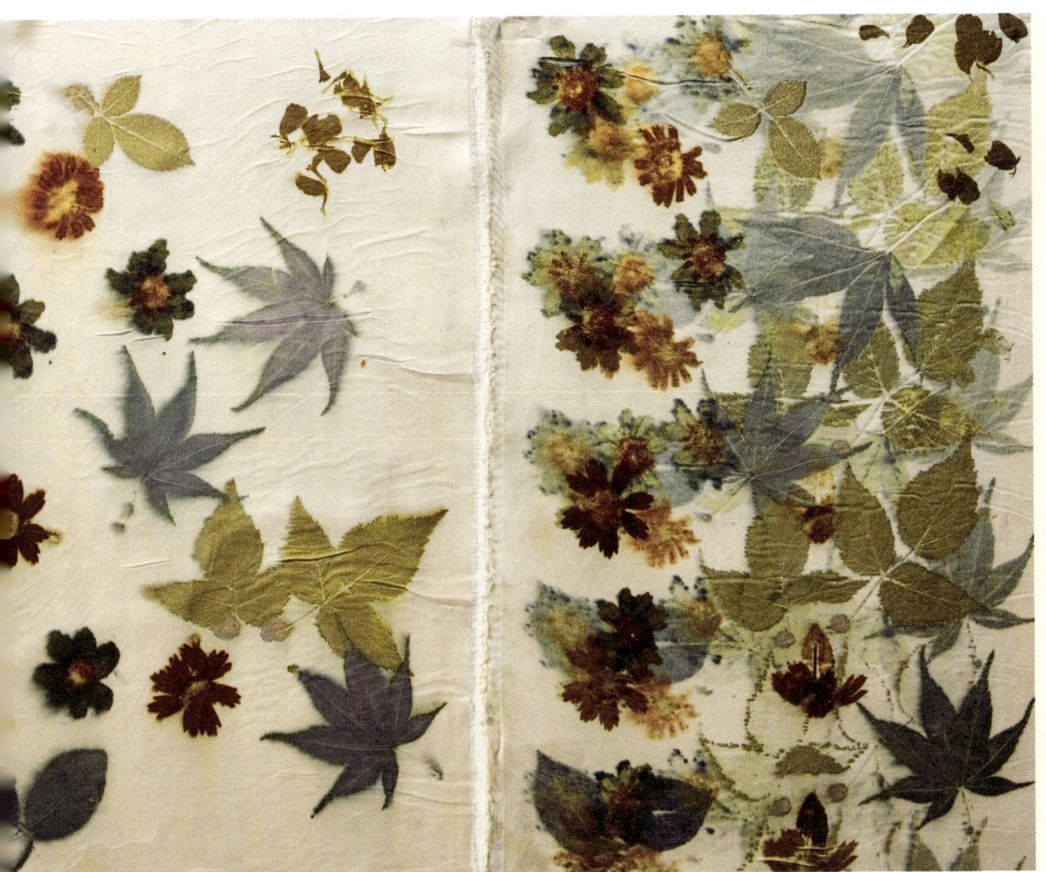

TO USE A BARRIER OR NOT?

Here we have two pieces of silk charmeuse that were printed with leaves and flowers. The sample on the left was rolled with a barrier in place before bundling, leaving a clear background. The sample on the right was rolled without a barrier, allowing the color to seep through and create repeats and bleeds. Both are beautiful in their own way.

Rolling and Wrapping the Bundle

To achieve quality prints, it is crucial that bundles are rolled tightly and securely, without any wrinkles or bubbles between the target, blanket (if using), and barrier. Using consistent pressure is key while rolling up the bundle.

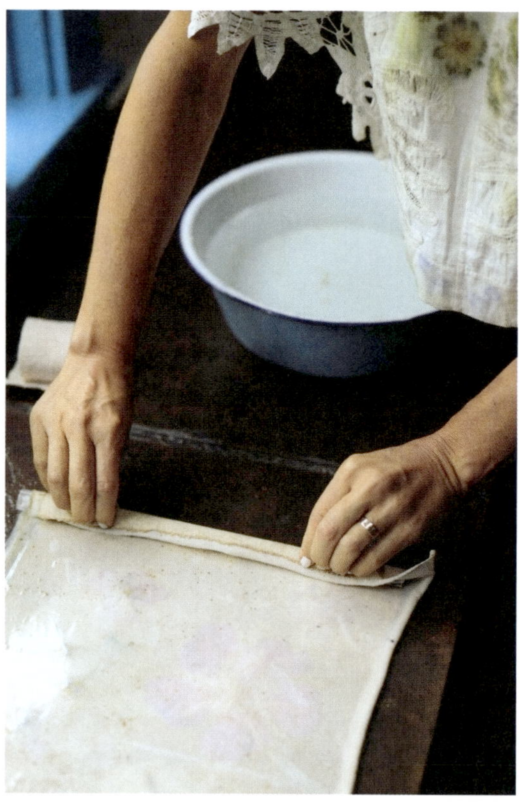

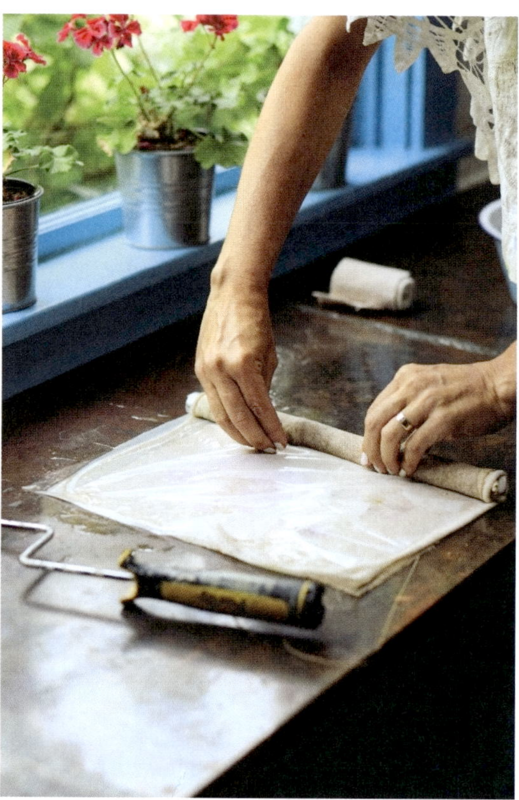

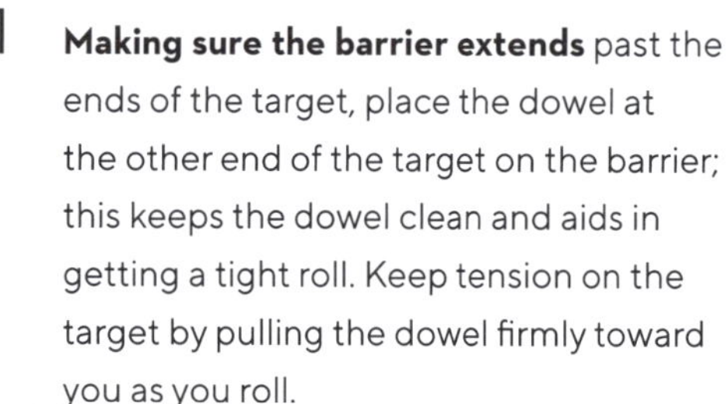

1 **Making sure the barrier extends** past the ends of the target, place the dowel at the other end of the target on the barrier; this keeps the dowel clean and aids in getting a tight roll. Keep tension on the target by pulling the dowel firmly toward you as you roll.

2 **Smooth out any bubbles** or wrinkles to ensure compression and connection of vegetation and target. When you reach the end, roll any remainder of the barrier around the bundle.

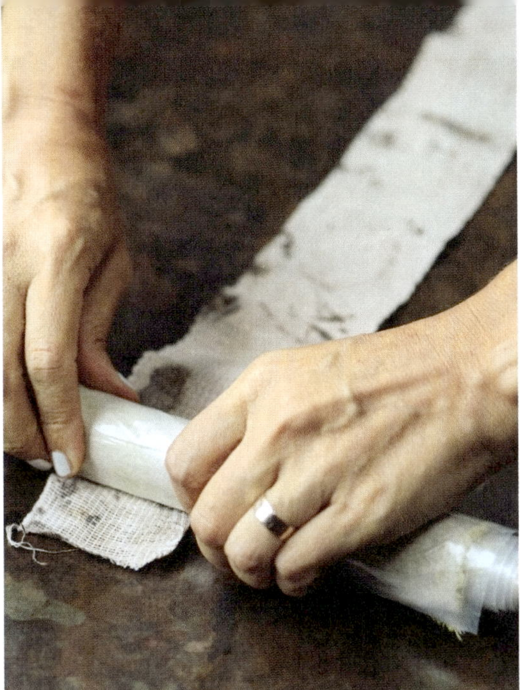

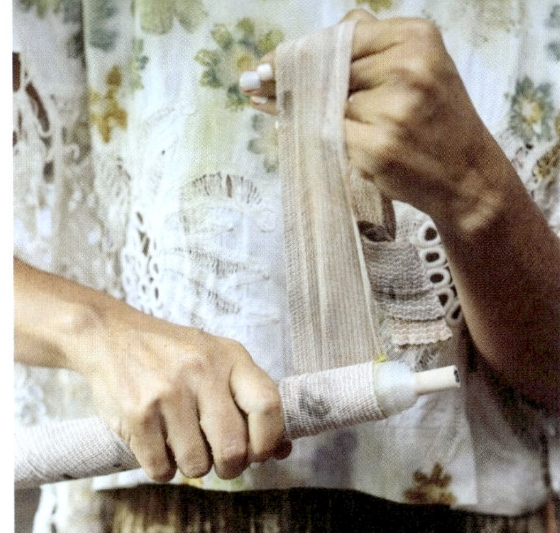

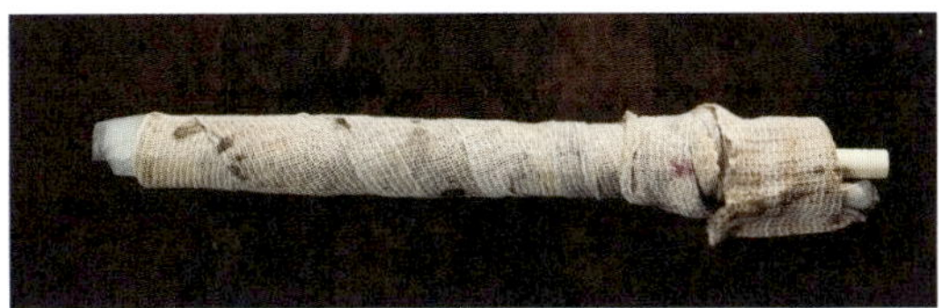

3 **The tightly rolled bundle** must now be wrapped to compress the materials more firmly and keep everything together. Using a stretchy bandage (like an Ace bandage with Velcro closure) or supple T-shirt yarn, begin at the middle of the bundle. Secure one end by winding the bandage over itself.

4 **Roll the bundle** toward your body, pulling tightly on the bandage for resistance. Wrap from the center to one end, then back to the other end. Secure with the Velcro end or a rubber band, or tie a simple knot. You can also step on one end of the bandage while wrapping to create resistance, as shown below.

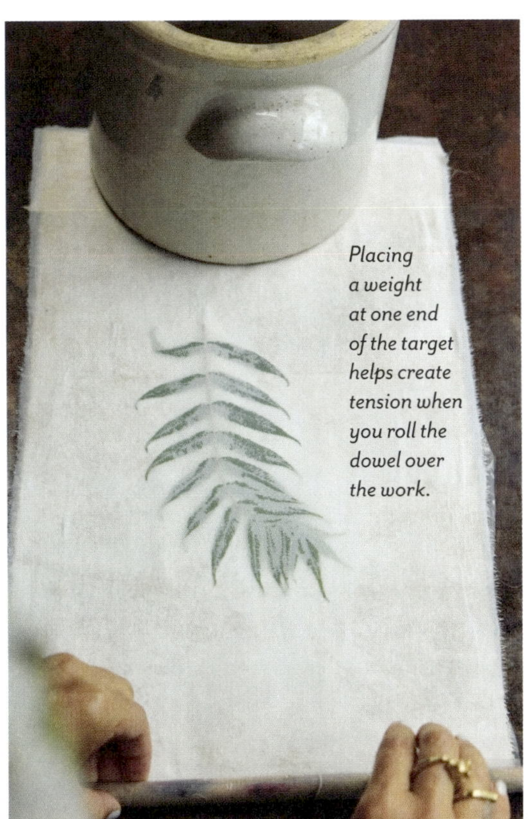

Placing a weight at one end of the target helps create tension when you roll the dowel over the work.

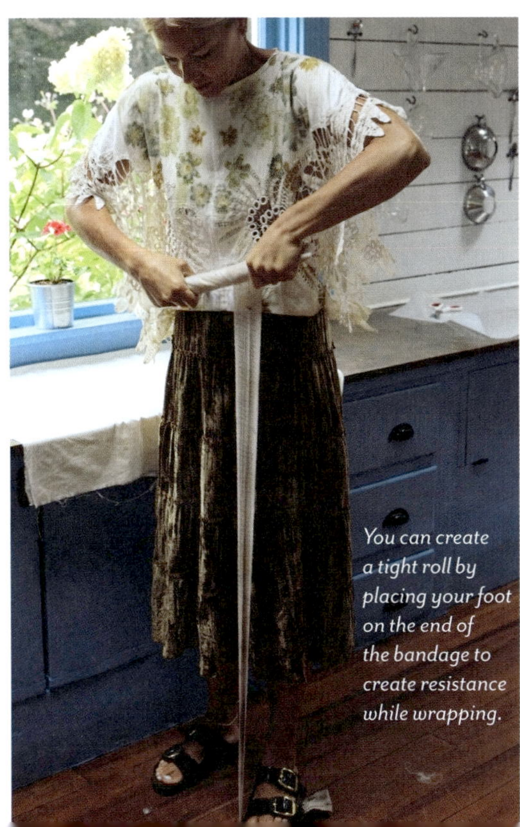

You can create a tight roll by placing your foot on the end of the bandage to create resistance while wrapping.

Steaming the Bundle

Steaming the bundle above the water line in a pot with a lid completes the transformation of transmuting pigment, shadow, and imprint of the botanicals into the target. When steaming, keep at least 3 inches of water in the pot to ensure it won't all evaporate while simmering. Steam bundles at a slow to medium simmer with the lid on. A rolling boil is not necessary.

Steaming times vary for different plants, and people have differing opinions as to how long to steam bundles. Most flowers transmit their colors to the target within about 30 minutes, and leaves take about 45 minutes. Eucalyptus is an exception; it needs at least 90 minutes of steaming to fully transfer that magnificent color. I use these guidelines—and I always use an insistent timer that I cannot ignore!

- **Bundle with fresh flowers, without leaves:** 30–45 minutes at a low simmer with the lid on
- **Bundle with flowers and leaves, and no eucalyptus:** 45–60 minutes at a low simmer with the lid on
- **Bundle with eucalyptus:** 90 minutes at a medium simmer with the lid on

STEPS

1 **Add 3 to 5 inches of water** to the steaming vessel, keeping the level below the steaming tray. Place the pot on the heat source and bring to a gentle simmer.

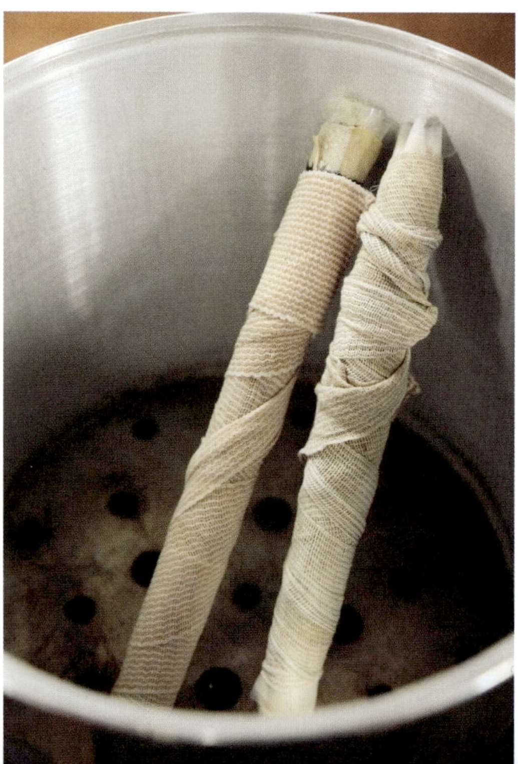

2 **Using tongs** and heat-resistant gloves, place the bundles into the pot and put on the lid. Set your timer for the desired length of time. When the time is up, turn off the heat and allow the pot to cool. To speed up the cooling process, carefully remove the lid, avoiding the escaping steam. Remove the bundles when they are cool to the touch (after 20 minutes or so).

Drying and Rinsing the Target

When the bundle has cooled sufficiently, unwrap the binding and unroll the bundle. Peel away the barrier and carrier blanket (if using), and gently remove or shake off any excess vegetation. Allow to dry fully.

Once dry, a quick rinse in cool water with pH-neutral soap is sufficient to wash and rinse the fabric. Hang or lay flat to dry again in the shade. Ironing with steam on the backside of the fabric will remove any wrinkles from the printing process.

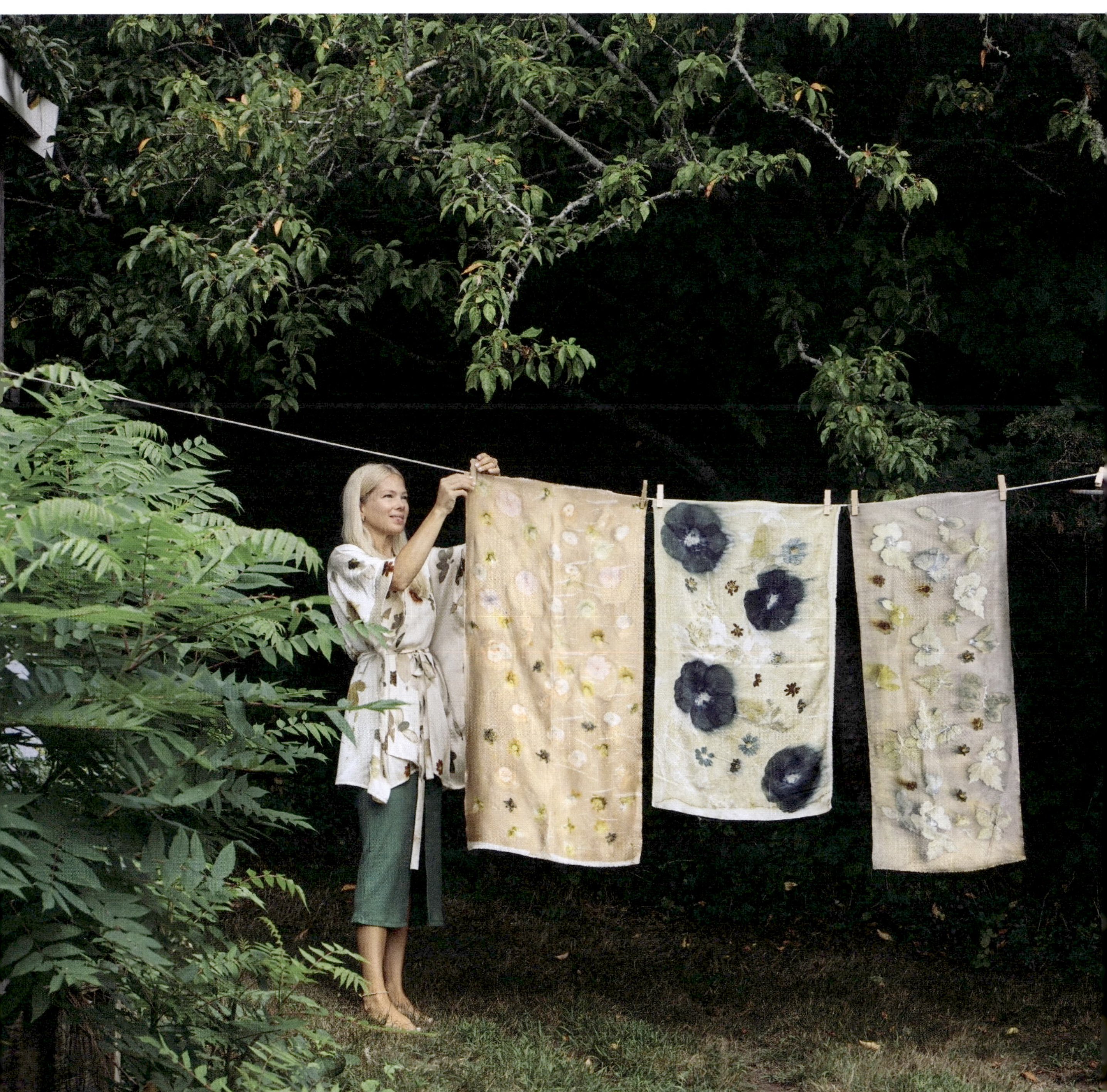

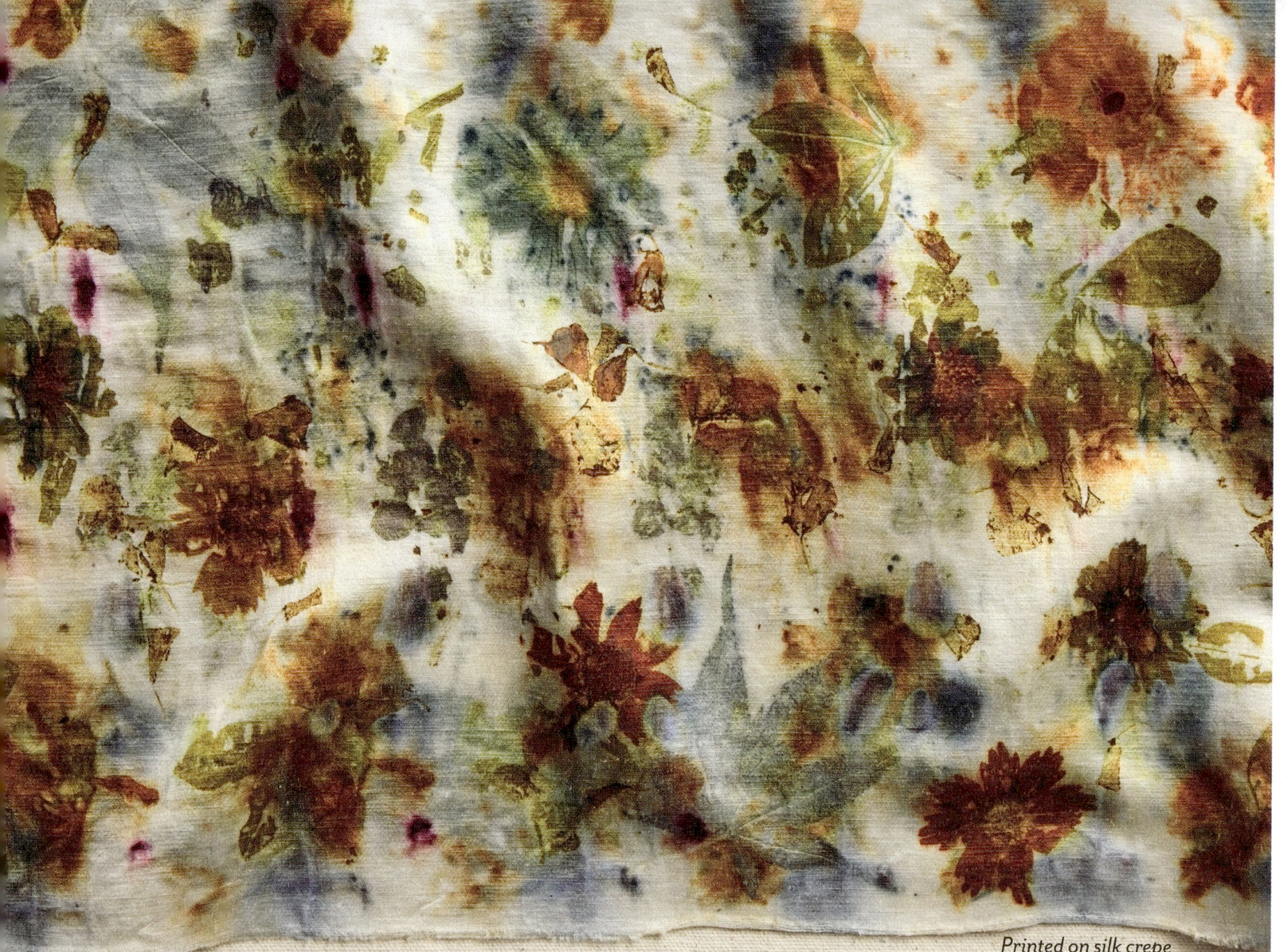

Printed on silk crepe

TECHNIQUE 1

BASIC BUNDLE DYEING

Bundle dyeing uses dried and fresh botanicals to create allover prints in a "Jackson Pollock" style—full of repeats, layers, and pops of color allowing for pigmentation to bleed through and create patterns throughout the textile. This method can be implemented with no repeats by using a barrier when rolling the bundle. It is often the first technique one will try when experimenting with natural dyes, as it is the simplest and most straightforward process.

Practice is key to discovering which plants you like best and how you like to work with them. Bundle dyeing is a great method to practice on used or stained clothing and textiles, as the colorful botanicals may cover up any imperfections.

SET UP FOR SUCCESS

Scour the target unless the fabric is labeled as "ready to dye" (essential if using cellulose fabric). Optional for cellulose: Soak the fabric in a soy milk bath (page 129) before printing.

Mordant the target with the recipe of your choice, using one with ferrous sulfate if printing with leaves to ensure a good print. When printing with just flowers and dried botanicals, the Fundamental Mordant recipe without iron (page 118) is suitable.

Gather all your materials. Place leaves in a bowl of water to keep fresh and allow better contact with the target. Fill your steaming vessel with at least 3 inches of water and set to simmer.

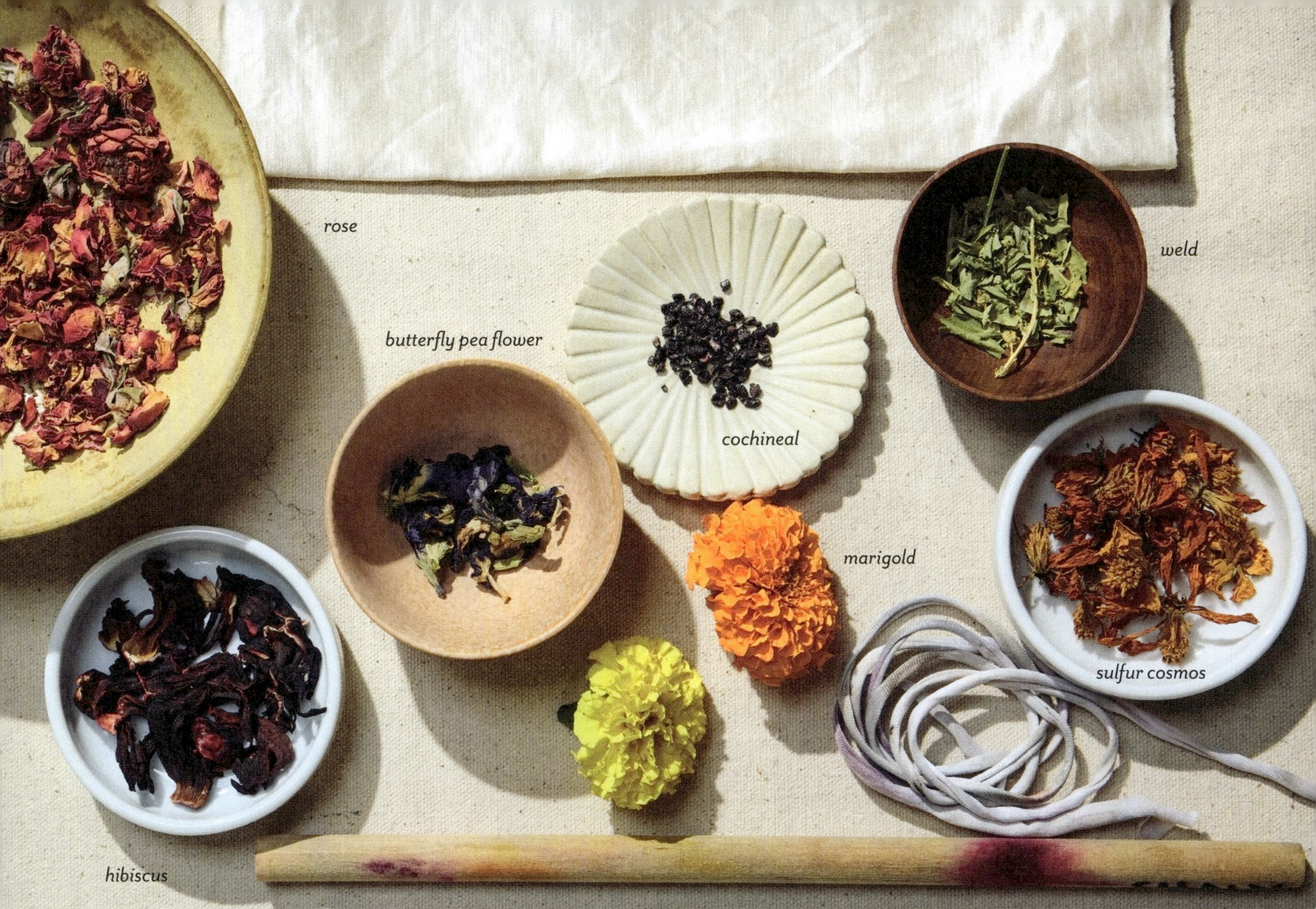

Suggested Botanicals

Bundle dyeing works excellently with dried flowers. Try rose, hollyhock, butterfly pea flower, marigold (dried or fresh), coreopsis, cosmos, pincushion, hibiscus, dahlia, black rose mallow, tulip, iris, pansy, violet, goldenrod, bidens, and/or weld flowers.

You may also get nice imprints from fresh leaves. Try rose leaves, chestnut leaves, raspberry leaves, eucalyptus leaves, false indigo leaves, and plum leaves. If the textile has been mordanted with iron, experiment with other fresh leaves.

Here is a guide should you wish to impart specific colors.

Reds and pinks: Ground madder root, Japanese maple leaves, brazilwood powder, safflower, sappanwood, dried hibiscus

Oranges: Marigolds, coreopsis, annatto seeds, yellow onion skins, turmeric powder, kamala powder, Himalayan rhubarb, eupatorium powder, fustic powder

Yellows: Dyer's broom, ground Osage orange, marigolds, zinnias, bidens, buckthorn powder, chamomile

Greens: Weld flowers, false indigo leaves, rose leaves, plum leaves, rose of Sharon, red onion skins, Himalayan rhubarb (when iron is present), myrobalan

Blues: Butterfly pea flowers, black rose mallow, black beans, dried alder berry

Purples: Logwood powder, red onion skins, cochineal bugs, lac powder, black tea, alkanet

Browns: Tannin and walnut powder, ground pomegranate rinds

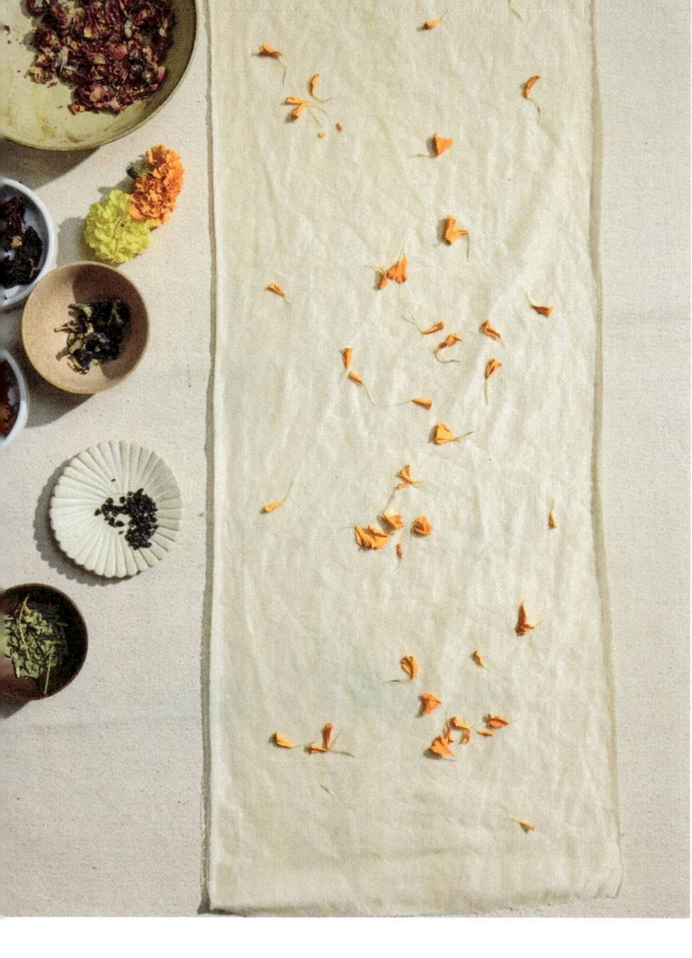

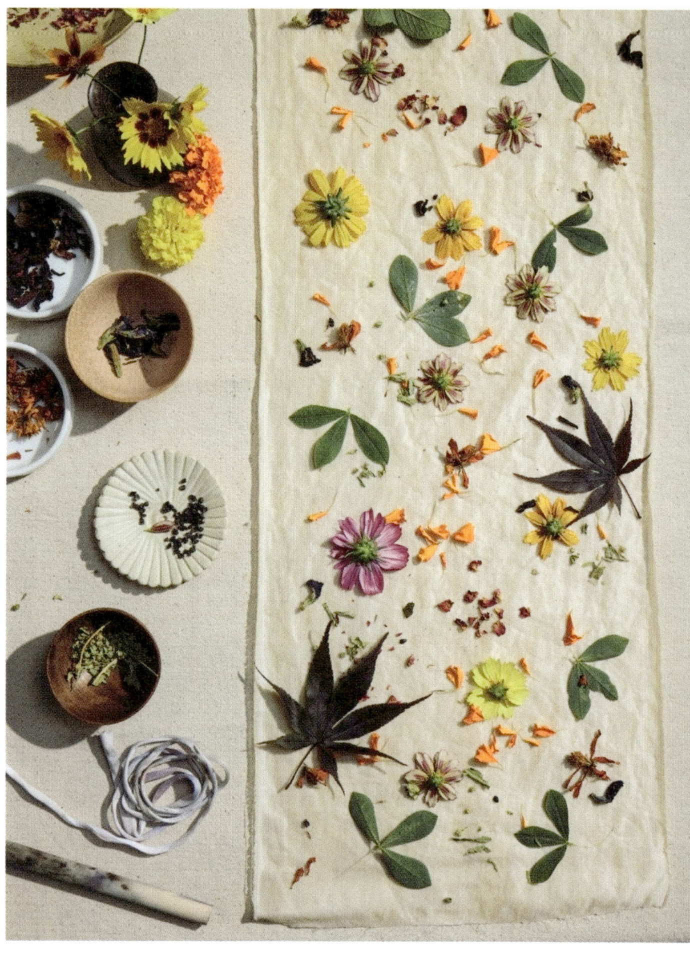

DECORATE THE TARGET

1 **Wet out the textile** and gently wring it out until it is damp (not dripping). Lay it out on a clean, protected worktable. Smooth out and make as flat as possible.

2 **Create your design.** This can be an active meditation as you decide which vegetation to use, how much, and where to place it. Use a wide range of colors with a combination of dried flowers and fresh leaves. Dried botanicals can be broken up into bits and sprinkled onto the target. When bundle dyeing, I sprinkle as much as 75 percent of the surface area with many different types of plants, but the choice is entirely up to you.

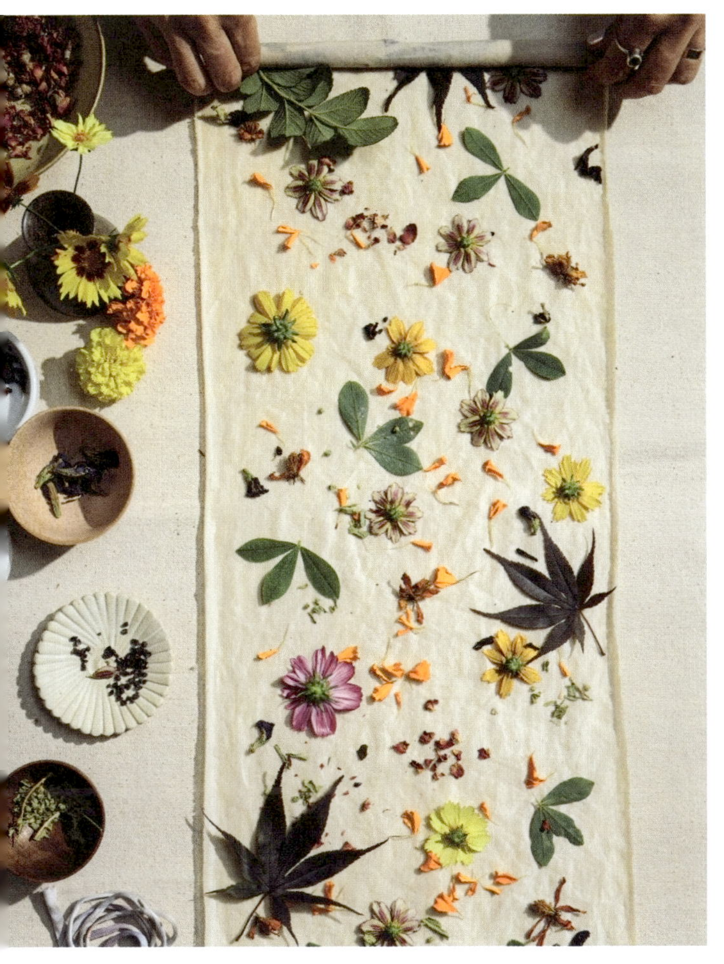

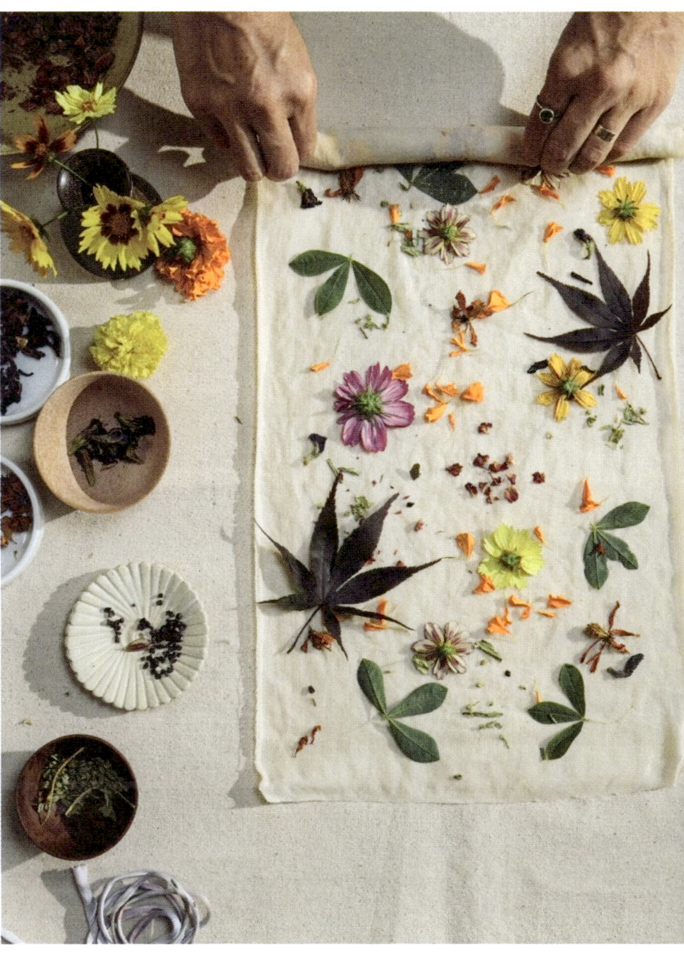

ROLL AND WRAP THE BUNDLE

3 **Roll the target tightly** and securely around the dowel. Begin by rolling one edge of the target around the dowel. Firm, consistent pressure is key. (If it's too wide, the fabric may need to be folded lengthwise to fit into the dowel. Folding creates more saturation and coloring by allowing the pigments to bleed through the layers of fabric onto the opposite side.)

4 **Pull the dowel toward your body** when rolling to increase the tension of the bundle. Keep pressure consistent throughout the process. Smooth out any bubbles or wrinkles to ensure compression and connection of vegetation and target. Roll any remainder of the barrier around the bundle.

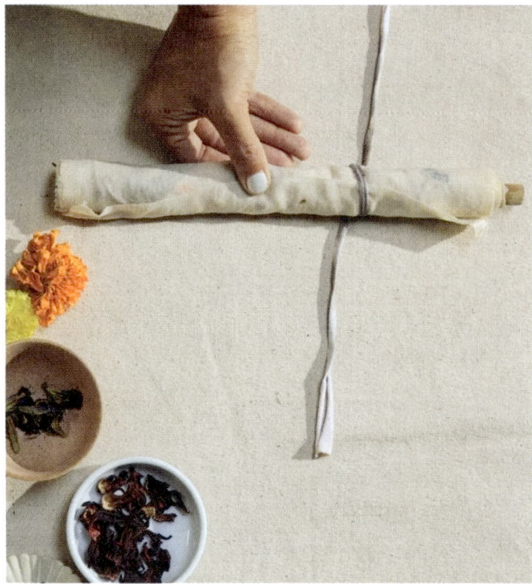

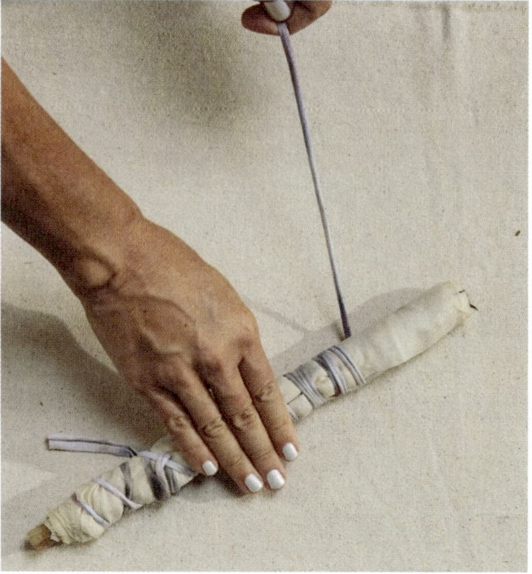

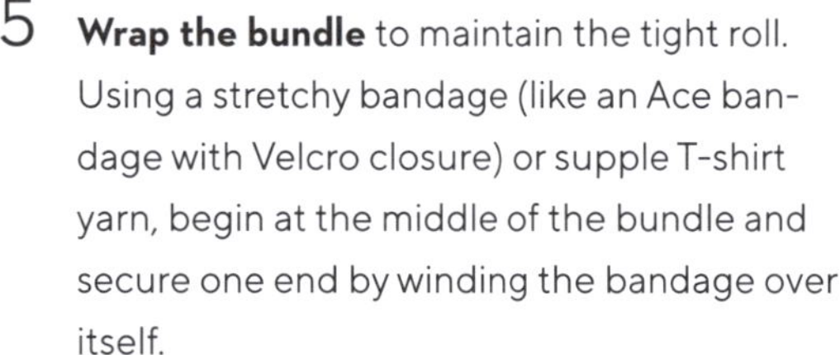

5 **Wrap the bundle** to maintain the tight roll. Using a stretchy bandage (like an Ace bandage with Velcro closure) or supple T-shirt yarn, begin at the middle of the bundle and secure one end by winding the bandage over itself.

6 **Lay the bundle** on the table horizontally and roll the bundle toward your body while pulling tightly on the bandage, creating resistance. Work your way to one side, winding around the bundle, then to the opposite end and tie off. If using bandage, make use of the Velcro end to secure in place, or tie a simple knot.

STEAM THE BUNDLE

7 **Put the bundle in the pot,** keeping it above the water level. Bring the water to a simmer, not a full boil. Steam for 30 to 90 minutes, depending on the chosen vegetation, with the lid on. Check the water level halfway through and add more if necessary.

- **Just flowers:** 30–45 minutes
- **Flowers and leaves:** 45–60 minutes
- **Any composition with eucalyptus leaves:** 90 minutes

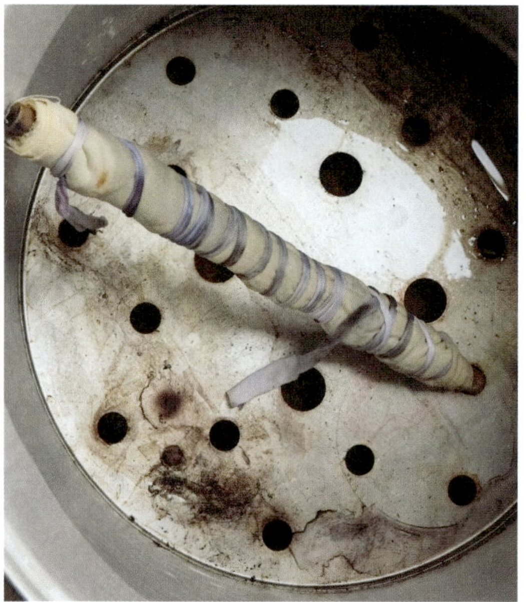

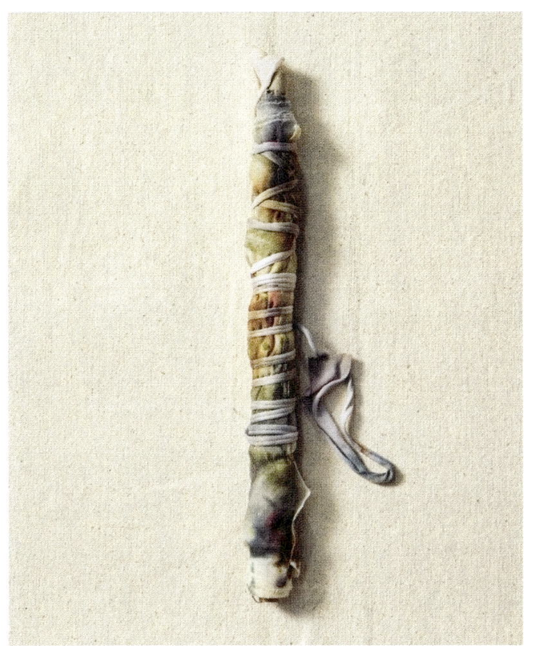

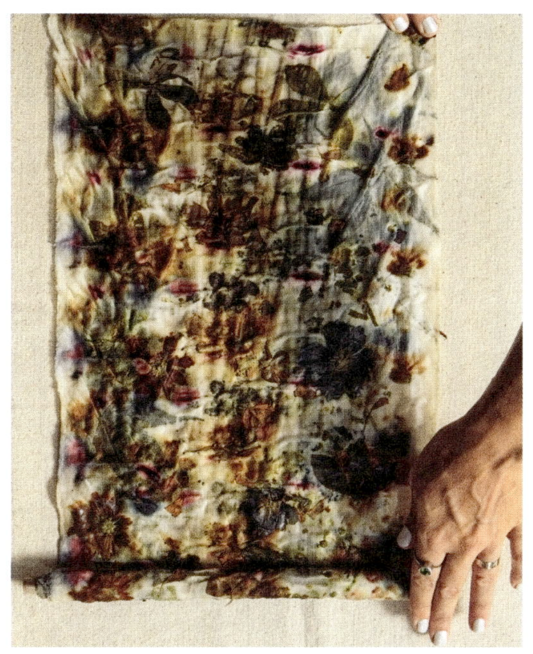

8 **When your timer goes off,** turn off the heat, remove the bundle from the pot, and allow to cool. You will see how color has seeped into the fabric.

9 **Unroll the bundle** and shake off the vegetation. Enjoy the reveal! Allow the textile to dry completely before rinsing.

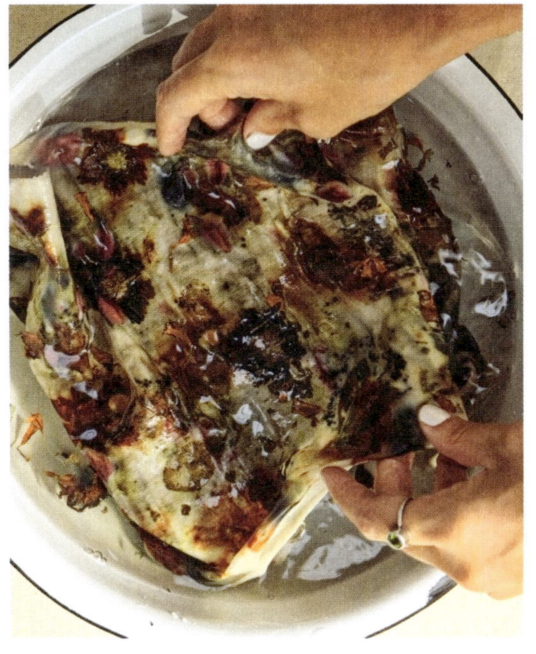

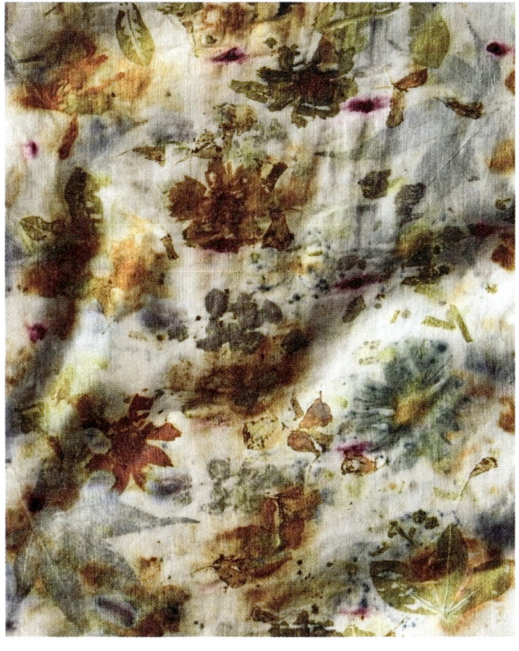

10 **Rinse the textile in cool water** with a dash of pH-neutral soap. Be gentle; it does not have to be scrubbed! Gently wring and hang to dry in the shade. Iron with steam for the best finishing results.

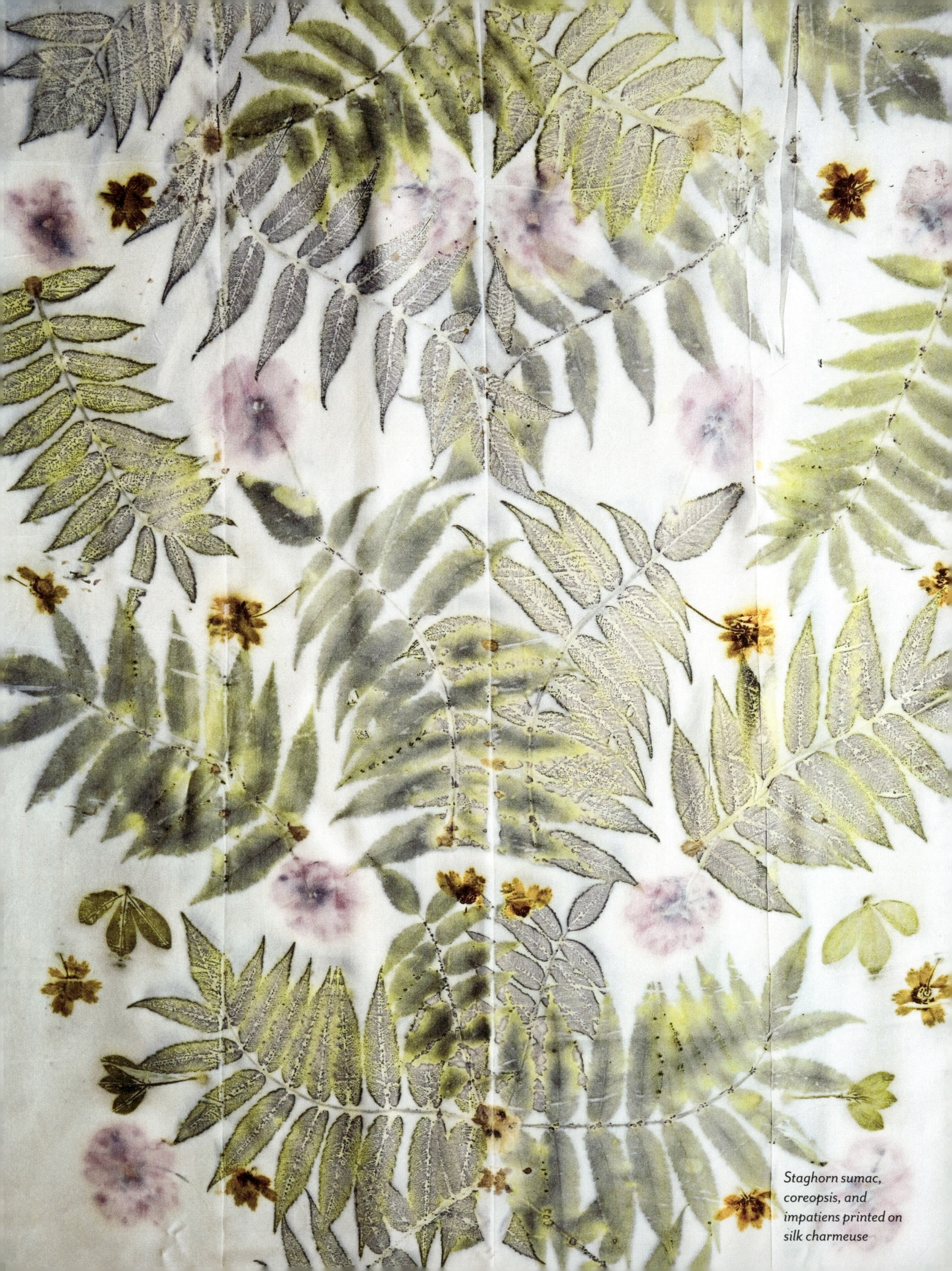

Staghorn sumac, coreopsis, and impatiens printed on silk charmeuse

TECHNIQUE 2

Printing a MIRROR IMAGE

Mirror-image prints are created by decorating one side of a piece of fabric with botanicals. The opposite side is then folded over the decorated side to create a print where the fabric accepts the pigment from both sides of the vegetation. I love this technique and use it frequently for printing fabric that I want to make into apparel, as the symmetry of the composition often elevates the design.

This technique works well for fabric that is too wide to fit onto a dowel and needs to be folded anyway. You can use any of the mordant recipes in this book, but be sure to use one with ferrous sulfate if printing with leaves.

SET UP FOR SUCCESS

Scour and mordant the target textile. If using leaves, use a recipe with ferrous sulfate (iron) for best results.

Cut a barrier that is slightly wider and at least 10 inches longer than the target.

Optional: Cut a cushioning blanket that is half the width and slightly longer than the target.

Gather all your materials. Place leaves in a bowl of water to keep fresh and allow better contact with the target. Fill your steaming vessel with at least 3 inches of water and set to simmer.

Design Notes

Use this technique to create symmetrical designs on a white background. Use plants that are reliable printers and offer color on both the sun and moon sides so that the composition is balanced.

Keep in mind that if the vegetation touching the fold line will be "kissing" its mirrored image, you may wish to use this to your advantage! This looks especially nice when the tips or stems of leaves meet in the center.

Flowers tend to look more harmonious when placed farther out from the fold; they can look murky as mirror images right next to each other.

Use both sides of the leaves and flowers while creating your design so there is balance on the mirrored side.

Overlapping leaves and flowers within the layout can make for interesting variations.

Suggested leaves: Fresh rose leaves, castor, raspberry, blackberry, strawberry, eucalyptus, false indigo, cotinus, staghorn sumac, vitex, maple, peony

Suggested fresh flowers: Hollyhock, butterfly bush, marigold, coreopsis, cosmos, pincushion, hibiscus, dahlia, impatiens, begonia, rose of Sharon, African violet, bidens

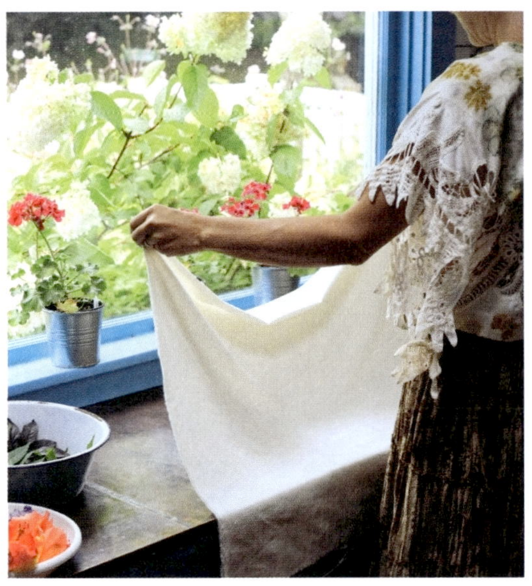

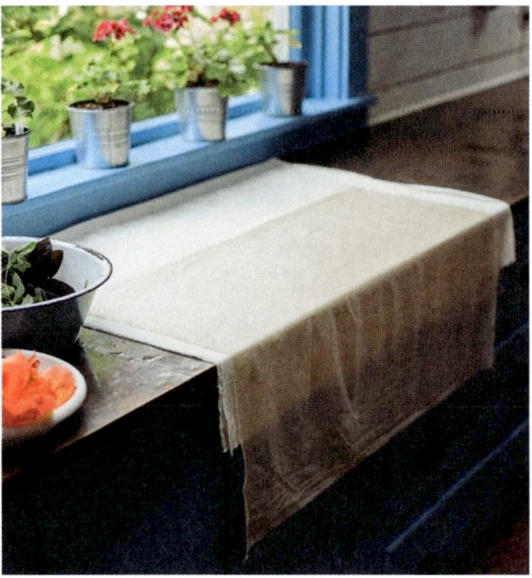

DECORATE THE TARGET

1 **Wet out the textile** and gently wring it out until it is damp, not dripping. Lay it out on a clean, protected worktable. Find the center by folding the fabric in half widthwise, selvedge to selvedge. If the fabric has a "right" side, that should be facing upward to be decorated.

2 **Fold the overlapped side** away from you so as not to decorate it and mark the center. I hang the opposite side over the edge of the worktable to clearly mark the center.

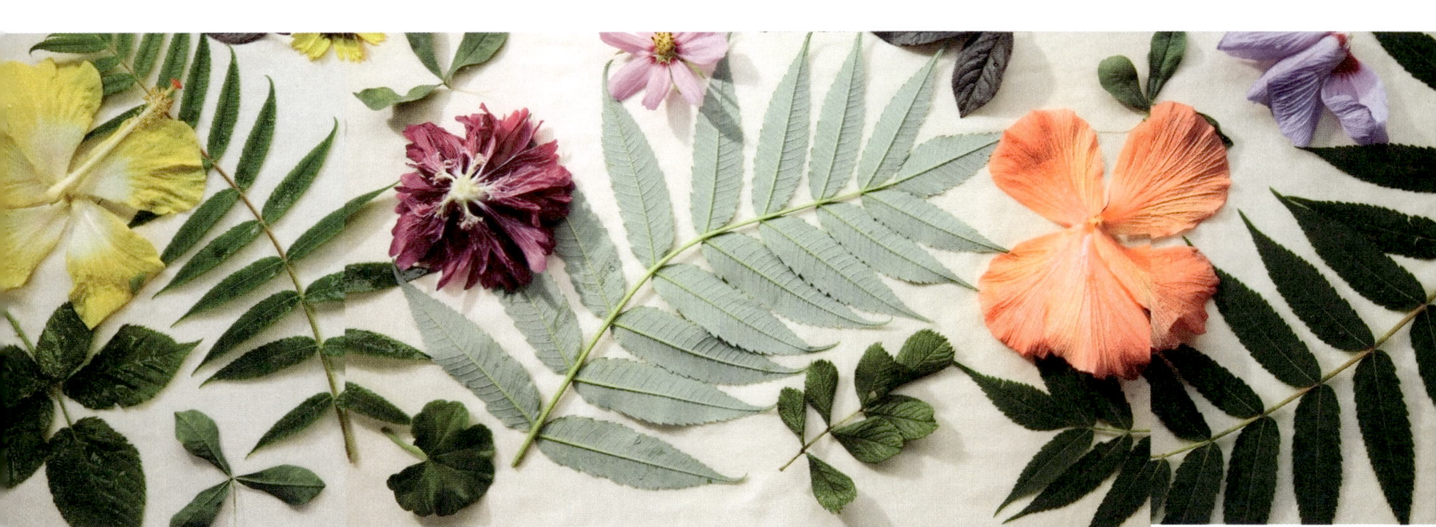

3 **Decorate one side of the textile** with botanicals, going right up the fold line in some places. Aim to cover 50 to 75 percent of the target with vegetation for a balanced composition—don't forget about placing some vegetation toward the outer edges. Vegetation can extend past the edges, if so desired.

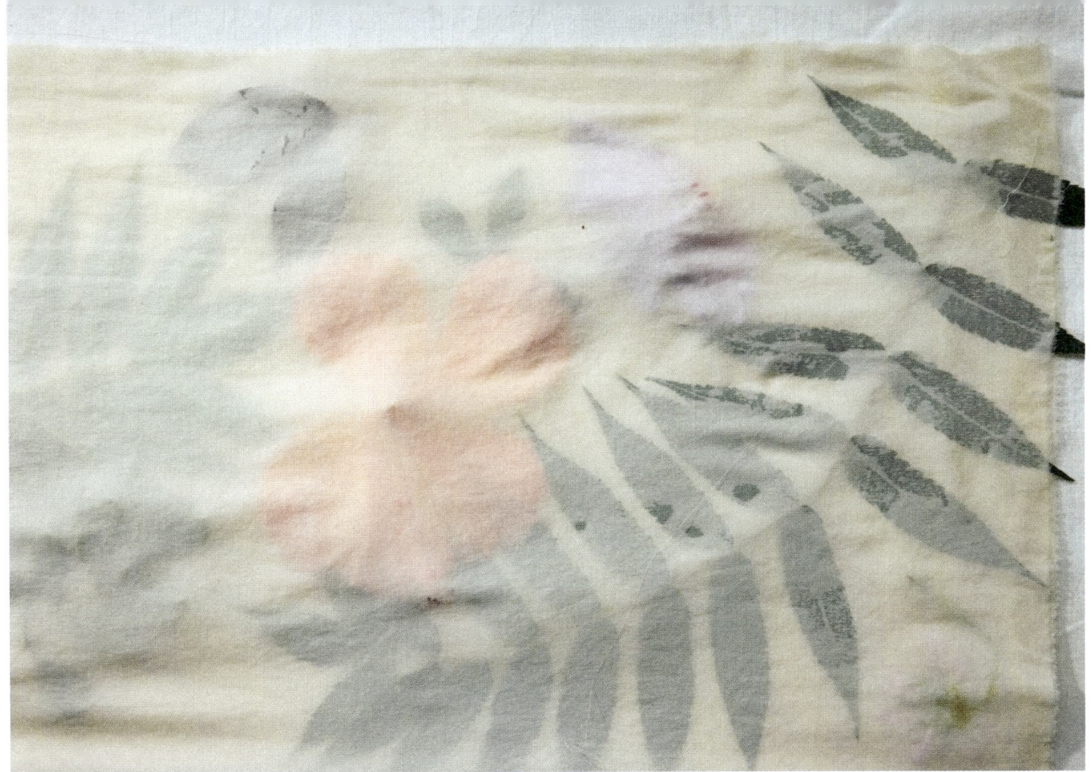

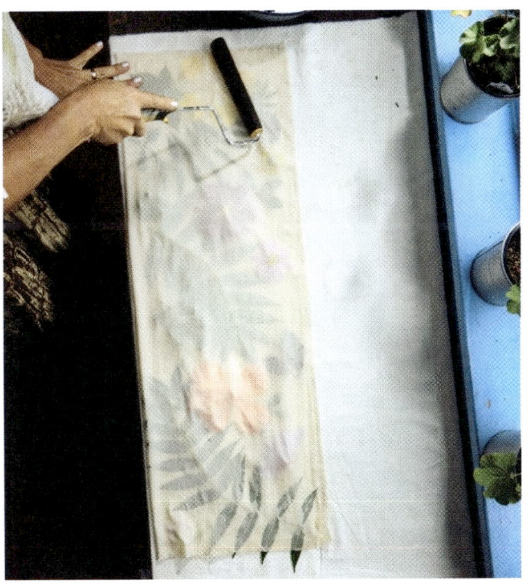

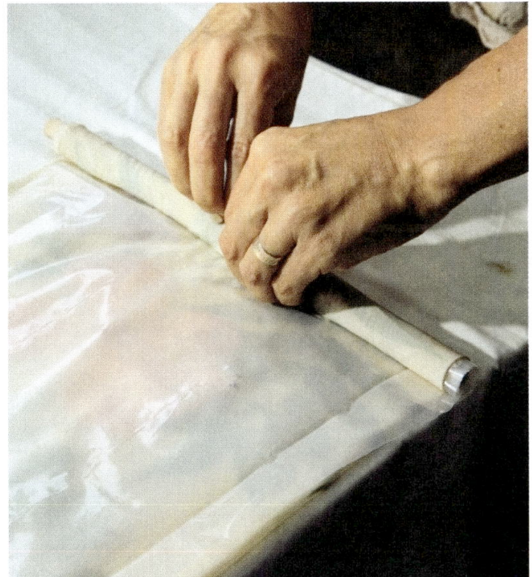

ROLL AND WRAP THE BUNDLE

4 **When satisfied with the design,** fold the opposite side over the decorated side. Smooth with a roller, eliminating any bubbles, folds, or wrinkles, compressing the vegetation between the fabric. Look at the fold to check if any of the vegetation is kissing the center or has folded back on itself—fold backs and overlaps can be lovely but can cause bulk when bundling.

5 **Lay the barrier on the target,** leaving a bit of excess length on the far end. Carefully roll the textile, barrier, and cushioning blanket around a dowel and secure tightly with an Ace bandage or supple T-shirt yarn.

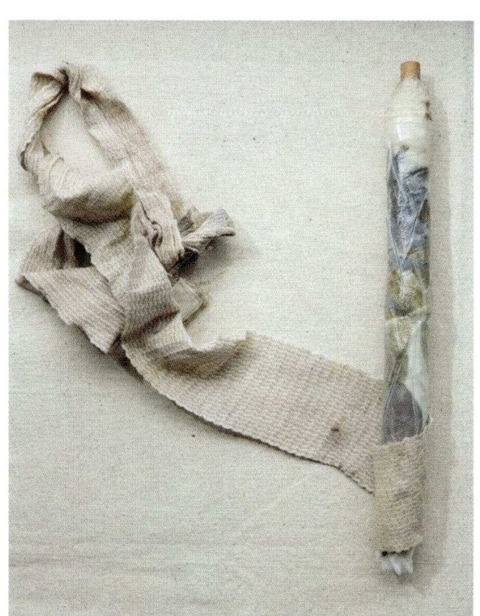

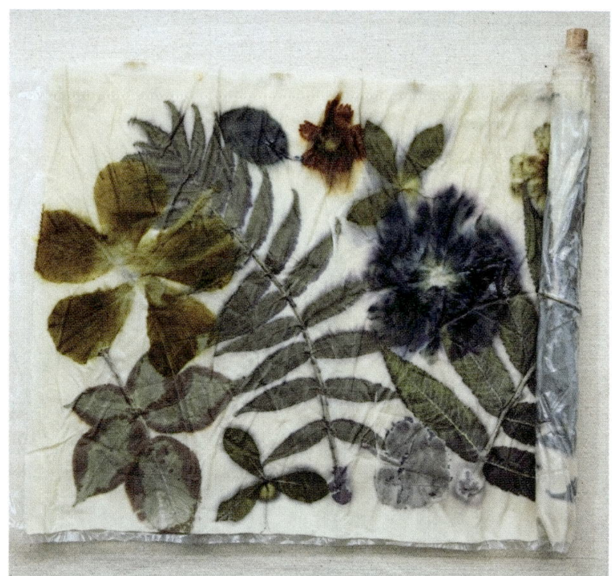

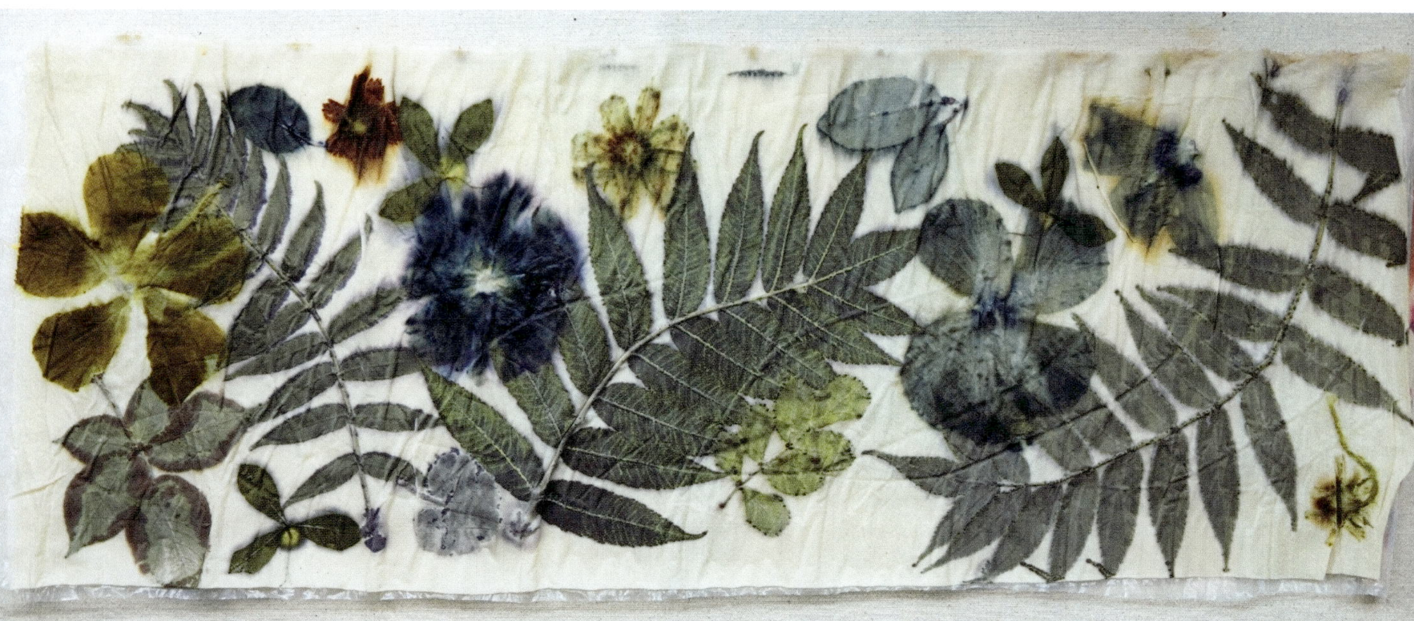

STEAM THE BUNDLE

6 **Put the bundle in the pot,** keeping it above the water level. Bring the water to a simmer, not a full boil. Steam for 30 to 90 minutes, depending on the chosen vegetation, with the lid on. Check the water level halfway through and add more if necessary.

- **Just flowers:** 30–45 minutes
- **Flowers and leaves:** 45–60 minutes
- **Any composition with eucalyptus leaves:** 90 minutes

Once your timer alerts you, turn the heat off and allow the bundle to cool. Unravel and revel in the results!

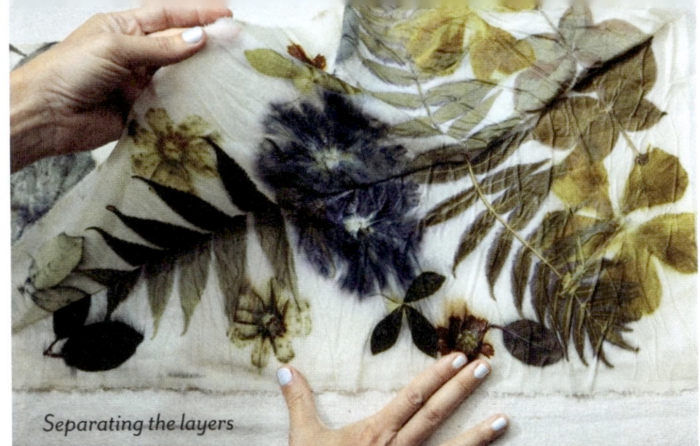
Separating the layers

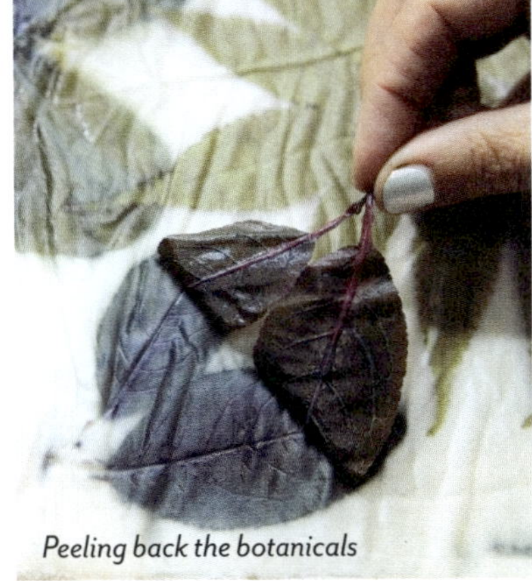
Peeling back the botanicals

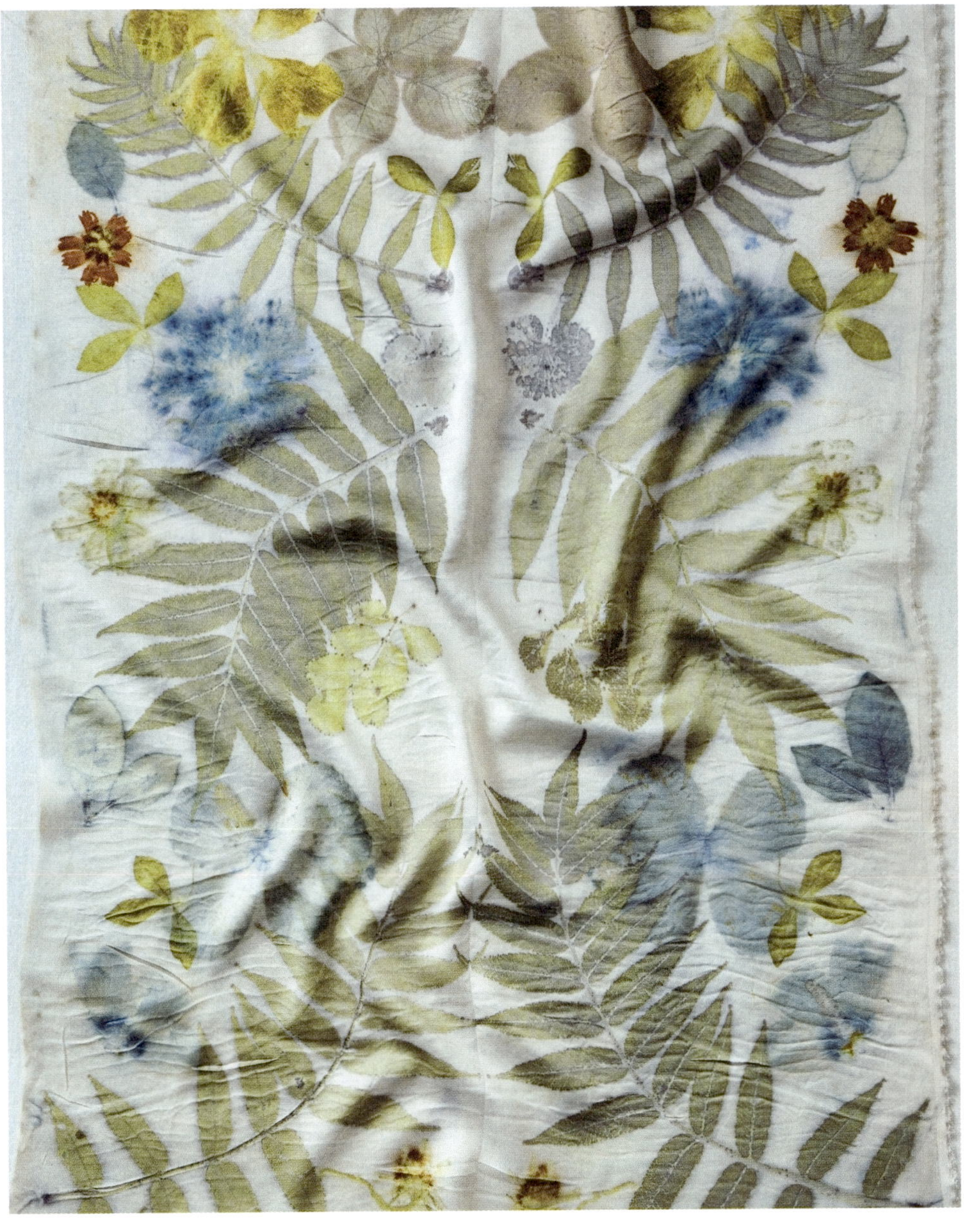

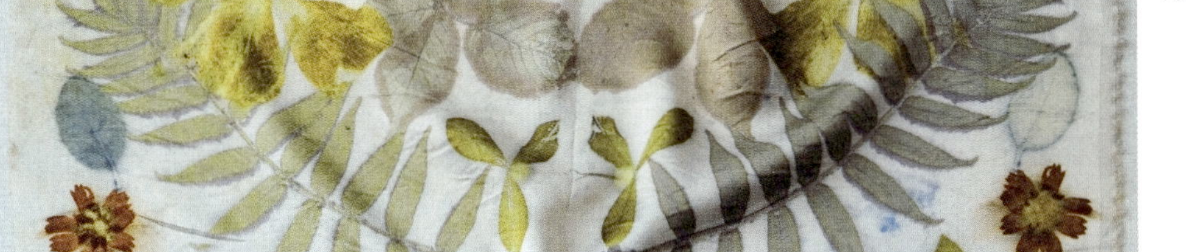
The finished result

7 **Allow the textile to dry** completely before rinsing. Rinse the textile in cool water with a dash of pH-neutral soap. Be gentle; no scrubbing necessary! Hang to dry in the shade and iron with steam on the back side for the best finishing results.

TECHNIQUE 3

Using a CARRIER BLANKET

Botanical printing with a carrier blanket introduces a captivating layer of color to the work. This technique involves placing a dye-soaked carrier blanket atop a target fabric adorned with plant matter, forming a creative sandwich. The dye from the carrier blanket permeates the target textile, creating a vibrant and unique background that beautifully frames the delicate patterns formed by the plants. The plant material acts as a resist, enhancing the contrast and allowing for striking visual effects.

Cotton flannel, French terry, and medium-weight jersey are good choices for a carrier blanket. Stretch fabrics such as jerseys can be helpful in molding themselves around any bulbous or protruding plant parts. Use white, natural, or light-colored pieces of cloth for the blanket so that no unwanted coloring or dye transfers to your work.

Carrier blankets can be reused, although it is impossible to remove the original tannins and pigmentation entirely. Before reusing one, wash it in the washing machine with soda ash, detergent, and hot water to remove any residual coloring. I reuse blankets by color; I'll store one for browns, or reds, or yellows, keeping the blankets within the same color families to avoid any unwanted color transfer.

A used carrier blanket itself can provide the background to a beautiful work of art. To preserve the color, mordant the carrier blanket using the Fundamental Mordant recipe *before* soaking in the dye bath, thus allowing it to accept coloration from the printing process.

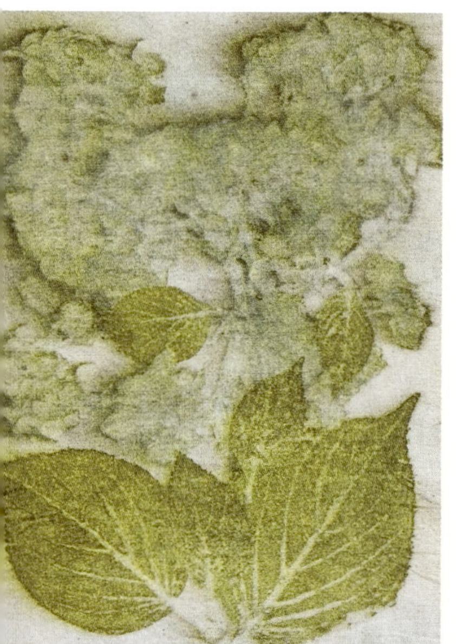

USING AN IRON CARRIER BLANKET

An iron carrier blanket is a piece of fabric that has been soaked in ferrous sulfate. The addition of an iron blanket can result in darkened outlines around the vegetation, creating more definition in your prints. Playing around with percentages of how much ferrous sulfate to use will determine how bold the outlines become, and how darkened ("saddened") some colors may appear.

Start by using ferrous sulfate at 1 to 2.5 percent weight of the iron blanket. Traditionally, the iron carrier blanket has been placed on top of fabric or paper that has been simply mordanted in PAS, or PAS and tannin, then decorated with tannic leaves. The result is a bold outline at the edges of the leaves, where the tannic acid and iron create a marked reaction, as if the leaves had been outlined by a pen.

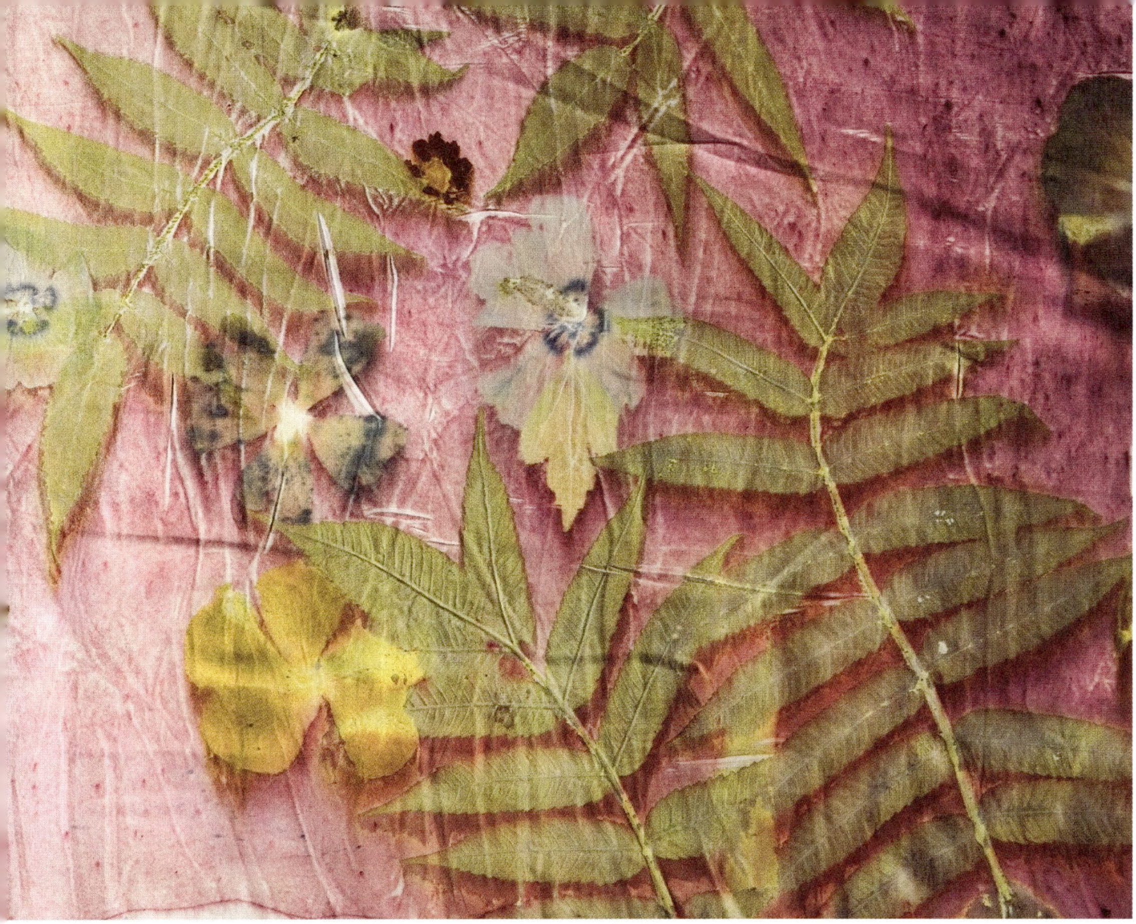

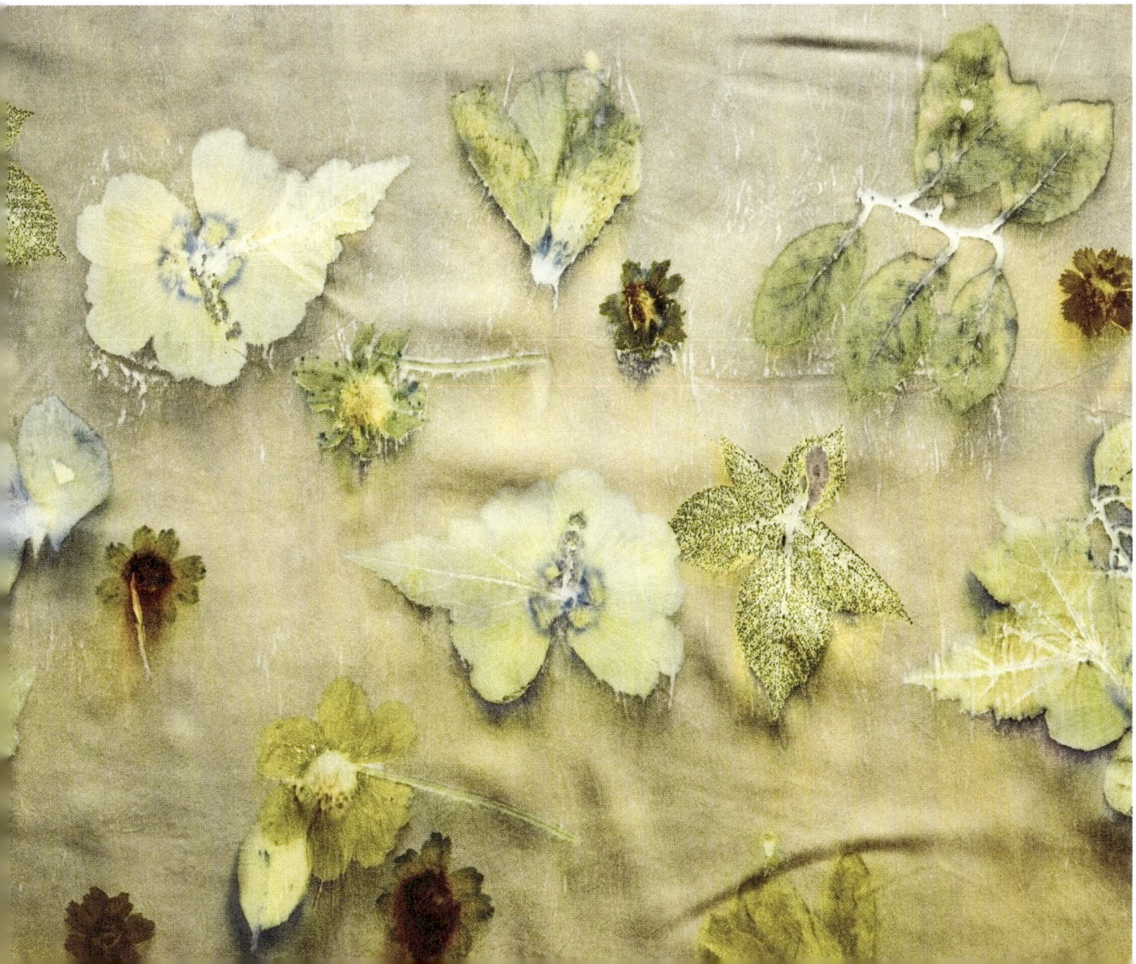

This piece of silk charmeuse was mordanted in the Compound Mordant Bright Outcome recipe and the carrier blanket was soaked in sappanwood dye for a saturated pink background color.

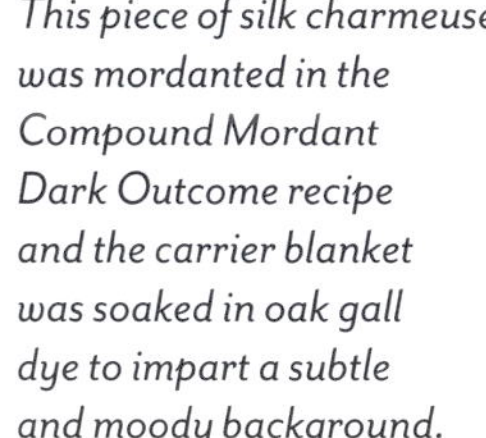

This piece of silk charmeuse was mordanted in the Compound Mordant Dark Outcome recipe and the carrier blanket was soaked in oak gall dye to impart a subtle and moody background.

MAKING A CARRIER BLANKET DYE BATH

All measurements in dyeing are based on the weight of fiber (WOF) to be dyed. Weight of fiber offers a simple method to determine how much dyestuff is needed for a given shade, regardless of whether the dyer wants to dye a small swatch of fabric or several yards. The weight of dyestuff is expressed as a percentage of weight of fiber.

The amount of dye to be used is determined by the weight of the carrier blanket when dry. This number, in grams, is multiplied by the percentage of dyestuff recommended by the retailer or by researching what percentage is most used. For every 100 grams of fiber, I use 1 liter (1 quart) of water.

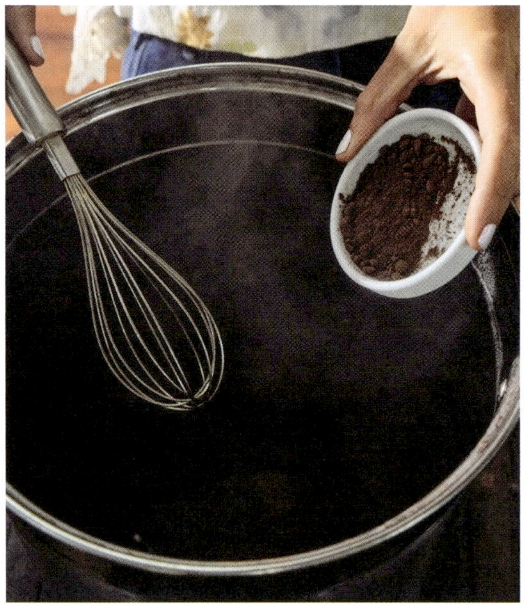

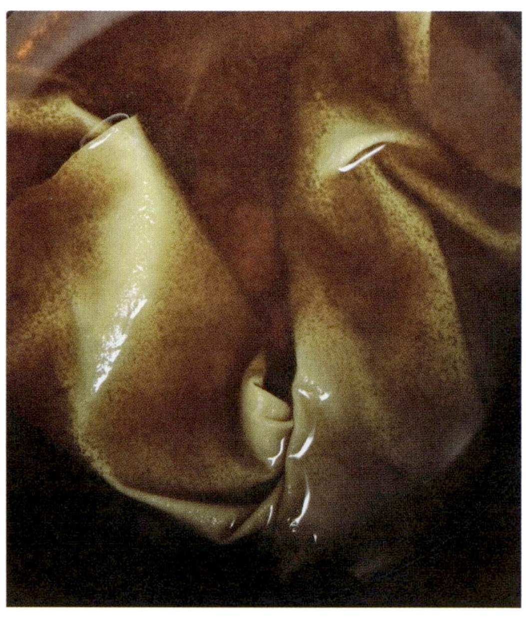

1 **Make the dye bath** by following the manufacturer's instructions. Allow it to cool.

2 **To dye the carrier blanket,** wet out the fabric, wring it out, and place it in the dye bath for 30 to 60 minutes prior to printing with it. For the carrier blanket to become fully saturated, you may need to add a small amount of water and leave the blanket to soak freely within the liquid. The blanket can soak in the dye for a couple of days if the temperature is cool enough to discourage the growth of mold, which can grow within a few days in very hot weather. Make sure it is saturated with color and there are no dry or blank spots on the fabric. Before using the carrier blanket, remove it from the dye and wring out until it is damp (not dripping).

PRINTING WITH A CARRIER BLANKET

On the following pages I outline two different processes that yield distinctly different results, achieving prints that are either vibrantly colorful or dark and contrasted. The first process uses the Compound Mordant Bright Outcome recipe on page 126. With it, you can experiment with many natural dyestuffs and extracts to obtain your desired color palette. The second one uses the Compound Mordant Dark Outcome recipe and tannin-rich dyes that interact with the elevated levels of iron in the mordant to create a luxurious, dark background.

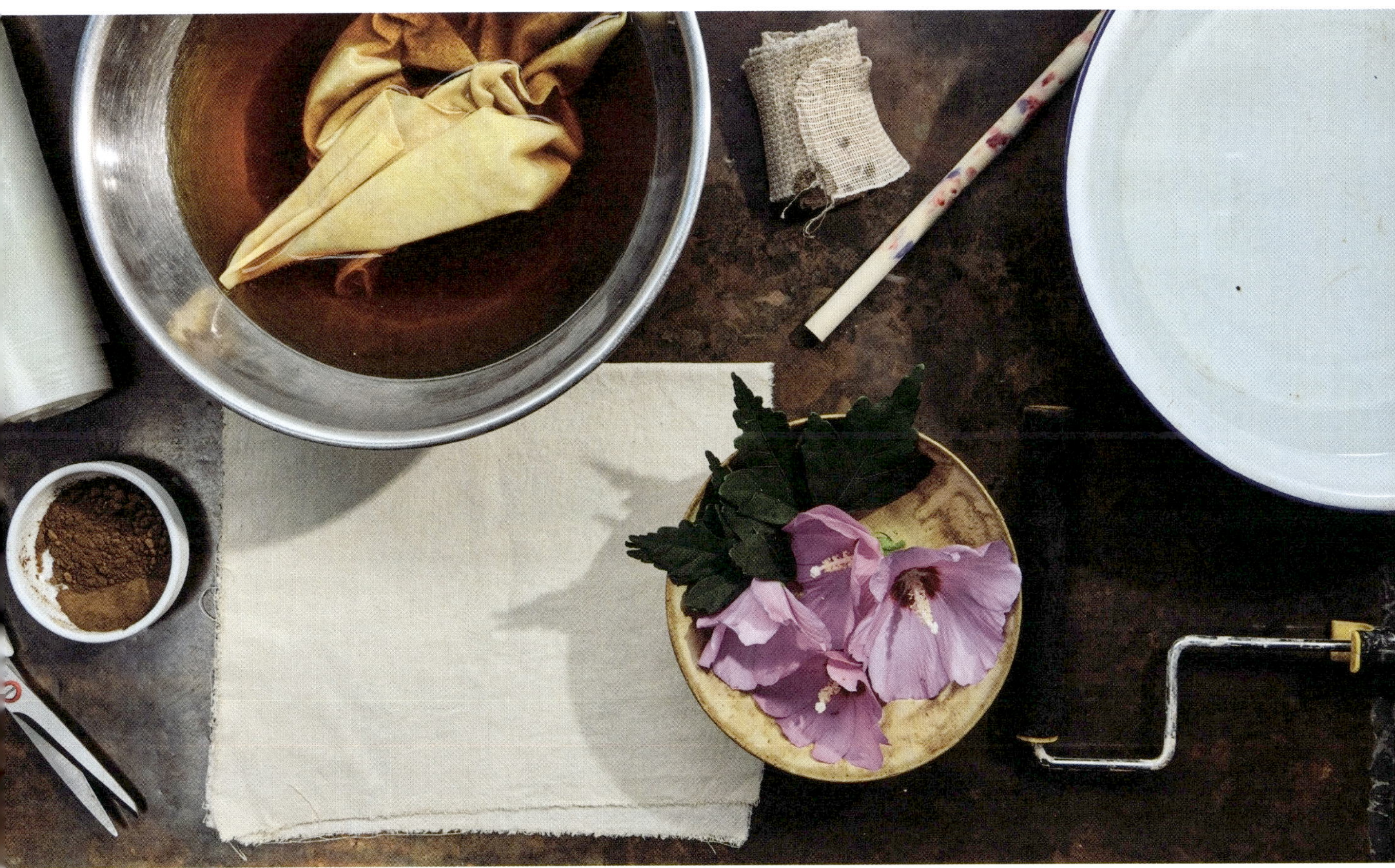

CREATING A BRIGHT AND COLORFUL BACKGROUND

Creating a vibrant and colorful background can be achieved through an array of botanical dyes that expand beyond the traditional tannin-specific options. While some of these dyes contain tannin, they also introduce a broader spectrum of colors, allowing for diverse outcomes. This guide highlights various botanicals and their potential color combinations, providing a road map for both novice and experienced dyers to explore and experiment with. Use these suggestions to enhance your natural dyeing projects, and feel free to explore beyond this guide to create your own diversity of color.

Suggested Botanicals

Reds: Madder root, lac, annatto seed (peach)

Oranges: Kamala, turmeric, yellow onion skins

Yellows: Marigold, myrobalan, Osage orange, pomegranate, buckthorn

Greens: Weld, Himalayan rhubarb, chlorophyllin extract, henna, dyer's broom, fustic

Blues: Saxon blue indigo extract, woad

Purples: Cochineal (lavender to magenta), logwood, purple onion skins, alkanet

Pinks: Quebracho rojo, safflower, brazilwood

Browns: Walnut, quebracho moreno, cutch

Blacks: Oak galls, pomegranate

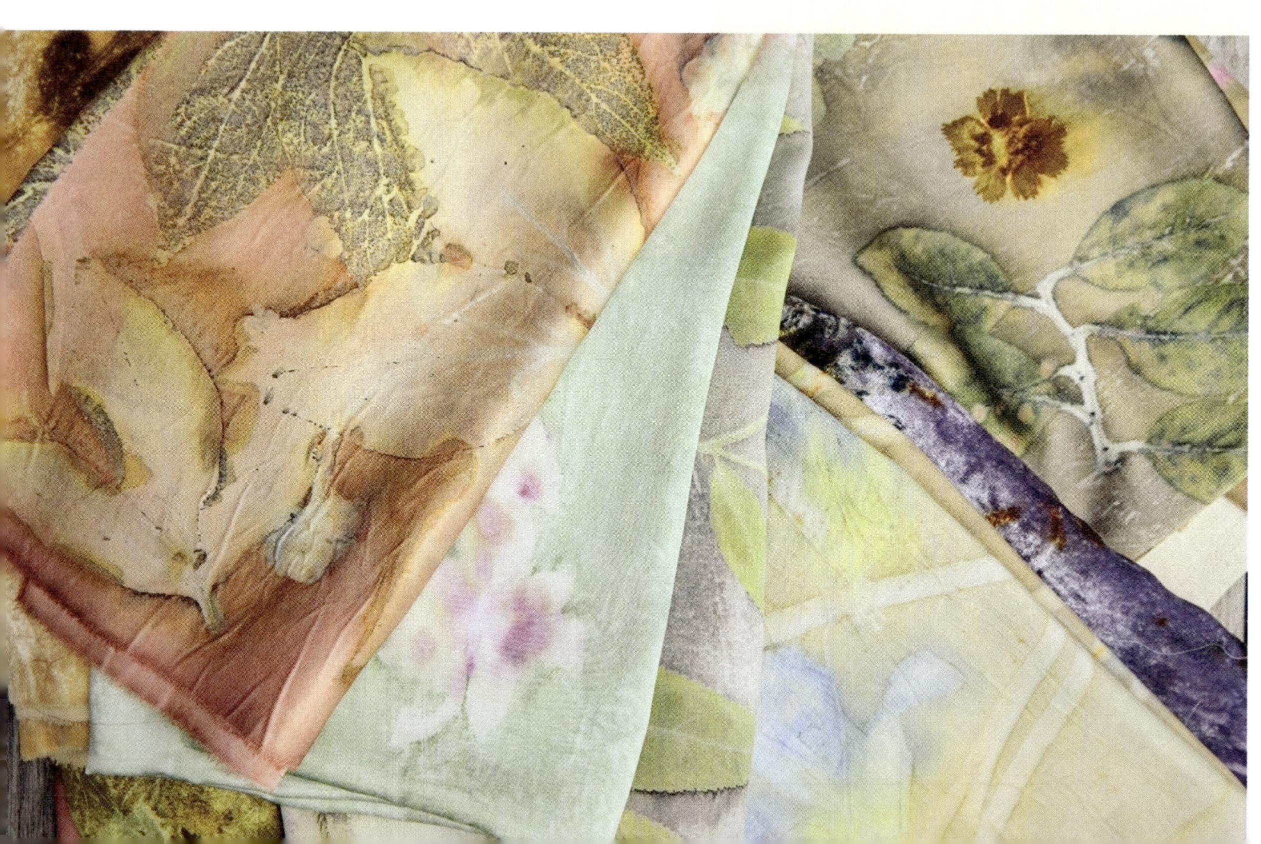

CREATING A POTENT AND DARK BACKGROUND

Tannin-rich dyes derived from plants produce complex, earthy colors, typically in shades of brown, yellow, or red. When paired with mordants like PAS and iron, the depth and intensity of the color are enhanced: PAS brightens and intensifies hues, while iron darkens and deepens them, offering a wide range of tonal possibilities.

These dyes are easy to find and forage for, as tannic plants are common in nature. For convenience, powdered tannin extracts, often a mixture of catechins, are available from vendors and can be used to achieve deep, vibrant colors in dyeing and printing, enhancing the final result.

Suggested Botanicals

Gallic tannins: Gallnut (oak gall), tara, and some sumacs are light-colored and clear. Contact with iron shifts their coloring to cool blues, dusky lavender, and grays.

Ellagic tannins: Myrobalan, pomegranate, black oak, and fustic are yellowish green. When combined with iron, they can turn mossy green, burnt yellow, and a near black.

Catechin tannins: Cutch, mimosa, quebracho moreno, tea leaves, and some sumacs are in the warm reddish brown family. When mixed with iron, these dyes remain true yet become richer and a few shades darker.

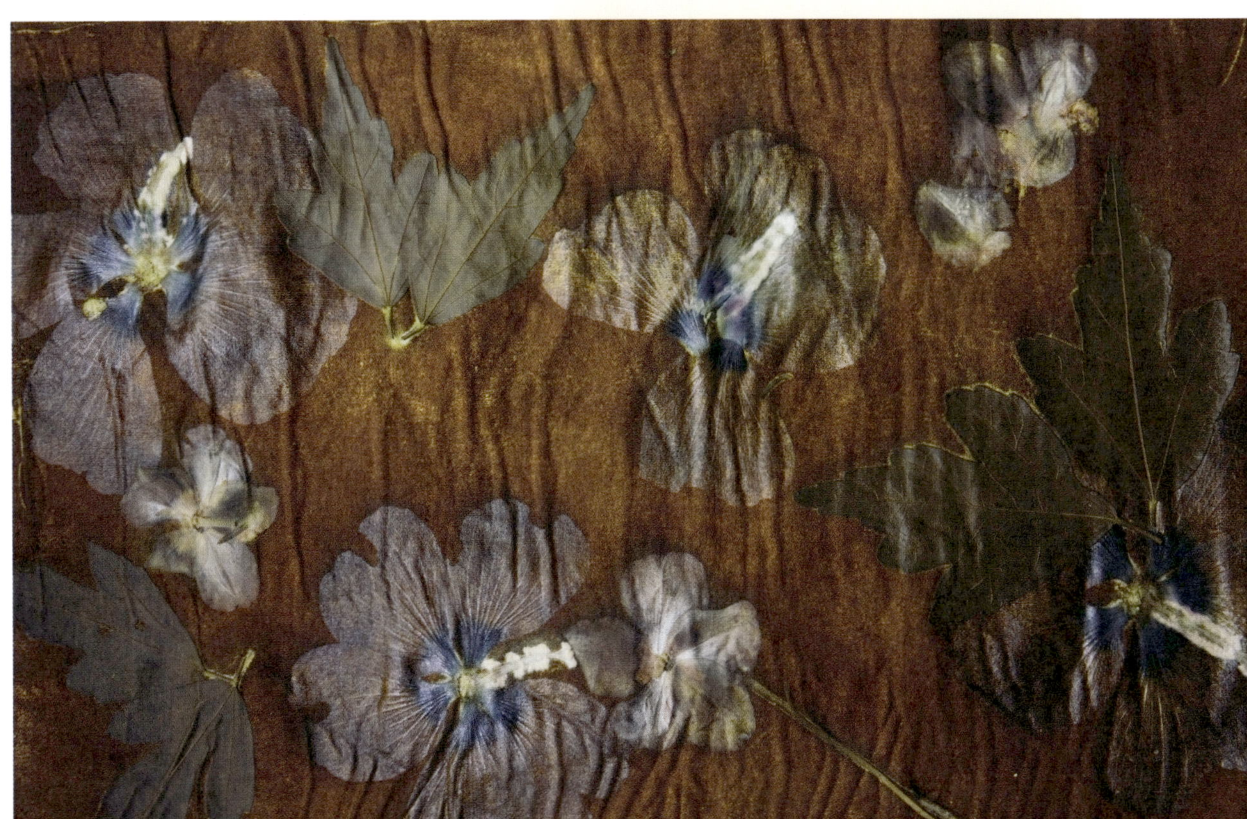

SET UP FOR SUCCESS

Scour the target unless the fabric is labeled as "ready to dye" (essential if using cellulose fabric). Optional for cellulose: Soak the fabric in a soy milk bath (page 129) before printing.

Mordant the target to achieve your intended result.

Cut a barrier (painter's plastic or parchment paper) that is slightly wider and at least 10 inches longer than the target.

Cut a carrier blanket that is the same width and length, if not slightly longer, as the target. Dye the carrier blanket according to the instructions on page 154.

Gather all your materials. Place leaves in a bowl of water to keep fresh and allow better contact with the target. Fill your steaming vessel with at least 3 inches of water and set to simmer.

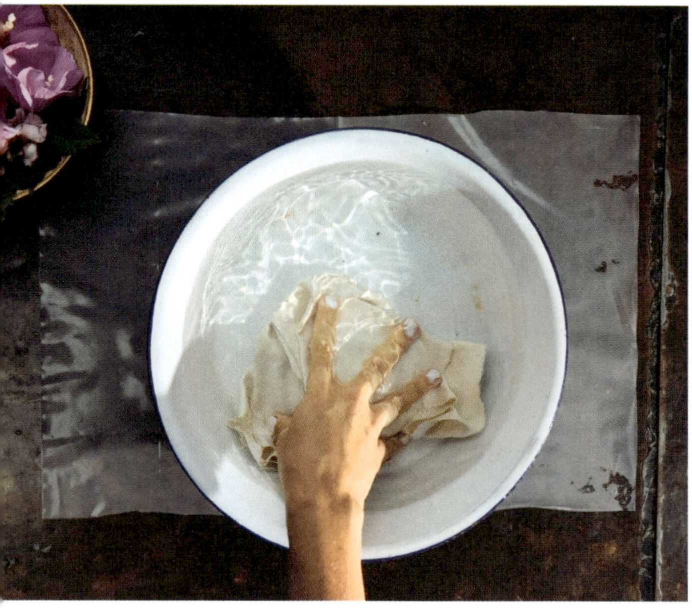

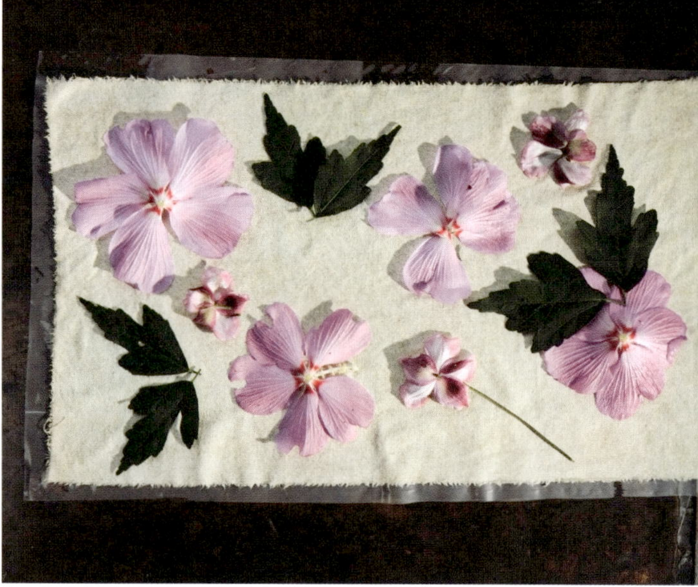

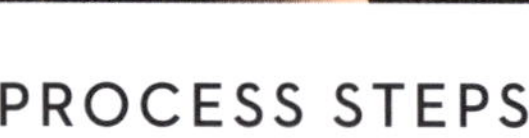

PROCESS STEPS

1 **Lay the barrier on the table.** Wet out the textile and gently wring it out until it is damp (not dripping). Lay it on top of the barrier, leaving excess on all sides. If the textile has a nubby or textured side, as with terry cloth, lay the smooth side carefully on the barrier.

2 **Decorate the textile,** aiming to cover 60 to 75 percent of the target with vegetation for a balanced composition. Don't forget about placing some vegetation toward the edges (vegetation can extend past the edges if desired).

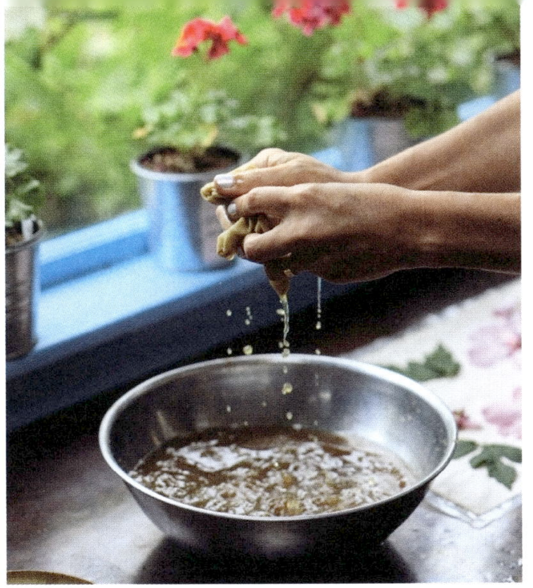

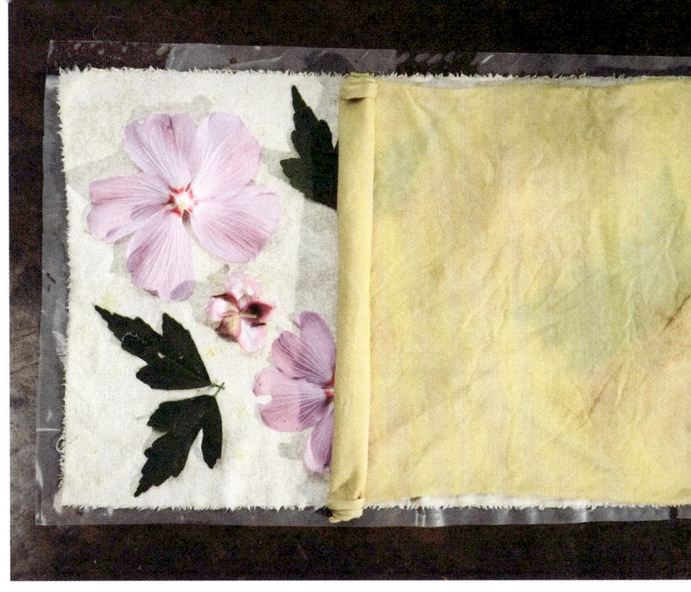

3 **Remove the carrier blanket** from the dye bath and wring out until it is damp (not dripping).

4 **You can place** the blanket directly on top of the target, but I find it easier to roll it into a tube first and then unroll it over the target.

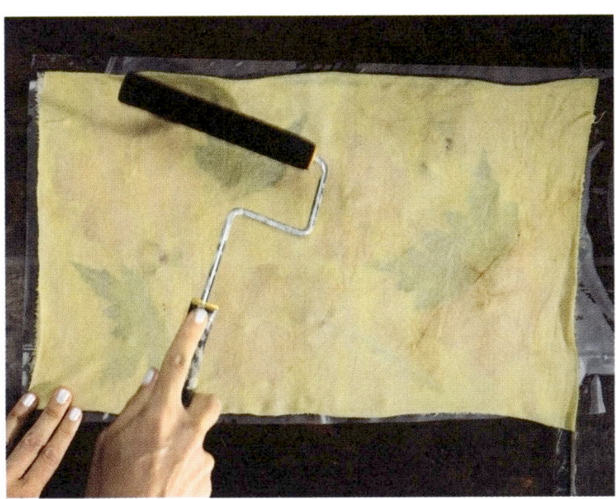

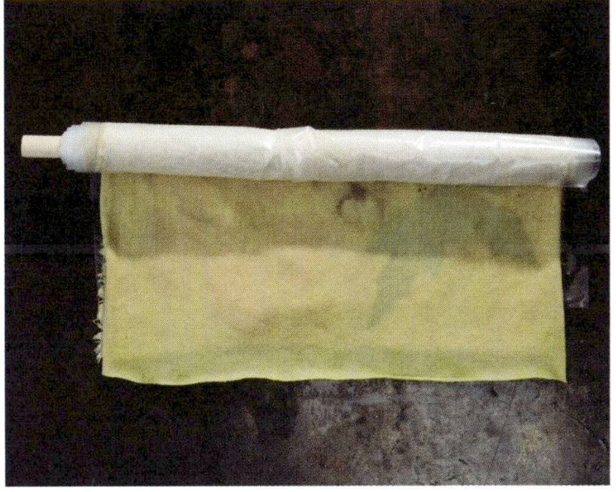

5 **Once the blanket is placed on top of the target,** use a roller to remove any bubbles or wrinkles. Compression is key to a crisp and saturated print; aim to get each layer of fabric as flat as possible.

6 **Carefully roll the barrier,** target, and carrier blanket around a dowel and tightly secure with a bandage or string. Steam the bundle with the lid on for 30 to 90 minutes (depending on the vegetation).

- **Just flowers:** 30–45 minutes
- **Flowers and leaves:** 60 minutes
- **Any composition with eucalyptus leaves:** 90 minutes

When the time is up, turn off the heat and allow the bundle to cool.

Once cool, unwrap the bandage or string and enjoy the reveal. Shake out any excess vegetation and hang to dry in the shade.

TECHNIQUE 4

Printing on CLOTHING AND GOODS

This technique outlines how to create botanical contact prints on clothing and other premade goods. For cellulose fibers, I recommend the Compound Mordant recipe (page 122) for the best results. The options are endless when it comes to variations in color, flowers, leaves, compositions, and layouts. Practice on sample fabric before printing on the final target to ensure that the plants and fibers form a strong bond, resulting in clear prints.

The best techniques for printing clothing and goods are bundle dyeing or mirror-image printing.

SET UP FOR SUCCESS

Scour the target unless the fabric is labeled as "ready to dye" (essential if using cellulose fabric). Optional for cellulose: Soak the fabric in a soy milk bath (page 129) before printing.

Mordant the target by following the recipe of your choice, using one with ferrous sulfate if printing with leaves to ensure a good print. When printing with just flowers and dried botanicals, the Fundamental Mordant recipe without iron (page 118) is suitable.

Gather all your materials. Place leaves in a bowl of water to keep fresh and allow better contact with the target. Fill your steaming vessel with at least 3 inches of water and set to simmer.

If printing a garment using barriers, cut a barrier that is the same length and half the width of your garment. Optional: If you do not wish color to bleed through to the other side, cut barriers to the same size and shape of the insides of the garment, such as the torso area and sleeves.

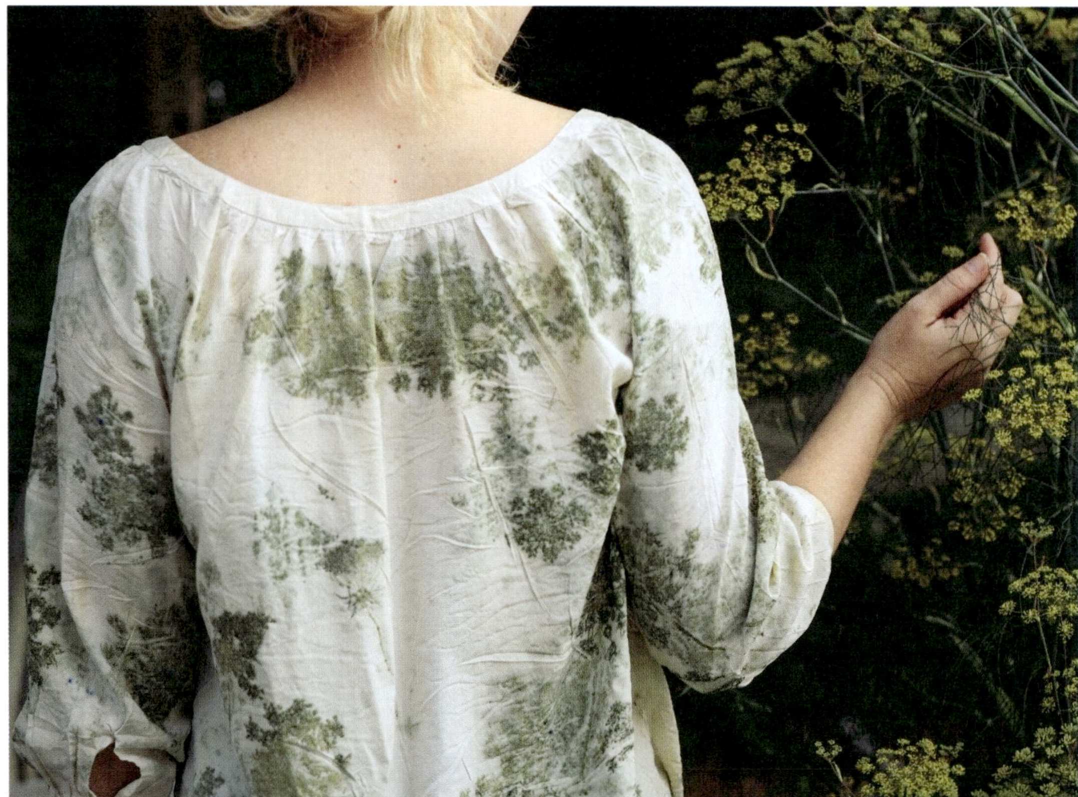

PROCESS STEPS

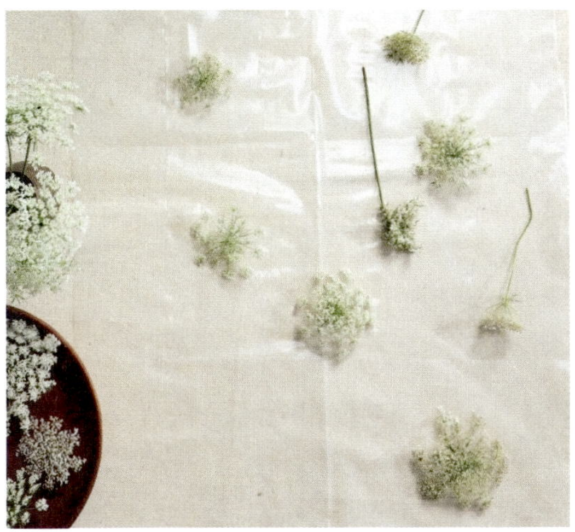

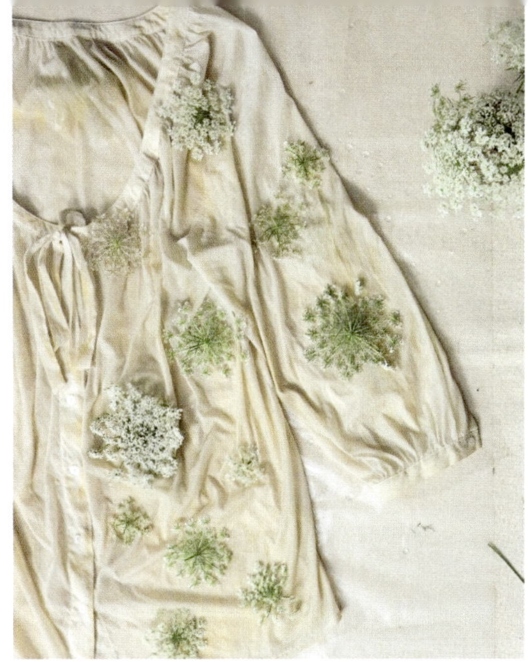

1 **Lay the barrier on the table.** Decorate the barrier as if it were *one half* of the back of the garment.

2 **Place half of the target** *on top* of the vegetation (e.g., the left backside of the shirt, including the arm). Now decorate the front side with vegetation.

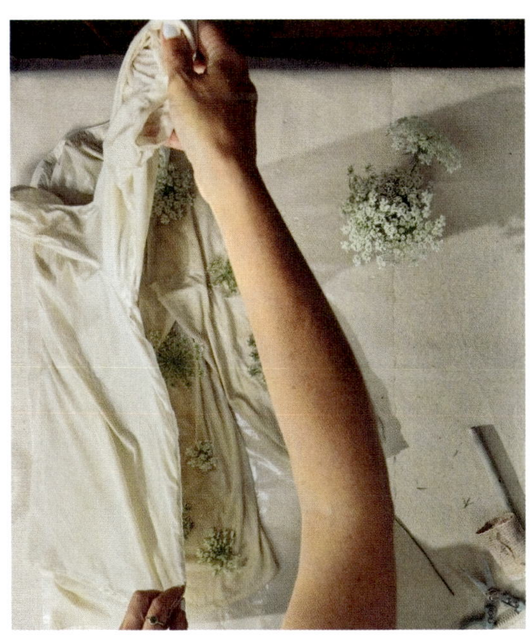

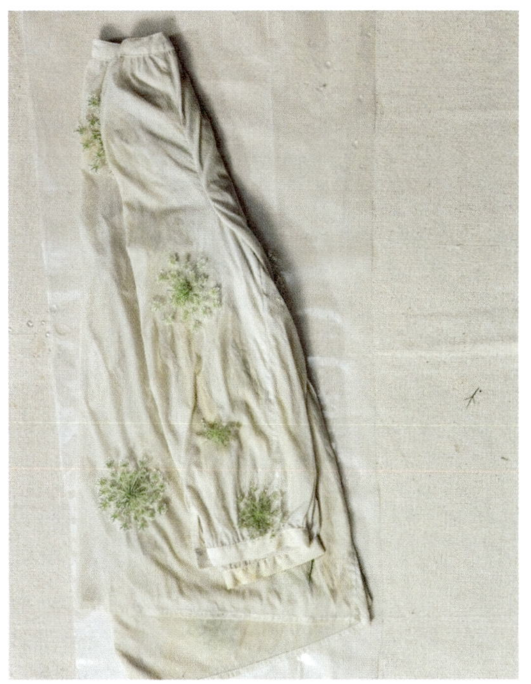

3 **Fold the other half** of the garment onto the decorated side. If printing on a shirt or another garment with sleeves, line up the sleeves and center front line.

4 **Decorate the side** that is now facing up, using a similar design as the other side. To fit the target on the dowel, you may need to fold sleeves (if applicable) on top of the garment or even fold the entire garment widthwise.

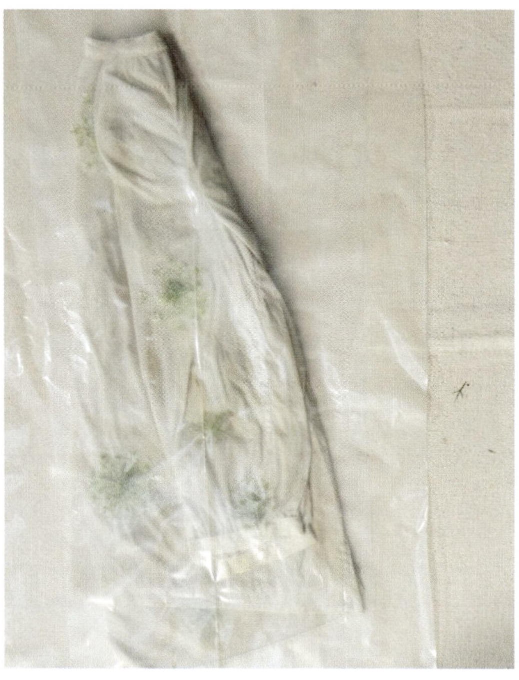

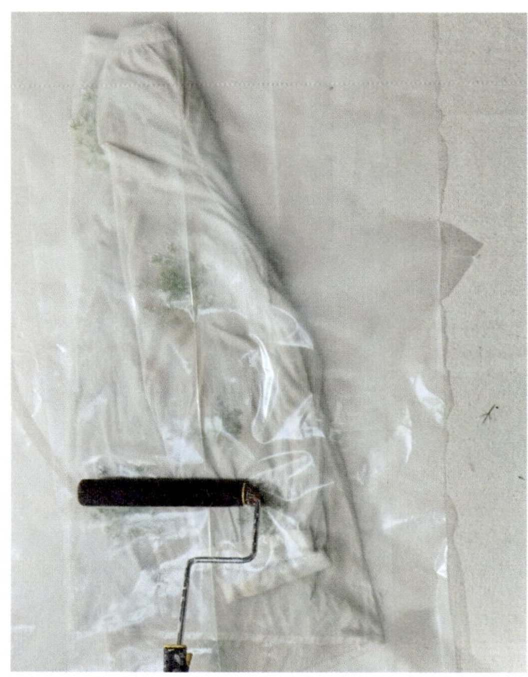

5 **Place barriers on top** of the garment, if using. Use a roller to compress the layers.

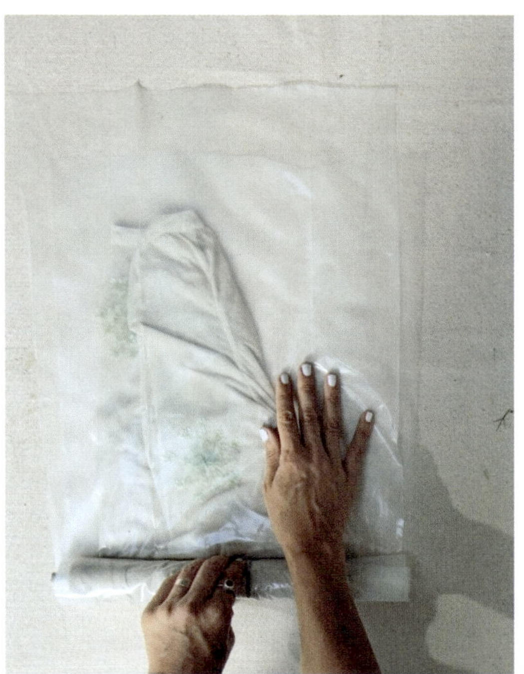

6 **Beginning at one end,** roll the garment tightly around the dowel, keeping it as compressed as possible. You can also roll the garment without a dowel, allowing for more flexibility when placing it in the steamer.

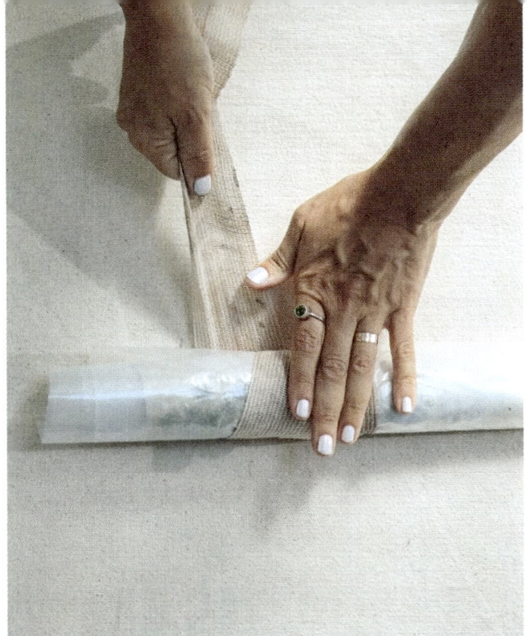

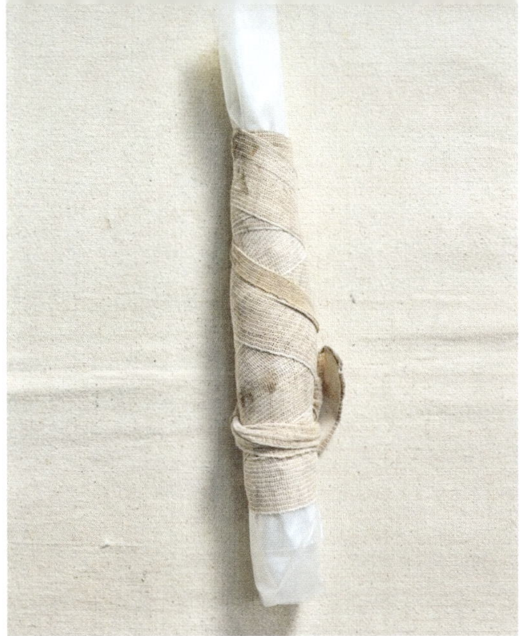

7 **Securely wrap** the bundle with an Ace bandage or T-shirt yarn. Steam the bundle with the lid on for 30 to 90 minutes, depending on the vegetation:

- **Just flowers:** 30–45 minutes
- **Flowers and leaves:** 45–60 minutes
- **Any composition with eucalyptus leaves:** 90 minutes

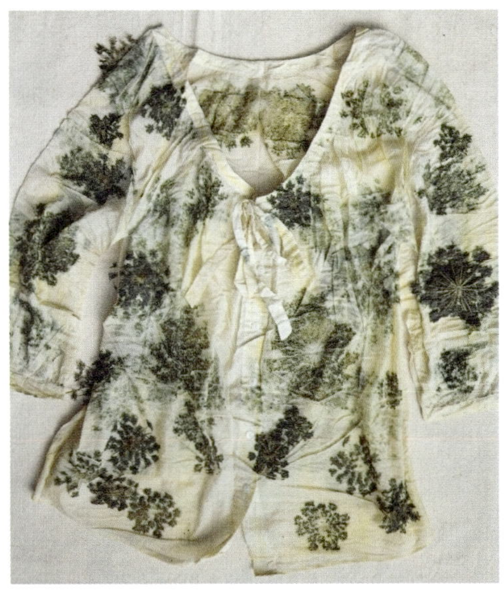

8 **After the allotted time,** turn off the heat and allow the bundle to cool. Unwrap the bundle and shake off excess vegetation. Let the textile dry completely before rinsing. Rinse the textile in cool water with a dash of pH-neutral soap. It does not have to be scrubbed; be gentle. Hang to dry in the shade and iron with steam for the best finishing results.

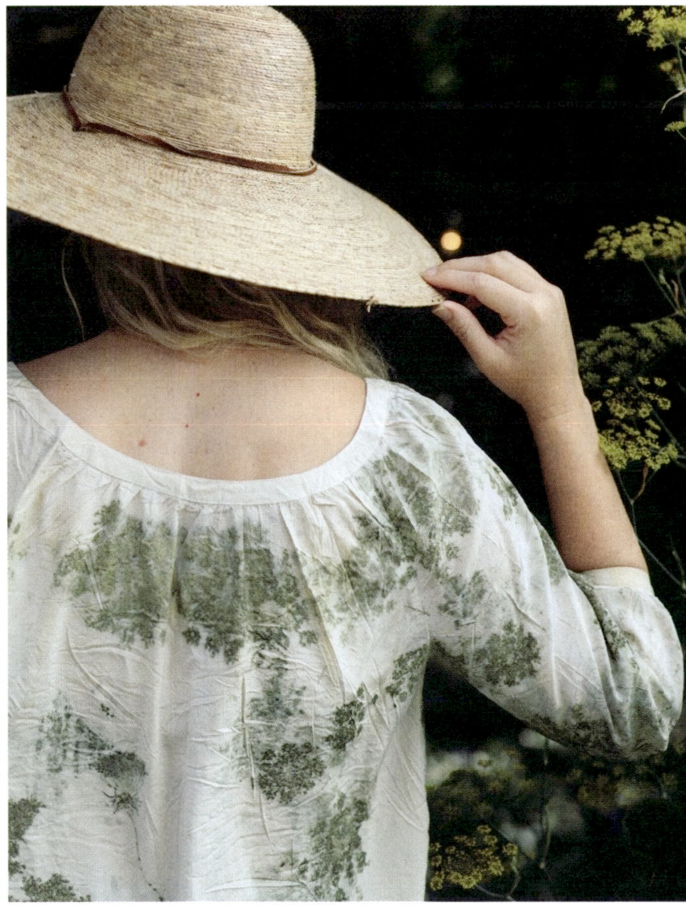

QUICK INDIGO DYEING WITH SAXON BLUE

Saxon blue, first created in Germany in the 1740s, is a remarkable dye derived from natural indigo, converted to a liquid dye using a strong acid to achieve a unique coloration. Unlike traditional indigo vat dyes, Saxon blue offers an easier application method, exclusively suited for protein fibers. This vibrant hue, characterized by its greener undertones compared to regular indigo, serves as an excellent base for crafting a diverse palette, including teal, aqua, cornflower, periwinkle, lilac, and medium value purple.

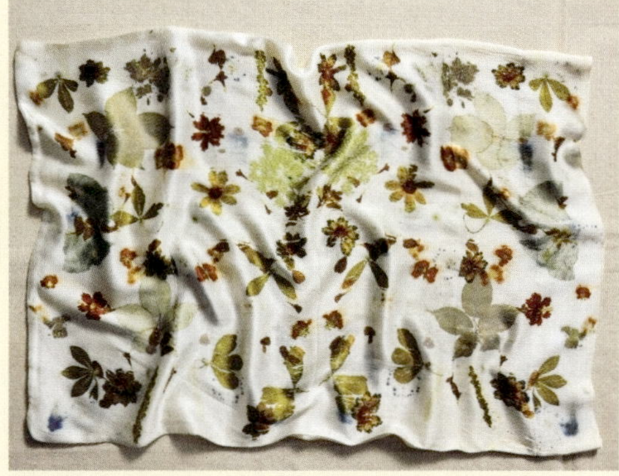

This silk charmeuse pillowcase was bundle dyed with various flowers and leaves. A quick dip into a Saxon blue dye bath will dramatically transform the coloring. To create your own quick indigo dye bath, follow these steps.

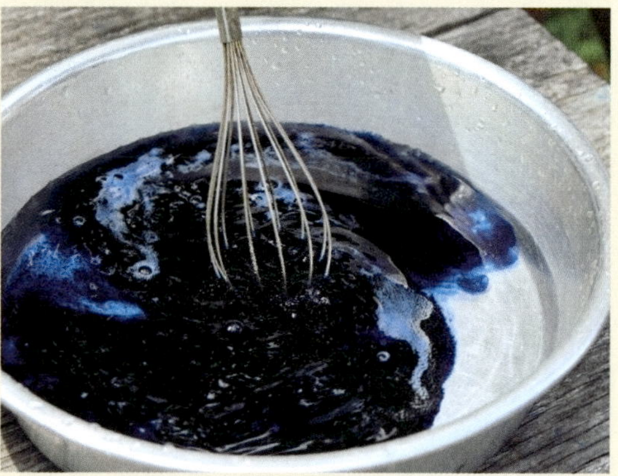

1 **Weigh your target dry** to calculate the amount of dye needed: 25 grams of Saxon blue will dye about 285 grams (0.625 pounds) of fiber to a very rich blue shade. Measure out the liquid dye and pour into a bucket or bowl of water with enough liquid to immerse your target. Mix well.

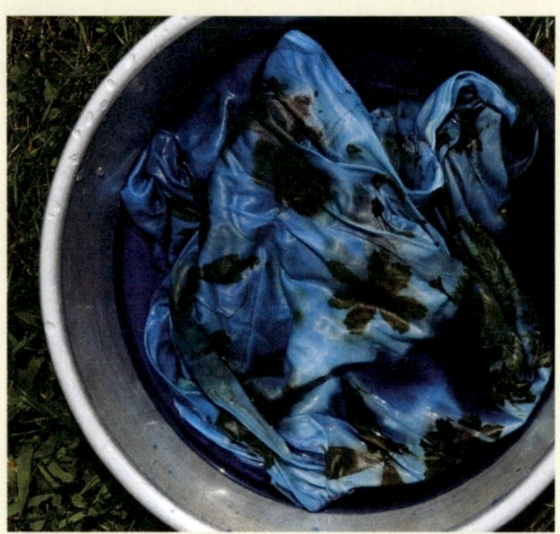

2 **Wearing gloves,** add the fabric to the vessel and work it in with your hands, ensuring full saturation. The transfer of dye to fabric happens quickly; after a minute the target has reached full saturation.

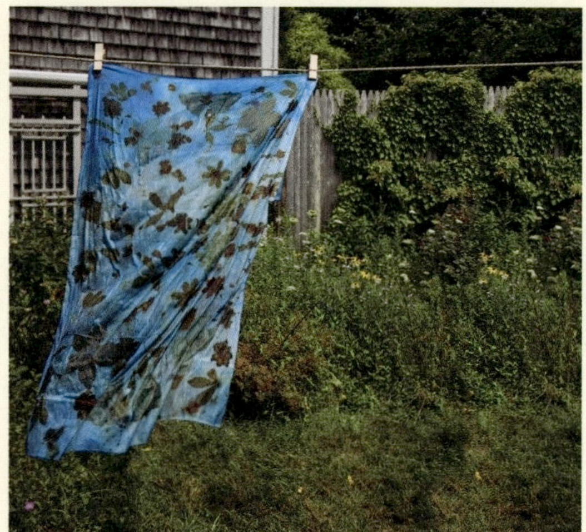

3 **Wring the target out** and hang to dry fully. Once dry, rinse with cold water to remove any excess dye. Dry again, then iron with steam on the back side.

How to Care for Fabric After Printing

Careful handling and mindful maintenance will ensure the longevity and beauty of your exquisitely printed textiles. I always opt for handwashing botanically printed fabrics to ensure they are treated carefully. Fill a vessel large enough to accommodate your fabric with cold water and add a small amount (1 teaspoon) of olive oil soap, pH-neutral dish soap (such as Seventh Generation or Dr. Bronner's), or a sulfate-free shampoo. Immerse the fabric in the water for a few moments and agitate gently. Rinse and hang to dry in a shaded area away from direct sunlight.

To keep your fabrics looking vibrant, consider using a steam iron, rather than washing, for a gentle refresh.

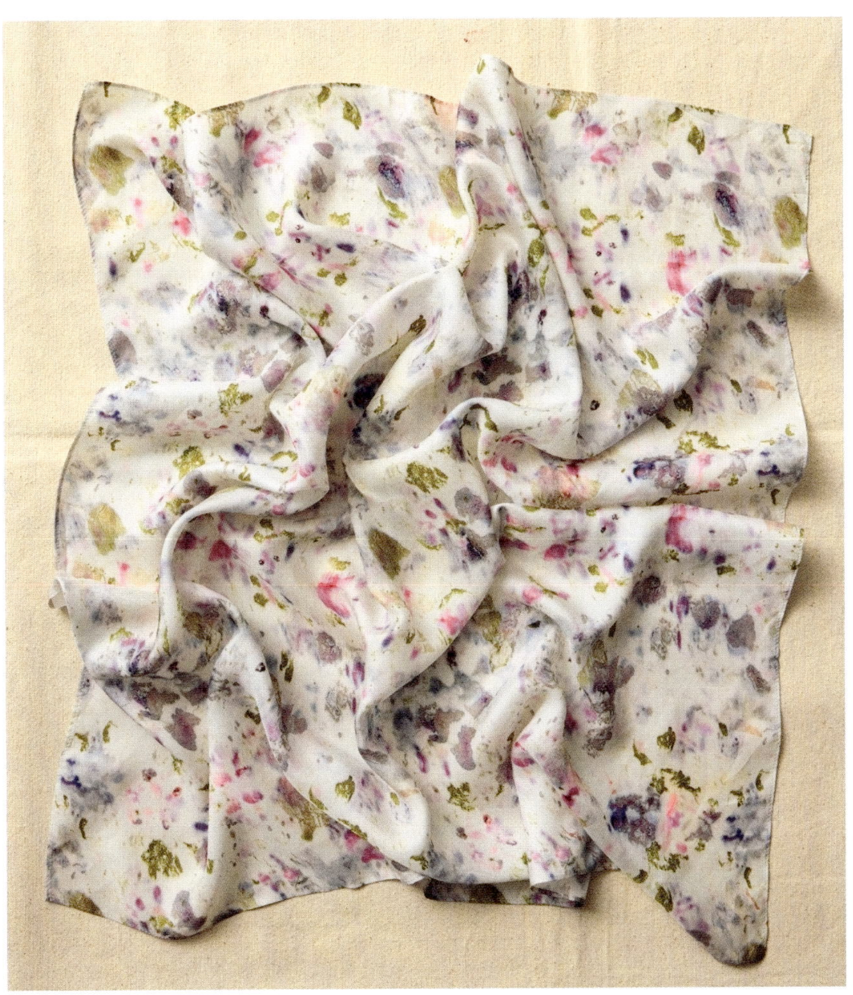

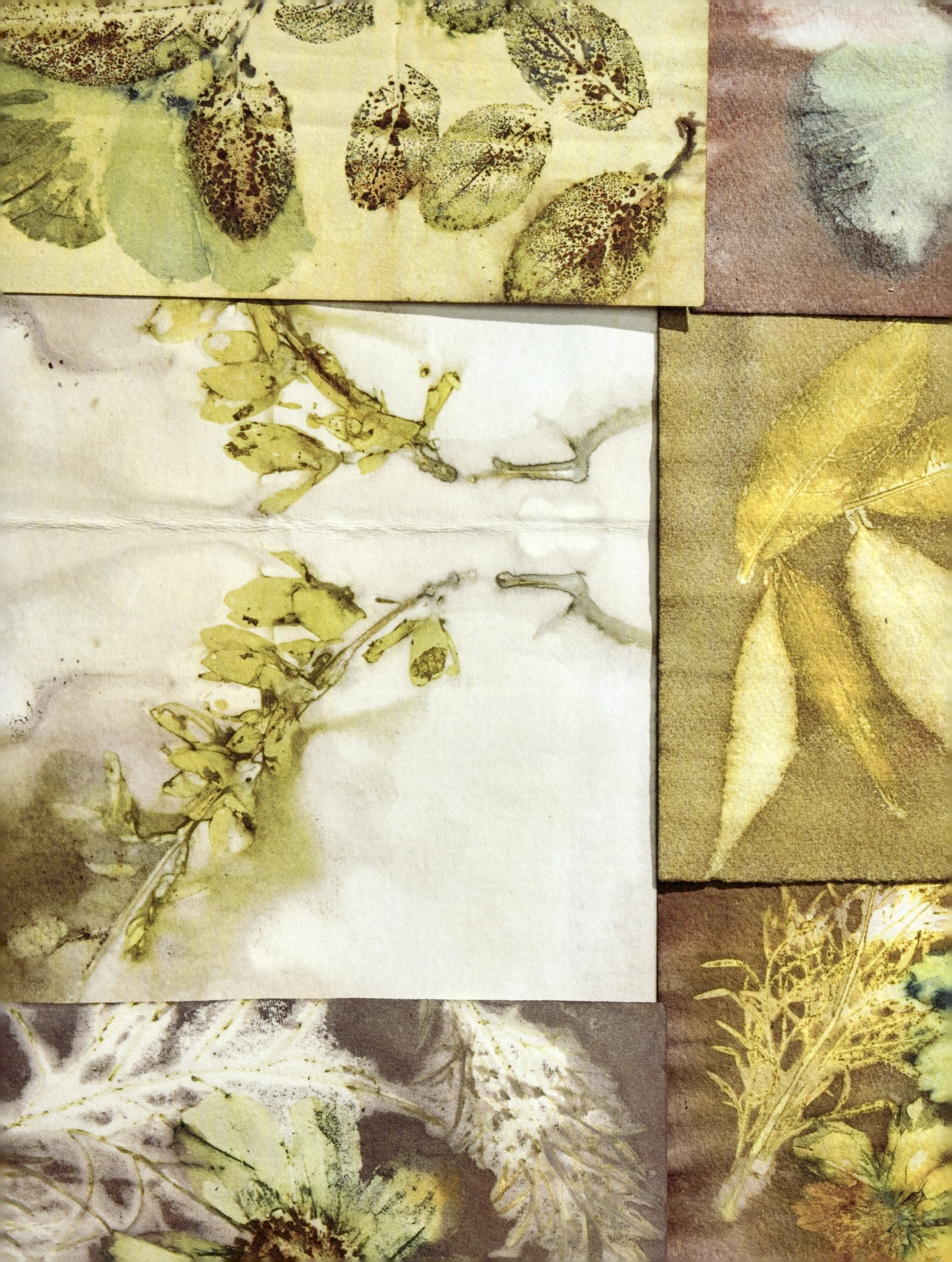

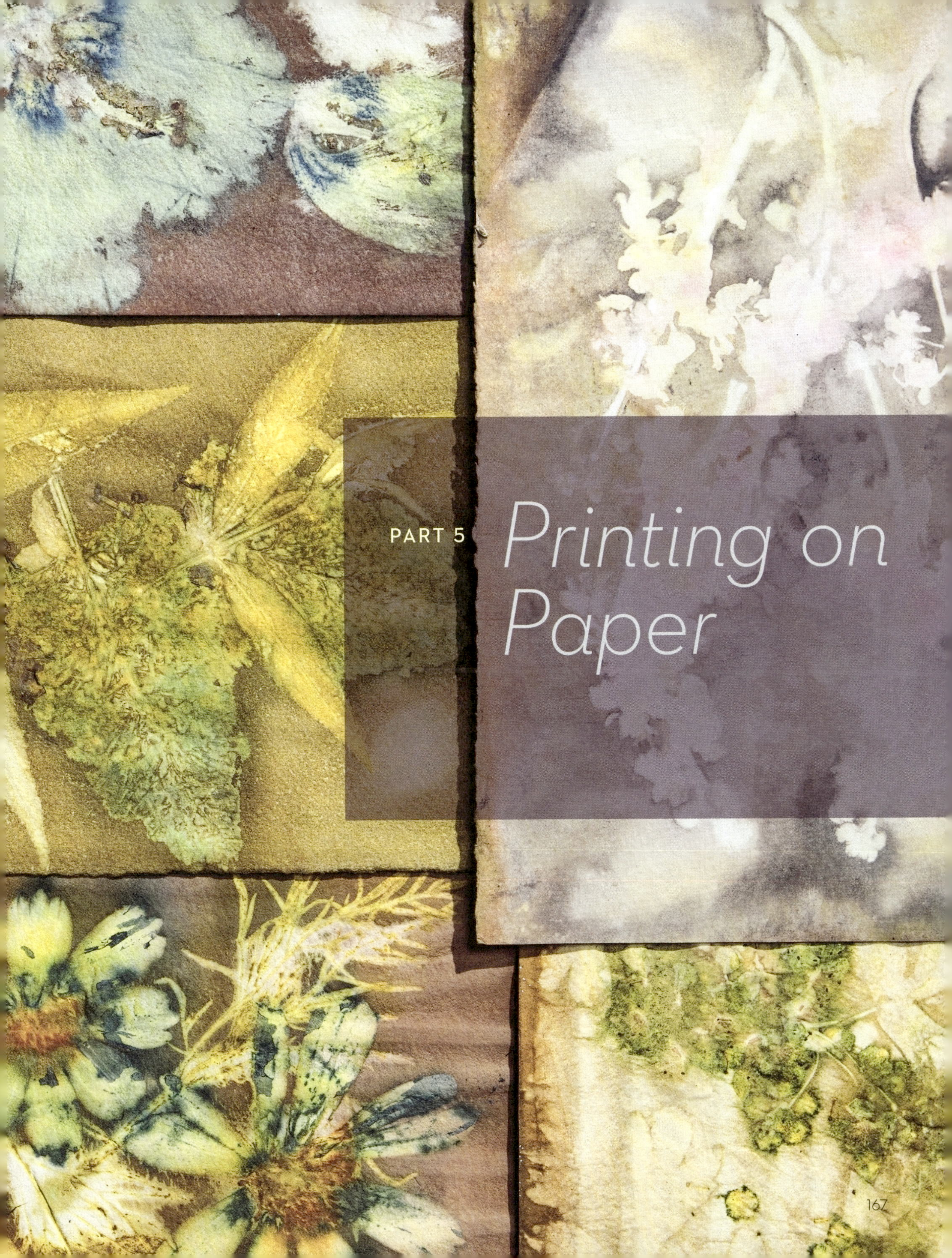

PART 5

Printing on Paper

Techniques for Printing on Paper

Botanical contact printing on paper is similar to printing on fabric. Many of the same materials and ingredients can be used for both processes. Paper is an excellent medium for experimenting with natural dye techniques due to its manageable size and affordability. Unlike fabric, paper allows for easy practice without the cost concerns often associated with textiles. Additionally, paper is readily available, making it a sustainable choice—perfect for utilizing all that paper sitting in your recycling bin.

I outline two processing methods here. The first is rolling, bundling, and steaming the target above the water level on a steamer tray, just like processing fabric. This technique uses a cushioning blanket to yield crisp, realistic results. As with fabric, you can print on paper with or without a carrier blanket. If not using a carrier blanket, aim to use plants that are reliable printers to achieve distinct coloring or markings on plain white paper.

The second method is immersion printing, in which the decorated paper is wrapped around a pipe or a tin can and placed directly into a simmering dye bath. The dye bath can be made with iron, tannin, a botanical dye based on a specific color choice, or raw dye materials, such as onion skins, avocado pits, or pomegranate skins (a new way to compost!). Immersion printing can be quite unpredictable, making for dramatic compositions that are painterly and surprising.

You can use cushioning and carrier blankets to print on paper, just as you can with fabric.

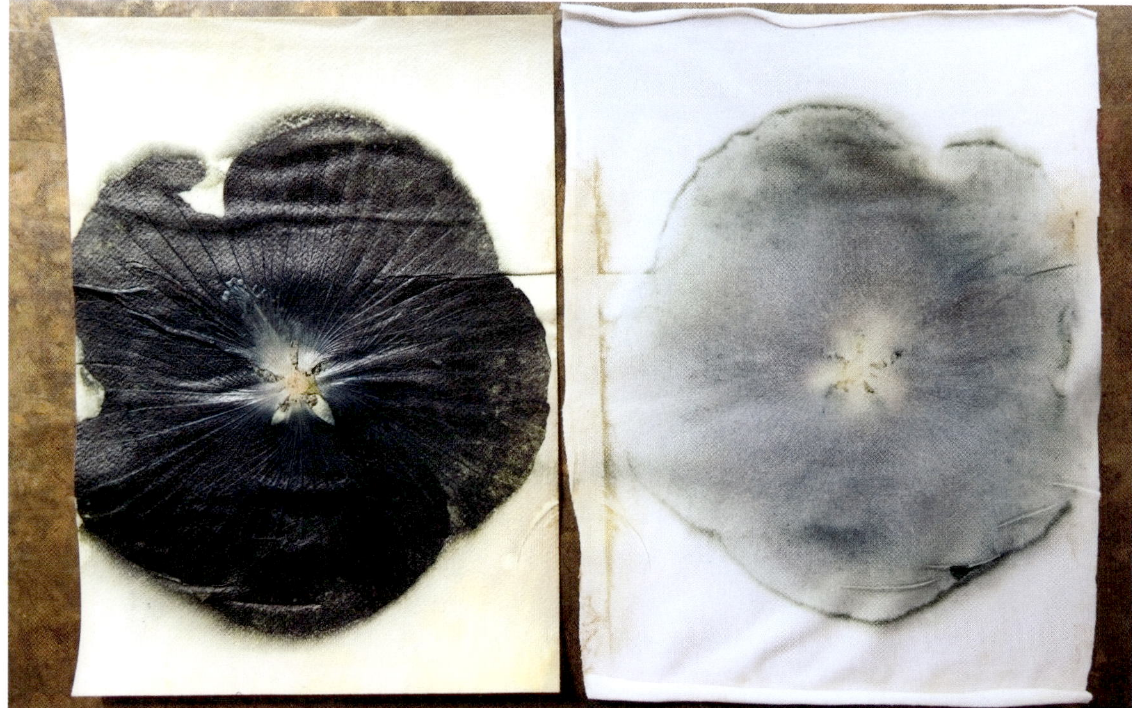

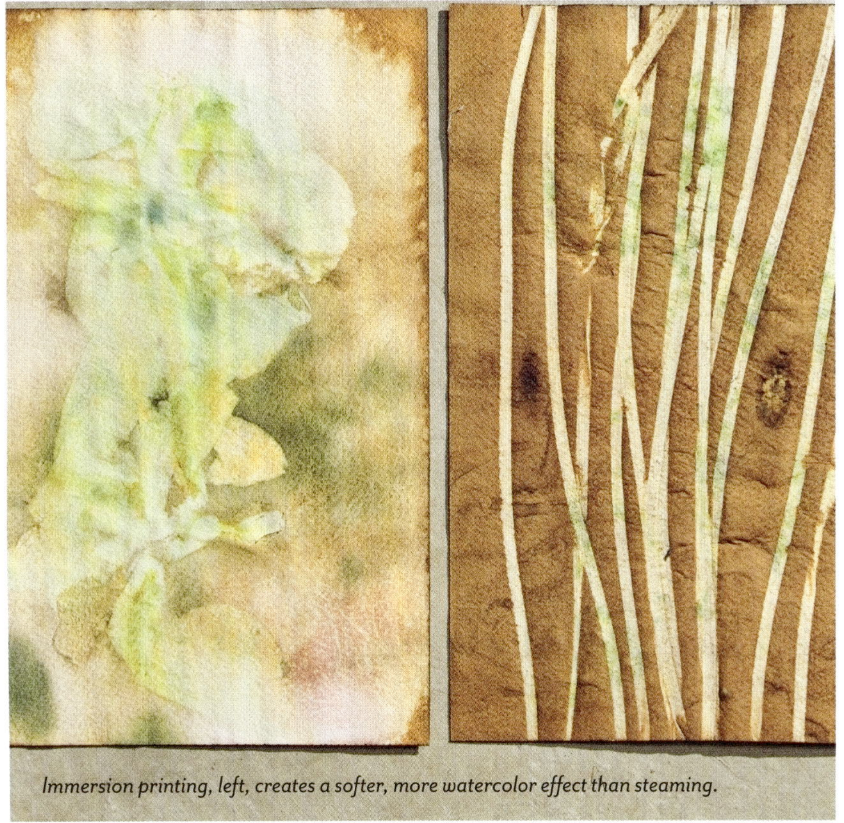

Immersion printing, left, creates a softer, more watercolor effect than steaming.

Choosing Paper

When printing on paper, as with all botanical printing, experimenting is key to discovering what's possible. By exploring various plant materials and printing techniques, you can unlock unique shades and compositions that capture the beauty of nature.

Begin your journey with materials you already have; printer paper, scrap paper, and even pages from old books make excellent starting points. By testing your mordants and the printing abilities of various plants on these options, you can refine your techniques without the fear of wasting more luxurious paper.

Paper is a cellulose fiber, much like cotton fabric, and requires mordanting before printing in order to enhance pigment transfer. I typically use hot-pressed watercolor paper, which often comes sized with starches, PAS, or synthetic ingredients. This sizing can act as a beneficial aid in botanical printing, improving the adhesion of the mordant and plant pigments, resulting in beautifully saturated prints. Regardless of whether the paper is sized, I always mordant it to ensure the strongest outcomes.

WATERCOLOR PAPER

Consider weight and quality when you are choosing watercolor paper. This paper can be rough (nubby texture), hot pressed (a very smooth surface with almost no tooth), or cold pressed (slightly textured, a cross between rough and hot). White or light-colored paper will best display your prints. Many of the projects shown in this book were printed on a paper that I love for its satinlike surface: Arches Aquarelle hot-pressed watercolor paper, 140-pound weight, gelatin-sized.

Most watercolor paper is made from either 100 percent cotton or wood pulp and comes in two different weights: grams or pounds per square meter. I prefer a medium weight between 140 pound and 240 pound; it rolls more easily than thinner paper and is a bit more workable than thick, heavier-weight paper.

How to Mordant Paper

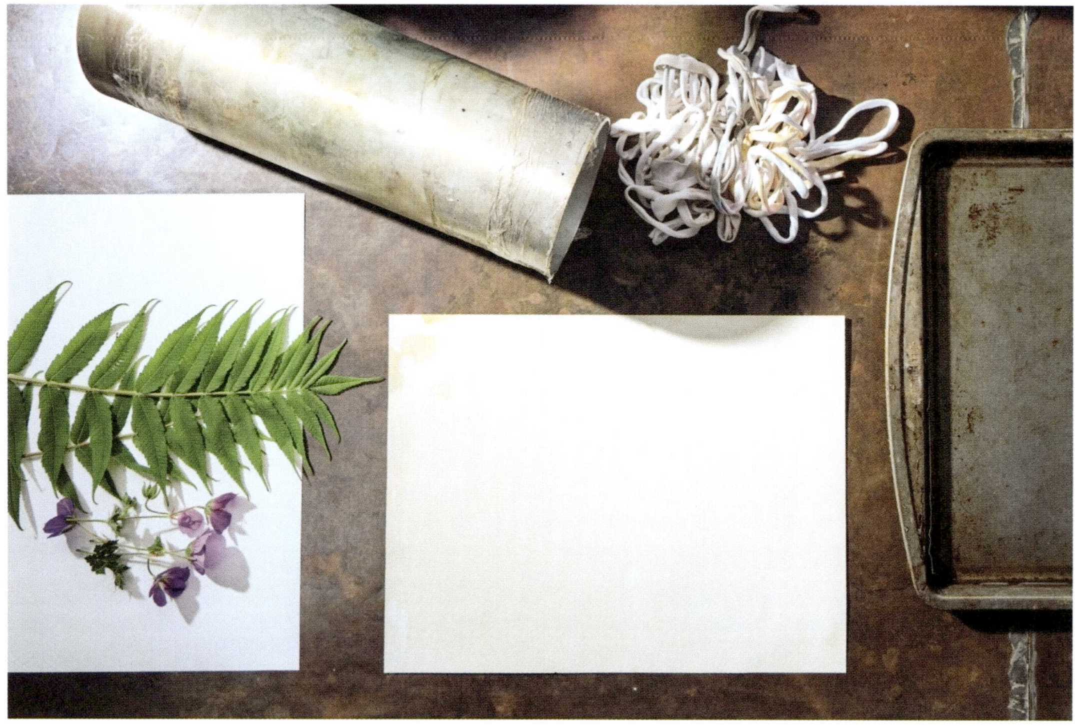

In this method, paper is mordanted in a carefully balanced solution of PAS, ferrous sulfate, and soda ash, mimicking the traditional fabric mordanting process. First, the paper is thoroughly immersed in the mordant solution and then suspended to dry completely. Then the paper is treated with an oatmeal or wheat bran bath to remove any residual mordant molecules lingering on the fibers. This essential process not only enhances the bond of the mordant to the paper but also facilitates a superior uptake of color from the vegetation, resulting in stunningly rich and dynamic prints.

I usually mordant a stack of paper at once so that I have a supply on hand whenever I need it.

COMPOUND MORDANT RECIPE

This solution is sufficient to process approximately ten 11- × 14-inch pieces of 140-pound watercolor paper. Excess solution can be stored in a sealed jar for later use.

- ½ liter (½ quart) distilled white vinegar
- 50 grams potassium aluminum sulfate (PAS)
- 4–8 grams ferrous sulfate (more ferrous sulfate will darken the prints)
- 20 grams soda ash

STEP 1: MORDANT

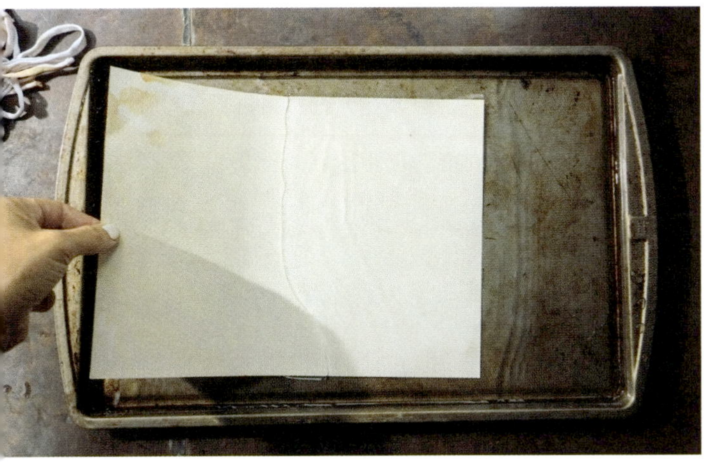

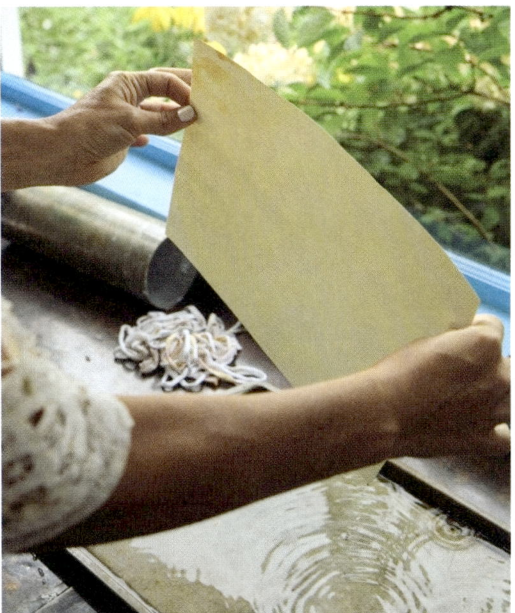

1 **Pour the vinegar** into a measuring cup or mixing vessel (nonreactive glass, steel, or enamel). Add the PAS and whisk until dissolved. Add the ferrous sulfate and whisk until completely dissolved. This prevents the mordant from becoming murky with the addition of soda ash. Add the soda ash a little bit at a time, stirring until all particles are dissolved. Soda ash may have a fizzing and bubbling reaction. Wait until the bubbling has stopped.

2 **Pour the mordant solution** into a shallow plastic tub or cookie sheet that is larger than the sheets of paper being mordanted. Run the paper through the mordant solution for at least 30 seconds. Thicker paper can be left to rest for a few minutes. Hold the paper above the solution to allow excess mordant to drip off before laying it flat or hanging it to dry.

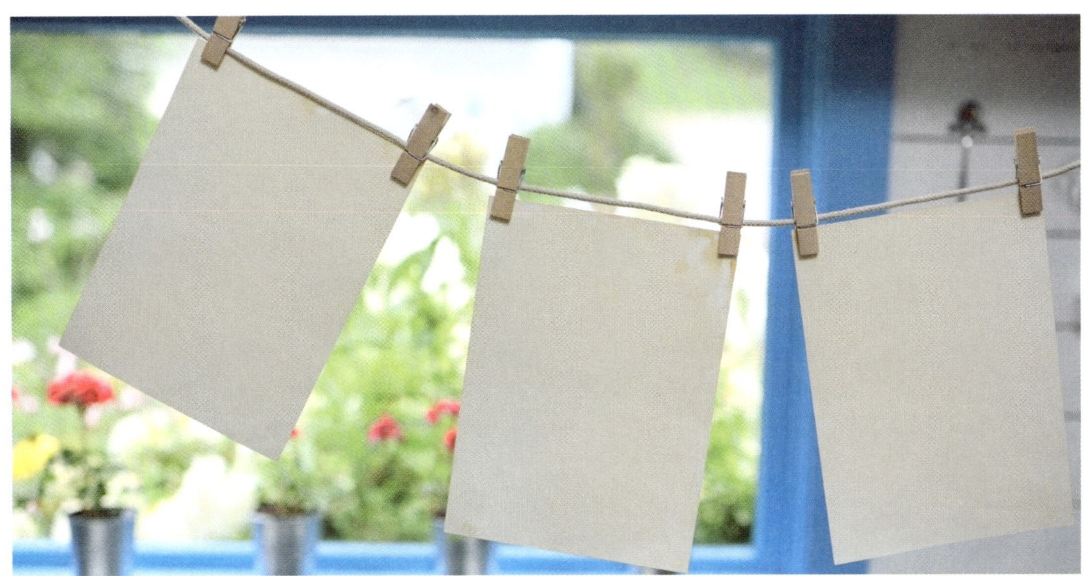

3 **Allow to dry completely** before proceeding with the oatmeal bath, following the steps on pages 127–128.

TECHNIQUE 1

Steaming with a CUSHIONING BLANKET

In this process, vegetation is steamed into paper using a cushioning blanket to create distinct, clean, striking imprints. If your aim is a pure imprint on a white background, use a barrier to ensure there will be no bleeding or unwanted marks. With a wide enough dowel, like a large can or pipe, the paper will not overlap itself and you won't need a barrier (as shown here).

SET UP FOR SUCCESS

Cut a cushioning blanket from a supple fabric, like jersey or French terry, to the same dimensions (if not slightly larger) as the target paper to ensure coverage, and dampen it before use. If using a barrier (painter's plastic or parchment paper), cut it slightly wider and longer than the target.

Gather all your materials. Place leaves in a bowl of water to keep fresh and allow better contact with the target. Fill your steaming vessel with at least 3 inches of water and set to simmer.

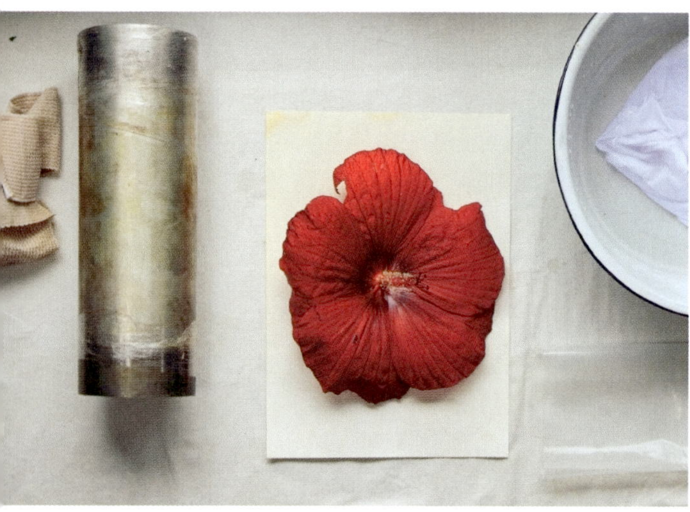

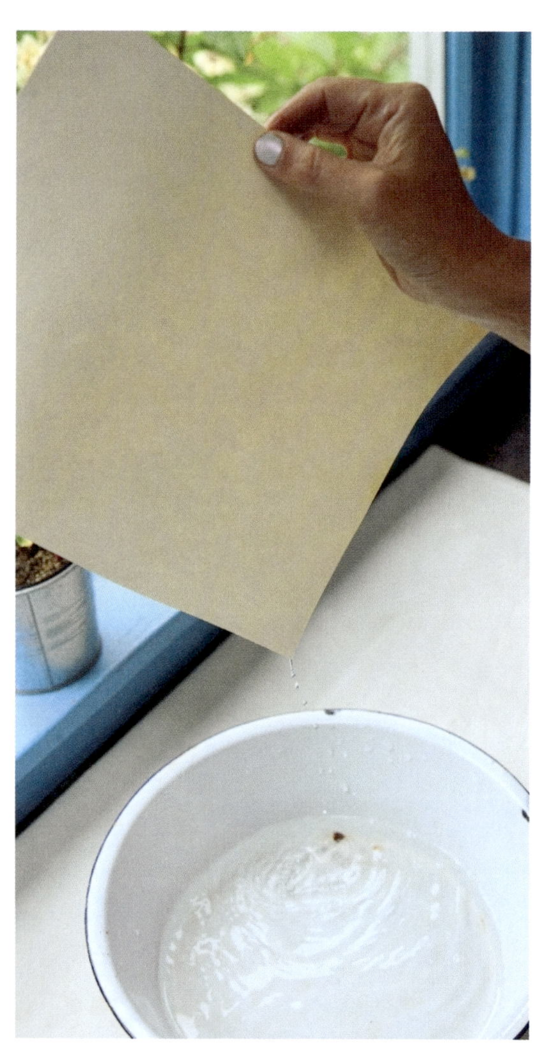

PROCESS STEPS

1 **Lightly wet the mordanted target** by spraying it with water, running it quickly under a tap, or dipping it into a container of water. Lay the paper flat and blot excess water with a clean towel—it should be damp but not dripping.

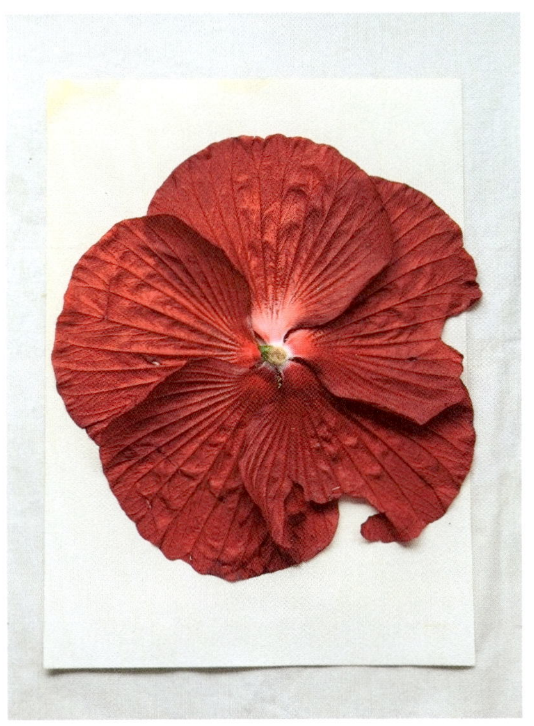

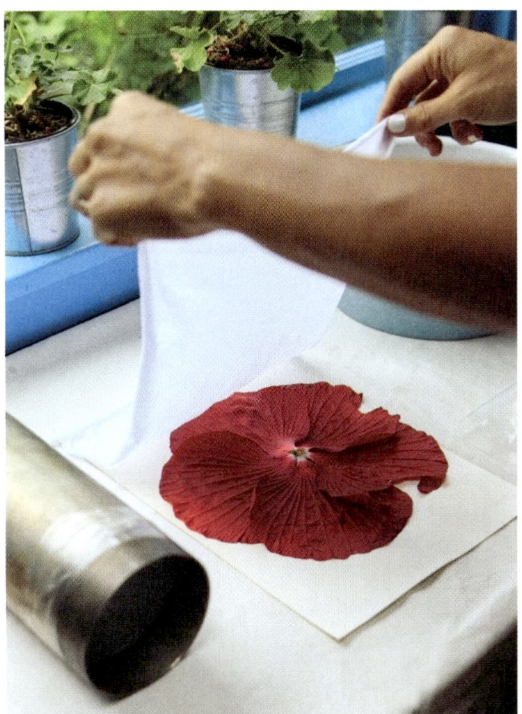

2 **Place the paper** on a clean workspace (and on top of the precut barrier if using one). Decorate the target with the chosen botanicals. Be sure to place flowers face down onto the paper. If you're looking for high contrast, place the leaves moon side, or vein side, down; some sun sides of leaves won't impart much color or imprint.

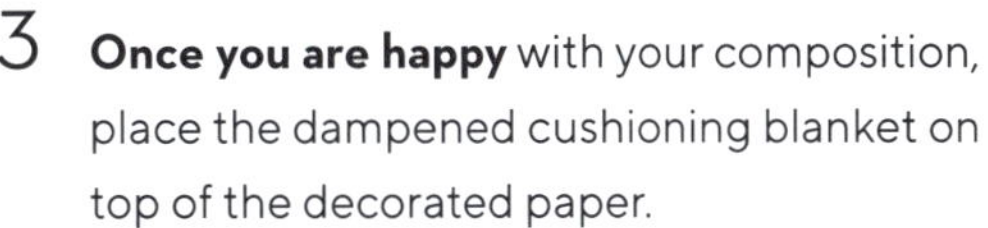

3 **Once you are happy** with your composition, place the dampened cushioning blanket on top of the decorated paper.

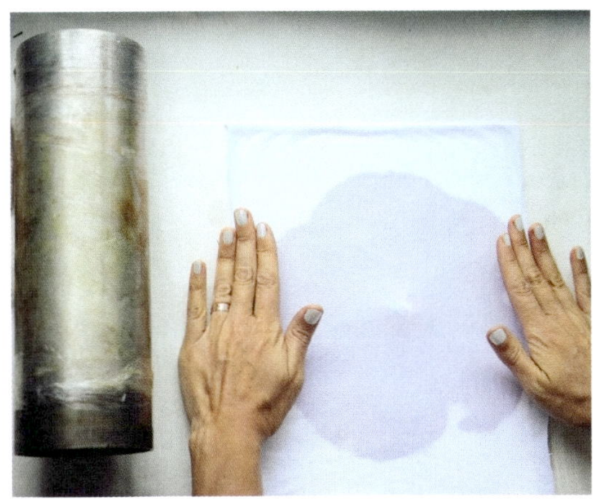

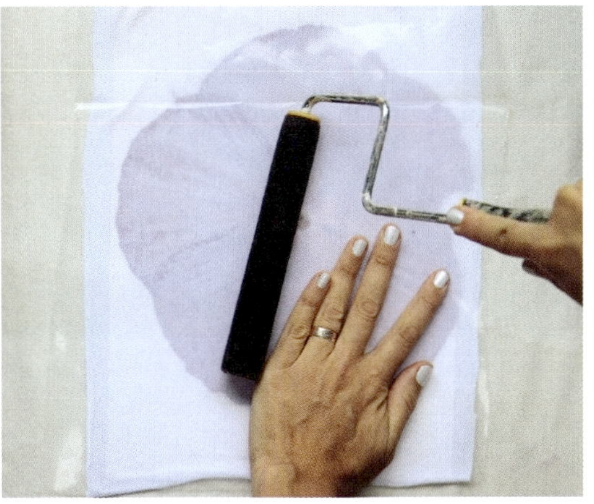

4 **Use a roller** to compress the vegetation between the target and blanket.

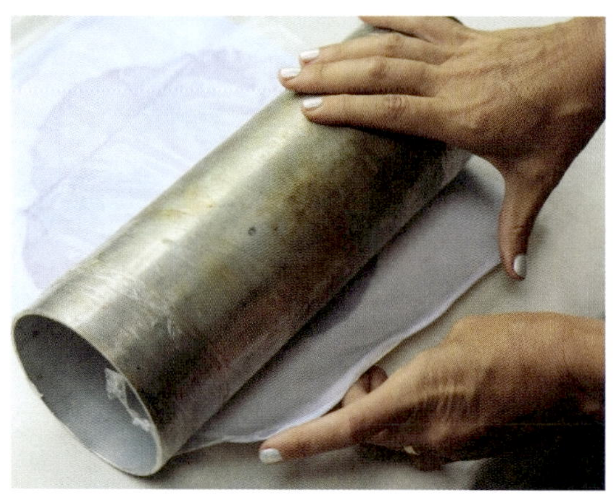

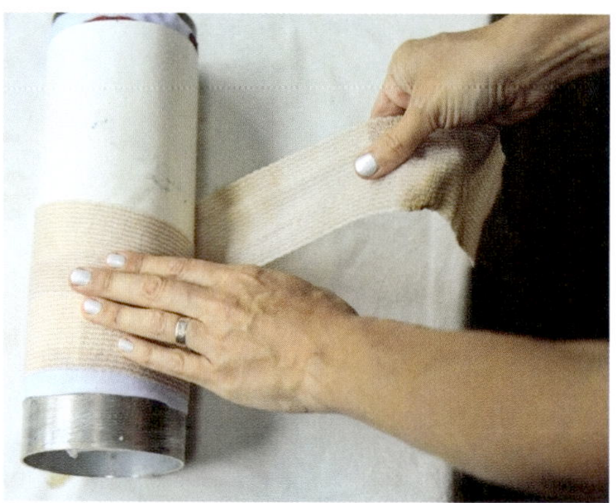

5 **Starting at one edge** of the paper and blanket, begin to roll them onto the dowel, keeping the bundle nice and tight.

6 **Secure the bundle** with an Ace bandage or T-shirt yarn.

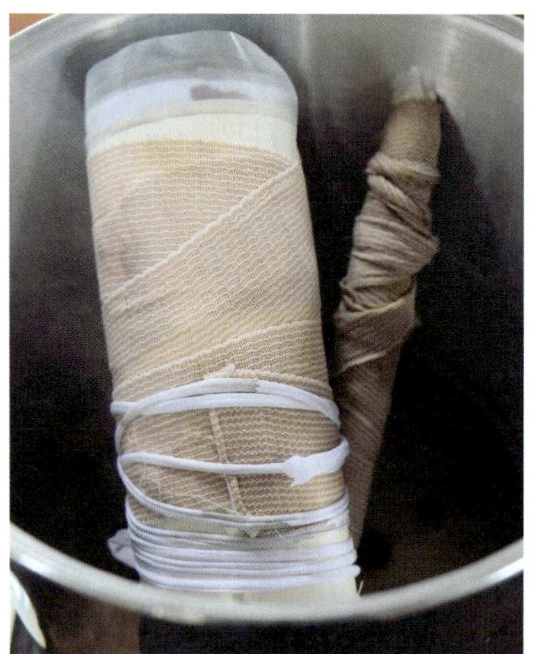

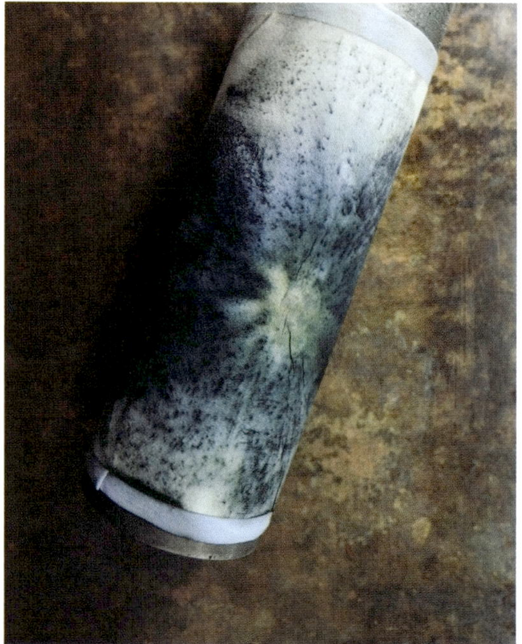

7 **Put the bundle** in the pot, keeping it above the water level. Bring the water to a simmer, not a full boil. Steam for 30 to 90 minutes, depending on the chosen vegetation, with the lid on. Check the water level halfway through and add more if necessary.

- **Just flowers:** 30–45 minutes
- **Flowers and leaves:** 45–60 minutes
- **Any composition with eucalyptus leaves:** 90 minutes

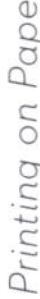

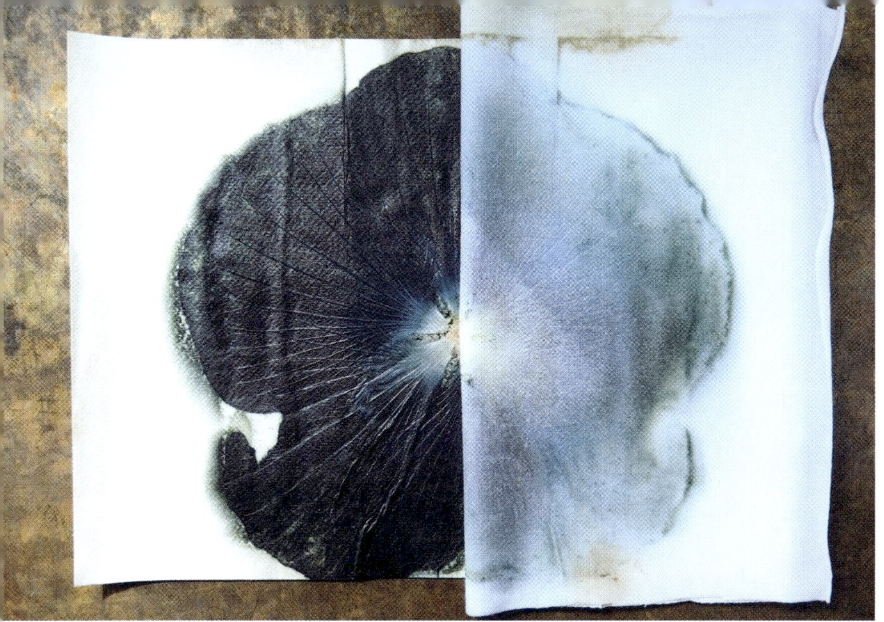

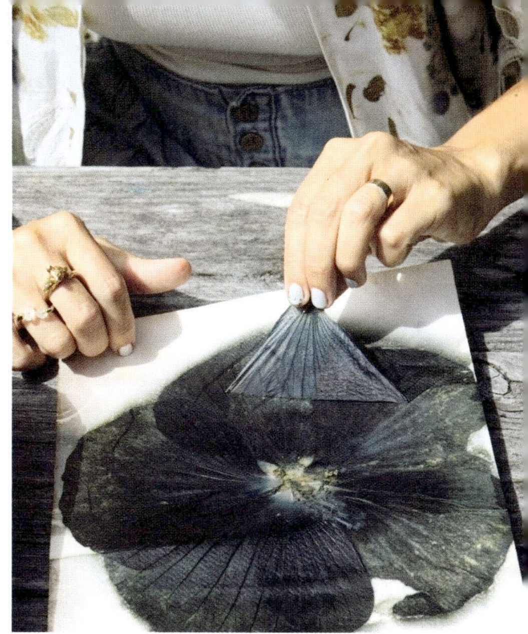

8 **When the time is up,** turn off the heat and allow the bundle to cool. Carefully unwrap the bundle and open the paper. Remove the vegetation that peels off easily by hand but be careful not to smudge anything—the rest will come off when dry.

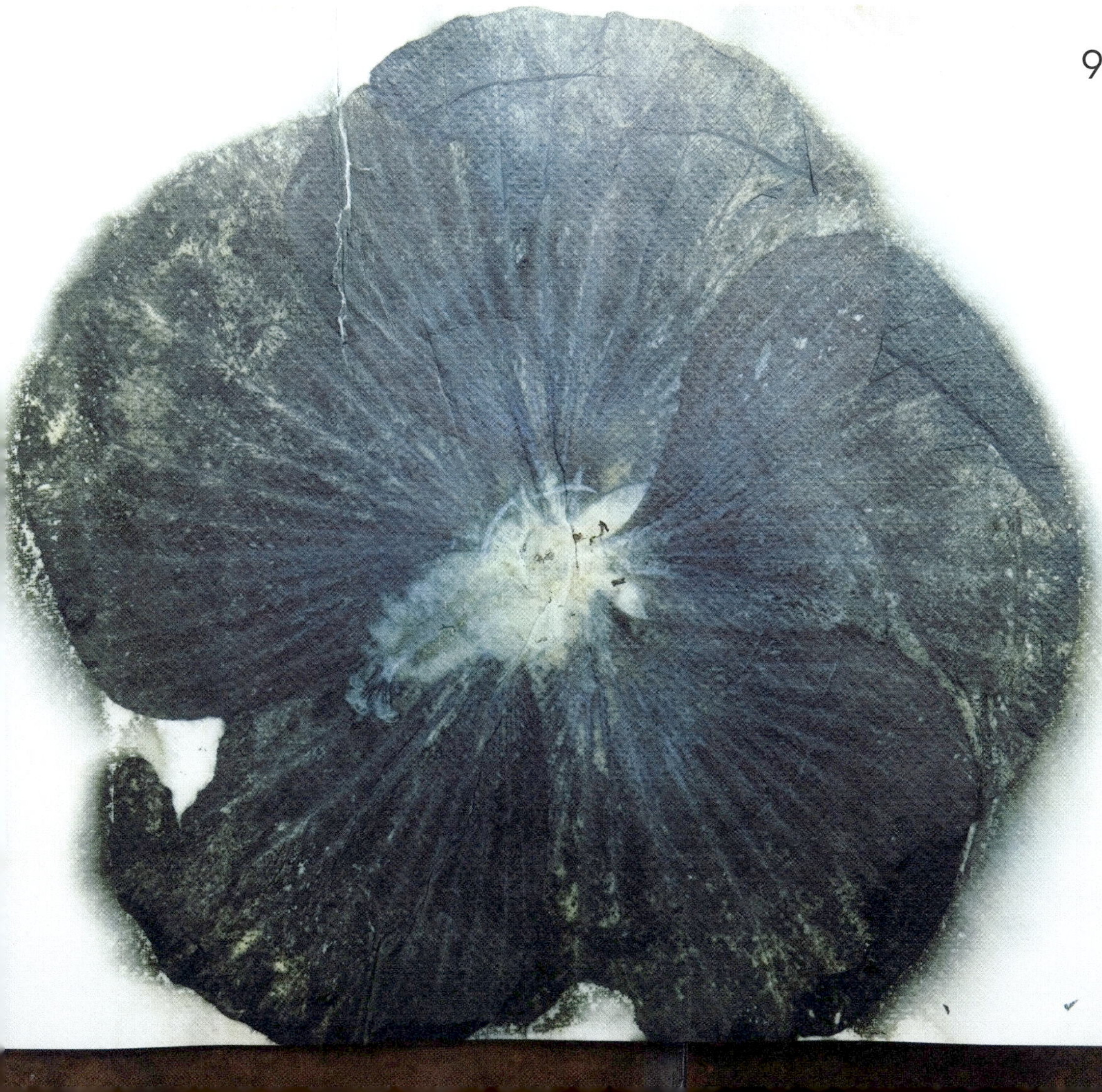

9 **Hang or lay flat** to dry in the shade. Allow the paper to dry completely, then carefully remove any excess vegetation. Use a dry sponge or toothbrush to coax off any stuck pieces. If the paper appears to have buckled or does not lie flat, place a piece of cotton fabric over the dry paper and run an iron over it a few times at medium heat with steam to flatten it. Store between heavy books or in a binder to keep flat.

TECHNIQUE 1 VARIATION

Steaming with a DYED CARRIER BLANKET

In this process, pigment is steamed onto the paper with a dye-soaked carrier blanket, which provides a colorful background to the botanical design. Depending on the size of the dowel, a barrier of plastic may be required to prevent the carrier dye from bleeding through to the opposite side and discourage oversaturation. The options for colorful backgrounds are many, so have fun experimenting with dyes you love.

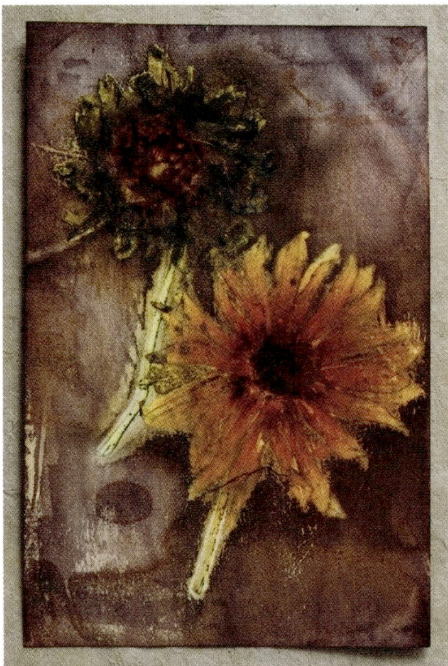

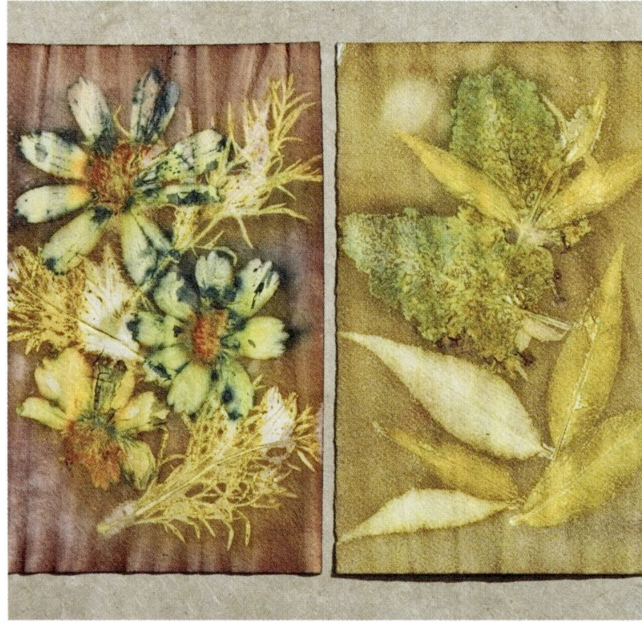

SET UP FOR SUCCESS

Cut a cushioning blanket from a supple fabric, like jersey or French terry, to the same dimensions (if not slightly larger) than the target paper to ensure coverage.

Cut a barrier (painter's plastic or parchment paper) that is slightly wider and at least 10 inches longer than the target.

Cut a carrier blanket that is the same width and length, if not slightly longer, as the target. Make the carrier blanket dye bath by following the steps on page 154. Put the carrier blanket in the dye bath to soak.

Design Notes

Place flowers face down onto the paper and leaves moon side, or vein side, down, if you're looking for high contrast, as some leaves' sun side won't impart much color or imprint.

It is okay to overlap some vegetation, as it may add an interesting dynamic to the print.

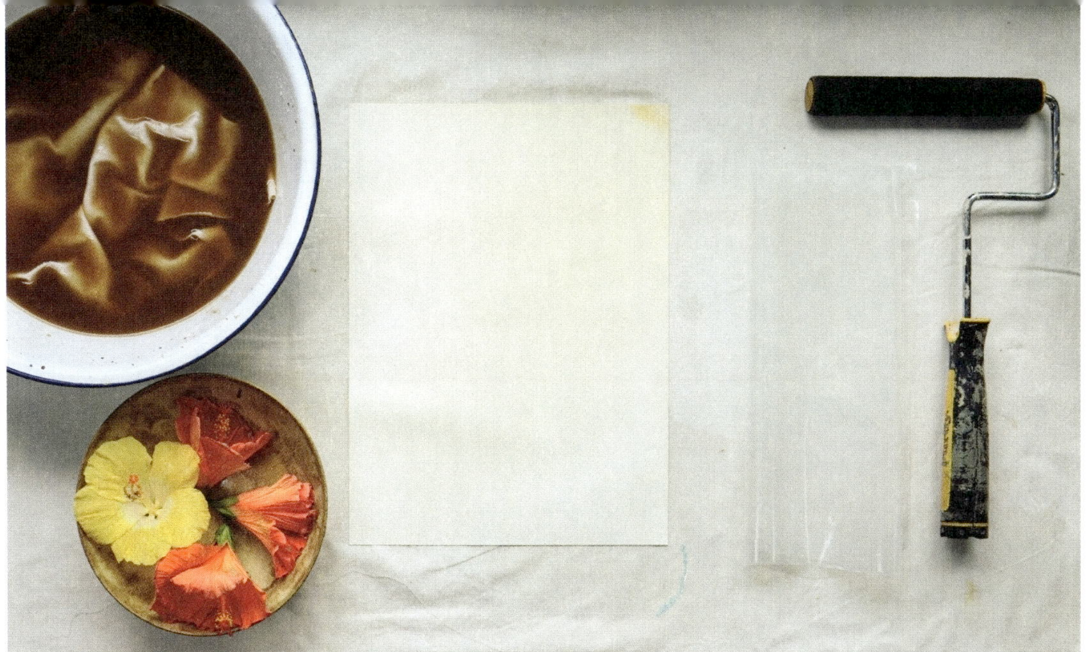

Gather all your materials. Place leaves in a bowl of water to keep fresh and allow better contact with the target. Fill your steaming vessel with at least 3 inches of water and set to simmer.

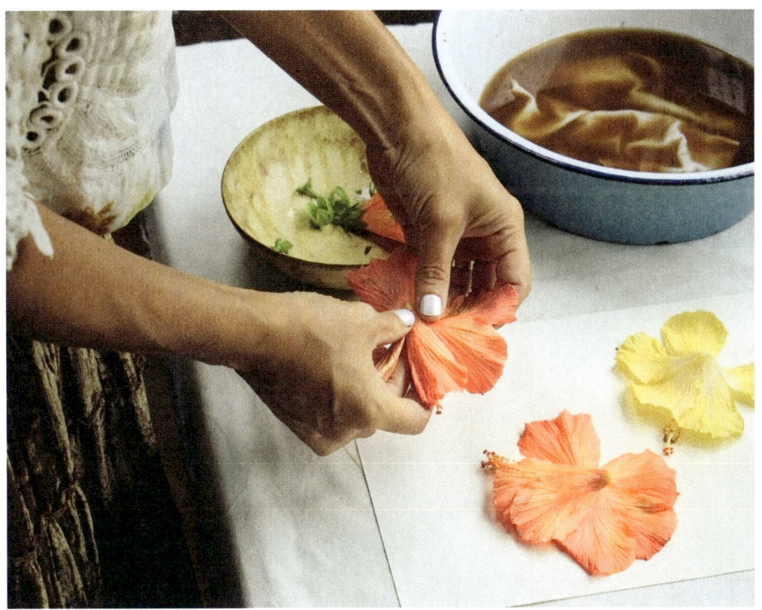

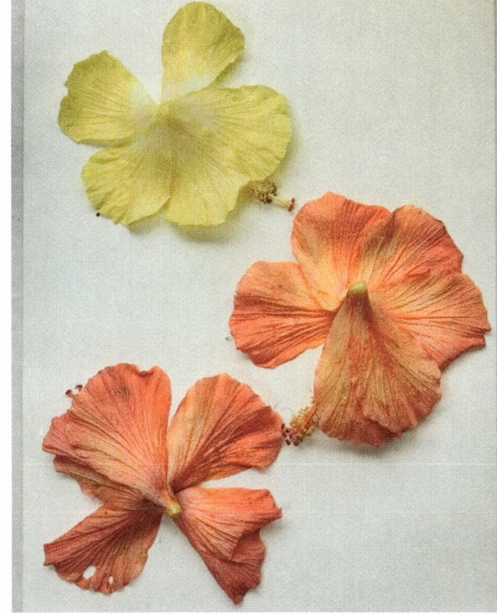

PROCESS STEPS

1 **Lay the barrier,** if using, flat on the workspace (not necessary with the large dowel used in this project). Lightly wet the mordanted target by spraying it with water, running it quickly under a tap, or dipping it into a container of water. Lay the paper flat and blot excess water with a clean towel—it should be damp but not dripping. Place the paper on top of the plastic barrier, lining up the bottom edges of the paper and the plastic. Any extra plastic should be at the top edge of the paper. Decorate the target paper with the chosen botanicals.

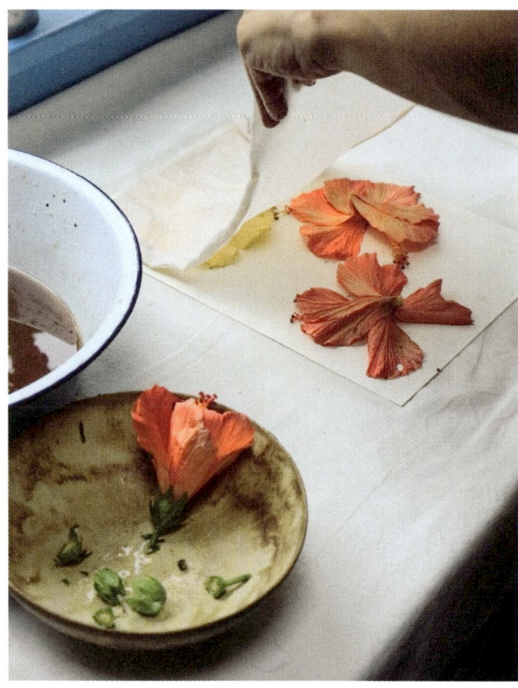

2 **With gloves on, wring out** any excess moisture so the carrier blanket is damp but not dripping. Place the carrier blanket on top of the paper. Try to sandwich the vegetation tightly between the paper and blanket without any bubbles or too much space.

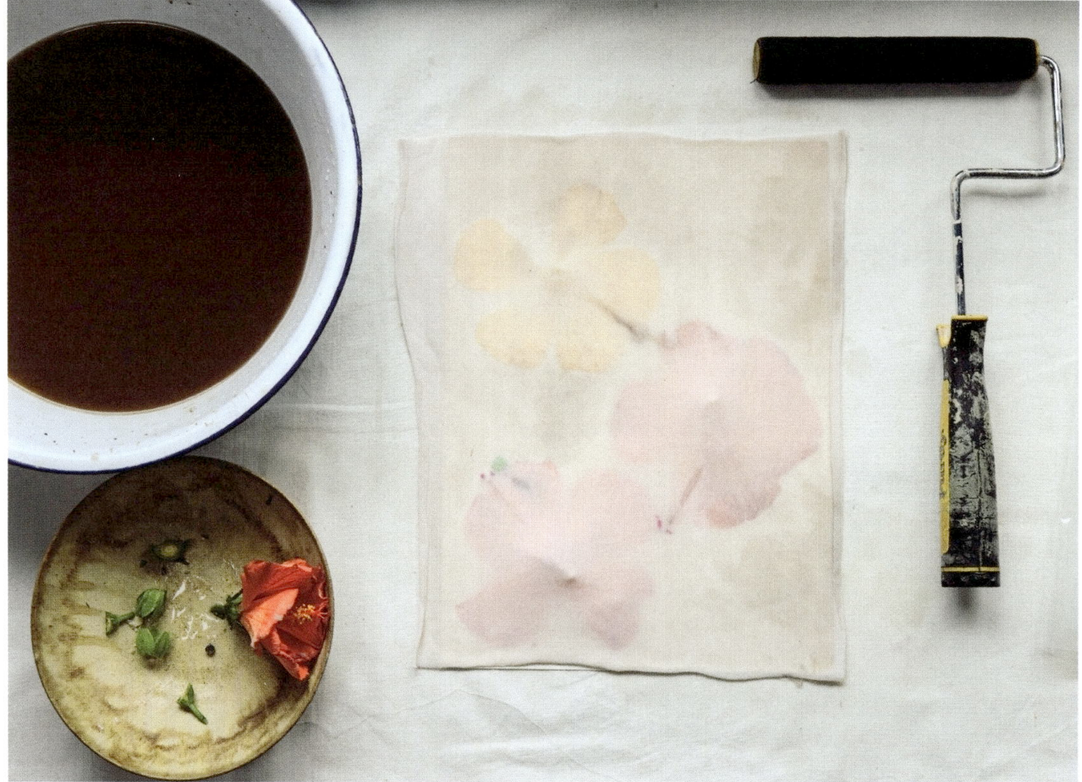

3 **Use a roller** to flatten out bubbles and bulges. As the iron in the mordant reacts with the carrier dye, the background will take on more color. Rolling helps enhance this process.

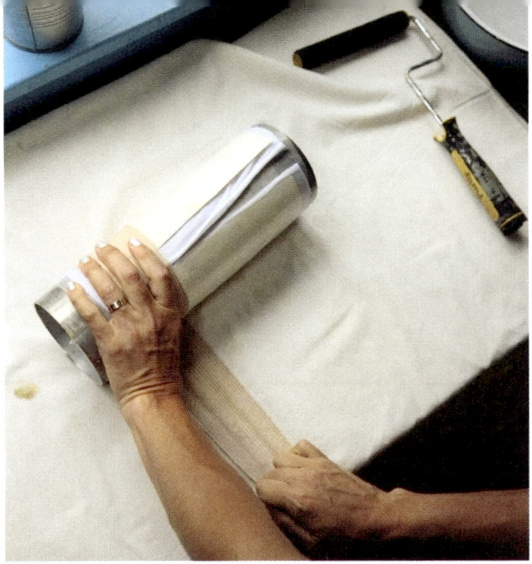

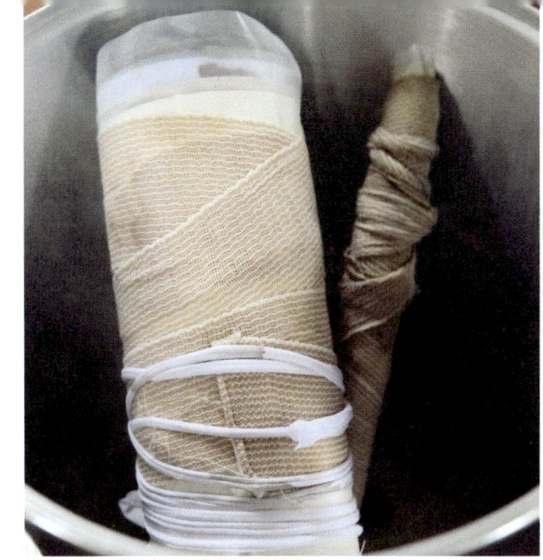

4 **Using a dowel,** roll the barrier, paper, and blanket together, from the bottom edge to the top edge of the paper, keeping the bundle nice and tight. Wrap any extra length of barrier around the bundle and secure with an Ace bandage, rubber bands, or T-shirt yarn.

5 **Put the bundle in the pot,** keeping it above the water level. Bring the water to a simmer, not a full boil. Steam for 30 to 90 minutes, depending on the chosen vegetation, with the lid on. Check the water level halfway through and add more if necessary.

- **Just flowers:** 30–45 minutes
- **Flowers and leaves:** 45–60 minutes
- **Any composition with eucalyptus leaves:** 90 minutes

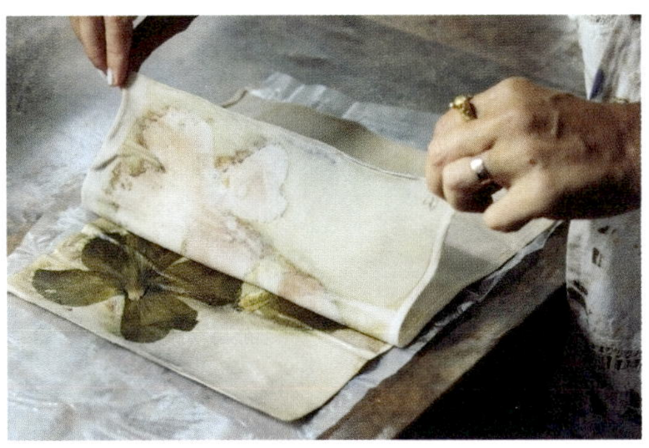

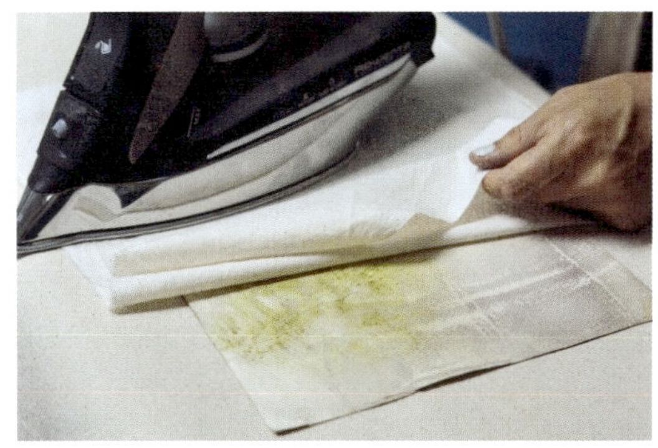

6 **When the time is up,** turn off the heat and allow the bundle to cool. Carefully unwrap the bundle and open the paper. Remove the vegetation that peels off easily by hand but be careful not to smudge anything—the rest will come off when dry.

7 **Hang or lay flat to dry** in the shade. Allow the paper to dry completely and carefully remove any excess vegetation. Use a dry sponge or toothbrush to coax off any stuck pieces. If the paper is buckled or wrinkled, place a piece of cotton fabric over the dry paper and run an iron over it a few times at medium heat with steam to flatten it. Store between heavy books or in a binder to keep flat.

TECHNIQUE 2

IMMERSION PRINTING

Immersion printing is a technique for printing on paper that utilizes binding and then simmering in a dye bath rather than steaming. This process is done without a barrier to allow the liquid dye bath to penetrate the paper. The dye bath is made with highly concentrated botanicals: powdered extracts, raw dyestuffs (e.g., onion skins, roots, bark, leaves), and liquid dyes. Results can vary from soft watercolor-like imprints to bold and highly contrasted visuals, depending on the type of dye chosen.

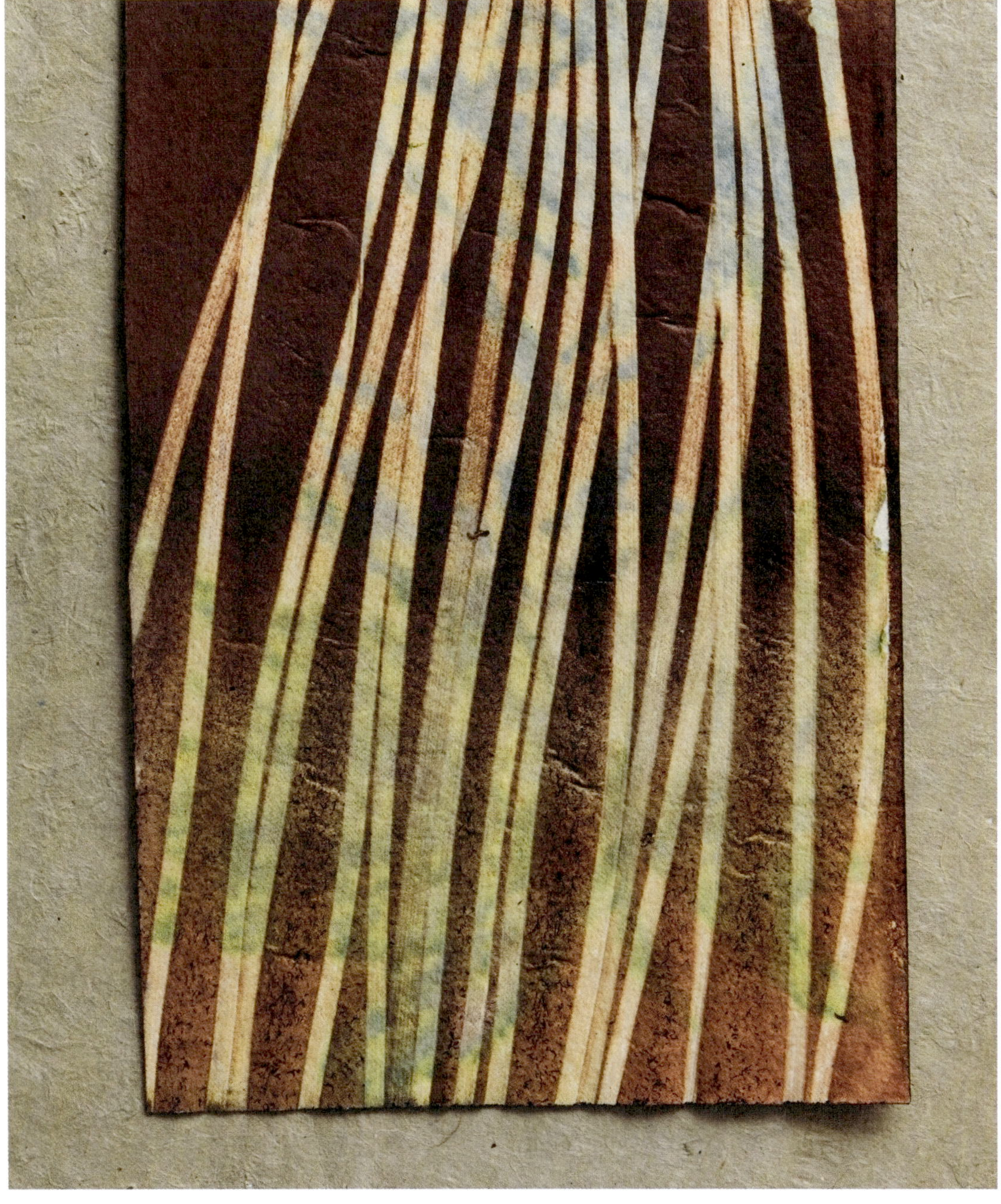

Wrapping the bundle with thin binding, such as T-shirt yarn, to expose some parts of the paper to the dye creates striking lines of contrast and adds a visual surprise to the backside of the work.

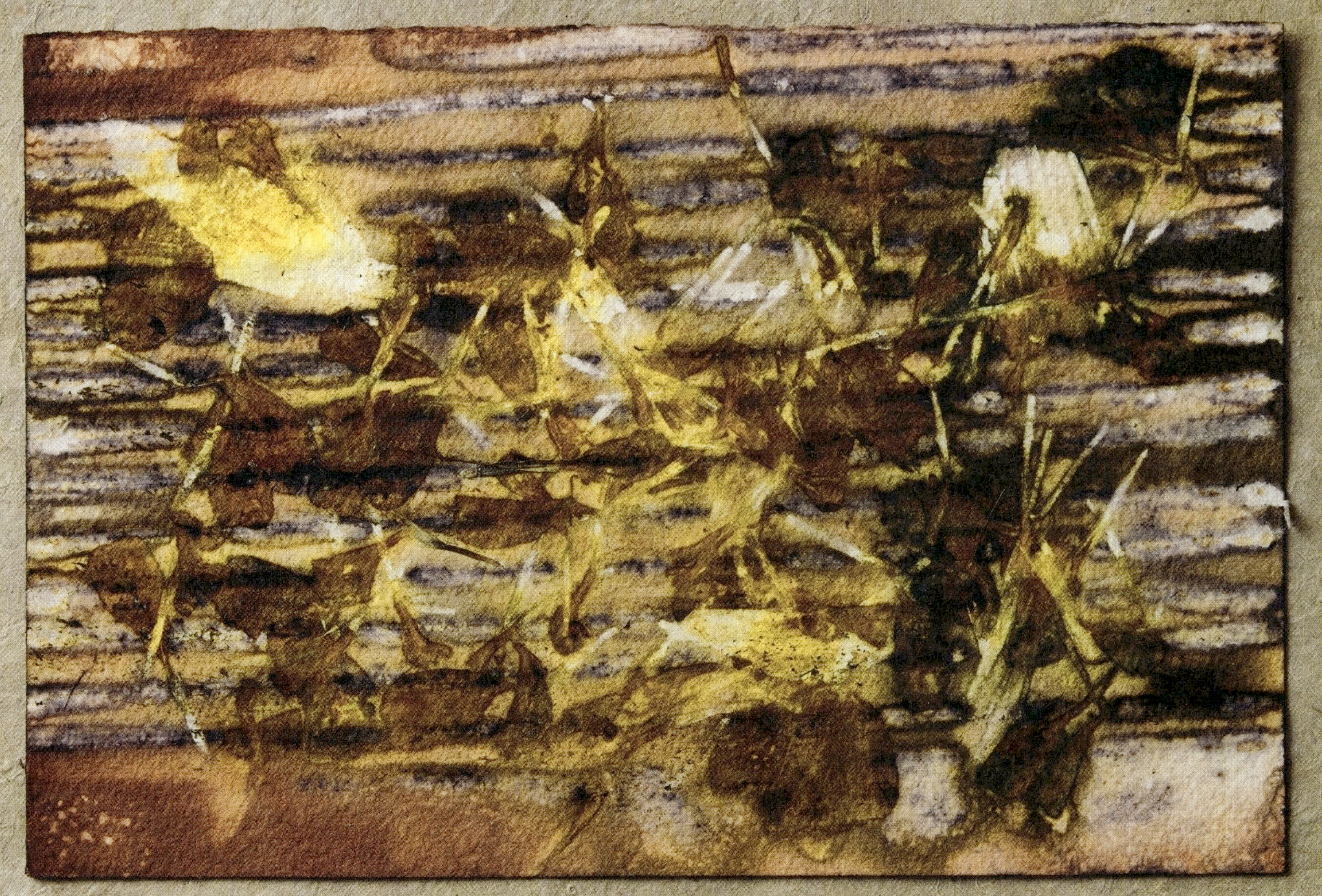

Suggested Botanicals

A tannin dye bath uses tannin-rich botanicals intended to interact with the ferrous sulfate in the mordant, creating dark and bold backgrounds and/or edges of the paper. The chemical reaction between iron and tannin creates beautifully tinted colors, outlines, and shadows. Using leaves that contain a lot of tannin, such as eucalyptus, maple, oak, or sumac, and simmering the bundle in an iron dye bath can work just as well.

Try these tannic powdered extracts and raw materials to achieve specific color ranges.

- **Browns:** Cutch, mimosa, quebracho moreno, walnut, chestnut, tannin blends
- **Dark grays to black:** Sumac, oak galls, pomegranate rinds or extract, eucalyptus leaves, black tea leaves, wattle (*Acacia* spp.)

A colorful botanical dye bath uses pH-sensitive dyes as well as other saturated botanicals to create beautiful pops of color. Here are a few suggestions to experiment with.

- **Pinks to reds:** Brazilwood, madder root, safflower, sappanwood
- **Oranges:** Kamala, marigold, fustic
- **Yellows:** Himalayan rhubarb, Osage orange, dyer's broom, chamomile
- **Greens:** Myrobalan, henna, weld, yellow onion skins
- **Blues:** Indigo, butterfly pea flower
- **Purples:** Lac, logwood, black mallow flower, red onion skins

SET UP FOR SUCCESS

Gather all your materials. Fill your steaming vessel with at least 3 inches of water and set to simmer.

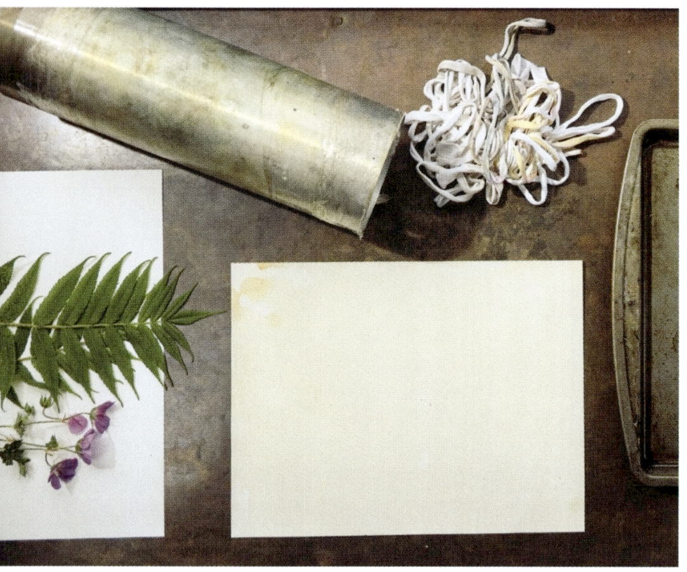

MAKE THE DYE BATH

Making a dye bath for immersion printing is quite like dyeing fabric a solid color or making a carrier blanket dye bath, except instead of weighing the paper you use a grams-per-liter recipe based on the type of botanical dye. Dye baths can be reused until they no longer impart color.

For raw dyestuffs (such as vegetable skins or leaves), weights can vary widely: Onion skins weigh practically nothing, so instead of trying to get 100 grams of onion skins, start with 1 cup of skins and see how much color is extracted when simmering. Keeping the raw dyestuff in the pot during the printing process may enhance and add more color to your prints. Here is a rough guide for making 4 liters (1 gallon) of dye.

Raw dyestuffs: approximately 100 grams
Natural dye extracts: 10–20 grams
Liquid dyes: 10–20 grams

1 **Add the water** to the dye pot, making sure there is enough to partially submerge the bundle. Bundles will float, so full submersion is not necessary.

2 **Add the raw dyestuff to the pot** and stir well. Bring the water to a gentle simmer (around 185°F/ 85°C). Raw dyestuffs require at least 45 minutes to fully saturate the dye bath. Dissolve powdered extracts in about ½ cup of hot water before stirring them into the pot of water. Liquid dyes can be stirred directly into the pot.

PROCESS STEPS

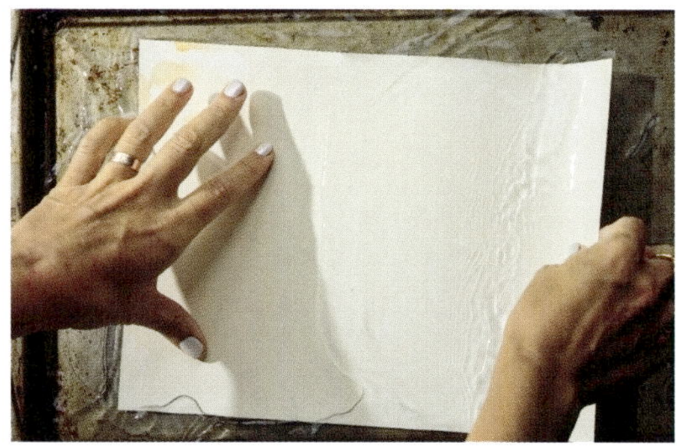

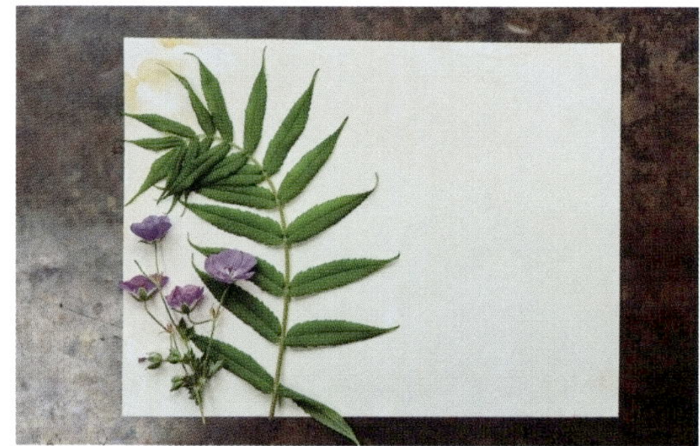

1 **Lightly wet** the mordanted target by spraying it with water, running it quickly under a tap, or dipping it into a container of water. Lay the paper flat and blot excess water with a clean towel—it should be damp but not dripping.

2 **Decorate** with the chosen botanicals. You may decorate the whole sheet, or fold over one half of the paper to create a mirror image.

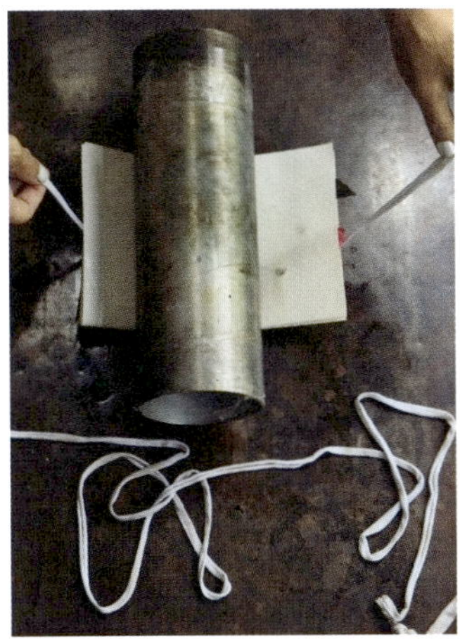

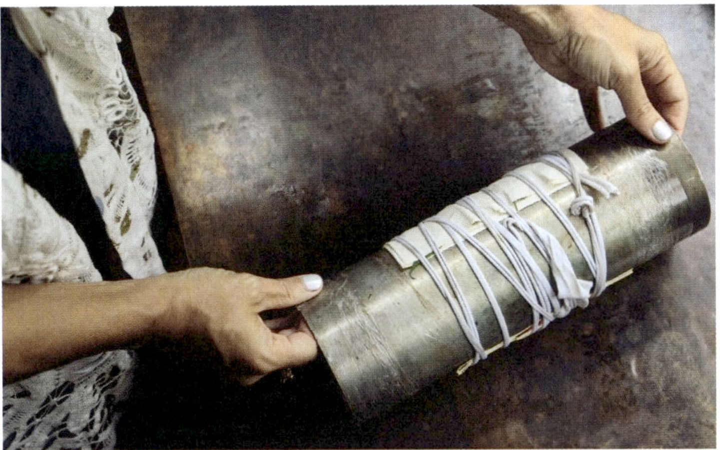

3 **Roll the paper onto the dowel** and secure with T-shirt yarn, starting at the center and working outward toward one edge, then the other. The more spaces you leave between the wrapping, the more the dye will penetrate the paper (which is what you want).

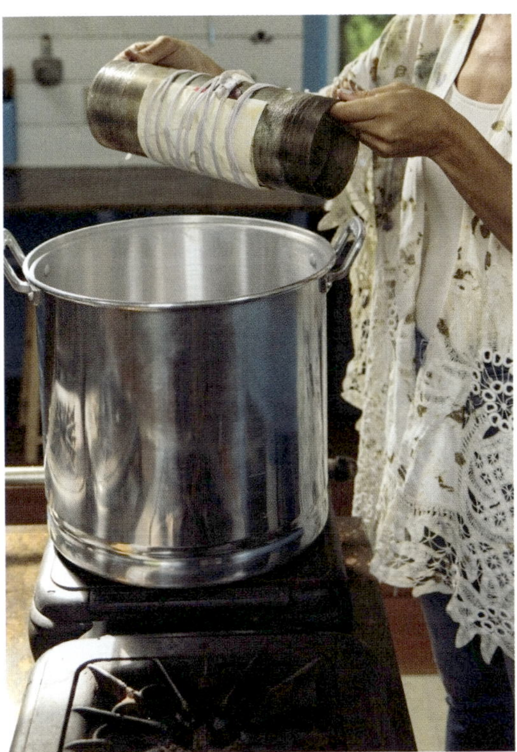

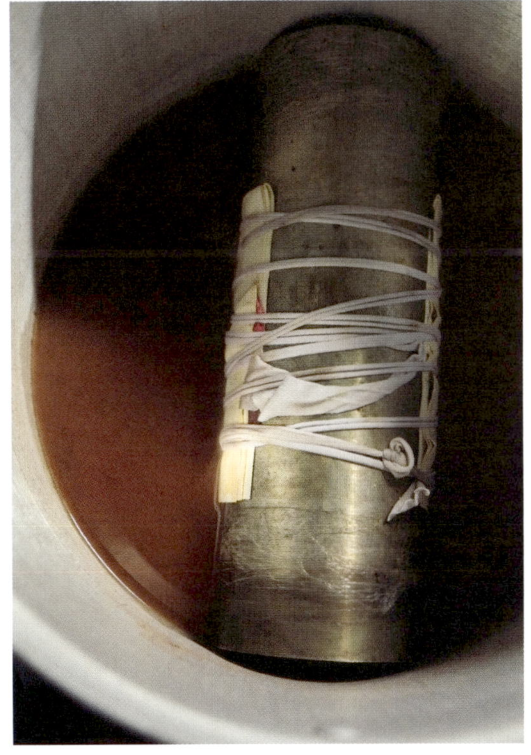

4 **Put the bundle in the dye pot** and simmer with the lid on for 30 to 90 minutes, depending on the chosen vegetation. Check the water level halfway through and add more if necessary.

- **Just flowers:** 30–45 minutes
- **Flowers and leaves:** 45–60 minutes
- **Any composition with eucalyptus leaves:** 90 minutes

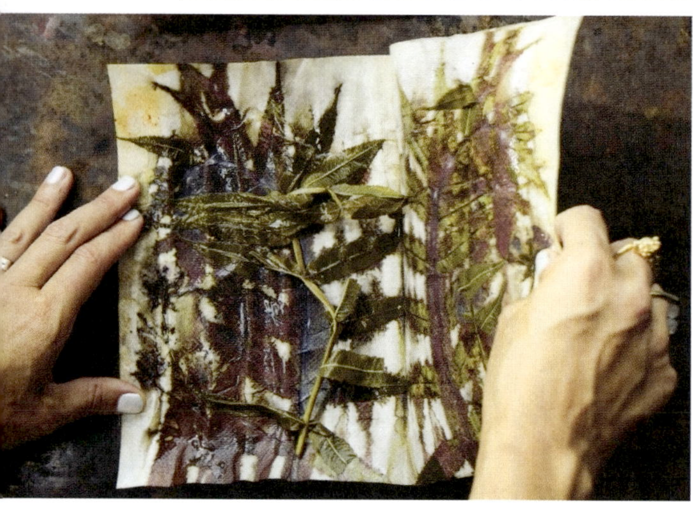

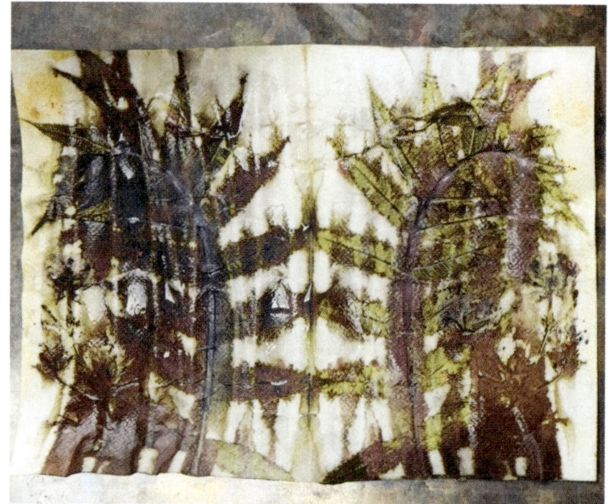

5 **When your timer goes off,** turn off the heat, remove the bundle from the pot, and allow to cool. Carefully unwrap the bundle and open the paper. Remove the vegetation that peels off easily by hand but be careful not to smudge anything—the rest will come off when dry.

6 **Hang or lay flat to dry** in the shade. Allow the paper to dry completely and carefully remove any excess vegetation. Use a dry sponge or toothbrush to coax off any stuck pieces. If the paper is wrinkled or buckled, place a piece of cotton fabric over the dry paper and run an iron over it a few times at medium heat with steam to flatten it. Store between heavy books or in a binder to keep flat.

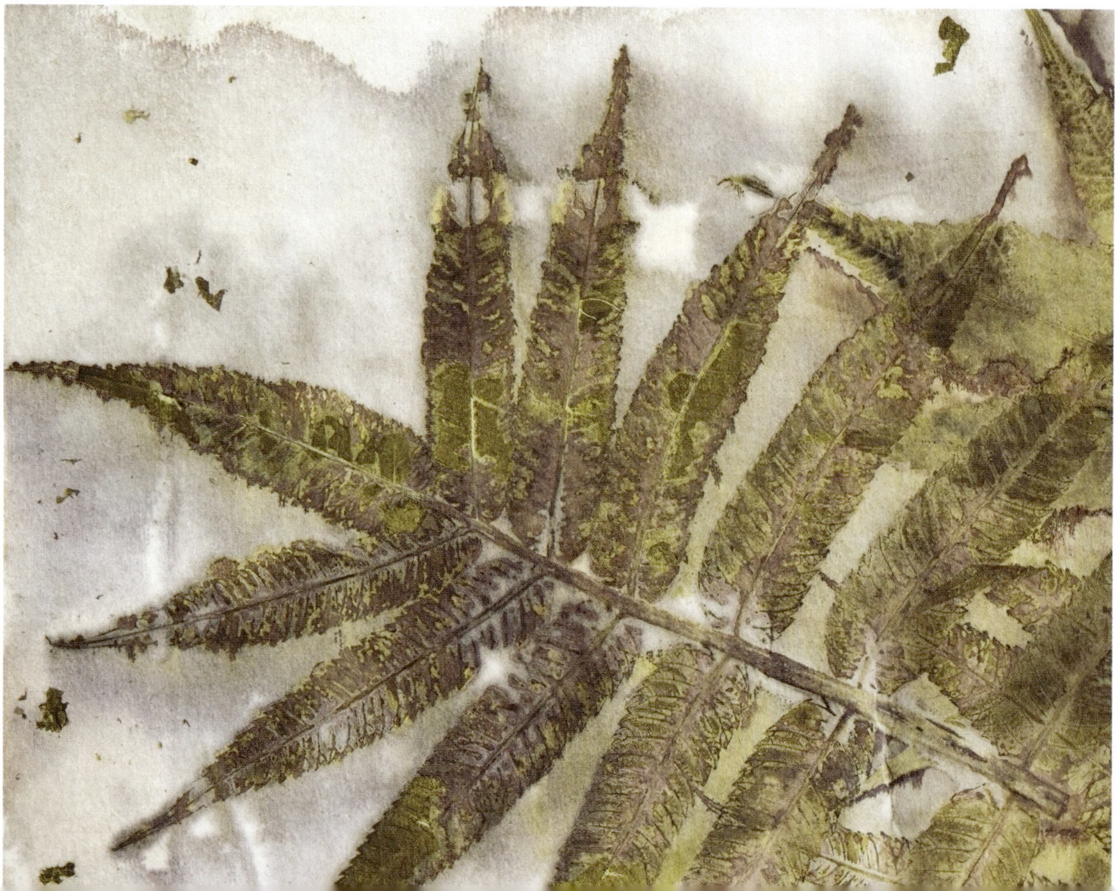

Acknowledgments

The journey of bringing this book to life has been deeply inspiring and meaningful. I am immensely grateful to so many people for accompanying me on that journey.

My dear family, Dane and Dolly, for their unwavering support and for putting up with my messes of dye pots, flowers, and fabrics. My mother, Karen, whose nurturing spirit and artistic influence planted the seeds for everything this book has become, and my sister, Megan, whose encouragement means more than words can say.

At Storey, Diana Rupp helped bring my idea for this book to life, and Lisa Hiley guided me in describing complex processes in accessible ways. It was a true pleasure to collaborate with artistic director Carolyn Eckert, whose talent and creative eye shine brightly throughout. I was blown away by the artistry and vision of Kristin Teig, whose photography is essential to this book. And I'm grateful to my agent, Kate McKean, for being a supportive presence all the way.

Thank you to Kathy Hattori of Botanical Colors for your generous offerings of natural dye materials and for the way you nurture and connect the natural dye community. To the team at Dharma Trading, thank you for your donation of fine fabrics used in several of these projects.

Amy DuFault, our conversations and flower-gathering adventures have been a wellspring of inspiration. Julia Dow, my fellow "grass girl," I am forever grateful for the spark and inspiration you bring to my life. Kirsten McCracken, walking and talking among the flower beds of Coonamessett Farm with you always rekindles my creative fire. And to all my dear friends and loved ones who have brought me flowers, shared books on natural dyeing, or simply cheered me on—thank you from the bottom of my heart.

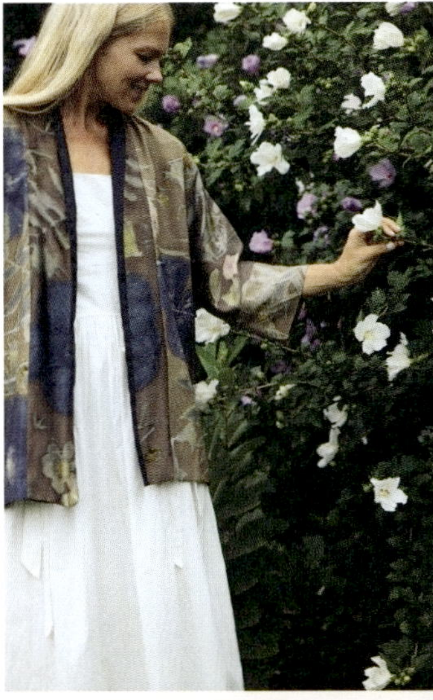

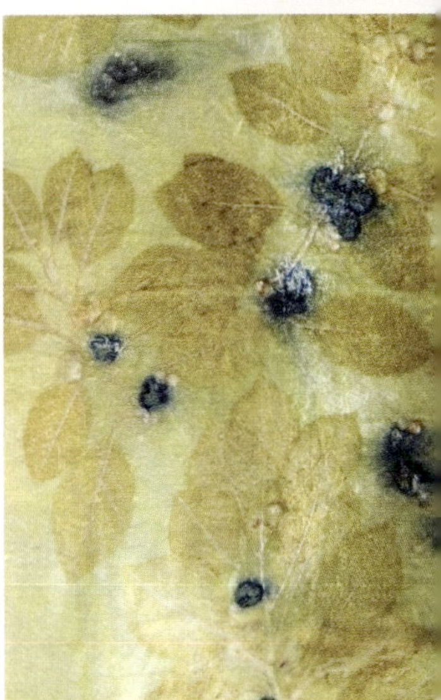

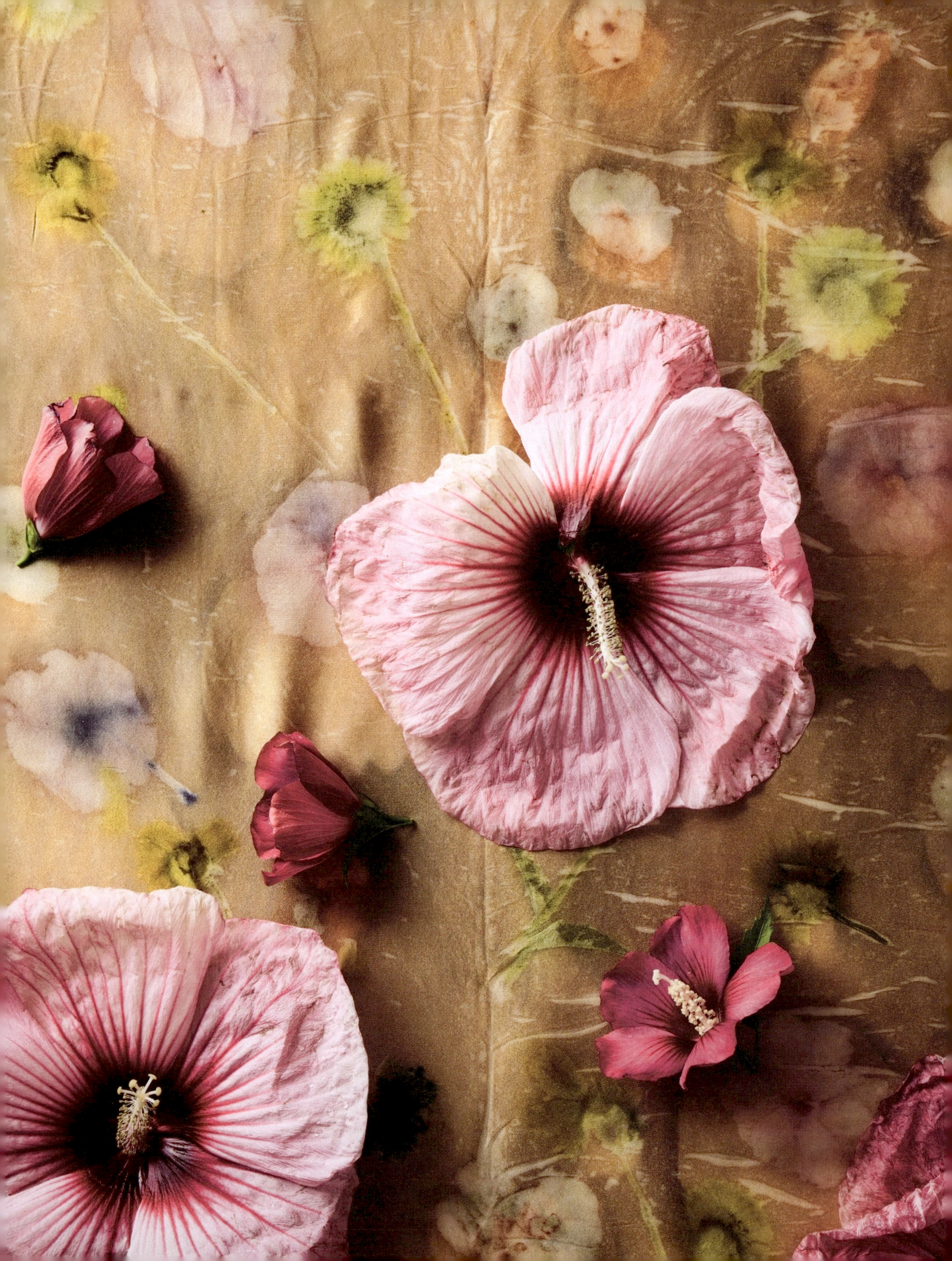

Index

Page numbers in *italics* indicate photographs.

D

E

F

T

V

W

Z

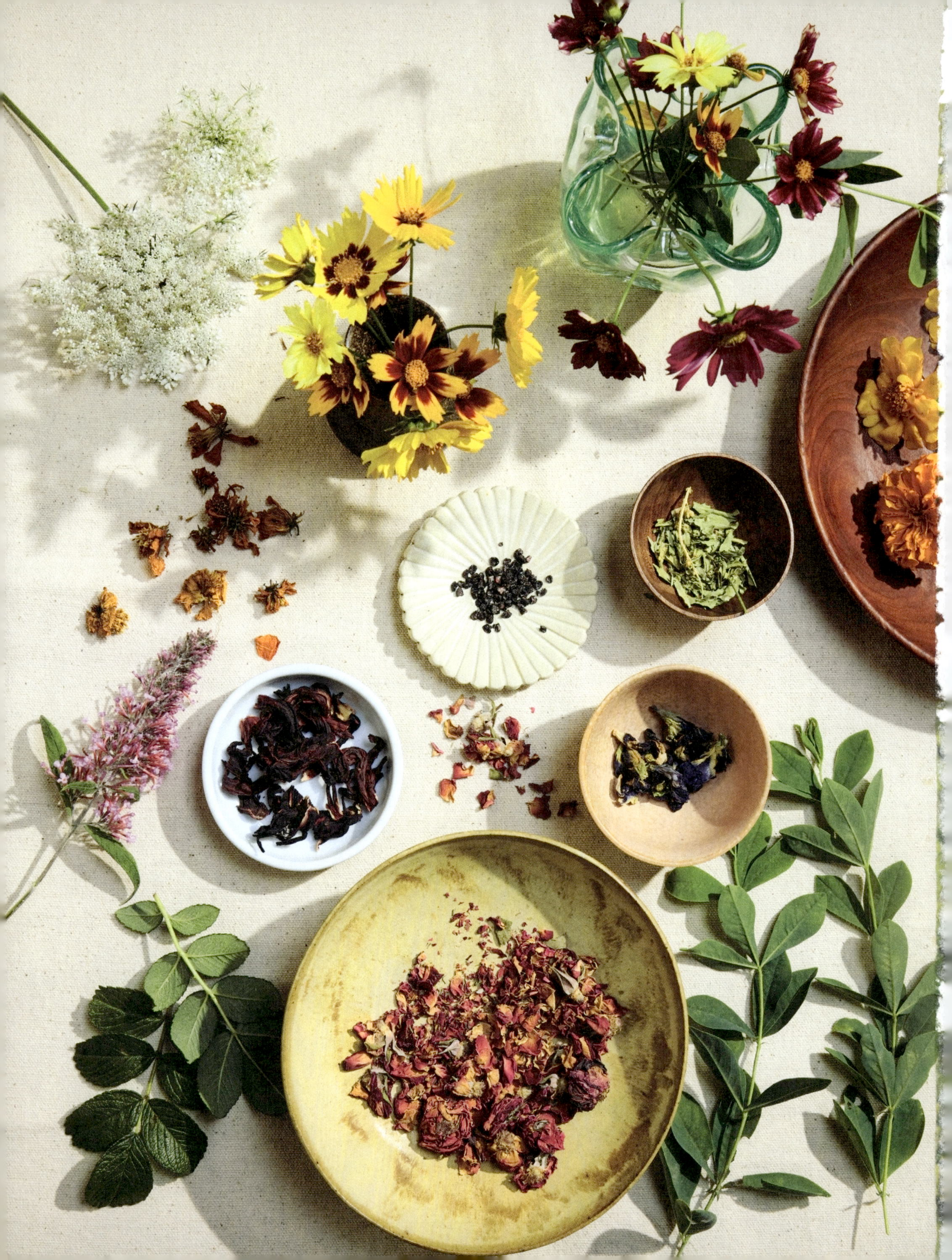

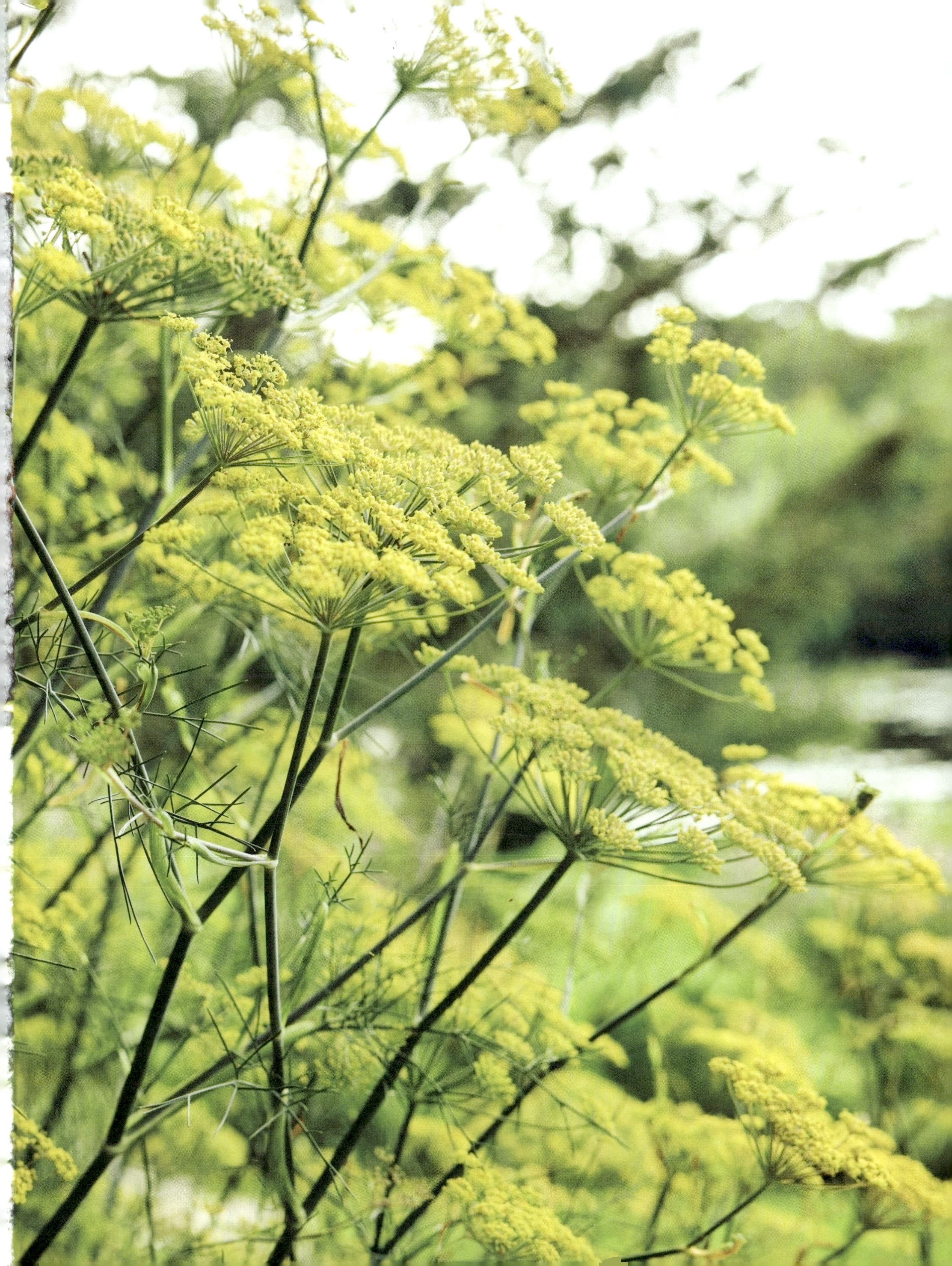

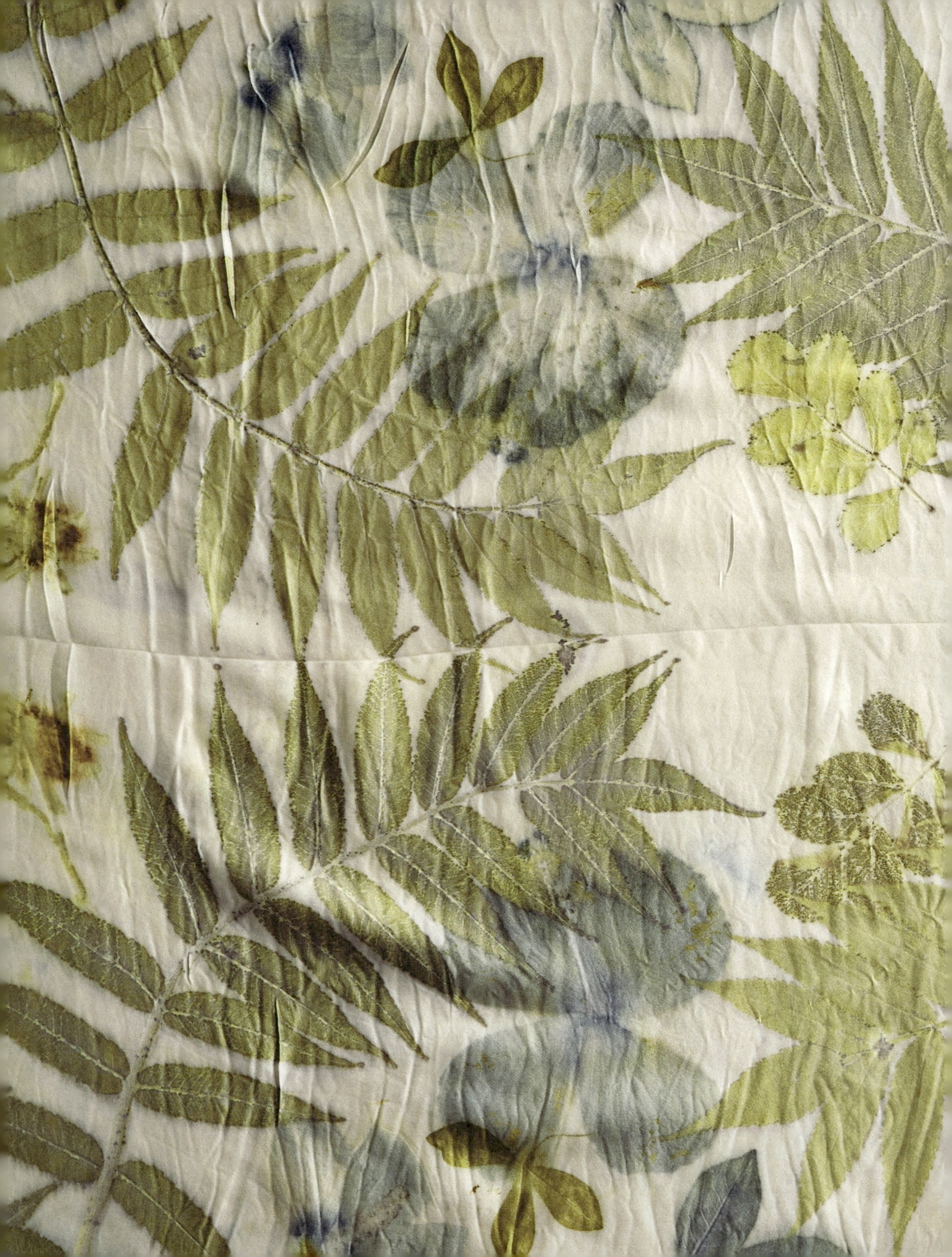